ELECTRIC SHEPHERD

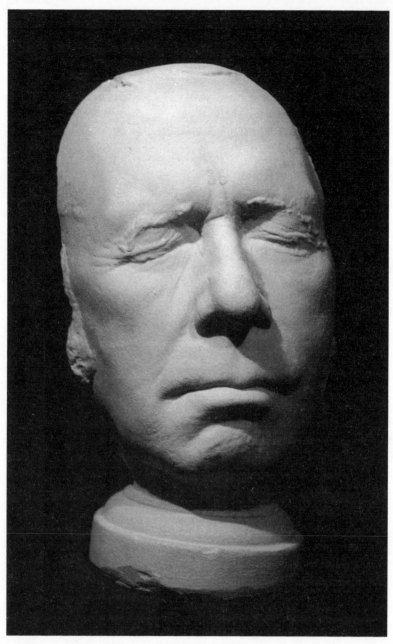

Death mask (or, more likely, life mask) of James Hogg

Electric Shepherd
A Likeness of James Hogg

KARL MILLER

faber and faber

by the same author

COCKBURN'S MILLENNIUM

DOUBLES:
Studies in Literary History

AUTHORS

REBECCA'S VEST:
A Memoir

DARK HORSES:
An Experience of Literary Journalism

First published in 2003
by Faber and Faber Limited
3 Queen Square London WC1N 3AU
Published in the United States by Faber and Faber Inc.,
an affiliate of Farrar, Straus and Giroux LLC, New York

This paperback edition first published in 2005

Printed and bound in Great Britain by William Clowes Ltd, Beccles, Suffolk

A CIP record for this book
is available from the British Library

ISBN 0-571-21817-2

2 4 6 8 10 9 7 5 3 1

Contents

———

List of Illustrations

———

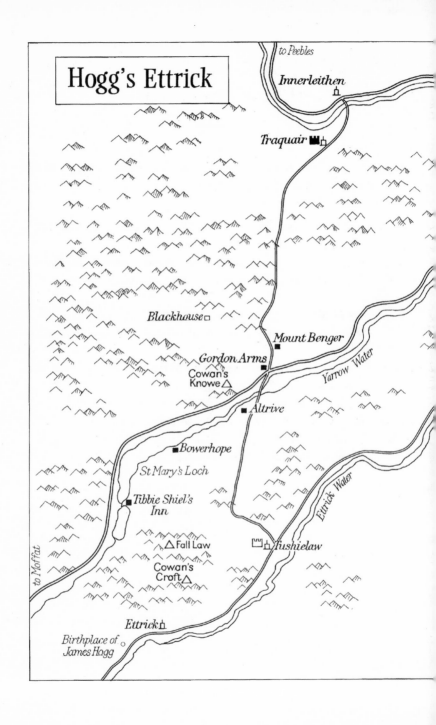

Hogg's Ettrick

to Peebles

Innerleithen

Traquair

Blackhouse

Mount Benger

Gordon Arms

Cowan's Knowe

Yarrow Water

Altrive

Bowerhope

St Mary's Loch

Tibbie Shiel's Inn

Ettrick Water

to Moffat

Fall Law

Cowan's Croft

Tushielaw

Ettrick

Birthplace of James Hogg

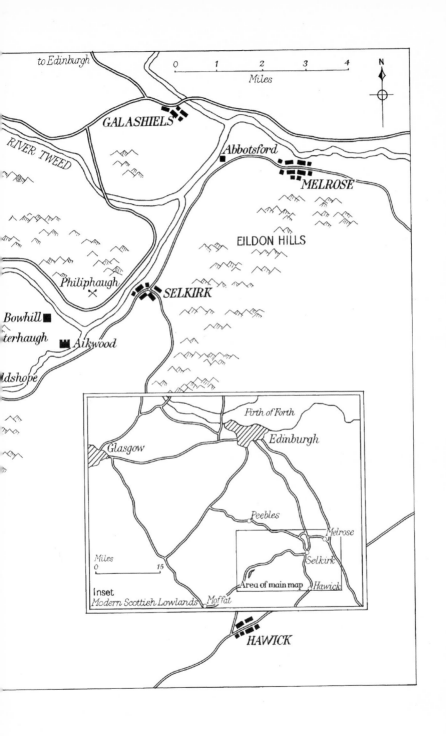

CHAPTER ONE

Hogg's Hole

Imagine him, as he was to imagine himself. Bare feet and a ragged coat. Behind him a hole in the ground, his bothy, which you have to stoop to enter and in which you can't stand up. Inside there's a bed of rushes for his rests, and for his literary work. His bed at night has often been in stables and cowhouses.

This is a self-portrait of the artist as he was in his mid-thirties, minding his master's ewes on the great hill of Queensberry in Nithsdale, Dumfriesshire, in the Scottish south-west. James Hogg is remembering a time when half his life was over, and when he stood staring at two strangers who were approaching him and whose walk was not the walk of shepherds. What could the matter be? 'I was afraid they were come to look after me with an accusation regarding some of the lasses.' His dog Hector, son of Sirrah, barked at the strangers in his usual way, and was silenced, this being 'the only servant I had to attend to my orders'. The younger of the two strangers bore himself as if Hogg were the Duke of Queensberry, and the other called him sir, whereupon Hogg glanced down expressively at his rags. These were the brothers Cunningham, also from the south-west.

Hogg, a man for likenesses, thought that the younger, Allan, of the brawny handshake, a stonemason's apprentice, looked like Robert Burns. The Cunninghams, admirers of his writings, had come to pay homage, and the three of them spent the afternoon on the rushes, in the darkness of the bothy, sharing his scrip and his bottle of sweet milk, moving on to the 'strong bottle' brought by the visitors, and talking about poetry. Allan Cunningham and Hogg became friends. Hogg's *Memoir of the Author's Life* refers to an attachment between 'two aspiring Scottish peasants, over which the shadow of a cloud has never passed', and which began 'at that bothy in the wilderness'. In later life Cunningham, too, remembered the occasion – the sunny, rainy day passed with Hogg and Hector 'at the foot of old Queensberry', at that 'little sodded shieling'.[1]

Over the hills to the north lay Ettrick Forest, where Hogg was born, at Ettrickhall farmhouse, and baptised on 9 December 1770, and where he spent most of his life. Around him were rough haggy roads and 'green, dumpling-looking hills', as he saw them, covered with grazing sheep. The drove road to the markets of England ran through the Forest at Tushielaw. But most Forest roads were all but impassable for wheels in 1792, and no better in 1820. A turnpike of sorts led north to the town of Selkirk, 14 miles off, beyond which, near Melrose and the Eildon Hills, Walter Scott was to raise his baronial Abbotsford; 37 miles from Ettrick was the city of Edinburgh, which a man might walk to in a day or ride to after dinner. Hogg's wilderness, where people were cut off for months at a time in winter, gave access to one of the intellectual capitals of the world, known in irony to the Westland novelist John Galt as 'the metropolis of Mind'.[2]

Two streams, the Ettrick and the Yarrow, flow north in parallel, the latter from St Mary's Loch, to join the Tweed near Selkirk, and the Yarrow ran between the two cottages inhabited by him in adult life, Altrive Lake (now embodied in the farmhouse of Eldinhope) and Mount Benger, which were a few hundred yards of path apart. Over the hills to the north of Mount Benger is the town of Innerleithen. Between his farms, at a crossroads, there stood, and still stands, an inn, the Gordon Arms. At the head of the loch stood, and stands, another inn, Tibbie Shiel's; on the summit of a nearby hill, Fall Law, Hogg located the suicide's grave investigated in his novel, the *Confessions of a Justified Sinner*. True to the doubling and riddling in the novel, a second hilltop, Cowan's Croft, is also proposed, and is then superseded, as the site of the grave – a local family, still there in Hogg's youth, having lent its name to features of the landscape. The names and places of this landscape helped him to write his book, in which there's a fall from grace, and Colwan is one of its sinner's two surnames.

The Forest was now treeless. It had once been a hunting-ground for Stuart kings, a killing ground and a singing ground, famous for chivalry and minstrelsy, courage and theft, for its raiders or mosstrooping reivers, its slain lovers, its dowy dens. These were associations which caused it to be seen, by Hogg and by Burns, as a region both classical and romantic. For some, it was the Arcadia of Scotland. For Hogg, it was more than that. It was the Sylva Caledonia of the Ancients and the Arcadia of Britain.

This was an ancestral countryside of Hoggs and Scotts; Walter Scott's friend, the explorer Mungo Park, born at Foulshiels near Selkirk, returned from the heart of darkness to live in Peebles. 'His Grace is the principal proprietor,' wrote Hogg,[3] referring to Selkirkshire and to the Duke of Buccleuch. Hogg's ancestors were feudally dependent on the Scotts of Harden, to whom Walter Scott professed fealty, while also kneeling to the more materially powerful Dukes of Buccleuch whose land-holdings were augmented by the acquisition of the Douglas estates in 1810, and who owned land throughout the kingdom, including the new industrial town of Grangemouth. Their house of Bowhill was in the neighbourhood, as was the castle of Aikwood, held by the Medieval philosopher, deemed wizard, Michael Scott, who has also been deemed the leading Western European intellectual of the earlier thirteenth century, and whose magic tricks and skinny shanks are to be found in Dante's *Inferno* (Canto 20). Buccleuch, the place, was a heap of rubble out there in the Ettrick beyond where the dominion of the clan had begun. One Scott forebear, the archetypal reiver known to Hogg as Wat o' the Cleuch, was also known as Flagellum Dei; another scourge of God was Auld Wat of Harden. Not for nothing were they remembered, by Walter Scott, as 'the rough clan'.

Hogg traced his origins to a Dark Age North Sea reiver named Houg, meaning Eagle, alias Hugo of Norroway. Other students of his name have stressed occupation. A hog was a sheep which has yet to be fleeced, as well as a pig. An ancestor was known as the Wild Boar of Fauldshope and he himself was known in Edinburgh as the Great Boar of the Forest, among other porcine cognomens, with the Metrical Psalms of David in mind, the 80th of these: 'The boar that from the forest comes doth waste it at his pleasure.'

'Thou Cherokee!' The Ettrick ragamuffin would in later years be wigwammed by an Edinburgh crony conscious of Hogg's role as a wild boy, a child of nature. Hogg was often to embrace the role. His seal was to consist of a harp, with the motto *Naturae Donum*. From quite early on, however, for all his savagery and educational slow start, he was more than nature's gift to literature. He has been relished as the exponent of an oral tradition as opposed to a print culture: but he was into writing and publishing by the turn of the century and the age of thirty. In 1807, a year after the Cunninghams' homage, he brought out the first instalment of the *Memoir* which, in the course of his life, subject to revision, accompanied instalments of his prose and verse, and in the same year there appeared his *Shepherd's Guide*, a 'practical treatise on the diseases of sheep', published by Constable in Edinburgh and John Murray in London, and printed by James Ballantyne, Scott's business partner, in Edinburgh.

He went to school for short spells, some six months in all, where he was made aware of the Bible, the Metrical Psalms of David, the Proverbs of Solomon, the Shorter Catechism. When he was six, his father went bankrupt: the price of sheep had fallen and a debtor had absconded. The leases of the farms of Ettrickhall and Ettrickhouse were forfeited, and Hogg's father was turned out of doors 'without a farthing'; but a neighbour, Walter Bryden of Crosslee, took the second of the farms and placed Robert Hogg there as a shepherd. James was put to service with a succession of masters: 'I was often nearly exhausted with hunger and fatigue.'

His sentimental education began. 'I have liked the women a great deal better than the men ever since I remember.' He was sent to herd cows, his half-yearly payment a ewe lamb and a pair of shoes. With him, when he was eight, went rosy-cheeked Betty, who was herding lambs. Hogg had a dog and Betty had none: so they were to stick together.

> Never was a master's order better obeyed. Day after day I herded the cows and the lambs both, and Betty had nothing to do but to sit and sew. Then we dined together every day at a well near to the Shiel-sike head, and after dinner I laid my head down on her lap, covered her bare feet with my plaid, and pretended to fall sound asleep. One day I heard her say to herself, 'Poor little laddie! he's joost tired to death,' and then I wept till I was afraid she would feel the warm tears trickling on her knee.[4]

Eventually he became a shepherd. He forgot the little he had learned at school and had to start again. There were remedial attentions. He was

4

coached by his mother, to keep him quiet when darkness and wet weather kept him indoors, and a diary owned by an Ettrick resident of the present day indicates that a neighbour, James Anderson, 'taught the Ettrick Shepherd to write, sitting on a corn kist at nights', the shepherd who was in turn to teach 'the wandering winds to sing'.[5] In later life he was ready to describe himself as having been for many years 'illiterate', but the word is misleading – it then meant untutored or uncultivated, and Hogg learnt to read and write in his teens, and caught up fairly soon. In time, he was climbing the hill with slates on which to compose, and with an ink bottle, for good measure, stuck in a hole in his waistcoat, together with a cork, a piece of string, the stump of a pen, and a sheet or two of paper folded and stitched. He went on composing in this way, and would later claim to be nothing without the slate. At fourteen, having saved five shillings, he bought an old fiddle and taught himself to play the old Scots tunes; a musician heard him practising, heard his own warbles being murdered by the tiro, and reckoned that the Devil and his waltzes were in the barn.

Border shepherds were notable for their piety, and for an intercourse with spirits and demons. And they were readers, who would lend each other books, leaving them in dykes for collection – sermons in stones. And they were debaters. The comparatively recent taste for clubs and forums had reached Hogg's native mountains. He was to struggle through the snow, on a 'very ill day' in 1794, 'a flaming bombastical essay in my pocket', to contribute to a debate in a remote shieling, where he failed to arrive: the debaters at Entertrony were then suspected of raising the Devil and bringing down the storm. A poetry competition was devised by Hogg, his brother William and their friend Alexander Laidlaw. The subject was 'the stars'. Judges were appointed. William won.

There were other clubs too – winter ones for curling on the ice and for evenings spent singing, fiddling, dancing and drinking. Burns's songs were a delight. Shepherds were footballers, runners and wrestlers, as well as wranglers. Athletic zeal 'presides in the shepherd's heart above every consideration,' wrote the young Hogg, 'bearing down on those affections which might prove far more immoral and debilitating'. Fear of spirits prevents 'many a night walk by the youth around, who verily believe them most apt to appear to people going about some ill end'. It did not prevent Hogg from going on many a night walk. The remoteness of Ettrick, he remarked at this point, 1802, had entailed 'a later and more sudden emergence from barbarity' than occurred elsewhere.[6]

This was not a barbaric or benighted life. He called it 'elegant and agreeable'. But it was also a hard one, as his *Shepherd's Guide* sufficiently illustrates. He was awake to the period concern with the pursuit of knowledge under difficulties (the pamphlet with that title appeared during his last years), and the treatise says more about his embodiment of the pursuit than the affirmations in his *Memoir*, by saying what it says about what shepherds did. The very names of the diseases which befell their flocks – braxy, sturdy, staggers – are formidable, and the treatise is replete with shepherds' warnings. He explains that in order to deal with 'water in the head', he bored holes in the skull and thrust wires up a nostril, which sometimes worked. And he explains how to geld his beasts:

> When the lambs are taken up to be cut, they should never be catched by the back or flanks, or any other part except the hough or neck, and lifted gently up by the legs. The operation ought to be performed as gently as possible, by slitting up or cutting the scrotum with a sharp smooth-edged knife, and starting the testicles by pressing both hands against the belly of the lamb. In removing them, the chords should be taken between the fingers and thumbs, while the backs of the hands are still kept steadily against the belly, and the stones drawn with the teeth somewhat upward until they separate. The operator must then pull its tail sharply two or three times, to replace the chords and vessels which have so violently been disarranged.[7]

Here was a man of feeling who used to bite the balls off sheep – at a time when the poet Cowper had declared that lambs and Negroes both were harmless things. He was thought to be a barbarian, flattered for that, while also commanded to be delicate, by those who belonged to the strongholds of refinement, of books and social advancement, north and south of the Border. He was close to the ground – as many people are, still, at a time when many others find such people outlandish, savage. He was a cherisher and a killer of birds and beasts, who was shocked by the piles of dead larks in Covent Garden market, and was the author of an 'Ode to the Skylark'; there were dogs who meant more to him than some of his friends did. As athlete, archer, drinker, he would not have been out of place in Beowulf's boat or Hrothgar's hall, any more than Houg would have been. He could show both the insentience and the sensitivity of such a man.

The treatise has no use for obtruded sensibility, but is not without feeling. It argues that 'sheep are the most suitable stock in the world for these countries' – the Highlands; but we must not 'drive the people from their poor but native huts and glens until some other source of industry is opened to them'. The Clearances had already started to drive the people out, and 'America hath been the resort and grave' of too many Highlanders (some of his own family would one day emigrate there, and to New Zealand). The treatise would not be Hogg's, moreover, without word of a little monster who haunts the hilltops and is called by shepherds Phaam.[8]

Sheep farming had expanded greatly in the later eighteenth century. On one of his trips to the Highlands Hogg noted that 'the whole of Glengarry was made over to sheep.' As an agriculturalist, Hogg was to complain about a Border reluctance to improve (not much in evidence in the Lothians and the Berwickshire Merse), but he doubted the utility of the introduction to the Border lands of the Cheviot breed, which had come 'in the room of the old rough, hardy, black-faced natives of the soil'. Cheviots lacked horns, and were unsuitable, he felt, to the Border environment. They were ghostly pale. A shepherd prayed to God in a style Hogg loved to reproduce: 'If it is thy will that black should become white, we have nothing earthly to say.' An Ettrick shepherd quarrelled with his neighbour's opinions on this subject: Hogg, he said, was not a man for whom facts are chiels that winna ding – won't bend or break.[9]

One of the faces of Lowlands improvement was the amalgamation of farms, a development which made employers, and magnates, of ambitious and competitive farmers – in the Merse, for instance. The difference between the gudeman and the hind was no longer, as it had once been, a difference of degree rather than kind. Historians have argued that the change was of benefit to the labour force in the 1820s, but Hogg was saying in his late fifties, at the end of the decade, that it had produced a debasement, an enslavement. Farms were joined up, while social classes were thought to have become divorced – for all the probability that chances to rise in the world were better than they had been. Laurance Saunders's *Scottish Democracy* of 1950 observes that 'social distance and class distinction were growing,' while Hogg's contemporary James Ballantine, poet, stained-glass artist and self-styled gaberlunzie or romantic vagrant, looked back, as others did, and as is often done, at a finer past: 'The different classes, although as well defined then as now, associated more with each other, a better feeling was kept up between the higher and lower orders.'[10]

An immense public drama of Hogg's lifetime was the quest for an improved Parliament in the 1820s and the passing of the first Reform Bill in 1832, which extended the franchise among middle-income elements and attempted to fashion a half-way representative urban electorate. The Scottish electorate increased thirteen-fold; 43,000 were now able to vote. Hogg was friends with those who felt that this was democracy, and the end of the world. But it did not put an end to the acutely class-conscious Scotland with which he was familiar. After Hogg's death, John Heiton wrote of Edinburgh, 'the pressure upwards has become a war of pride and envy between caste and caste,'[11] and Hogg himself could be remembered as something of an anomaly: 'it did not seem as if he had the slightest veneration for any one more than another whom he addressed, no matter what was their rank or position.'[12]

His adult life spanned the interval of forty-three years between the French Revolution and the Reform Bill. The first of these events brought a time of political oppression. For his contemporary Henry Cockburn it was the horror, and the hope, of Edinburgh citizens, their all-in-all for twenty years. There is no reason, however, to think that it was like that for Hogg, whose writings speak frequently of Jacobites, rarely of Jacobins. This is not to deny that his world was shaken by what occurred in 1789. For the Hogg impersonated in *Blackwood's Magazine*, as in the issue of October 1826, it was a topsyturvying, or tapsalteerying, of society and a rampaging of fiends.

In the course of Hogg's lifetime there were two industrial depressions – 1816–7 and 1827–8 – and a momentous shift from country to city. In the 1830s two-thirds of the population were still living in the country. Nevertheless, the proportion of Scots living in towns doubled over the fifty years from 1750. The national population was presently to rise by 88 per cent to 2.374 million, many of them servants and beneficiaries of an empire of 20 million, a quarter of the people in the world. Edinburgh was now two cities – an Old Town and a Classical New Town, where, in 1816, on the Regency promenade of Princes Street, Hogg's future publisher William Blackwood set up his new shop. Scotland had been two countries – Highlands and Lowlands – and there were now, with the advent of an industrialised central corridor, two sets of Lowlands.

The Edinburgh of his middle years found a new buoyancy and prosperity. The capital of North Britain had become a middle-class city, swollen though it was to twice its population size by Irish and other incomers: a city of books and book production, of concerts, a hive of professional activity, rather than a patrician faubourg or an aggregation of factories. The second decade of the new century brought a spell of financial disruption, and a new sense of political possibility. In 1830, the city went bankrupt, as many of its citizens had been doing. Two years later the ancien régime staggered from the blow of the Reform Bill, and by the particular zeal for its enactment shown in Scotland. The old world of rank and order, it was feared, had gone. Blackwood's writers, joined by Hogg from the country, were against 'the Jacobin Bill'. 'Let weel bide,' they cried. Let well alone.

His Tory friends were also against Britain's industrial proletariat. In 1821, Henry Glassford Bell, in due course editor of the *Edinburgh Literary Journal* and Sheriff of Lanarkshire, wrote Hogg an 'agreeable letter', according to Hogg's daughter Mary, which said: 'I am quite sure that the annihilation of twenty thousand of the mob in all the populous towns would do an immense deal of good, and nothing would give me greater pleasure than to see Wellington making a progress through the country with a few pieces of artillery for this purpose.'[13] Bell's shells were one way of dealing with a slavery of the towns which was becoming more of a threat than the slavery Hogg was to perceive in the country.

The arch-improver Sir John Sinclair's *Statistical Account of Scotland*, completed in 1799, contains a statement by a Selkirkshire minister, one of his informants, who spoke of 'the impolitic practice of adding farm to farm', and of 'the fatal operation of poors-rates'. Of the 1700 inhabitants of his countryside, town and hinterland together, forty-two gained from the compulsory provision for the poor to which he was opposed, as unfriendly to the cause of virtue. Enquiries into the problem of depopulation should bear in mind, he suggests, 'the dissipation of the lower ranks, which makes them afraid of marriage, and desirous of enjoying the pleasures, without the burdens of matrimony'. There they were on their night walks. His was a parish in which people were leaving for the town and for the Empire, and in which he heard 'the cries of starving infants'.[14]

The Rev. Robert Russell reported, in the *Statistical Account*, that the parish of Ettrick, from which he flitted next door to Yarrow at this point, 'possesses no advantage'. Lord Napier was patron of the kirk and owner of St Mary's Loch. Ten non-resident proprietors are listed. Barley, oats and potatoes are the sole crops. For months at a time, 'no intercourse with mankind'. Reporting from Yarrow in 1793, Russell calls for more Cheviots, and remarks that poors-rates are a 'noble institution': they give rise to squandering but relieve 'virtuous poverty and distress'.[15] Russell was to refuse Hogg's father, an elder of his kirk, a pair of boots from the collection-plate money, and was to become Hogg's friend.

Hogg's troglodyte youth, with its holes and hungers, imparted to his writings an interest in appetite which he shared with a circle of Edinburgh friends very few of whom can ever have starved. Since the great famine of the late seventeenth century, severe scarcities had returned, as in 1740, and harvests failed disastrously when he was in his twenties. When he was old, he referred to himself as a ravenous mountain man who has 'suffered sae muckle wi' hunger an' thirst'. In 1825, a poem of his was published,[16] 'The Grousome Caryl', written in the antique Scots he invented for ballad purposes, a poem in which Lord Annerdaille and his men chase an ogre, a cannibal king, holed up in the hills with his hellish brood. Their lair is not far from Queensberry Hill, and from the famous waterfall the Grey Mare's Tail, on the brink of Hogg's main Border region. ' "Who holdis this holle," cryit Annandaille.' The soldiers engage the ogre, take casualties, and are aghast at what comes next:

> For there they saw both wyffis and barnis,
>   Of frychtsome gyant brode,
> Come runnyng out of the horryde holle,
>   And drynke their kinsmenis blode.

A Border archer of renown is called in to exterminate the brutes. Hogg was himself to prove a Border archer of renown. He was also, in another of his incarnations, a kind of cannibal king.

A little earlier, in 1822, he produced a hunger story, rarely discussed, which is among his most marvellous pieces of writing. It forms part of a storytelling competition staged in his burlesque romance *The Three Perils of Man*, but it seems significant that he chose to republish it at the end of his life as an item in the collection *Altrive Tales*. It is certainly strong enough to stand on its own. The romance is set in the Middle Ages. A party of travellers is penned in Michael Scott's magic castle of Aikwood down the glen from Hogg's cottages. One of the party, a friar, is apparently the Franciscan Faustus Roger Bacon – in this context, a name to conjure with in more ways than one. Doublings, masquerades and metamorphoses break out, as does a feast at which one of the party is consumed. The competition stories are told, Scheherazade-style, under threat of starvation and death. This particular story, in a most energetic Scots, is that of the Laird of Peatstacknowe and is about a youth called Marion's Jock.[17] Marion is a single mother whose silly son, whose 'gilliegaupy of a callant', would have eaten the backside off a horse. He is voracious, bulimic. His pangs are a wonder.

Jock is put to work with a violent, 'grumphing' farmer, who is appalled by the boy's eagerness for a bacon ham, which he attacks with his gully knife and swiftly roasts. Goodman Niddery demands that the weapon be surrendered. 'Jock fixed his green eyes on his master's face. He could hardly believe him to be serious ...' The master knocks him down. 'The creature's bacon mad,' cries the goodwife. Jock is installed in his herd's hole, a 'small shieling' with kindling for a fire but with nothing to cook. 'Among Jock's fat sheep there was one fat ewe lamb, the flower of the flock, which the goodwife and the goodman both loved and valued above all the rest. She was as beautiful and playful as innocence itself, and, withal, *as fat as she could lie in her skin*.' Jock fondles the lovely lamb and is caught up in a murder which is written to resemble a rape. 'She struggled a little now and then, but finding that it availed not, she gave it over,' uttering no more than a single bleat. Jock tells her, 'I canna help it' – something Hogg was given to saying. 'Ye are suffering for a' your bits o' ill done deeds now.'

He eats the ewe in a long agony of delight. The following morning, the farmer asks him where she is and if he 'had her yestreen'. 'O yes! Jock was sure he had her yestreen.' By now, 'his strong appetite for fat flesh was somewhat allayed.' The farmer gets to know what has been done, as if to a man's daughter, by his 'carnivorous herd'. Jock dispatches his master and sprints for freedom, his apprenticeship over. 'Let me gang!'

Michael Scott notes that a maiden in the party is 'the favourite lamb' whom this storyteller 'wishes you to kill and feast on in the same delicious manner as did the hero of his tale'. For Hogg at times, and for some of his contemporaries, hunger and sexual desire were mirror images, in a Scotland where starvation had no friends and sexual abstinence came to be idealised by men who did not practise it.

Another of the storytellers, known as the Deil's Tam, identifies himself as the hero of this tale, and adds some further adventures in a story of his own.[18] 'I wish ye wadna always turn your green een on me that gate when you speak about your fat flesh,' says a companion. Tam is cannibal stuff. His tale 'goeth here and there, without bound or limit', as Friar Bacon points out, in a spirit of appreciation. Bounds and limits, freedom and deliverance, are constituents of an ethic and of an aesthetic in Hogg's writings. If the Deil's Tam is the hero of the heartfelt tale of Marion's Jock, so is Hogg, who is of the Devil's party on this occasion, as on some others. His works imagine for the human individual an internal division and diversity in which the Devil may take part.

Hogg's early and lasting friendship with his relative William Laidlaw, the poet who became Walter Scott's secretary, and Laidlaw's portrait of Hogg as a young man, are proof in themselves that his early life was far from a morass of hardship and ignorance. His person fascinated his contemporaries. He was pictured in a series of paintings and engravings, and of conflicting verbal descriptions. An equivocal icon, he was a man of feeling and a child of nature, his hair 'lissome as a woman's', and a man of the woods with buck teeth, or tusks, and stringy hair. He was both heaven-taught and earthy, both delicate and gross. He was and was not tall.

The early impressions, and the hagiographic after-images derived from these, are benign. Here is Laidlaw's account of his entries at the age of nineteen into the local kirk:

Hogg was rather above the middle height, of faultless symmetry of form; he was of almost unequalled agility and swiftness. His face was then round and full, and of a ruddy complexion, with light blue eyes that beamed with gaiety, glee, and good-humour, the effect of the most exuberant animal spirits. His head was covered with a singular profusion of light-brown hair, which he was obliged to wear coiled up under his hat. On entering church on a Sunday, where he was all his life a regular attender, he used, on lifting his hat, to raise his right hand to assist a graceful shake of his head in laying back his long hair, which rolled down his back, and fell below his loins. And every female eye was upon him, as, with light step, he ascended the stair to the gallery where he sat.[19]

The minister in the pulpit may have had long hair too. The Rev. Robert Russell followed the fashion of the time and used curl papers on Saturday nights in preparation for the Sabbath. 'Hogg and I were unbounded laughers' in their youth, said Laidlaw, 'when the occasion was very good'.[20]

Poor Hogg, as he was to be constantly referred to in time to come, was evoked in a novel of 1824, *Scotch Novel Reading*, 'by a Cockney' – Sarah Green. This belongs to the school of the anti-romantic fictions of the day, such as *Northanger Abbey* and Eaton Stannard Barrett's *The Heroine*. The romance of Scotland is seen in the novel as so much quackery. Green's heroine is an English Regency belle who goes about speaking a patois learnt from the Waverley novels ('I maun say, I am unco fashed to hear your lack o' guid taste'), in pursuit of an 'airy dream of Scotch perfection' which includes 'the sunny ringlets floating over the rosy cheek of poor Hogg', of the distressing surname, who was then in his fifties.[21]

Many writers have pretended to be shepherds. Hogg really was a shepherd, while also, at times, a pretender, a role-player. His writings contained within them an extraordinary achievement, which it took a revolution in taste to uncover. It can also be said of them that they were both cause and consequence of a rise to notability in the divided world of the United Kingdom – the United Kingdom he inhabited and accepted, Scots patriot though he always was. His was a precarious rise, and there were falls. Walter Scott said of his writings that they were like those of a man on a tightrope. He became a husband and father, and a master of servants, but was never rich and often poor. He moved from bare subsistence as Jamie Hogg to international fame as 'the Ettrick Shepherd', from starvation and from shieling disquisitions to the 'Noctes Ambrosianae' symposia in *Blackwood's Edinburgh Magazine*, which were real feasts, sited in Ambrose's tavern, as well as barmecidal or imaginary ones, and in which his conversation was mimicked by John Wilson, alias Christopher North, and John Gibson Lockhart, Tory scriptwriters assisted by the man himself, and his vicarious presence was the chief attraction. He was to show, and to affect, the 'innocent rusticity' and 'blunt simplicity' that sophisticates expect from country folk and men of action; and yet he was to project a psychology – whereby the idea of a collective humanity is married to that of an individual multiplicity – which has contributed to the way we think of ourselves now.

Out of his holes, out of the deep past, out of the oral and the immemorial, he has come to take his place in the business of posterity, the transactions of modernity. Expressions of his anticipate later usage. In one of his parody poems he wrote of 'the sexual intercourse of things'. In another poem, where a knight encounters an enchantress,

> She took so moving a position
> That set his soul in full ignition.

And he was a wielder of the figurative electric shocks which became fashionable during his lifetime and have been current ever since. Scott used the metaphor with reference to the fond kiss exchanged by George IV, at his Coronation, with his brother the Duke of York – an embrace that 'approached almost to a caress, and impressed all present with the electrical conviction, that the nearest to the throne in blood was the nearest also in affection.' Soon after this, Scott went to Ireland and kissed the Blarney Stone. At the time of the king's visit to Edinburgh after his Coronation, a welcome given to Sir Walter on the High Street impressed Sir Robert Peel with a notion of 'the electric shock of a nation's gratitude'. As for the first number of the Whig *Edinburgh Review*, that, too, was 'electrical' – Henry Cockburn's word for this event of 1802. And 'the force of the shock was increased on each subsequent discharge.'[22]

CHAPTER TWO

First Poems

To turn back to Hogg's early years is to meet the eye of his strong mother. His mother Margaret, he was made to say in *Blackwood's*, or said there, in another of his anticipations of the future, was no 'regular smoker', and it is possible to think of her, with her occasional or notional pipe, her lore, her hereditary connections with the spirit world, as a little witch-like. She and her son James, and her brother, another William Laidlaw, furnished Walter Scott with material for his *Minstrelsy of the Scottish Border*, but she was displeased with what she saw of its first two volumes, and upbraided Sheriff Scott. By printing her songs he had broken a charm. 'Ye hae spoilt them a'thegither. They war made for singing, an' no for reading; and they're nouther right spelled nor right setten down.' This comes, complete with its semi-colon, from Hogg's *Memoir*,[1] and suggests that his mother can't have been wholly unable to read. She had been known to cry over the education she had been denied, but was said to have had much of the Bible by heart and to have taught the Psalms to her son James. She lived to a great age, as did her husband, and when she died at eighty-three, he grieved, *en poète*, that he would now have no one to be kind to.

In a manuscript letter of 1813 to a bookseller, Bernard Barton of Woodbridge, Suffolk – a bank clerk and poet, a friend of Charles Lamb's – Hogg refers to patronage matters, to another literary contact, the poet and historian William Roscoe of Liverpool, and to his mother's death: 'I have lost the warmest, the sincerest and in a word the best friend that ever I had in this world or am ever likely to have. My old mother to whom my attachment was such as cannot be described is no more and I am just returned from paying the last sad duties to her to whom I owed everything that a son could pay and from comforting an aged father who is now left right solitary. I have however this solace that her existence was lengthened while it could be comfortable to herself, valuable to her friends it always was.' Her death has caused him to delay replying to a letter from this member of his circle of supporters and correspondents; such 'indolence', he adds, is 'notable even to a proverb among my friends'. Barton later gave out that Hogg had intimated to him that he was the author of Scott's anonymous 'Tales of My Landlord'.[2]

His mother's songs, ballads and stories 'formed the groundwork of my intellectual being'; she was a 'living miscellany' of this material. Hogg's brother William wrote correctively of her indifference to 'the best pieces of English poetry' read to her by William, and of his father Robert's ear for a 'fine description'.[3] The Hogg parents had four sons, of whom James was the second. The family's ancestral connection with the Scotts of Harden was commemorated in an old rhyme quoted by Hogg and by Walter Scott:

> If ye reave the Hoggs of Fauldshop
> Ye herry Harden's gear;
> But the poor Hoggs of Fauldshop
> Have had a stormy year.

If you raid the Hoggs, you raid these Scotts, that is to say; and it's also to say that the Hoggs were controlled by the Scotts.

Fauldshope, to be distinguished from Phawhope or Phaup, was a tract of heath, winds and waters, four miles south-west of Selkirk. Nearby was the wizard's castle of Aikwood (the present Lord of Aikwood is the Liberal Democrat politician David Steel). On top of the hills sat a thick, dark cloud, and lots of spirits had been seen there in Margaret Hogg's time. Hogg's parents lie buried in Ettrick churchyard, and so does their son James, and so does his maternal grandfather, 'the far-famed Will o' Phaup, who for feats of frolic, agility and strength had no equal in his day', according to the blithe epitaph on the gravestone shared with his daughter and her husband. This William Laidlaw was a shepherd, a runner, a fighter, a drinker, and, according to his grandson, both a 'welcome guest' and a truth-teller, a 'man of probity' who was also the last man in this wild region to converse with the fairies.[4]

James Hogg both believed and disbelieved in fairies. 'Several of the wives of Fauldshope were supposed to be rank witches,' he wrote, and a famous one got the better, at a cost, of Michael Scott, in a clash of spells, by turning him into a hare and hunting him with his own dogs ('Shu, Michael, rin or dee'), until he was forced, some said, to 'take shelter in his own jaw-hole'. Michael instructs a servant to place above the woman's lintel 'a line written in red characters', which turns her into a dervish, dancing naked round the fire with her kin. The note is removed, the madness lifts, but 'poor Lucky', Hogg's forebear, dies overnight.[5]

The spirits of the glen had given way to the light of the Gospel. But only up to a point, and only very recently. They were not forgotten, and were indeed not gone, for ghosts, brownies and bogles, 'awful, terrible bogles', were 'as plenty as ever', while some still alive 'have had intercourse with fairies, and the stories of their pranks and gambols are listened to with more attention, and as much faith annexed, as the gospel according to Matthew.'

The letter in which Hogg says this is one of the series of articles in the *Scots Magazine* (1802-3) which describe a Highland journey. On his way he overtook a beggar woman. She had been born in America of 'good' family, and had experienced adventures, 'or misadventures, as Sancho called them', which forced her 'to beg for a precarious existence amongst the mountains of Scotland'. On top of the Border hills, to the east of the Ettrick summit of Phaup-penn, she fell and broke a leg, in February 1801: 'Here she lay crying until her voice failed, but no help appeared; and finding that she must soon perish of cold, she took some few appendages, necessary to her occupation, and fastening them round her waist, tried her last effort to save a wretched life. Night was now coming on . . .' She crawled for two days, till at last she was spotted from the 'led' or amalgamated farm of Broadgarehill, a red napkin tied round her head. 'The people seeing such a horrible phaenomenon approaching them, and knowing that no such monster inhabited their mountains, readily concluded it to be the devil, and began a dispute which of them he was come in quest of.' They fled, all but one lad, who went up and touched the stranger, still uncertain as 'to what class of beings she belonged'. She proved to be flesh and blood, and was received by the parish, attended by a surgeon, and 'then, poor creature! was again turned on the wide world to beg her bread from door to door!'[6]

Will o' Phaup's dealings with the supernatural are recounted by his grandson in his *Shepherd's Calendar*, where he mentions that – like

17

Marion's Jock – Will beat his master, then sprang up and bounded away to the hill. On another occasion, as he sat by his shieling at Old Upper Phaup, he was visited by three fairies in the likeness of children. 'Good e'en t'ye, creatures,' he greeted them. Perhaps they were 'some gentleman's sons come from his master'. They ask to be put up for the night, and astoundingly explain that they are commissioned to demand from him a silver key. 'A silver key? In God's name, where came ye from?' At this pronouncement of the name of God the creatures disappear in the twinkling of an eye. Nothing more has ever been heard of the silver key.

On a further occasion, Will creeps into an opening in a hill scarcely big enough to admit a man, and finds himself in a magic barn; the villagers were afterwards unable to locate it. These meetings are associated with Tam o' Shanter rides back from market-day drinking in Moffat to the 'outskirts' of Ettrick Forest, 'quite out of the range of social intercourse, a fit retirement for lawless banditti, and a genial one for the last retreat of the spirits of the glen'. He beheld them once, in grass-green bonnets, sitting with their queen in seven circles: he had been drawn to them by 'their mysterious whisperings, of which he knew no word, save now and then the repetition of his own name, which was always done in a strain of pity'. Hogg's poetry has many fairies. But none is more persuasive than those glimpsed in the prose he wrote about his grandfather.

The world was told that when Hogg was about to enter it, a midwife or houdy was sought by a timid rider, afraid to cross the Ettrick. The Brownie of Bodsbeck unhorsed him, carried the houdy home, and gave a wild shout when Hogg was shown to his parents. Another magic trick entailed sharing a birthday with Burns by postponing his date of birth to 25 January 1772. He spent his life believing in this false birthday, and was only disabused in 1833.

William Hogg said of his brother that in the playground he would race and wrestle with the bigger boys, undiscouraged, but that when he grew up, 'writing out his songs was a more serious affair than a race or wrestling-match. He first stripped off his coat and vest; yet, notwith-standing, his wrist took the cramp, so that he could rarely make out more than six lines at a sitting.' In later life, sheep-smearing cost him days of stiff fingers. James would one day mistake himself, in a London mirror, for his observant brother. At sixteen he was in the service of one of the region's Laidlaws, with whom the Hogg family was intricately connected: at Willenslee, where there were books. He read with immoderate fondness Hamilton of Gilbertfield's modernisation of Blind Harry's poem about the liberator Wallace, finding in it a word that was to be applied to himself, the future apostle of duality: 'aefauld', meaning single-hearted or loyal. The original poem has, in Wallace's lament for his dead comrade Sir John the Graham, the undying line: 'My a fald freynd, quhen I was hardest stad!' This Ettrick shepherd also read *The Gentle Shepherd*, by Allan Ramsay, Scotland's premier pastoral; and the *Theory of the Conflagration of the Earth*, an apocalyptic cosmogony which he attributed to Bishop Burnet, but which was the work of the enquiring Thomas Burnet. Said Hogg: 'All the day I was pondering on the grand millennium, and the reign of the saints; and all the night dreaming of new heavens and a new earth – the stars in horror, and the world in flames!' He still had trouble reading some of his books. He was like the man from Eskdalemuir who borrowed a dictionary and returned it with the words: 'I dinna ken, man, I have read it all through, but canna say that I understand it; it is the most confused book that ever I saw in my life!'[7]

In 1790, at the age of twenty, he was taken on by another of his Laidlaw masters, a relative, with whom, at Blackhouse, he remained for a period of ten years, which made all the difference to him, in coaxing his literary flame. Around 1793 he began to write poems. 'I about this time began to read with considerable attention; – and no sooner did I begin to read so as to understand, than, rather prematurely, I began to write.' The house had a fair library, on which this self-styled 'illiterate' fed, while also subscribing to Mr Elder's 'collecting library' in Peebles, and the son of the house was the poet William Laidlaw, who became Hogg's fast friend, and Scott's fast friend, factor and amanuensis. A letter to him of 1800 reports on a visit to Perthshire and closes with: 'You must pardon my inaccuracies as they proceed from haste and wearyness. I am Dear William at whatever distance, Yours sincerely, James Hogg.'[8] They were indeed dear to each other, and Laidlaw did as much as anyone, including Scott, to advise and assist Hogg. Both Laidlaw and Scott wanted him to take more pains. The former, wrote Hogg, 'hath often remonstrated with me, in vain, on the necessity of a revisal of my pieces; but, in spite of him, I held fast my integrity.' To the Blackhouse years belongs the James Hogg of the *espièglerie* noted by Laidlaw, of the sparkling eye and floating hair, who would captivate the kirk where he would later be the precentor, his collie howling along with the hymns.[9]

Laidlaw took pains with his poem 'Lucy's Flittin", which was one of the most celebrated of the Scottish nineteenth century but which has escaped the notice of subsequent anthologists; no doubt it has been seen as a precursor of the Kailyard school of later in the century, as an example of the sentimentalising of country life which gained ground with the industrial revolution. The poem certainly has, against the grain of its dactylics, a premeditated and excessive pathos. But it's an excellent piece of work, for all that. The opening stanza carries a subtle Scots rhyme, in line three, worthy of Hugh MacDiarmid's Lallans of the 1920s, a poetry which arose only a few miles from Queensberry Hill, and from Thomas Carlyle's Ecclefechan:

> 'Twas when the wan leaf frae the birk tree was fa'in,
> And Martinmas dowie had wound up the year,
> That Lucy rowed up her wee kist wi' her a' in't,
> And left her auld maister and neebours sae dear.

Orphan Lucy had served her summer term as a farm servant: such terms were commonly settled at hiring fairs and servants were used to flitting. Everyone is as sad as she is over her departure, and the poem gives no clue as to why her contract hasn't been renewed. Has she been looking to improve herself?

> If I wasna ettled to be ony better,
> Then what gars me wish ony better to be?

She has received a blue ribbon from her friend Jamie, but the suggestion is that they won't be seeing each other any more. They could always have kept up. Rumour identified Lucy's situation with the Laidlaw family, and also had it that she had been deserted by her master's son. At all events, there's a fatalistic relish for misfortune in the poem. When Hogg included it in a collection of verse by various hands, *The Forest Minstrel*, he added eight lines (condemned by John Buchan, understandably enough) in which he compounds Lucy's bad time by killing her off. The farm Lucy flits from, the Glen, was near Innerleithen. Later in the century a new-made industrialist, Charles Tennant, built a castle there of that name, where the twentieth-century novelist Emma Tennant was to spend some of her girlhood.

Hogg's first published poem, 'The Mistakes of a Night' (subtitle of Goldsmith's play *She Stoops to Conquer*), is very different from 'Lucy's Flittin''. It is not a caring poem. It's a song in Scots for an old Scots tune, and it shows the rough countryman, having a laugh. Geordie hies off over the moor to court shy Maggie and unknowingly sleeps with her widowed mother instead. Nights can be very dark in Yarrow. He tells himself that he has tamed his 'skittish elf', Maggie, but is then haled before the minister. The 'grand mistake' is cleared up. Cursing and ruing, he marries the widow, who is about to 'turn a mammy'. The poem ends ineptly with healths drunk to all concerned and with the wish that

> warse than happen'd Geordie Scott
> Meet ev'ry f—r.

Fornicators, may they rot in hell, were more frequent than phoenixes in the Borders, and the poem invites a glance into the abyss which was often to separate practice and profession in the sexual life of his society. The poem also inaugurates Hogg's engagement with the subject-matter of dissimulation, error and disguise which was to mean much to him.

This is a swaggering work which is confident of its audience and of its Scots words. Hogg was later to move to a poetry predominantly in English, and to an accommodation with the charges of indelicacy which his writing incurred from the beginning; but he was never to foreclose on the desire to write like a Scottish Borderer, and one of the last poems he wrote was even 'coarser' than this one, whose merits are highlighted by the apology which accompanied its appearance in the *Scots Magazine* for October 1794. The editor was disposed to encourage a young poet: but 'we hope he will improve, for which end we advise him to be at more pains to make his rhymes answer, and to attend more to grammatical accuracy.'

Among his earliest poems is one of his best-known: the patriotic bawl – virtually a recruiting song – 'My name it is Donald McDonald', written among his lambs on Blackhouse Heights. Donald, with his kilt and feather, sword and buckler, is a Highland bravo who did it for the Jacobites and is now all for George in his struggle with Napoleon. The song took like a charm and passed into folk possession. Hogg got no money for it and, for a time, no authorial credit. He heard it sung by a soldier tramping through a wood; a General McDonald had it roared in the mess, under the impression that it was a tribute to his own valour; and when Hogg sat through the encores in a Lancaster theatre for a rendering of the song augmented by an even more chauvinistic, British Empire verse by someone else, he informed a Yorkshire manufacturer that he, Hogg, had done it. The Yorkshireman thought him a half-crazed Scots pedlar.

During the first year of the new century, Hogg explains, 'Jamie the Poeter', as he'd become in the Borders, 'most sapiently determined on publishing a pamphlet, and appealing to the world at once'. In the autumn of that year he went to Edinburgh to sell sheep, and on the Monday of the week in question the sale was slow. He was left with some animals, which he placed in a park, meaning to try again on the Wednesday. With time to kill, he found a printing-shop and wrote out a few of his pieces from memory – 'not the best, but those that I remembered best'. Such were his *Scottish Pastorals*. In January 1801, back in the Forest, he wrote downcast to William Laidlaw to say that his health seemed to have 'gone into Edinburgh to see what is become of my poems'.[10] He says in his *Memoir* that he was mortified to find misprints and omissions in an early copy or proof copy of the book: this was an earnest of the anxieties that were to attend his dealings with publishers and his contested accounts of these dealings. No great harm was done on this occasion. He seems to have made corrections, and the text as it now stands could do with more.

Problems of a different order had also arisen. These pastorals are intensely local, and it was felt that local feelings might be hurt or inflamed. Should the publisher have been allowed to call him a farmer? He was a lesser man than that. Nor was he a tenant. His father, to whom he had by then returned, was the tenant. Would Francis, Lord Napier, seventh Baronet, be offended by an inoffensive reference to him? Hogg spoke to Laidlaw of fighting a duel with this proprietor, with rocks, on his lordship's hillside. A 'pickle' for Lord Napier that would be. 'I don't give a farthing for him nor any nobleman in Scotland.'[11] Duels were to be an aspect of his future.

Elaine Petrie, editor of a modern edition of the *Scottish Pastorals*, is right to praise them for their vigour and their candour. They consist of seven items, 'mostly written in the dialect of the South', according to a subtitle – Scotland's South. A man's memory might have written them all down between markets, while making them new as well, and forgetting bits: Border memories were long, and Walter Scott's has been termed eidetic, which can mean of a hallucinatory vividness, or, perhaps, 'photographic'. They are in Scots and in English, sensibility's polite English for the most part, and in both at once. Scots and English are branches of the same language, and in Hogg's hands, as in those of others, the two are often one. The first item is a lively comic dirge for a gypsy fiddler, Geordie Fa; the next is an eclogue, 'Dusty, or Watie an' Geordie's Review of Politics', which opens with an echo of Burns's poem on his birthday. Hogg writes:

> On June, the year, nor less nor mae
> Than eighteen hunder a' but twae ...

The topicalities in the poem, begun in 1793, were updated over the years that followed. Watie and Geordie are complainers. Watie, of a Cameronian or Covenanting turn, asserts that religion has become a laughing-stock. Geordie says the time-honoured thing: 'My dear dear country gaun to ruin.' 'We've a liferent,' he goes on, 'O' slav'ry o' the hardest kind.' And 'the French ir comin' to invade us.' The tax on dogs is deplored, and Geordie has been forced to hang his faithful collie, a gruelling scene (which Hogg treats as expectable, though the dog could always have been spared).

'Willie an' Keatie' is a pastoral romance, fast and fresh, like a tumbling burn, in the style of Ramsay. A 'lovely bloomin' shepherd' tells a story which Hogg said was true to his own life. Willie prepares to go wooing:

> Now my yellow hair I plaited,
> Gae my downy chin a shave,
> Thrice my tales of love repeated,
> Fearin' I would misbehave.

Keatie affects to marry a rich man in order to test her shepherd, and a friend disguises himself as a fortune-teller in order to sound her out. The poem closes with

> Constancy an' perseverance
> Ever will rewarded be.

Walter Bryden of Crosslee, the neighbouring farmer who had stood by the Hoggs at the time of their fall from what they later described as opulence, was killed by 'the stroke of a tree'. A 'rose of gratitude' is bestowed here, in 'Dialogue in a Country Churchyard', on his tomb.

Two songs round the collection off. In one, a grand youth vows marriage to a country lass; his father won't mind. In the second, a shepherd is accosted by a grand youth who wants to know the way to Traquair. He's down in the Borders for the lasses and to sing with the swains. Now he is leaving 'this modern Parnassus', having seduced a certain Jeanie. The shepherd is angry: 'Afore I forgie her I'll pit out her breath.' Jeanie then sheds her disguise, and the shepherd wraps her in his plaid.

In November 1798, in the midst of these thriving poems, Hogg's breath was very nearly put out by a bowel complaint. A close call. According to the *Scots Magazine*, his ghost – 'or wraith, as we call that nonentity' – was seen.[12]

The *Scottish Pastorals* would not be what they are without the example of his elder brothers in the Muses, Ramsay and Burns. Hogg's claim never to have heard till 1797 of the latter, whose songs he had been singing, and whose poems he had been learning from, is a pose which belongs to the fiction of the feral child which induced him to defer, in his *Memoir* and elsewhere, the starting-point of his literate and literary life. The claim is made in the *Memoir*, where he says he first heard of Burns a year after his death:[13]

> One day during that summer a half daft man, named John Scott, came to me on the hill, and to amuse me repeated Tam O' Shanter. I was delighted! I was far more than delighted – I was ravished! I cannot describe my feelings; but, in short, before Jock Scott left me, I could recite the poem from beginning to end, and it has been my favourite

poem ever since. He told me it was made by one Robert Burns, the sweetest poet that ever was born; but that he was now dead, and his place would never be supplied. He told me all about him, how he was born on the 25th of January, bred a ploughman, how many beautiful songs and poems he had composed, and that he had died last harvest, on the 21st of August.

The effect on him of 'Tam o' Shanter' was 'electrical', wrote Sir George Douglas in the last year of the nineteenth century.[14] He shed tears over the genius and fate of Burns. What was to hinder him from succeeding Burns? he asked himself. 'I too was born on the 25th of January, and I have more time to read and compose than any ploughman could have, and can sing more old songs than ever ploughman could in the world. But then I wept again because I could not write.' Nevertheless, he resolved to be a poet and to follow in Burns's footsteps. He tells the story again in the notes to an edition of Burns's verse which he did with William Motherwell. In this version a sceptical old man is quoted: 'Humph, where hae ye been a' your days that ye never heard o' Burns?'[15]

The young Hogg who wanted to be like Burns, and to excel him in some things, went to live, on Queensberry Hill, not far from where Burns had last lived, and where Allan Cunningham had heard him recite 'Tam o' Shanter'; having shared a pew with her in Dumfries, he came to admire Burns's widow – he had 'scarcely ever met a woman, either high or low, who improved as much on acquaintance'. 'She had a great deal of good sense and good nature.' And a pair of 'fine eyes'.

Hogg's minister, Robert Russell's son James, of Yarrow kirk, speaks in his *Reminiscences* of Burns's walk in the Borders with a friend in 1787. The two men reached Selkirk one afternoon and sought 'refreshment' at its 'principal inn'. Hearing 'loud sounds of merriment proceeding from the apartment above', Burns, 'with a tone of irony, said to the waiter, "My lad, you seem to have a prayer-meeting up-stairs."' These were farmers and their friends, enjoying themselves 'at a kind o' club they have'. Burns sent up to ask if two tourists might join them. The company wanted to know from the lad what sort of people they were. 'Very like country drovers,' said the lad. Ah well. 'Naturally enough, thinking they would be no great accession to the already hilarious circle, the members of the club instructed him to say that it would not be convenient.' The company was later 'chagrined above measure' to discover they had missed 'a nicht wi' Burns' – an expression Russell places in quotation-marks: Burns suppers and souvenirs had long been on the scene.

Hogg, master of disguise and of the traditional theme of the monarch incognito, supplied a version of the story in the notes to his edition of Burns, a version whose focus is the chagrin of one of the snubbing Selkirk worthies, Hogg's friend and Burns's fan, the surgeon Ebenezer Clarkson, who had been informed at the Forest Inn that 'the one spoke rather like a gentleman, but the other was a drover-looking chap.'[16]

This is a story about Hogg, as well as about Burns. He lived in a country whose adored writer, Walter Scott, suffered from 'a too high devotion' to titled rank, according to Hogg, from an adoration that approached servility. According to Scott's friend Lady Louisa Stuart, of the blood royal, Scott had 'too partial a regard for aristocracy'.[17] Such a partial regard was well within the sympathy, observance and convenience of many Scots, including Hogg, who was both democratic and deferential. He, too, was a sufferer, in his very different way, where rank was concerned. He rose in the world but never really left the Forest, and his 'low' birth is at the root of the disparagements to which he was subjected, both during his lifetime and long after he was dead.

Witness to this is the much-suspected Hogg of Edith Batho's study of 1927.[18] She suspects him herself, and blames him in a way that seems to owe something to a consciousness of class. 'He is a figure comic even in his iniquities.' She commends the shrewdness of an American visitor, who reported: 'His face is very pleasing, and shows much good nature and self-complacency. His light grey eye, when at rest, would not be distinguished for either quickness or brilliancy; his lips rather large, and not firm, seem to lack decision – if it were not for his noble forehead he might pass in a crowd for an ordinary man – a respectable farmer – but his is a broad and lofty brow, denoting both judgment and imagination.' The visitor thought he looked very like Scott, though Scott's was the higher brow. Edith Batho comments: 'The mouth not too firmly set might have been suspected' – like so much else of his. She suggests that the tale of Marion's Jock 'ought to have brought punishment on the teller' – Gibbie or Hogg. And she ends her book by saying that he was 'not undeserving, in spite of some lapses, of the affection which he received from better men'.

CHAPTER THREE

Ballad Work

Hogg was a collector of ballads. So was his mother, and his uncle William. So was Walter Scott. And so was Allan Cunningham, who relayed Scott's view that 'the Border was once peopled with poets, for every one that could fight could make ballads, some of them of great power and pathos. Some such people as the minstrels were living less than a century ago.'[1] In that last respect, ballads were for Hogg like fairies – only very recently deceased, if not still alive. Two theories of the Border Ballads and of their emergence from the past – by word of mouth and exercise of memory, in many cases – vied with each other in his youth, and were associated, respectively, with Bishop Percy and Joseph Ritson: that they were the work of a single author, a bard, a praiser of chiefs and exalter of war, and that they were communal, multiple. The distinction, and the absence of distinction, between writing (and remembering) as the exercise of a collective will and as the utterance of an individual were to be of importance to Hogg's literary life, and to his rogue membership of a literary coterie, the *Blackwood's* collective, with its composite compositions.

Both theories had to make what they could of a process of change deemed to have inflected or distorted the ballads in their passage down the years. An anxiety of the text, more appropriate to the first than the second of the theories, produced talk of impurity and corruption, and even – as in Edith Batho's treatment of Hogg's delivery of ballad material to Scott – of criminality. Such talk tends to be misplaced. Ballads were discovered in Hogg's day, and they were also freely imitated and invented, patched and copied. In a sense, all such ballads are imitations. To transmit is, in this context as in most, to create. An older Hogg told one of his many visitors that he'd taken Wattie in with certain of his discoveries, and an earlier Hogg admiringly suspected that his friend Allan Cunningham's *Remains of Nithsdale* and *Galloway Song* was the work of Allan Cunningham, an accomplished writer of verse whose parlour shanty 'A wet sheet and a flowing sea' was another good poem of the Scottish nineteenth century to fall from favour in later times.[2]

Hogg wrote ballads which could be and were called imitations, but which are his own work and were offered as that. They are among his best poems. Some represent an ironising and grotesquing of his sources, a self-mockery which is equally a burlesque of the tradition they perpetuate. 'Gilmanscleuch' is a tale of the Ettrick Forest, 'founded upon an ancient family tradition'. It has its native wood-notes, some very sweet.

> O weel to you, my little flower,
> That blumes in desart wilde.

It's about vassalage and internecine clan strife; a mysterious beggar man tells of a brash brother and of a Jock of Harden foully slain. The last stanza reads:

> A Scott must aye support ane Scott,
> When as he synketh low;
> But he that proudlye lifts his heide
> Must learne his place to knowe.

Once upon a time the Hoggs had known their place as feudal adherents of the Scotts, and that relationship had not been altogether effaced and forgotten. Hogg may be thought to have supported Walter Scott by gathering ballads for him as a form of service, a tithe, which was also a form of social advancement, and Scott was often to support Hogg, glad to do so and nobly obliged to do so.

Hogg said that during a respite from a night fishing, a salmon-spearing on the Tweed, he repeated 'Gilmanscleuch', got stuck and was helped out by the eidetic Scott, who explained that he'd once recited its eighty-eight stanzas from memory, having heard it 'sung' by its author on an earlier occasion. Scott was no singer, but his memory does seem to have been prodigious. It is hard to believe, to the letter, in the second of these feats, but it serves to indicate how oral transmission would have worked – with recourse, surely, to improvisation and omission. Writing to Louisa Stuart in 1801, Scott described himself as 'a ghost ballad writer', in words that seem to lean towards an expression of the present time.[3] It does no harm to take him at his word, and say that this is what he was, and what Hogg was, at times, in their engagement with the minstrelsy of the Scottish Border. They were minstrels themselves, after all, carrying on the good work.

In 1800, Hogg flitted from the Blackhouse Laidlaws in order to run Ettrickhouse farm for his father, a stay that lasted three years. A letter to William Laidlaw of that year mentions work in progress – a tragedy, *The Castle in the Wood*, and a comedy, *The Scots Gentleman*, neither of them completed – and lets him know that 'the people of Ettrick seem greatly to despise me,' because of his lack of worldly consequence: but 'I'll show them what company I keep.'[4] For both men, Walter Scott was a badly needed window of opportunity.

He may first have met Scott in Edinburgh, at the time when he drove his pastorals to market, together with his sheep. Lockhart's *Life of Scott* states that he met Scott shortly before the Grassmarket trip. John Sutherland's *Life of Scott* (1995) has it that their first meeting happened later, in 1802. At all events, Hogg had some months before the meeting read the first two volumes (published in Kelso in February 1802 and expanded to three for the second edition of 1803) of Scott's *Minstrelsy of the Scottish Border*, and had been sending him material through Laidlaw. Hogg was already a published poet when he met Scott, who was a year younger.

In 1802, the Hogg family at Ettrickhouse was visited by the young Sheriff-Depute (or principal law officer) of Selkirkshire, Walter Scott, who was threading its wilder regions in a round-up of old songs. Stanzas of a ballad he coveted, 'Auld Maitland', had been spoken to William Laidlaw by a servant girl, a Lucy, at his farm, and Hogg had then sent Scott a full version, vouched for by his mother, and obtained from his uncle, another William Laidlaw, and before him from yet another, agile Will o' Phaup.

These transactions have been more than once memorialised.[5] William Laidlaw gave an account, long unpublished, which tells of the arrival in the region, in 1802, of Scott and his co-collector John Leyden. When his visitors were struck by an 'alpine' view of St Mary's Loch, Laidlaw felt 'the same sort of pleasure as when I found that Walter Scott was delighted with James Hogg.' Scott noted 'poor Hogg's address', and the party called at Laidlaw's cousins, Walter and George Bryden of Ramseycleuch. Hogg 'came to tea', carrying an 'MS of some size': 'the penmanship done with more care than ever the poet bestowed on anything before'. Hogg sang – the themes of his songs 'too local, and perhaps of too low a caste'. The next morning Scott, Leyden and Laidlaw visited Hogg and his parents; old Robert may have thought these song zealots 'crazy fools'.

Scott, said Hogg, in one of the two versions he gave of the trans-actions, was 'in some dread' that parts of 'Auld Maitland' might have been forged. The dread was shared by Leyden, a gifted scholar cele-brated by Scott and Lockhart as a half-savage man of the people. Lockhart saw him as 'uncouth' and as almost entirely self-educated, though he was a graduate of Edinburgh University, and Edgar Johnson calls him 'a wild-looking scarecrow-figure with unshorn sandy hair and staring eyes',[6] which is almost word for word what journalist friends were to say about Hogg.

At Scott's table Leyden ate up a plate of raw beef to spite the vegetarian Ritson, whose neck on another occasion he threatened to thraw, till Scott shook a feather duster about his ears. His voice had its 'saw tones', said Scott, and when Hogg came to praise the verse of the impatient Leyden, 'the Harp of Teviot', he took this into account:

> Though false his tones at times might be,
> Though wild notes marred the symphony.

With reference to Hogg's contributions to the *Minstrelsy*, Leyden's 'saw' delivered the enquiry, with a reining-in of the black horse of the equestrian song-seeker: was he a poet? 'Very beautiful verses,' enthused Laidlaw, which showed 'great facility'. 'Let him beware of forgery,' rasped Leyden.[7]

A letter to Scott from Hogg at Ettrickhouse, dated 30 June 1802, is all support for Scott's labour of love, his 'raids' into the uplands of the Forest in search of ballads about ancestral raids into Northumberland. He is Scott's 'most humble and affectionate servant', who asks pardon for 'the freedom I have taken in addressing you'. And his tone is certainly quite free for a man of inferior rank not yet well-acquainted with his correspondent. He would be 'proud' of a visit: 'yet hang me if I would know what I would do wi' ye.' Here and elsewhere, deference puts on a quizzically bold face.

He remarks in the letter that the first two volumes of the collection were 'the first book I ever perused which was written by a person I had seen and conversed with'. He compares his mother's version with various items printed in these volumes. Of 'Auld Maitland' he writes: 'I am surprised to hear that this song is suspected by some to be a modern forgery; this will be best proved by most of the old people having a great part of it by heart.' He tells how his uncle William lost interest in ballads when he got religion. He had poured out a deluge of sermon talk on being primed with a 'hearty glass'. 'The mentioning a song put him in a passion.'[8]

'Auld Maitland' is a patriotic work, of the sort Scott classified as historical. He judged it of 'very high antiquity', as dating from Plantagenet times, and as perhaps 'the most authentic instance of a long and very old poem' preserved by traditional, oral, means alone. It was in a perfect state of preservation, like Tollund man, altogether free from illegal substances. It concerns the exploits of Maitland's three sons:

> We be three lads o' fair Scotland
> That fain wad fighting see.

They see it. King Edward's nephew's siege of the 'darksome house' of Leader-Town (Lauder) is beaten off. Later, there's carnage all round, and young Edward is done to death by a Maitland lad:

> Its ne'er be said in France, nor e'er
> In Scotland, when I'm hame,
> That Edward once lay under me,
> And e'er gat up again!

Carnivorous Leyden liked the idea of all that Southron blood being shed. A note by Scott agrees with his 'ingenious correspondent', a man 'in the humble situation of a shepherd', about the authenticity of the poem. The word 'portcullize' would not have been introduced by 'a modern ballad-maker'.[9]

Scott's visit to the wise woman, Mrs Hogg, is described by her son in a piece which was taken into his *Memoir* after it had appeared in the

Edinburgh Literary Journal (1829), and which appeared, authorially revised, in the *Familiar Anecdotes of Sir Walter Scott*, published in America. The second version is the more revealing. Both versions have Hogg hoeing at Ettrickhouse in the summer of 1801. An old man, Wat Shiel, tells him he must go down to Ramseycleuch. There are gentlemen who want to see him: 'I'm thinking it's the Shirra an' some o' his gang,' says Wat. At the Hoggs' house Margaret delivers her rebuke to Scott for spoiling her songs by printing them. Hogg writes:[10]

> 'Take ye that, Mr Scott,' said Laidlaw.
> Scott answered with a hearty laugh, and the quotation of a stanza from Wordsworth, on which my mother gave him a hearty rap on the knee with her open hand, and said, 'Ye'll find, however, that it is a' true that I'm tellin' ye.' My mother has been too true a prophetess, for from that day to this, these songs, which were the amusement of every winter evening, have never been sung more.

A profound print pessimism, not confined to the Hogg family, is registered here.

On his way down to Ramseycleuch, Hogg ran into Scott's groom, 'a greater original than his master'. This makes him sound like Tom Purdie, whom the Sheriff did not meet till 1804, when he appeared before him for poaching, so the story goes, and was invited by Scott to serve as his shepherd. This groom asked: 'Are ye the chap that mak's the auld ballads, an' sings them sae weel?' Hogg replied: 'I could not say that I had ever made ony very auld ballads.' A wonderful reply. In a certain sense, making and singing were the same for Hogg. He took part in the dynamism which produced the ballads. He spoke – and with one of his pens wrote – the language spoken by those who made them. He was what they were. He did what they did, adding and subtracting.

Hogg's accounts lack the astringent Leyden and lay stress on his mother's chaunting. In his 'Lines to Sir Walter Scott' he casts his mother as an 'ancient minstreless', who brings tears to Scott's nut-brown cheeks with her rendering of a martial vaunt from Maitland's sons.

> With fervid voice, and kindling eye,
> And withered arms waving on high,

she turns the words into an eldritch shriek which has Scott's fist banging the table: 'By —, sir, but that is the thing!'

Commentators have suggested that mother and son, and Laidlaw, may have patched and supplemented the ballad. Hogg says that his mother supplied a pedigree: she had heard it from her father and her brother William and from auld Andrew Moore, or Muir, a well-known authority, who'd heard it from auld Baby Mettlin – a 'corruption' of Maitland – 'wha was housekeeper to the first laird of Tushilaw'. Baby was a singer of the old songs, 'said to hae been another nor a gude ane', no better than she should be sexually, or perhaps a witch. This sounds like the voice of Hogg's outspoken mother. It does not sound like that of the forger of a pedigree. Edith Batho writes that, according to Andrew Lang, 'a seventeenth-century Maitland forged the ballad,' and that it was 'a really old ballad which has suffered from keeping bad company'.[11] Can she be referring to humble, dubious Baby Maitland, 'another nor a gude ane'?

A preface by Hogg to a ballad in his antique style, 'The Two Men of Colston', retails the activities of a Cumberland balladmonger, out to make a fortune.[12] The poem is a dialogue between a Hanoverian farmer and a Jacobite who speaks up with unction for the men-women, the he-brides, of the skirted clans, and for the true prince. The preface tells how two Scotsmen come to a widow's house 'in search of old songs'. She says she has plenty, but they are all written by her brother Twommy, 'whoy had mwore lear nwor wot to guyde it'. She warms to her account. 'Aweel, thoul't no hender Twommy, but he'll patch up a' the feyne ould sangs i' the weyde warld, and get them prentit in a beuk.' After a lifetime of 'gathering and penning' he is stuck, scolds his sister, with 'a batch o' scrawls, that nay body can read but the sell o' thee'. But perhaps the visiting Scotsmen will make a bid. Here is a caustic description of *The Minstrelsy of the Scottish Border*.

Scott has long been suspected of helping out his ballads, no one much minding. A copy of the *Minstrelsy* which I received in the 1940s, for a school essay on Scott's poetry, has inked-in evidence of my feeling that his poetry had taken part in his minstrel finds. 'She belted him with his noble brand' was 'perhaps interpolated by Scott'. Modern scholars have declared the 'ancient dirge', 'The Twa Corbies', to be largely his own work. It had, to be sure, been preceded by a similar poem, identified by

Ritson in a seventeenth-century printing. Scott's was better; it is, I shouted at sixteen, 'great, great poetry'. Hogg's suspected interpolations were hunted up more assiduously than Scott's – as those of a crafty peasant capable of passing off his own efforts as the work of some early harper, or of the folk. Writers are gentlemen. Peasants interpolate.

If Hogg and Laidlaw can sometimes be thought to have joined the Shirra's gang, as dependants, they were both to remain their own men. Something of this is evident when the *Memoir* turns to the visit to the minstreless, and then turns to the 'sociality' of the evening at the Brydens', to the discussion there of sheep, which Ettrick divided into the long – who were Cheviots – and the black-faced short, the original Forest breed, and to an excursion of the day after. 'Putting on his most serious calculating face', Scott enquired of Walter Bryden of Ramseycleuch: 'I am rather at a loss regarding the merits of this very important question. How long must a sheep actually measure to come under the denomination of a long sheep?' Walter replied, in 'the simplicity of his heart', that it was a matter of the wool: 'The lang sheep hae the short woo, and the short sheep hae the lang thing.' Scott's grave face gave way to 'a hearty guffaw'. The scene alerted Hogg to the identity of the anonymous Waverley author when a version of it appeared in *The Black Dwarf*. When Scott noticed, at Altrive, a volume marked 'Scott's Novels', he observed: 'Jamie, your bookseller must be a stupid fellow to spell *Scots* with two t's.' And Hogg replied to the tease: 'Ah, Watty, I am ower auld a cat to draw that strae before.'[13] Some claimed that Jamie never came down lower than 'Walter' in addressing Scott.

The following day, a party rode off to hunt for relics at what was left of the Scott strongholds of Buccleuch and Mount Comyn. 'We came to one half of a small pot, encrusted thick with rust. Mr Scott's eyes brightened' – rather as his voice took on a burr, a Scots note, when the Maitland manuscript was inspected. A tar pot, Laidlaw declared it, used by local farmers. 'Sir Walter's shaggy eyebrows' – always of barometric interest to Hogg – 'dipped deep over his eyes' in disappointment. Then, suppressing a smile, he strode off saying that 'we had just rode all the way to see that there was nothing to be seen.' The comedy of these incidents is not servile, though kind to the Sheriff's guffaw – which may have been an interpolation.

Each of these old songs is, in a further sense, at once ancient and modern: modern in its open-endedness, its textual indeterminacy, its very imperfection; modern, too, in its exemplary leaps and leanness, its avoidance of expostulation, and of any parade of feeling. In this respect, as in others, the ballads were to be a lesson to later writers. 'From among a hundred corruptions,' wrote Lockhart of Scott's ballad work, he 'produced strains in which the unbroken energy of half-civilised ages, their stern and deep passions, their daring adventures and cruel tragedies, and even their rude wild humour, are reflected with almost the brightness of a Homeric mirror, interrupted by hardly a blot of what deserves to be called vulgarity, and totally free from any admixture of artificial sentimentalism.'[14] The fanciful poetry that Hogg was thereafter frequently to write – the poetry, for instance, that earned him the name of Poet Laureate of the Fairies – is by no means free from sentimentalism. But many of his ballads, his own ballads, tell a different story: their rude wild humour, their irony and tartness, suggest that he had learnt a lesson from the ballads he collected and helped to write, a lesson he was apt to forget in other regions of his song.

Taking part in the collective anonymity of the ballads was a baptism which led to an enduring engagement with questions of personality and individual identity. Anonymity, pseudonymity, parody, dual personality – these were the pursuits, the avocations, of an egotist and star who sought liberty in concealment, and of the friends he found in Edinburgh. One man might behave like another, might envelop and ingest another. Cannibalism and journalism and plagiarism can seem at times, in Hogg's world, near-allied.

He had 'attained to considerable celebrity' by the age of thirty, according to an article in which Hogg is likely to have had a hand, and which appeared in the *Scots Magazine* of July 1805. He was by now a writer, and someone other than Scott's sorcerer's apprentice. In 1801, he made his way on foot to Edinburgh and was benighted at the village of Straiton, where an encounter with an idiot boy (together, perhaps, with Wordsworth's 'The Idiot Boy', published three years before) inspired the poem 'Sandy Tod', which appeared in the *Edinburgh Magazine* the following year. That same year saw him off on one of his Highland journeys, the journey described in letters to the *Scots*

Magazine over 1802–3. The letters, in which he describes another Wordsworthian encounter, the one with the American beggar woman, are introduced by 'SW', presumably Scott, who speaks of Hogg's having to contend with the 'pride of lettered rank'.

One of the letters says that the Royalist general Claverhouse, Bonny Dundee, of the seventeenth-century 'killing time', is mentioned in Ettrick 'with horror'. Claverhouse is then addressed by Hogg: 'thou art now in the true world and I in the false.' In the false world of everyday reality his dealings with lettered rank were to be a source for Hogg both of pride and of pain, and Claverhouse was to be a matter of dispute between himself and Scott. Hogg had a greyhound whom he named Claverse. One day, as he sat at the Altrive parlour window with Scott, Claverse dashed past, pursued by a maid who believed that he'd stolen her black puddings. 'Sir Walter laughed heartily, and slyly insinuated that he feared poor "Claverse", like his great namesake, got the credit for crimes which he perhaps did not deserve.'[15]

Lettered rank disgraced itself in Holland during the summer of this trip to the Highlands. In a letter of 25 August 1802, the Whig economist Francis Horner, a contributor to the *Edinburgh Review*, referred to a newspaper report concerning 'three Anglois'. These Anglois were Ecossais, friends of Scott. One of them, Adam Ferguson, son of the philosophical historian of that name, was a close friend; a friend of Hogg's too, and, it would seem, of Horner's. Scott arranged to have him knighted at the time of George IV's Coronation visit to Scotland, and he became the Keeper of its Royal Regalia. The three Scotsmen, perhaps drunk, entered an Amsterdam synagogue, which may have been the city's principal synagogue, among the most ancient in Europe. 'One of them broke into a fit of laughter, at some part of the ceremony, which was of course Adam Ferguson,' wrote Horner. A Jew was knocked down by another of the three.[16] Ferguson was widely liked, and was known to the author of *Ivanhoe* and to other friends as 'the Merry Knight'.

Hogg's humble origins were apparent in his very name. In the Borders, his name enrolled him in a close-knit community of kinship and shared occupation. Elsewhere, he could seem to be the wild boy of Ettrick, whose vanished woods stood in a line of descent from the wilderness by which cities had felt themselves surrounded. But he was also the hearty Borderer who was liked for his humour, and good humour, as Adam Ferguson was. He spent much of his time in action and in the open air. There was more of that then than there is now, among Scotsmen of all conditions; even Lockhart of the midnight oil got out, and behaved as a sportsman and soldier. There Hogg was, at the heart of the Border lands, surrounded by Laidlaws and Chisholms and Scotts, who were at once a hierarchy and a democracy, and who had fought their ancient fights with the Robsons and Charltons over the border. His writings look back to a past of reiver raids and bad barons, slaughters and sieges, the lifting of widows' cattle, and forward to a time when the same clans and names have played rugby and football with the old ardour. But his writings were also to look forward to the literature of modernity. He was a complicated, bluff man who became an expert in complication and who belonged to an age in which complication, needless to say, was familiar enough. His was a Scotland in which a passion for sound sense and plain speech did not prevent duplicity, in which boldness and physical force, a foreign and domestic settlement by the sword, did not drive out disguise.

Hogg's relationship with Scott was certainly complicated. This was a pool in which a monstrous fin or two would occasionally surface. He could be hurt by Scott. He sometimes resented him. He could be sycophantic, and he wrote him begging letters ('your poor, unfortunate, Hogg'). He received help which he was capable of denying that he'd received. Theirs was a bond, however, which difference of class served to strengthen and define, as well as to impair. Lockhart's *Life of Scott* introduces Hogg with an attention to the duality of the man which reveals in their fullness – as Scott's letters seldom do – the awe and affection Scott felt for him: 'Under the garb, aspect and bearing of a rude peasant – and rude enough he was in most of these things, even after no inconsiderable experience of society – Scott found a brother poet, a true son of nature and genius, hardly conscious of his powers ... well as Scott knew that reflection, sagacity, wit, and wisdom, were scattered abundantly among the humblest rangers of these pastoral solitudes, there was here a depth and a brightness that filled him with wonder, combined with a quaintness of humour, and a thousand little touches of absurdity, which afforded more entertainment, as I have often heard him say, than the best comedy that ever set the pit in a roar.'[17] The account opens with Lockhart's own word for it: Hogg was perhaps 'the most remarkable man that ever wore the *maud* of a shepherd'. A shepherd's plaid was to be his hallmark costume, in Ettrick as in Princes Street, Edinburgh, and London's Mayfair and Holborn.

Lockhart's account is worth comparing with Scott's words of 1817 to Lord Montagu, the brother of Charles, Duke of Buccleuch, who died two years later: 'There is an old saying of the seamens every man is not born to be a boatswain and I think I have heard of men born under a six penny planet and doomd never to be worth a groat. I fear something of this vile sixpenny influence has gleamd in at the cottage window when poor Hogg first came squeaking into this world.' As early as 1806 Scott described him, in testimonial vein, as an old friend – 'by the unpoetical name of Mr James Hogg'. He remained, with intermissions, a friend, of whom Scott said many years later that he lacked judgment and too much wanted to seem the interesting eccentric. At a low point in the trajectory of Hogg's career he said of his prose works: 'Truly, they are sad daubings, with here, and there, fine dashes of genius.' Wilson, too, applied the word 'daubings' to Hogg's work.[18]

Towards the end of 1803 Hogg made one of those entries of his into a drawing-room which became notorious. Displeased with the 'Imitations of the Ancients' in the *Minstrelsy*, he had hoped to do better. According to Lockhart, 'he says, in one of his many Memoirs of himself, "I chose a number of traditional facts, and set about imitating the manner of the ancients myself." '[19] He now meant to incorporate these efforts in a further collection of verse, *The Mountain Bard*, and waited on Scott for advice at his town house in Castle Street. He and Will Laidlaw were asked to dinner. Lockhart indicates that Mrs Scott was pregnant (with her daughter Anne).

> When Hogg entered the drawing-room, Mrs Scott, being at the time in a delicate state of health, was reclining on a sofa. The Shepherd, after being presented, and making his best bow, forthwith took possession of another sofa placed opposite to hers, and stretched himself thereupon at all his length; for, as he said afterwards, 'I thought I could never do wrong to copy the lady of the house.' As his

dress at this period was precisely that in which any ordinary herdsman attends cattle to the market, and as his hands, moreover, bore most legible marks of a recent sheep-smearing, the lady of the house did not observe with perfect equanimity the novel use to which her chintz was exposed. The Shepherd, however, remarked nothing of all this – dined heartily and drank freely, and, by jest, anecdote, and song, afforded plentiful merriment to the more civilised part of the company. As the liquor operated, his familiarity increased and strengthened; from 'Mr Scott', he advanced to 'Sherra', and thence to 'Scott', 'Walter', and 'Wattie', – until, at supper, he fairly convulsed the whole party by addressing Mrs Scott as 'Charlotte'.

Lockhart was not present at this threat to Mrs Scott's chintz, and had yet to meet this regaler of 'the more civilised part of the company' – the rest of the room, in other words. Oral transmission had occurred over the thirty years before he came to write the story down – recite the ballad of Hogg's droll oddity and crudity, a sequel to Shakespeare's account of the behaviour and reception of Bottom the Weaver at the court of Duke Theseus.

On Christmas Eve Hogg wrote Scott a letter of apology, from Ettrickhouse, asking 'ten thousand pardons':

I am afraid that I was at least half-seas over the night I was with you, for I cannot, for my life, recollect what passed when it was late ... I have the consolation, however, of remembering that Mrs Scott kept in company all or most of the time, which she certainly could not have done, had I been very rude. I remember, too, of the filial injunction you gave at parting, cautioning me against being ensnared by the loose women in town. I am sure I had not reason enough left at that time to express either the half of my gratitude for the kind hint, or the utter abhorrence I inherit at those seminaries of lewdness.

Scott had previously warned him that his wife was a foreigner – French. 'As dark as a blackberry and does not speak the broad Scots so well as you and me.' The supper marred by his capture of the sofa seems likely to have been the occasion when Hogg went to Castle Street expecting to see 'a half blackamore whom our sherrif had married for a great deal of money' – a West Indian heiress, maybe. Judge of his surprise when he met a beautiful brunette who spoke English very well. 'She called me all her life Mr Og,' however. She did not like Mr Og, whose *Memoir* ignores or denies this: 'it was well known how jealous she was of the rank of Sir Walter's visitors yet I was all my life received with the same kindness as if I had been a relation or one of the family although one of the most homely of his daily associates!'[20]

Hogg's letter of apology moves to the matter of what poems are to be in his collection. The 'Pastoral' entitled 'Sandy Tod' had to be in – 'as I am Sandy Tod'.

CHAPTER FOUR

Sandy Tod

—

On a fine day, the distant prospect of Edinburgh, for a walker on his way there from his southern fastness, over the Moorfoot Hills, was enough to kindle the resolve of a turned-again Dick Whittington. Amid its Lowlands panorama, the city lay stretched out before him like a Shangri-La, with its volcanic bumps of Arthur's Seat and the Castle rock, its Old Town and rising Hanoverian New Town, its sky-blue Pentland Hills, the more than Border fastness of the Highlands shimmering away to the north, a smidgeon of sea to the east. When Hogg walked there in 1801 and spent the night at the inn in Straiton, Midlothian, in the lee of the Pentlands, he was staying in the mining village where I spent the first two years of my life.

The 1807 version of his memoir[1] tells that

> the landlord had a son deranged in his mind, whom his father described as having been formerly sensible and docile. His behaviour was very extravagant; he went out at night and attacked the moon with great rudeness and vociferation...
>
> Thinking that a person in such a state, with a proper cause assigned, was a fit subject for a poem, – before I reached home, I had all the incidents arranged, and a good many verses composed, of the pastoral tale of *Sandy Tod*. I think it one of the best of my tender pieces.

Edith Batho imagines an incompatibility between Hogg's saying that he was Sandy Tod and his later claim to have been inspired to write the poem by the boy who bayed at the moon. She also writes: 'The worst things in the volume are "Robin an' Nanny", which is weak, and "Sandy Tod", which is very weak, though Hogg had a tenderness for it.'[2] They are the best things in the volume, to my mind (the first of these was added in the 1821 reissue). 'Sandy Tod' belongs to the early work of which he could be fond, but of which he could also disapprove, surveying it from the high ground of the fanciful genteel. Bound together by their trochees and their ballad leaps and swiftness, the two poems have the fresh air of his *Scottish Pastorals*, and they have the merit of dealing with topics – prostitution and venereal disease, respectively – which literature had become less and less willing to treat.

Sandy is a blithe and sturdy lad, of blameless life. At the sight of Sally, 'dressed in hat an' feather', sitting in a nearby pew,

> Sandy's tender heart was smitten
> Wi' a wound that never healed.

He courts her, with some success:

> Sandy raze – his bonnet daddit –
> Begged a kiss – gat nine or ten;
> Then the hay, sae rowed an' saddit,
> Towzled up that nane might ken.

But Sally had been let down by a Westland farmer, and afflicted with another sort of wound 'that baffled healing', and when Sandy goes west to pay a visit he finds her in a shroud. He goes off his head and jumps off a cliff. From beyond the grave he implores the lovers who step over him to 'walk in Virtue's road'.

In 'Robin an' Nanny' a daughter Mary leaves the Highlands for the city, to go into service, and is picked up by a spark in his gig and led astray. Nanny worries over what may have become of her. Robin is cross with his wife: 'Lye i' peace, or lye your lane.' But he departs to search for his daughter in amazing Edinburgh, all lords and dukes: 'Where's the folk gaun a' sae fast?' He finds her pleading to be let back into a brothel, out of the cold, into one of the seminaries of lewdness against which Scott had warned Hogg, where she had been refusing to do as she was bid. She is restored to her shieling. This is a touching and harrowing homiletic poem, not much harmed by what there is of an effusiveness hardly characteristic of the old songs. Hogg did well to ask for forbearance in respect of 'female innocence o'ercome'. The exposure of women in poverty to disease and death as sexual slaves was a disgrace which doctors, rather than writers, had begun to address by 1840, when Edinburgh was reported to have two hundred brothels.

Hogg said of *The Mountain Bard*, published by Constable, that it was 'designed solely for amusement', and the notes are often as amusing as the poems. More than one commentator has pointed out that this can happen with Hogg, and it may be considered the deficiency of a period marked by the production of large amounts of poetry which failed to be interesting even to those who published it, much of it the soft-hearted, high-minded poetry of risers in the world: Lockhart was right to complain that *Blackwood's* carried 'a cursed deal too much of poetry such as every human being can write and nobody ever will read'.[3] In Hogg's case, this is to speak, not of his poetry as it always is, but of the gentleman's poetry which he would sometimes think was expected of him. His notes display the bard's dependence on local lore and oral learning. Ettrick's famous Calvinist divine, Thomas Boston, is cited as having laid the ghost that appears in 'The Pedlar'. Boston's servant was the balladist Andrew Moore.

The collection has far too much amusing carnage. In 'Willie Wilkin' a wizard knight kills his own mother:

> Her blood was sprinkled on the wall,
> Her body was on the floor;
> Her reverend head, with sorrows gray,
> Hung on the chapel door.

The poem cribs from 'Tam o' Shanter' when this mother surprises a coven carrying on in the kirk: 'The riot rout then sallied out...' The bloodshed is relieved by a moment of compunction – when the Englishwoman Lady Derwent turns her eye to Borrowdale and is chilled by the sight of the Scottish bands. In a later edition of the book, Hogg's nephew Robert Hogg has a ballad, 'The Tweeddale Raide', which plies a similar carnage: Norman Hunter of Polmood 'blindit mony a Southron ee' with his braid-bow (Norman Hunter of Leeds United was praised by the football fans of modern times for his ability to 'bite yer legs'). Hogg would seem to have felt little hesitation in pressing this violence on a readership which, as he'd been advised, included many females insistent on delicacy. He was more nervous about offering them lasciviousness. When 'Mess John' describes the undoing of a pre-Reformation priest by the Devil in the shape of a lovely girl, who assures him that girls are 'fervid' for 'ardent' kisses, a note informs his 'fair readers' that these assurances must be understood as the blandishments of a fiend.

In 'The Fray of Elibank', which contains an ironic fealty to the chivalry of the Scottish Border, bold Juden Murray, lord of Elibank, has his cows rustled by bold Willie Scott of Harden, son of the celebrated Wat, with support from a Hogg, the Wild Boar of Fauldshope (discussed in the notes in terms identical with the epitaph on Hogg's grandfather, Will o' Phaup), who is, however, missing, perhaps culpably, from the scene when his lord is captured. The lord is given the choice of a rope or of marriage to Juden's daughter, Muckle-Mou'd Meg. Both here and in a poem by Louisa Stuart on this same shotgun marriage, the pair are thought to have lived happily after, and Hogg says that a great deal of good blood flowed from the union.

With one part of him, he was in love with the exploits of the warrior past. The Yarrow minister James Russell tells a story about Auld Wat of Harden, this late sixteenth-century bandit chief of particular rapacity, a story which he heard from Hogg and which Hogg employed in his novel *The Three Perils of Man*. Wat 'had gone on one of his foraging expeditions across the Border, and plundered one of the noble houses of Northumberland ... The young heir of the estate had been carried off too, and placed on top of the baggage. The return party prospered till they reached the Ettrick, when on crossing the boy dropped into the river unperceived and was drowned.' The forager, 'bitterly grieved', built a bridge at the Ettrickbridge ford, that 'the one life lost should be the means of saving a hundred'.[4]

The ballad 'May of the Moril Glen' was placed in a posthumous edition of *The Mountain Bard*, having appeared in 1827 in *Blackwood's*, in the full panoply of his antique spellings. May is the embodiment of a sinister chastity, a serpent châtelaine of ample means, with a mysterious daughter. This virgin queen is courted by the King, on whom she looks as on something 'that ought not to have been there', and by his noblemen. She turns out to be a right royal Belle Dame sans Merci. Keats's poem, published in 1820, contributes to Hogg's: like clothes hung out to dry, rejected suitors lie around 'right woe-begone', pale and wasted in the manner of Keats's knight (whose enchantment has been linked to a disease like the one suffered in 'Sandy Tod'). The King, too, is affected, bewitched: 'What ails, what ails my royal liege?' After wrecking the glen, and the flower of the Scots nobility, May sets sail in a ship whose mast is of beaten gold, a ship that takes flight. This is an aerial and an artful poem. There is 'a speire' (a question) in her every smile; later, the lightning of that evil eye is 'sharper nor the sharpest spear in all Northumberland'. The pun is assisted by Hogg's system of antique spellings, where the two constituent words are spelt the same.

Keats, a favourite dish for the *Blackwood's* cannibals, the purveyor of a lower-class 'drivelling idiocy', in Lockhart's view, was an influence on Hogg's verse. But the principal influence on the second phase of his poetry, now in train, was Scott. Hogg and Scott were in some sense doubles, the high and the low of one another, with Hogg every so often perceptible as Scott's id or savage self. Each did what his Border fellow did. They went bankrupt together, with Hogg's poor man's insolvencies ranking as fecklessness and bad character. Both their houses were plagued with admirers, spongers, 'sorners'; of both their houses it was said by inmates that they were like hotels; they were hotels where you didn't have to pay, with Altrive ill-advised to emulate Abbotsford in that respect. And both men came out with poetries compounded of the chivalric and the supernatural. Scott's example – as distinguished from that of the old songs he collected, his Border minstrelsy – was in many ways a false light for Hogg, as were the examples of John Wilson's verse and of Ossian.

It seems a shame that he did not, on setting out, take more notice of the vernacular poetry of Robert Fergusson. But the vernacular Burns was an early influence which remains potent in *The Mountain Bard*. 'The Author's Address to his Auld Dog Hector' is patterned on Burns's great 'The Auld Farmer's New-Year Morning Salutation to his Auld Mare, Maggie', which has

> Mony a sair darg we twa hae wrought,
> An' wi' the weary warl' fought!
> An' mony an anxious day I thought
> We wad be beat!
> Yet here to crazy age we're brought,
> Wi' something yet.

Hogg's Address has

> For mony a day, frae sun to sun,
> We've toiled fu' hard wi' ane anither.

Written beneath 'Queensb'ry's lofty height', the poem reveals a 'forlorn', a poor Hogg, deserted by friends, and even by Meg, who'd once made misogynistic Hector jealous, as 'thou placed thee by her other leg' in a fraught threesome. Hector proves truer than Meg, who will be succeeded, though, by some further 'sweet lovely breast' – 'to me a balm for every ill'. Sweethearts are both balmy and betraying, while friends, 'by pop'lar envy swayed', are ten times worse than any enemy.

Hogg's forlorn state takes part in the Highland journeys which he performed over the first decade of the new century, and which he described in the *Scots Magazine*. From time to time, these pieces show a carnival Hogg, and a comedian of errors. Around the table at Ambrose's tavern the word would be that error can be a good thing. But one of his errors of the decade proved hard to be happy with.

He had been visiting the Highlands since the end of the last century. Subsequent visits were to involve a plan to settle with his parents, and with a fellow Borderer, on a sheep farm at Shelibost on the island of Harris, further to a grazing agreement reached with a Mr William MacLeod. Two hundred pounds, saved over the Blackhouse years, were to be sunk in the project. A 'Farewell to Ettrick' was written, along the lines of the farewell written by Burns to lament an expected emigration to the West Indies. There was an argument of the time that the Highland economy needed saving and might be saved by the importation by landlords of sheep and shepherds from the south. The native inhabitants should be left in place and other forms of husbandry encouraged. Hogg would not have felt himself to be an accomplice of the Highland Clearances.

The series of letters to the magazine, 1802-3, to which reference has already been made gives accounts of Ettrick and Edinburgh, of a performance there of *Hamlet*, and of his American beggar woman, and then proceeds to Perthshire. In the summer of 1803 he set off for the Highlands and the Isle of Lewis, 'a morass', and wrote about it in letters which went unpublished until 1888.[5]

These letters are addressed to Walter Scott, whose wand had begun to wave him towards another world, that of power and possessions. 'O Mr Scott, Mr Scott, thou wilt put me stark mad some day.' Introduced by his friend to the castled Duke of Argyll, 'I was struck with a sense of my inferiority, and was quite bamboozled.' Inferior at Inveraray, he felt ill, and glancing down at a mirror by his leg, saw a chapfallen, 'extraordinary red face', a monster's. But the letters are far from chapfallen, in their supply of incident and sentiment. 'I wish from my heart that the distinctions of Englishmen and Scot were entirely disannulled and sunk in that of Britons.' Might 'disannulled' imply a more divided heart than the sentence seems intended to express? Probably not. Again: 'I could not help being a bit of a Jacobite in my heart.' On Loch Duich, he wraps a Miss Flora in his plaid – not the only such use of the plaid on his Highland tours – and wonders if he might not fall in love with her. But she goes down with flu and is unable to dine with him. A landlord explained that he was loth to send all his tenants away to America, but they paid him only half of what sheep would bring. The Trossachs, said this traveller by foot and coach, were the 'most confused piece of Nature's workmanship that I ever saw'.

In an inn in Glenshiel he was, for all his precautions and bravado, robbed. He got the best bed, but it was hard and was the 'hereditary domain' of lots of tiny insects. Vagabond Highlanders, male and female, burst in and drank whisky and made a din. He wrapped his watch and his money in his waistcoat and placed it beneath his head. 'I heard one distinctly ransacking my coat which was hanging upon a chair at a little distance from the bed.' There would be no pickings for the vagabond there: 'but not knowing where this might end I sprung to my feet in the bed, laid hold of my thorn-staff, and bellowed aloud for light ... I reprimanded the landlord with great bitterness.' Six letters of introduction were lost.

James Boswell's experience overnight in nearby Glen Moriston, where he and Samuel Johnson had been supplied with sheets by Mrs Boswell, who feared that they might 'catch something', was not in all respects dissimilar. Since then, problems of accommodation for travellers in the Highlands had not eased. They were a feature of what Hogg called an 'unfortunate journey' to the region, written up in letters to the magazine

(1808-9) and performed in the summer of 1804. He was accompanied by two friends, whose initials suggest William Laidlaw and John Grieve, a cultivated Edinburgh hatter, son of a Cameronian Border minister. Grieve may be characterised as a man of sorrow and acquainted with Hogg, whom he supported and accommodated and by whom he was at times sorely tried. The party first went to Greenock, where they met up with a remarkable circle of young people then in literary and intellectual cahoots, which included James Park, Latinist and poet, and the novelist John Galt, a little dandyish in his frock-coat and new top-boots, whom Hogg came to admire, and to designate 'this most original and most careless writer'. In the second of the letters Hogg confided: 'I would rather be the first man amongst the shepherds of Ettrick Forest, than the second in Edinburgh: but the great loss is, that I will never be the one or the other.'

Presently he stepped into a boat in which were 'two country girls of the better order from Lorn', and offered one of them his plaidie to the angry airt. I laid me down, reported the man of feeling, 'on the bieldy side, desiring the prettiest of the girls to take up her birth [*sic*] in my bosom. She complied without hesitation, and I screened her with my mantle. O! how my companions envied me my situation.' But they then found they were in the wrong boat. 'We were all obliged to shift, and I being farthest in, was last in getting out, and lost not only my dearest bosom-friend, but every tolerable seat in the boat, being forced to sit grinning with my face in the weather all the way.' The anonymous author of the next piece in the journal on that occasion (September 1808) alludes to a lower order of girl: it is said of him editorially that he 'concludes with remonstrances on the hardships endured by the class of women called Bearers, who bring up the coal from the pits, and recommends the use of horses in their stead'.

Off the island of Egg the party endured a storm, sea-sickness and famine. His 'rashness' cost him a 'grievous' facial wound. During this unfortunate journey he mentions 'the unfortunate Prince Charles Stuart', the conventional expression of a time when it was customary to talk of 'poor Hogg' and of poor many other people too, not all of them poor. Then came an accommodation problem. They spent the night in a house where there were two heather beds without hangings, and a woman and some children. 'Mr W' flew into a 'terrible passion'. The women and children 'slid away; the beds were made up with clean clothes, and we were obliged to spend the night on them the best way we could.' At least he had 'the advantage of a feather bed above the heath'. Later, Mr W flies into a passion at the impertinence of some people who had to go off to attend a funeral.

On the way to the Hebrides they 'never' walked an hour without being drenched to the skin and muddied to the knees, never went to sea without facing accidents and perils, never, on leaving Greenock, 'proceeded one day by the route we intended'. On Harris, Hogg appears to have missed seeing the proprietor of the farm with whose tacksman he had been dealing: had he done so, 'a great deal of my ensuing misfortunes' would have been avoided. As it was, he and his partner were to lose their savings. Having bought a stock of sheep, they were notified that the tacksman's right to dispose of the farm was under challenge and that a plea had been entered at the Court of Session. The plea went against them.

In one of the letters he remarks that he has no doubts about the authenticity of Ossian, James Macpherson's Celtic bard. By now he may have had doubts about his own authenticity. Was he still the lowest of the low? Was he a farmer any more? Was he a writer? Was he mad? But he resolved to let bygones be bygones. The 'elastic' shepherd admired at this point by his biographer Thomson spent a while wandering round the Lakes to avoid his creditors, and then went back to the Borders. He felt he'd better steer clear of Ettrick, where questions had to be faced, and he travelled south with his dog Hector to herd sheep for Mr Harkness of Mitchell-Slack in Nithsdale, where, unaccommodated man on the Queensberry Hill heath, he received his visit from the Cunninghams.

A visit of 1805 to the counties of Stirling, Perth and Kinross was chronicled in the autumn of that year, again in the *Scots Magazine*. A woman 'with an air of travelled importance said, I was once at Stirling.' A man acquired 'a most unaccountable veneration' for Hogg, which made him nervous. The man warned: 'You'll no think muckle of Stirling.' He then fell in with two Englishmen who thought muckle of everything they came across in Scotland. What was their game? 'At length the word *artist* escaped from them as applied to themselves.' They were intent on 'taking' or 'getting' picturesque views, and 'began to converse in a language which was quite new to me. Fine *distance*, but no *foreground* – there's *character* for you – what an *interesting* lime-kiln.' Hogg's was not, in fact, an innocent eye. He was already interested in looking at landscape through the Claude glass of sensibility.

When Hogg was in Nithsdale, Scott thought of making him chief shepherd, and 'manager of all his rural affairs', on a Selkirkshire estate he was contemplating, but 'the plan misgave', said Hogg; Scott's bid for the estate failed. Lockhart associates the thought with a different Border estate, Scott's Ashestiel. Scott then recommended him to Lord Porchester, continuing to see his friend as a farmer rather than a writer, wishing him to attend to his muttons, and seeking to impose, Hogg reckoned, the proviso that 'I was to put my poetical talent under lock and key for ever!' The proviso was resented in *The Queen's Wake*:

> O could the Bard I loved so long
> Reprove my fond aspiring song!

The *Familiar Anecdotes of Sir Walter Scott* comments: 'I never knew any gentleman so shy and chary of his name and interest as Sir Walter was.' What rankled here was Scott's reluctance to review his work, or 'bring me forward in any way by the shortest literary remark in any periodical'. Scott explained that he felt they were so much of the same school that it would be like applauding himself. Hogg had a reply to that which cracks one of his vertiginous vanity jokes: 'Dear Sir Walter ye can never suppose that I belang to your school o' chivalry? Ye are the king o' that school but I'm the king o' the mountain an' fairy school which is a far higher ane nor yours.'[6]

Scott was a seeker of favours for family and friends; for him, as for others, 'making interest' was a way of doing things. In the spring of 1806 he wrote to the Buccleuchs, to Lady Dalkeith: 'Our Ettrick Shepherd has laid by his pastoral reed for the more profitable employment of valuing Sheep Land in which he has given great satisfaction to those who engaged him being a remarkably clever fellow in the line of his business.' Hogg wanted the future Duke Charles's patronage, as a valuer, and Scott then found that he'd taken the liberty to apply for it to his wife directly.

Lady Dalkeith, as she then was, formerly Harriet Townshend, a sprightly Englishwoman, used to summon Hogg to play cards with her, of all 'singular' things, a source of surprise to Scott. Hogg, though, was to be disappointed on this occasion. A little later, Scott sent the Lichfield poetess Anna Seward a copy of *The Mountain Bard*: the author was 'upon the whole a very interesting person' – 'not only a good Ballad writer but a most excellent shepherd. I know nobody who understands the diseases of sheep so well or faces the tempests more hardily.' He is 'deeply interested in his fate now that he is about to emerge from his state of Servitude'. Anna Seward was not impressed: 'James Hogg – luckless name!' With further reference to Hogg, he also wrote to her at this time to say: 'Such a night as last always sends my mind to the desert hills where my poor countrymen must be all night driving the sheep with their faces to the wind to prevent their lying down & being smothered.'[7]

Two years later, Scott tried to dissuade him from going after an ensigncy in a militia regiment, as Lockhart's *Life of Scott* explains. He wrote 'capital war-songs', Lockhart notes, but his nerves were not 'heroically strung' – he was a peasant, after all.[8] When he failed of an epaulette, he threatened to enlist in a marching regiment as a common soldier. Three years after that, Scott forwarded a copy of Hogg's *Forest Minstrel* to Lady Dalkeith, fearing that 'your Ladyship will find but little amusement in it for the poor fellow has just talent sufficient to spoil him for his own trade without having enough to support him by literature.'[9] For the Scott of the letters and journal, Hogg was the braver of storms, and the honest grunter. He can be Wamba the clown, and Gurth the swineherd, of *Ivanhoe*, which tells of the half-instinctive devotion to his noble master of the palpably more intelligent jester. He can be the good shepherd – *pastor fido*, as a *Blackwood's* crony teasingly murmured – who was liable to miscarry, and the interesting man who deserved help. As for Hogg, he worried that Scott might die, and was alarmed when he fell ill. He once advised him to apply a little gunpowder to ease his stomach cramps. Scott was his chief, his friend and his rival. There was bound to be trouble.

Other events of the year 1806, when Hogg's welfare and vocation had become a taxing issue, included the unsolved murder, on a dark November night in Edinburgh, of James Begbie, porter to the British

Linen Company's bank, an event which was to wind itself into the mysteries made by the *Blackwood's* circle. Henry Cockburn's *Memorials* discusses the murder, which resembles in its haunting indeterminacy another Canongate murder, that of the good brother in Hogg's *Confessions*. Cockburn writes: 'All that was observed was by some boys who were playing at hand ball in the close; and all that they saw was that two men entered the close as if together, the one behind the other, and that the front man fell, and lay still; and they, ascribing this to his being drunk, let him lie, and played on. It was only on the entrance of another person that he was found to be dead, with a knife in his heart, and a piece of paper, through which it had been thrust, interposed between the murderer's hand and the blood. The skill, boldness, and success of the deed produced deep and universal horror.'[10] Among Scott's treasures was the knife in question.

In January of that year, in the course of some 'Letters on Poetry' in the *Scots Magazine*, he set down thoughts on the plays of Shakespeare. He was drawn, as was Scott, to Edinburgh's Theatre Royal, which was holding out against pious hostility, an old aversion which had survived the ascendancy of the Moderates in the Kirk, and he was to write dramatic pieces of his own. The fairies in *A Midsummer Night's Dream* are said here to be elegantly and accurately evoked: 'Yea so accurately do they suit our notions of these flimsy spirits, that the oldest man in Ettrick or Eskdale, although they have seen and spoke with the fairies many a time, cannot impress you more with the reality of their existence, altho' the one believes he tells you the truth, and the other knows he does not.' The play's fairy flights are natural, while the clowns and rustics are its 'most unnatural characters'. This is expressive both of his divided sense of the supernatural and of his divided society. There is something of Bottom in Hogg, who was to know before long what it was to perform for courtiers who liked him and laughed at him. No wonder he didn't take to the pastoral play-within-the-play, 'Pyramus and Thisbe'. Hogg's pig, you might say, was Bottom's ass.

When he called on the publisher Constable, Scott's publisher, hoping to make a deal for *The Mountain Bard*, Scott went with him. Constable was publishing's 'Czar', Thomson's 'Aristarchus of our metropolitan publishers', 'the Crafty', as he was known to his *Blackwood's* rivals: a rash mountain of a man perceived by the young Disraeli, a precocious judge in such matters, as exceptionally ostentatious. His was a craftiness which enabled him to publish the *Edinburgh Review*, and to refuse to publish Galt's *Annals of the Parish*, one of the period's most commercially successful novels, brought out by Blackwood instead. He received Hogg 'very kindly, but told me frankly that my poetry would not sell. I said I thought it was as good as any body's I had seen.' Constable insisted that poetry was a drug on the market, but that, 'as I appeared to be a gay, queer chiel [gey queer?], if I could procure him two hundred subscribers he would publish my work for me, and give me as much for it as he could.' Hogg gathered more than five hundred subscribers, Constable improved his offer, while also handing him 86 pounds for 'Hogg on Sheep'; but a third of the subscribers omitted to pay up.

Hogg's memoir goes on:

> Being now master of nearly three hundred pounds, I went perfectly mad. I first took one pasture farm, at exactly one half more than it was worth, having been cheated into it by a great rascal, who meant to rob me of all I had, and which, in the course of one year, he effected by dint of law. But, in the meantime, having taken another extensive farm, I found myself fairly involved in business far above my capital. It would have required at least one thousand pounds for every one hundred pounds that I possessed, to have managed all I had taken in hand; so I got every day out of one strait and confusion into a worse. I blundered and struggled on for three years between these two places, giving up all thoughts of poetry or literature of any kind.

These circumstances are termed 'laughable' in the memoir. The two Dumfriesshire farms he mentions were Locherben, which he took with a friend, Adam or Edie Brydon, and, before that, Corfardin.[11] Scott said in June 1808 that 'James Hogg has driven his pigs to a bad market. I am endeavouring as a *pis aller* to have him made an Excise officer that station being with respect to Scottish geniuses the grave of all the Capulets.' Hogg was 'totally destitute', Scott said in October.[12] Giving his creditors what he could, Hogg went off for a while, more buoyant than might have been expected: 'I was generally most cheerful when most unfortunate.' But when he got back to Ettrick, 'even those I had loved, and trusted most, disowned me, and told me so to my face.'

His thirties were a compulsion to repeat mistakes and re-experience rascals, a tissue of serial discouragements, disappearances and disputes, of Highland journeys and returns to Ettrick, of deals that went sour and of descriptions of them that daunt the spirits. The springtime of the unbounded laugher was gone.

His was a society in which climbs had become commoner than before, but in which falls from the cliff-face, and the cliff-hangings of Micawbers, had become a prominent feature of the record. It was an age of financial instability, and of insolvency, among both high and low. Scott went bankrupt. So, less resonantly, did Cockburn, whose friend George Joseph Bell wrote a timely standard work on the subject. Hogg's friend R. P. Gillies became a virtuoso debtor. William Laidlaw went bankrupt too, and so did the city of Edinburgh.

CHAPTER FIVE

A Scene in Romance

―――

'I am that individual,' said Hogg, plaided, shoeless, on a warm day in 1805, at Mitchell-Slack, on Queensberry Hill, to another enquiring visitor – like Allan Cunningham, a south-west Scot. John Morrison was an aesthete and man of parts, a topographer, a surveyor for the engineer Telford and for Scott at Abbotsford, a painter and a poet. In 1805 he was on a surveying expedition, and was told by his host, to whom he may have given ideas about turning surveyor: 'The devil a wheel-carriage road you will ever get from this to the water of Daar.'

A patron of Morrison's, an aesthete Earl of Selkirk, assured him that 'constant application to the sternly useful would drive me stupid.' But he was stern enough in matters of principle and taste. 'I am a Whig and Cameronian,' he told Scott, who, in 1819, wanted to raise Volunteers to put down riots (one projected force of the period was entitled the Buccleuch Legion) and sought to enlist him as an engineer. Scott had previously enlisted him as a prospector of 'fine old rhymes': in Upper Clydesdale, suspected Scott, 'there is much valuable wreck still floating down the stream of Time.' Morrison illustrated one of the Waverley novels, *The Monastery*, and Scott once wrote him out a list of the 'most interesting objects' for him to 'take' on a Border tour.

Morrison's 'Reminiscences' of 1843 are stern about Abbotsford: 'a strange jumble – if he had searched all over his property, he could not have built on a less interesting spot.'[1] And about the inflamed politics of Scott's later years. An opinion on that subject is attributed to a Border innkeeper and athlete by the name of Harper, whose 'gallant halbert' Scott wanted, in 1819, to launch against lower-class subversion. A letter of Scott's to Willie Laidlaw supposes Morrison to have 'volunteered':[2] but Morrison refused to serve, and so did Harper. In 1830, Harper said of Scott, 'O! man, it's *waesome* to see so good a man in other respects in such a state of bewilderment,' and Morrison told Scott, with reference to

'The Visionary', a pamphlet of Scott's last years, prophesying national disaster at the hands of reformers, that 'it was my business to prevent such principles being circulated in my native country.' Scott replied: 'I have been endeavouring to prevent the rascals from pulling down the old house about their ears; and some of my best friends will render me no assistance.'

Laidlaw was another of his friends with rascal sympathies, and it is admirable of this visionary Scott to have kept on terms with them. Morrison, like Harper, was in no doubt that Scott was a good man. But he was quick to criticise him. His piper, John of Skye, is found wanting. A Highland friend is quoted – 'his drones are not in tune with his chanter' – and so is Scott's uncle Thomas, himself a piper: John of Skye's ear was false, but his nephew liked a good-looking man, and John could make a noise – which was all that was necessary. Morrison listened to Scott reading his poems: 'even the burr had a charm.' He observed to him that the Scotts were banished from his native Galloway for stealing sheep, and Scott replied: 'they continued to practise the business on a pretty large scale when they settled in our country.'

After leaving Queensberry Hill in 1805, Morrison went to Edinburgh to give crime-scene evidence, and it was there that he first met Scott, who told him that Hogg was 'a wonderful man'. Later he took to saying that he was afraid Hogg would neglect his hirsel with his poem-making, and that 'he is, I am informed, an indifferent practical shepherd.' Morrison was to join Hogg's growing network of friends, patrons and literary correspondents, which included John Grieve, the Edinburgh hatter, Bernard Barton of Woodbridge in Suffolk, and General Alexander Dirom of Mount Annan in the south-west of Scotland, who took part in the subjugation of Tipoo Sultan's Mysore, and who introduced Hogg to William Roscoe of Liverpool, poet, historian, banker, bankrupt and Whig MP.

To Locherben, near Moffat, where Hogg was to be found in 1809, together with hard-drinking Edie Brydon, came Morrison on one of his visits. His self-assertive accounts of these are among the revealing memorials of the time, as are his conversations with Scott.

He rode up on his pony with a parcel for Hogg and was greeted by a good-looking girl. 'I have two masters, but I own the authority of Jamie only.' A bottle was set down, and a handsome high tea. Jamie was away, and was too often away. After sunset she pressed the visitor to stay on for a while. It would be light enough for him to ride on to his next place: 'It is the longest day, and it never is dark.' Morrison learnt from the housekeeper that 'the farm was understood to be high-rented, and, even with the most prudent management, would have enough to do' to survive. 'She had left her father's house in a pet,' and had reason to regret she'd done so, though the work was easy enough.

He went to Edinburgh, and to Scott, who had received a letter from Hogg, which the surveyor pocketed, 'by some mistake', and which had this to say:

> Our friend Morrison called at Locherben, and left with my house-keeper six pounds, which is far too much. I was from home; but he found things, I suppose, pretty comfortable; for he drank tea and toddy, and passed the evening, if not the night, very agreeably; and has left a dashing character behind him. I have little doubt that he was presented with the *deoch-an-doruis* on his departure. I have also observed that my housekeeper wears a brooch in her breast, which used not to figure there.

Walter Scott then made an enquiry of Morrison.

> 'Pray,' said Mr Scott, 'what kind of looking wench is this same housekeeper?'
> 'She is,' said I, 'a very comely, courteous, modest-looking damsel, as heart could wish, or eye look on. Her age may be twenty years. My expedition to Locherben is more like a scene in romance than an adventure in real life, and has given me a high opinion of Mr Hogg's taste.'
> 'Happy rogue!' said he. 'I am well informed that he has put more pretty girls through his fingers than any fellow in Ettrick Forest.'

Scott also remarked that Hogg evidently bore Morrison no malice.

When Morrison returned to the farm, 'my pretty housekeeper' was gone. Masters and men were answering the challenge of a sheep-shearing by sitting round a cask of whisky with tea-cups in their hands; he spent the night on his papers, while listening to the sound of revelry next door.

'The establishment at Locherben was soon after broken up – how could it stand?'

Hogg had earlier leased the farm of Corfardin, seven miles to the west, in the parish of Penpunt. Morrison spied him out there too, like someone from the Inland Revenue, and noticed that all the sheep were on the wrong side of the hill. Snow was on the ground and they had nothing to eat. 'Hogg was absent, and had been so for some days, feasting, drinking, dancing and fiddling, &c, with a neighbouring farmer. His housekeeper was the most ugly, dirty goblin I had ever beheld.'

Hogg got back just as he was about to leave, and, over their whisky, the two men talked. Morrison urged his friend to give up and come to Edinburgh and see to the publication of *The Mountain Bard*. Hogg agreed, and added that he had in mind a long poem about Mary Queen of Scots. But then again he might engage as a shepherd. Impossible, in Morrison's view – 'one who neglected his own flocks is not likely to manage well those of another' – unless he got a job as one of the King's shepherds in Hyde Park or Windsor Forest, a glorious sight with his chequered plaid and his new dog Lion lounging behind him. Morrison would like to be in charge of the gate for a week at a shilling a head. Half of London would be out to see him. 'One day of it would make Hogg's fortune.' In the meantime the shepherd had been warned. The morning sky was red.

In 1807 and 1810 two children were born to him, 'two very lovely daughters who bear my name', of whom he spoke in a letter to John Aitken of 1817. 'I have myself stood with a red face on the Stool of Repentance,' he wrote. The fine animal had entered the kirk to mount this pedestal, as Burns had done before him. The mothers married

> men much more respectable in life than ever I was ... and even with their nearest relations I have never been for a day out of favour. The aunt of one of the young ladies ventured in full assembly of friends to propose marriage to me with her lovely niece. I said I was sure she advised me well but really I could not get time. She said I had had plenty of time since Candlemass. 'O yes said I that's very true but then the weather was so wet I could not get through the water' at which they all burst out a laughing, the girl herself among the rest and there

was no more of the matter nor was there ever a frown on either side. If you now saw my Keatie at church in her hat and feather and green pelice you would think it the best turn ever I did in my life.

A remarkable essay by Gillian Hughes, published in 2000, has uncovered some of the circumstances relating to the birth of these children. At Whitsunday 1805 he went to herd sheep for Harkness at Mitchell-Slack and re-engaged there a year later, worried that his parents might be hurt by any further show of idleness. By a year later still he had moved to the farm of Corfardin, leased on the strength of his author's earnings. On 7 June 1807 Catherine Henderson appeared before the local minister to confess herself pregnant by Hogg, who was also summoned, and who gave two written acknowledgements of paternity. He promised Catherine's brother to 'take care of her and it'. The child, Kate, was baptised in Hogg's name and must be the Keatie of his letter to Aitken. Her mother afterwards married Hogg's cousin David Laidlaw. Kate grew up in Ettrick, on his doorstep.

In 1810, Margaret Beattie confessed before the same Closeburn kirk session to a like 'uncleanness'. This child, Betsy, was conceived at a point when Hogg was at Locherben, and her mother may well have been the pretty housekeeper memorialised by Morrison. The birth took place shortly before Hogg left Ettrick for Edinburgh – running away from his master, 'smitten with an unconquerable thirst after knowledge', as he was to describe the event. 'She must do for herself,' he said of Betsy, but is known to have given help and advice: 'Read your Bible.' She was at one time a servant in Aitken's household and elsewhere. Such were 'the rubs of life', he observed to John Aitken of Dunbar, banker, bankrupt and man of letters, who had been in the same boat. Hogg may have been uncertain as to whether this second child was his.

Hogg informed Margaret Phillips of the existence of the children when he was about to marry her, and she responded to the confession in a letter of 26 October 1819: 'Is it from a principle of honesty and candour, or does it proceed from (as you express yourself) a wish to get off with honour?' – break off the engagement. 'Keep your resolution,' she urged him in her resolute way – 'to repair as much as lies in your power the injury done. I am done with the subject, at least ever to reproach you.' Hogg wrote to her on 16 November to say that he had wished to tell her what might otherwise reach her. He was aware that the subject of illegitimacy was to her a 'heart-rending' one.

Hogg himself was not done with the subject. William Blackwood asked him to review for his journal an autobiography by an illegitimate son, but turned down the review in a letter of 26 August 1830: 'Your unsparing attack upon the bastard brood would if it appeared in Maga be considered political,' and it might anyway seem to the son harsh if a slating of a book of this sort which Blackwood himself had published were to figure in his magazine. The review was then published in the *Edinburgh Literary Journal.* It said that seven out of ten natural children are 'not like other people, either in body or mind; either they are decripit and misshapen in the one, or crooked or perverse in the other.' Of this autobiographer Hogg wrote: 'Sandy had nothing ado to intermeddle with the justice or injustice of his father's feelings towards him.'[3]

The girl who is seen at church in hat and feather in the poem about Sandy Tod comes to a very different end from Hogg's Catherine. This points up the complacency of his letter to Aitken of 1817, which in turn points up how far from complacent are many of his poems about sexual matters.

This poetry of his is insistent, repetitive, blithe, and also very bleak. Love can be anxious, and women witches.

> Love is like a dizziness!
> It winna let a poor body
> Gang about his business!

And there's a poem of his, 'I'm a' gane wrang', in which love and sickness memorably coincide, in which love may be an 'ailment that I daurna name', its 'dizziness' fatal. Another poem, 'I'm gane a' wrang, Jamie', has one of his impostures. Peggy is told off by Jamie for going to bed with a strange man, who proves to be none other than Jamie himself. Jamie then proposes marriage, as the best they can do in the circumstances. There's some cannibalising here of a poem associated with Burns, 'Ye hae lien a' wrang, lassie'. Among the writings by Hogg which deal with the half-submerged subject of venereal infection is his poem 'The Mermaid', published in 1819, the year in which Keats's accordant 'Belle Dame sans Merci' was composed. The mermaid is landlocked, one of the spirits of the countryside. She warns:

> Were you to reave a kiss from me
> Your life would not be lang.

A kiss is stolen, and the lad takes to his bed with a burning breast. The mermaid then weeps over the grave of a true love, but a morrow of resurrection and reunion is promised.[4]

To the pious inn-keeping matriarch Tibbie Shiel, who had been a servant in his mother's family, and in whose house he once woke up thirsting for St Mary's Loch, he later tendered good advice concerning a paternity action against her son:

> I really wish Thomas would take that poor girl's child. I advise it most seriously as if I were advising my own son. Was there ever a young man disgraced by acknowledging a child? Or was there ever a man who stood out and brought it to oaths and witnesses who was not disgraced? I have taken it upon me to stop the law proceedings for the present for two very good reasons. In the first place the examination of all the family as witnesses is going to make one of the most ridiculous exhibitions ever made in Selkirk. And in the second place after every consultation I can assure you and Thomas both that the girl's oath *will* be taken and the child sworn upon him.

Acknowledging the child is far the 'best way of settling a disagreeable business between near relations and a way that I have chosen to do myself when sensible that the child was not mine'. Tibbie would certainly have known of the existence of at least one child born out of wedlock who *was* Hogg's.[5]

Later in life too, in 1830, came a story of his, 'Seeking the houdy', [6] which acknowledges such children, together with the obstetric offices of the Brownie of Bodsbeck at his own birth. The story is told by a shepherd, Robin, who rides out one night to fetch a midwife for his wife Jean. His mare is unhappy about leaving her foal and drives Robin to an excruciating abuse of her. 'Robin thus found out a secret not before known in this country, on which he acted till the day of his death; namely, "that the best way to make a horse spring forward is to strike it on the face."' The horse halts. Poor Robin. 'What was our forlorn shepherd to do now?' He shouts into the darkness: 'Be ye devils, be ye witches, or be ye Christian creatures, rise an' shaw yoursels.'

A woman starts up, whose gestures in a heather bush suggest that 'the gypsy yaud has been murdering that poor bairn!' 'Yaud' could mean both a woman and a horse: 'it was nae wonder my auld yaud was frighted.' The weird woman tells him that 'it is a queer thing for a father no to ken his own daughter,' and adds, hailing him as 'daddy Robin!', that Jean has given birth to a daughter. 'You may be sure she has, else I could not have been here.' She explains: 'I am Helen Grieve. I was weel brought up, and married to a respectable farmer's son; but he turned out a villain, and, among other qualifications, was a notorious thief; so that I have been reduced to this that you see, to travel the country with a pack, and lend women a helping-hand in their hour o' need. An', Robin, when you and I meet here again, you may be preparing for another world.'

The woman gets up behind him on the mare, which flies off into the night in magical style. She is thrown from a precipice: 'I just gat ae glisk o' her as she was gaun ower the top o' the birk-bush like a shot stern, an' I heard her gie a waw like a cat; an' that was the last sight I saw o' her.' The English-speaking narrator says that the woman with the pack had identified herself as Robin's daughter, and that he had never had a daughter till that meeting occurred. That night Jean gives birth to a child, who grows up a Helen Grieve, and 'the midwife's short history of herself has turned out the exact history of this once lovely girl's life.' Just before his death Robin is visited by a female who may or may not be his lost daughter by Jean. 'Seeking the houdy' is the bewildering tale of a painful bewilderment. What happened on the heath in the way of an apparition or premonition transmits grief and guilt at the loss of a child.

Late marriage could be preceded, in the countryside, by a variety of partners and by the birth of illegitimate children. The realities of country life could be represented, by lettered rank, as the sexual life of savages, or, more relentingly, as a version of pastoral, where Jamie and his rosy ewe-milkers were the nymphs and shepherds of the Scottish Arcadia. These representations were a means of subordination, and they can also seem both like an endorsement and a scorn of the reprimands administered by the Church, by such men as the Selkirk minister, mentioned earlier, in the *Statistical Account*, who saw his parishioners as, 'in the prime of life, unclogged by families, indulging themselves in every species of debauchery common to that rank of life'. The truth of the matter is at once expressed and evaded in Hogg's writings; it was for long largely inadmissible by his biographers, for whom his only children were his lawful ones.

'Hypocrisy is a charge which has frequently been brought against the Scottish nation,' wrote William Tait, a doctor, in his study of prostitution, *Magdalenism* (1840).[7] Was Hogg a hypocrite? This man, famous for passing girls through his fingers in the Forest, became a fan of chastity, his concern with the subject an aspect of his climb from the lower depths and of the delicacy owed to a readership in which bluestocking opinion and female vulnerability had to be respected. At the end of his life a long poem of his, 'Love's Legacy', manages an outright repudiation of the senses.[8] The poet is in love:

> But not for worlds, in play or freak,
> Would I have kissed her dimpled cheek,
> Or trained my sordid arms around
> The form in which my heart was bound.

It was not like that when he was young, however, and this is made perfectly clear in his often directly autobiographical prose fiction. Of 'Love Adventures of Mr George Cochrane', a first version of which appeared in 1810,[9] he said that 'those who desire to peruse my youthful love adventures will find some of the best of them in those of "George Cochrane".' George is a bachelor curmudgeon who recalls his several affairs, and who addresses his readers as if they too were bachelor curmudgeons: *de te fabula narratur*, he says, quoting Horace. This is one of his most enjoyable tales. 'Carnality's the mother o' invention,' intones a Cameronian mother. 'It is the edder on the hill, that sooks the laverack out o' the lifts. It is the raven i' the wilderness, that cries, flesh, flesh, from evening to morning, an' the mair that ye feed her, the louder is her cry.' Carnality George's readers get to watch him at a hoped-for assignation, peering at a beloved from the bushes while assembling a spell-like poem:

Then I would take her in my arms
Like a new clippit yowe.

William Tait's *Magdalenism* looks deploringly at scenes of the utmost wickedness and of desperate squalor, inhabited by creatures no more unequivocally human than the beggar woman who crawled into Ettrick. In his seminaries of wickedness were part-time or 'sly' performers, and he makes much of the horror that struck when a gentleman encountered his housekeeper in one of them. Both on moral and medical grounds, he argues, these scenes must now be dismantled.

A notable murder, of interest to Hogg and his urban friends, was committed in a brothel run by 'Lucky' McKinnon, who was convicted for it, on insufficient evidence, in 1823. She had fallen, at thirty, Cockburn writes in his *Circuit Journeys*,[10] into 'the condition of being the mistress of a disorderly house in Edinburgh. But still she was not all bad; for a strong and lofty generosity, by which she had been distinguished before she fell, neither the corruptions, nor the habits of her subsequent life could extinguish.' Cockburn describes her execution: 'She had an early attachment to an English Jew, who looked like a gentleman, on the outside at least.' On parting from him on her last evening, 'she cut an orange into two, and giving him one half, and keeping the other herself, directed him to go to some window opposite the scaffold' and 'to apply his half to his lips when she applied her half to hers. All this was done; she saw her only earthly friend, and making the sign, died, cheered by this affection.'

The friend was left the sum of four or five thousand pounds. He took the money but refused to pay the costs of her defence, which had to be 'screwed out of him' by means of an action. Three years later Scott conveyed in his journal his dislike of the Jewish broker who had screwed out of him money owed at the time of his crash. Scott's ambivalence about Jews, evident in *Ivanhoe*, is echoed in the 'Noctes Ambrosianae', where a rabbi has his beard set on fire but is an exotic rather than an inimical presence.

Hogg's ambivalence in the field of sexual morality is seldom difficult to relate to the rival codes observed by the different classes of a sharply divided society, and the same is true of other hesitancies communicated by his life and work. He thought, as we have seen, that Scott cared too much about the old aristocracy of the country, and declared that 'the Whig ascendancy in the British cabinet killed Sir Walter,' 'affected his brain and killed him'.[11] Such comments came from a man who could appear to be affected in no very different fashion by the Whig ascendancy, and would speak up for the values of the party of aristocracy. A deference to rank could be expressed even by dissidents, and Hogg deferred. But then again he did not. This was the man who wrote a letter to the future Baron Napier who had been banning boats on St Mary's Loch, according to Hogg, a letter which apologised for irreverent mentions of an ancestral Napier, and of the future baron himself, in successive editions of *The Queen's Wake*, and which contained the sentence: 'though I regard you as a most noble fellow I cannot help thinking there is something peculiar in your character.' He was a man who wrote to Lord Byron offering to 'pop in on you some day'. Of his contacts and correspondents of a higher class, Byron stands out as the least class-conscious, in that way the most relaxed.[12]

Then there was this business of slaughter. He distrusted soldiers while thinking of joining them; he rejoiced over the destruction of wild life while wanting it preserved. Late in life, he eloquently criticised the third Duke of Buccleuch, who had introduced mole-catching into Scotland. Moles or mowdies were a good thing for ecological and commercial reasons, and mole-catching was an English thing. The Duke 'let the moling of his princely domains to a company or companies of Englishmen'. Moling has caused pining and foot-rot among sheep. Has he any proof? 'Neither have I that the tides of the sea are ruled and affected by the changes of the moon. But while I see the one always attendant upon the other, without the smallest deviation, then I am forced to admit that there must be some sympathy between them.' Tenants have petitioned 'their young Chief' to 'spare the remnants of their old friends the mowdies, and suffer them to breed again'. He goes on to say here that 'the change that has taken place in our country in the course of the last thirty years is truly melancholy to an old fellow like me. Our beautiful ever-green gairs, which were literally covered with mole-hills every summer, on which the ewes lay and the lambs sported, and on which the grass was as dark green and as fine and finer than any

66

of the daisied fields of Lothian, alas! where are they now? All vanished and become the coarsest of the soil, and thus the most beautiful feature of the pastoral country is annihilated.'[13]

He deprecates, on this nostalgic occasion, 'the system of extermination with regard to any class of creatures with which the all-wise Creator of the universe has seen fit to stock a country'. But then: 'How Benjy did laugh,' says a story of his, 'as the rabbit screamed and Cocket shook him by the throat.'[14] No slur on the sport is intended. 'Master,' said his maid once, 'aw wuss ye wud reise out o' yer bed, an' shoot thae cush doos.'[15] Poor doves. Poor moles.

He was with Scott in combining a Christian piety with a suspicion of the cloth. He took part in the comedy of the pulpit far from uncommon in the Scotland of his lifetime. For his local minister James Russell, Robert's son, he wrote a testimonial – 'I esteem him very highly as an associate, a gentleman, and a sound and eloquent preacher of the Gospel of Jesus' – while remarking to him, of a favourite preacher over at Traquair: 'I wadna like to hear yon man every Sabbath; he would mak me far oure guid.' James Russell, too, could smile. One day a parish eccentric was found occupying the Ettrick pulpit. 'Come down,' commanded the cloth. 'Na, sir,' replied Jock Gray, 'come ye up: they're a stiff-necked and rebellious people; it'll tak' us baith.'[16]

In all this, there was something other than a pathology of mental confusion, and some of these contradictions were shared, as I have implied, with the milieu he was to join in Edinburgh. Here, too, was an individual and a communal division. And something more, a further bond between Hogg and his magazine friends. Together, they were privy to an opening-up of personality which could at times seem to threaten its survival. Division went with dispersal, a pooling of identity, an abrogation of identity, as a consequence of their false names and false leads, parodies and plagiarism, deniabilities and mutual ingestions. Hogg was, in imagination, periodically eaten raw by the Witch 'Maga' – the cannibals' name for their anthropophagous magazine.[17]

He was – as Carlyle noted, with a stress on the ephemeral nature of his fame – a 'celebrity'.[18] Celebrity and personality can look like novelties at this point, and they have since come to stand to one another in a complex relation of affinity and hostility. Thanks to Hogg among others, the second term can now suggest a plurality, a more than one, self and alter, while the other term can suggest a less than one, the less than human. These meanings are prefigured in his experience of a rise in the world.

An emblematic figure of the period was the French ventriloquist Alexandre Vattermare, who performed at Abbotsford. For Scott, he was the 'arch deceiver', 'Alexandre & Co'. He was many in one. As a sheriff, Scott would have to bid him 'disperse'. Hogg's story 'Scottish Haymakers' causes Vattermare to imitate a crying child heard from under a pile of hay in a cart. Intellectual friends stand round while peasants toil in alarm to clear the hay. 'I wonder how they could fork a bairn up to me frae the meadow, an' me never ken!' cries one peasant. An afternoon of hilarity at the Hunter's Tryst is followed by a 'night of fun', with Vattermare behaving like a poltergeist and scaring the simpletons with the notion that a child has been corked up in a bottle. Someone seems to be coming down the chimney, maybe the Devil. All was not entirely well with multiple personality.[19]

Ambrosian adventures were, at times, Vattermare-like. These were laughers and hoaxers; for Hogg, at times, anonymity was a liberating joke. And they were liars. Hogg was scorned for being one, and he was one, and he said so. He told Byron that in one of his rows with Scott he had said things that were 'the reverse of truth'.[20] Hogg and the writers he came to know were given to saying such things, each with his own way of dinging or deflecting the facts.

The preoccupation with lies opens a back door to the romantic ethos as taught in this corner of Edinburgh. Blackwood's ventriloquists made the Shepherd say that there was something to be said for error, and that he could put up with a good deal of nonsense. It seems that Hogg believed some of this, and that the ventriloquists did too, though they were also using it to send him up. Hogg sent himself up, with his imaginative flights. Imagination showed the reverse of the truth in passing from this world to some other, and the poet Hogg took to looking down from space on the everyday world, from the fairy space of chastity and purity. Flight was another of the preoccupations of his day and age. When, in 1785, the Italian balloonist Lunardi was overflying Yarrow, he heard a Mr Scott calling up to him in the name of common sense and in the words directed at Jock Gray: 'Lunardi, come down.'[21] Hogg may be said to have gone up and to have come down. This is an aspect of his duality, and of a universal duality, very much alive in Ettrick and Edinburgh.

An Edinburgh friend, the High School master James Gray, had been a friend of Burns, and in a three-part discussion of the poetry Hogg was turning to, he maintained that Burns was a poet of manners and pathos and Hogg a poet of fancy.[22] The 'interesting valleys' of Ettrick and Yarrow had made Hogg a student of nature – one, however, who could mould every object into 'a thousand combinations that never existed but in his own mind'. The *Mountain Bard* poems, Gray wrote, were 'never uninteresting – the mortal sin of poetry'. But Hogg was at his most interesting in his flights of fancy.

Hogg agreed with this. When the London editor, William Jerdan,[23] a Borderer, praised him for putting 'two exquisite rural images into a single line, quite equal to anything in Theocritus', the poet asked: 'Hey, sir, what may thae be?' Jerdan replied, with feeling: 'The delicious traits of evening-fall, – when the lark becomes a clod, and the daisy turns a pea.' Hogg: 'Hey, sir, what's in that? – there's nae great poetry in that – so they do!' Jerdan wondered: 'Did he think that pure invention alone, and not an actual perception of beauties in nature, was poetry – imagination, not appreciation?' He told the story twice, in successive books. The second time round, Hogg accuses him of being daft: the lines are 'only joost true' – 'a plain description of what everybody can see'. Invention was much better. What never was and can't be seen was what mattered.

Jerdan supplied his version of what became a familiar topos, the homo duplex Hogg: 'a singular welding together of apt shrewdness and childish simplicity, of sound common sense and poetic imagination'. His poetry rose on the wings of the imagination, to the applause of his compatriots, in the approaching years of his life, and when the flight began to tire, and the readership to tire, he moved to prose. He did not always find John Wilson's verse interesting or even readable, but he became for a time the poet whom Wilson praised him for being – the poet-laureate of the Court of Fairy, who could almost persuade you that you were listening to the voice of one of the fairy folk. His ability to play with, and to extrapolate from, the plain truths of his environment produced a range of impressive results, in most departments of his work. But it is doubtful whether Wilson had more to say about the poet-laureate of the fairies than Tibbie Shiel did.[24] 'Aye,' she said, 'Hogg was a gey sensible man, for a' the nonsense he wrat.'

CHAPTER SIX

Mr Spy

For all the anguish, as James Gray called it, of the 1809 bankruptcy, Hogg was buoyant enough, a year later, to wind his plaid round his shoulders and trudge off for a fresh start to Edinburgh, where he was soon to launch a literary magazine. He had previously resolved to use his poetical talent as 'a staff, never as a crutch': a saying of the time, and of Walter Scott, whose staff turned to gold. Now Hogg would be trying to use his talent as a crutch. On getting to Edinburgh, however, he found it was rated nearly as low there 'as my shepherd qualities in Ettrick'. Border folk reckoned that his poetry had cast discredit on his husbandry, or so he felt, which made it worse that Edinburgh should prove indifferent to his verse.

He went knocking on the doors of booksellers – publishers, that is – and of editors. Not a farthing – a coin frequently invoked in the literary circles on whose threshold he stood – fell into his hat. He applied again to Constable, with a batch of songs, reclaimed from his youth, which was meant, Thomas Thomson thinks, to put heart into the minstrelsy of Scotland. Constable, Hogg believed, had a soft spot for him, but he had to wait on him three or four times before an arrangement of sorts was agreed for *The Forest Minstrel*, published in 1810. A thousand copies were printed at five shillings, and Hogg was to reap half the profits. In the event, according to his memoir, he got nothing, and, in trepidation, asked for nothing.

He was, though he said it himself, a natural songster. Scotland's lads and lassies sang his songs, and so did he. Some were words for established airs, and have in them the winter evenings when he could also be heard 'sawing away on the fiddle with great energy and elevation', a flourishing second fiddle to the violinist composers, the three Gows. Hogg's Cremona, a later acquisition, still survives, in its red leather case with the brass nails. After a rendering of the Strathspey

'Athol Cummers' in 1800, his mother asked him: 'Dear Jimmie, are there ony words to that tune?' 'No that ever I heard, mother.' 'O man,' she replied, 'it's a shame to hear sic a good tune an' nae words till't. Gae away ben the house, like a good lad, and mak' me a verse till't.'[1]

Never mind the farthings – Beethoven and Haydn supplied settings. 'The Highland Watch', on the Highlanders who fought at Waterloo, was printed with Beethoven's music in George Thomson's *Select Collection of Original Scottish Airs*, and was then to figure in Beethoven's *Schottische Lieder*, along with one of Hogg's liveliest lyrics:

> Could this ill warld have been contrived
> To stand without that mischief, woman!
> How peacefu' bodies wou'd have liv'd,
> Released frae a' the ills sae common.
> But since it is the waefu' case,
> That man must have this teasing crony,
> Why such a sweet bewitching face?
> O had they no been made sae bonnie![2]

Beethoven's setting is appreciably countryside-Scottish, and jolly. No great fear of the witch can be apprehended. George Thomson was the publisher for whom Burns did much of his invaluable work as a seeker of old songs.

Two-thirds of the *Forest Minstrel* songs were Hogg's, and the rest were by friends and correspondents: 'Lucy's Flittin'' is here, with Hogg's wrecking extra lines, and there are pieces by Allan Cunningham's brother Thomas. 'In general they are not good, but the worst of them are mine,' he said of the collection: he 'had never been once in any polished society – had read next to nothing'. The collection is divided into Pathetic Songs, Love Songs, Humorous Songs and National Songs. There's the poem about love's dizziness, and the mistaken-identity poem, 'I'm gane a' wrang, Jamie.'

The more humorous the poems are, and the more Scots-speaking, and the less delicate, the better. 'Ayont the Mow amang the Hay' is not delicate at all, and not Hogg's at all, but Thomas Cunningham's. 'Mow' can mean grain and it can mean sexual intercourse; and 'ayont' can be erotic too, when it refers to the placing of one body beside or beyond another in bed or barn. Hogg had a talent for poems about the senile suitor, seeing both sides of the issues raised. One of these poems, present here, is 'Gracie Miller'.

> 'Little, queer bit auld body,
> Whar ye gaun sae late at e'en?'

Gracie puts the question to an old soul on his way to woo her, but his senses let him down and he mistakes her identity. She accepts him all the same. He has taste, sense, and 'a dash o' amorous fire'. The poem says that women are easily flattered: but Gracie is just as much of a flatterer as her old soul.

The patriotic songs include the supercharged 'Donald McDonald', where Donald and his Highlanders will finish off the Corsican lad with bullets and stones. Tenderness had obliged them to support the unfortunate Prince. Had Hanoverian 'Geordie come friendless amang us', they'd have done the same for Geordie. An unsightly example of what Carlyle saw as the pervasive not-true, or affected, in the poetry of the age.

In Edinburgh, Hogg made up his mind to bypass the booksellers, 'enemies to all genius', and start a weekly paper without them. But no printer seemed willing to take him on without their backing. 'Damn them,' he said to himself: 'the folks here are all combined in a body.' (He is referring to trade-union action of a kind: the courts were later to acknowledge 'the innocence of mere combination'[3] where there was no coercing of fellow workers to strike.) John Ballantyne, James's brother, subscribed for copies, and Hogg finally persuaded James Robertson of Nicolson Street, printer and publisher, to take him on. On 1 September 1810 the first number of the *Spy* appeared, price fourpence.

The usual troubles that beset literary magazines were not long in making themselves felt, and were to persist when the magazine was transferred to another firm, A. and J. Aikman. Andrew Aikman issued a statement quarrelling with Hogg's account of the early difficulties when his memoir, incorporating the account, was reissued in 1832, and Aikman's statement was incorporated in a pamphlet by a brutish Whig enemy of Hogg's, Dr James Browne.[4] Aikman claimed that most booksellers were operating on the time-honoured (and long-lasting) sale-

and-return system, and that Hogg did not pass on, as agreed, subscription money that had been received. The fifty copies taken by John Ballantyne, to whom Hogg was in debt, went unpaid-for and unreturned, Aikman alleged. Hogg writes that, at the outset, a bad boy, meant to deliver free copies, charged for them, telling customers: 'I take nothing for the delivery, but I must have the price of the paper, if you please.' The coppers passed to Hogg by this boy were all he'd earned since his move to the city.[5]

The third and fourth numbers brought a scandal resulting from a piece describing youthful adventures suggestive of the idyll at Locherben: the 'correspondent' whose adventures these are looked very like Hogg to his Edinburgh readers, as did George Cochrane, a first version of whose amours appeared in the paper. In the piece in the third and fourth numbers, a Berwickshire farmer spends a night with his pretty housekeeper, who then bosses him about. He is no longer master in his own house; her impudent associates take over. A man is 'in a dangerous situation when he begins to parley with vice. His hand is indeed on a lion's mane.' While his neighbours praised his tunes and his songs, and drank his brandy, 'my housekeeper grew nearly double her natural thickness about the waist,' and he heads off for the revolutionary war in America, 'to help some of the people to fight with their neighbours'.

This would never do for the genteel or aspiring readership Hogg felt he had to interest: seventy-three subscribers cancelled. He was 'sorry at being obliged to curtail' the narrative, 'for want of room'.[6] Andrew Aikman spoke of the piece in 1832 as a sketch of Hogg's own life: 'a more shameful and indecent paper was never laid so barefacedly before the public.' Hogg believed that it set all Edinburgh against him – 'the literary ladies in particular'. This picaresque work later became 'The Renowned Adventures of Basil Lee', which starts the first of the two volumes of his collection of 1820, *Winter Evening Tales*.[7]

Braving these and other upsets, the magazine held on for a year. For Hogg, it was a place of trial runs – a testing-ground for his talents and preoccupations. And it gives a vivid picture of the Edinburgh of 1810, and of Hogg's acquisition, never quite consummated, of an appropriate street wisdom. This was a year of Napoleonic annexations, and of the expulsion of tenants by their Highland landlords, the year of an abortive Whig attempt at Parliamentary reform, and of Scott's *Lady of the Lake*, in which 'blows and blood' and trusted chieftains are glamorous and a king goes about in disguise. The Edinburgh of the *Spy* years, and of the several years that followed, was one in which Scott's Highland poem loomed large, in which there were 'classes', and an intense awareness of their existence, in which those keen on political reform could be taxed by opponents with religious infidelity, in which, for such opponents, God and King were one, in which jokes, games and sports were pursued, in which eating and alcohol were a fascination, and a special carnivorousness reigned in the expanding world of the media, where reviewers 'cut people up' and Constable could be said, by Hogg, to devour his writers, to feed upon the brains of his own species.

This was a romantic Edinburgh, as sung by Scott, and an unromantic one. Reason contended with a flow of soul, and 'the march of intellect' – a cant phrase of Radicals and others – had begun. The magazine unveils a city of common sense, and of its desertion, of ambitious poets, profligate students, ruined maids, of dinners, routs, cards. A quite new rampant consumerism and festivity are ascribed here to the wealthy, and thought to be trickling down to the city's risers and reachers. The 'low-bred' are unlikely to have relished a magazine which advised about servants, as this one did, and approved of the practice whereby they were permitted to 'go abroad', leave the house 'for the sake of attending church, at least one out of two Sundays'.

The *Spy* went every Saturday to subscribers whom Hogg hoped to entertain and who were on the look-out for indelicacies. Nothing should appear, he was early-warned by Scott's business partner and louche friend John Ballantyne, that might 'add the slightest tint of the rose-leaf to the modest cheek'. The first thirteen issues were brought out by Robertson, 'a kind-hearted, confused body,' said Hogg, 'who loved a joke and a dram', and who would accompany him 'down to a dark house in the Cowgate, where we drank whisky and ate rolls with a number of printers, the dirtiest and leanest-looking men I had ever seen'. Thereafter he took up with Andrew Aikman's better class of firm.

Scott dropped his eyebrows, according to Hogg, when this shepherd outlined his plans for a magazine. Was it not unwise to lay claim to ground once occupied by Addison, Johnson and Henry Mackenzie? 'No a bit!' replied Hogg:

> 'I'm no the least feared for that. My papers may no be sae yelegant as their's but I expect to make them mair original.'
>
> 'Yes they will certainly be original enough with a vengeance' said he.
>
> I asked him if he thought threepence would be a remunerating price? He answered with very heavy brows that 'taking the extent of the sale into proper calculation he suspected she must be a fourpenny cut.' He said this with a sneer which I never could forget.[8]

The supererogatory 'y' used here by Hogg was also assigned to him, as a piece of rustic speech and pastoral simplicity, in the 'Noctes Ambrosianae' serialised in *Blackwood's*, whose yeditor the Shepherd is mocked in the symposium for wanting to be: the former yeditor of the *Spy* alludes there, in his Shepherd capacity, to 'my yawtobeeograffy'. The ambivalence towards him which became a feature of the 'Noctes' conversations was already, in 1810, publicly apparent in Edinburgh and elsewhere. There were to be times when he could be seen both as a treasure and as a laughing-stock.

The activities of Hogg qua Mr Spy, and of the Ambrosians, formed part of the 'hoaxing and masquerade', the anonymities and clandestinities, which broke out in Edinburgh. Mr Spy, boulevardier and Addisonian essayist, purported to train a quizzical and magical eye on the inhabitants of the city – a purport which was to have consequences for his fiction of several years later: by looking at a face and imitating a posture, Mr Spy claimed to be able to penetrate and control the mind in question.

The second and third decades of the century brought to the place an extraordinary ludic surge, to which all that was comic, parodic and satirical in John Galt's magnificent novels of the early 1820s, carried in *Blackwood's*, lent momentum, as did the fiction of Galt's friend, biographer and bowdleriser, D. M. Moir, pen-named Delta. The 'Noctes', in particular, enthralled the young, some of whom were later lost when exposed to the paper's reactionary last stand over the Jacobin Bill of 1832.

These evidently gluttonous, Glenlivet-downing *Blackwood's* games-players, in all their proleptic political incorrectness, turned their symposium into one of the wittiest and wiliest of all accessions to the literature of journalism. And their love of the cryptic and covert, and of teases, is shown at a formative stage in the *Spy*. The magazine can be characterised by beginning at the end, with the *Spy*'s farewell to his readers, the monitor's farewell to his monitors, as he encourages one to put it, in which the eyeing boulevardier bows out, in which his sleights are acknowledged, in which the magician breaks his wand, for the time being. Earlier in the magazine, he had referred to himself as a 'monitor' in his editorial capacity, and he refers here to his friends as treacherous 'monitors' of his editorial performance. Late in life, he wrote a poem called 'The Monitors', where these are the omens that afflict an anxious old age.

Among the tricks played by Hogg the Spy is the insertion in the paper, half of which was written by himself, of passages from the essays of Samuel Johnson. Another late poem of Hogg's[9] targets a sermon delivered by a dandy clergyman:

> Twas all made up of scraps, from Johnson some
> And some from Joseph Addison...

Well, there are scraps from Johnson in the *Spy* too; the further debt there to Addison is more a matter of tips than scraps. For these borrowings, the farewell essay indicates, the Spy had his reasons.

It portrays him as illiterate, in the period sense of uncultivated, as a country 'nothing'. The not very telling Latin tags sprinkled about the magazine seem to have required the guidance of James Gray, and they do little to embarrass this strategy of disclaimer, adopted in order to deal with sneering friends and with a time when 'the whole of the aristocracy and literature of our country were set against me and determined to keep me down nay to crush me to a nonentity.' The bits of Johnson, he suggests, were put in to catch these friends out, to cause them to sneer at these bits as well as at the rest of the paper. He was an 'intruder', 'weak and friendless'. Friendlessness is, of course, a familiar trope. He did have friends. He was convivial, loved his joke and his dram. But this compiler of morals, manners and *faits divers* was no more of a connoisseur or strolling spectator than Johnson was, and he had a good deal to worry about. 'As his name became known,' he writes of himself here, 'the number of his subscribers diminished.' This last essay is, as such farewells often are, fraught and painful and combative.

The essay belongs to a literary work which speaks up for good nature, which harks back to the 'benevolism' of long before, of Addison's day, and Shaftesbury's. The magazine professes a delight in 'benevolent and friendly communications of the moving kind'. Kind writers address kind readers, urging them to avoid peevishness and other angers. They are under the eye of a benevolent God. That God, however, is admonition incarnate. People must *improve*.

A poem here by the editor, 'The Admonition', has a cotter who forbids a daughter to go roaming in the gloaming, where the late-marrying Hogg himself, the poet of an ethereal chastity, spent many a happy hour, as night fell on Ettrick Forest, where it was better to burn than to marry. The cotter points out that 'the pleasant way aft leads to death.' Soon after this, a ruined maid is put to service with a nasty old lady, and consoled by having her child of shame 'taken into a respectable hospital', presumably an orphanage.

These *Spies* belong to a community in which respectability was admired and advised, in which the poor were increasing, in which Juvenal's line 'Poverty makes men ridiculous'[10] was quoted among the upper orders, who used also to say how moving and good poor people were. The homage that vice pays to virtue was paid in Hanoverian Edinburgh, where, in matters of poverty and sexuality, hypocrisy can seem like a function of the divided mind perceived and pioneered in that city at that time.

The back-numbers of the magazine have been issued as a volume of the *Collected Works*. The first-publication text, together with its errors, is as far as possible preserved. At one point, a Georgian Gordian 'not' might perhaps have been noted. An essay – which turns into a story – on the deficiencies of Jacks-of-All-Trades arrives at a comment on the human mind: 'if it is bent upon any one object, and that alone, it is ten to one that it does not obtain it.' This is the material which was subsequently revised and elaborated as 'The Adventures of Basil Lee', where a sentence about the same human mind reads: 'if its course is bent towards *any one* object, it is ten to one that it obtains it.'[11] It would be hard to decide whether either sentence is more cogent than its opposite. Perhaps that is the way with admonitions, as with proverbs. As, too, with the duality of man.

A further admonition contains patches from Johnson's *Rambler*, to the point of resembling a cento, or a quilt. Here also the instability of advice is apparent. Johnson is warning against excessive forethought. Too much provision for the future takes from what is owed to the present – 'from the only time which we can call our own, and of which if we neglect the duties, to make provision against visionary' – that is, imagined – 'attacks, we shall certainly counteract our own purpose'. Hogg reverses the meaning by omitting the comma after 'duties'. The missing comma might seem to have flown to a later sentence: 'As I said before,' Hogg writes, about something that Johnson had said before, in an earlier *Rambler*, 'the recollection of the past, is most useful by way of provision for the future.'[12]

The *Spy* served as a provision for Hogg's literary future. Some of his best stories appear here in their pristine form: 'The Wool-Gatherer', for instance, in which a high-born girl pretends to be a low-born girl, sheds her disguise and gets married to the laird. Characteristic concerns are in evidence – those of a believer in community and in the uncertainty of the individual self. In the issue of 27 July 1811, the subversion of a man by his friend, and a 'dreadful dream' of convergent identities, give foretastes of the *Confessions*, twelve years ahead: 'You know, Sir, there is an old Scotch proverb, that "one had better dream of the deil than the minister"; but I dreamed of them both, and mixed them so completely together that they seemed to be one and the same person.'

An early essay by Hogg in the series expresses a hostility to critics and raises the question of Francis Jeffrey's treatment, in the *Edinburgh Review*, of two long poems by James Grahame, *The Sabbath* and his *British Georgics*, published five years later, in 1809. Hogg prefers the first and affects to think that Jeffrey's enthusiasm for the second was occasioned by a passing mood, or perhaps 'he had just been perusing *The Lay of the Last Minstrel* when he took up *The Sabbath* for inspection,' and perusing some inferior thing when he began inspecting the *Georgics*.

Jeffrey's review of the poem of 1809 was not, in fact, ardent. I once called it a measured account, in the course of discussing a letter to Grahame from Henry Cockburn. The letter predicts Jeffrey's review, which praised the poem while regretting its surplus of agricultural advice – not a fault that can be discovered in the poetry of Hogg.

'Sabbath Grahame', Jeffrey and Cockburn were friends and fellow Whigs, and Grahame, a Thomsonian poet strong against blood sports, and against the abolition of the Sabbath, which would adjudge 'to the rich the services of the poor for life', longed to review for Jeffrey's journal. Cockburn's letter tells him what it is to be an Edinburgh Reviewer, subject to the Jeffrey despotism, to Jeffrey the rewriter, and reassures Grahame about Jeffrey's approaching critique. Not long afterwards, this depressive Scotch bard, eager to be a Scotch reviewer, died.[13] Trained as a lawyer, Grahame was known to himself as 'the poor man's bard'. Such bards had become, since Burns, a fashion, both in Scotland and England. Some gave the sense of a one and only, but there were a number of them. The Northern chapter included Robert Tannahill, William Motherwell, William Nicolson, and William Thom, 'the weaver poet'. Their writings bore a likeness to certain of Hogg's, and he was kind to more than one of these men. Hogg and William Tennant, poet and professor, of Oriental languages, author of the accomplished fantasia of country life, *Anster Fair*, were seen by Jeffrey as prodigies of humble birth, and, according to Hogg, as self-taught geniuses. Hogg, thought Hogg, was the self-taught genius of the two. Tennant asked him to stay in 1829, wishing to see him 'in the real, visible, palpable, smellable beauty of your own person'.[14]

The poems printed in the *Spy* are prone to the language and landscape of sentiment, to love, loss and bloodshed, and to Scottish admonition. There's Hogg's poem about women as mischief, and as 'made sae bonnie', and another poem in Scots, 'The Twa Craws', which has been attributed to Robert Sym, Wilson's uncle, who figures importantly in the 'Noctes', dressed up as Timothy Tickler, the tall old caustic Tory wit. The poem is about the badness of shooting birds, and comes oddly from the hunting, shooting and fishing romantic carnivores of the *Blackwood's* connection, and perhaps from Sym in particular. It may be that not all Tories were mad for blood sports, and not all benevolent romantics opposed.

A thrillingly stern poem by James Park of Greenock consists of an imitation of Catullus. A Presbyterian Roman speaks ill of the imagination: what is seen has to be believed.

> Catullus, check thy useless grief,
> Nor seek in doubt a faint relief,
>   Believe what thou hast seen;
> Gone are thy joys, then think them gone;
> Nor vainly hope, when thus undone,
>   To be what thou hast been.

Not every one of its early readers would have expected this opening stanza to introduce a poem about being jilted.

Burns's friend James Gray here condemns – without naming him – the blame directed at Burns, as at Hogg, by monitors and detractors: 'He was a good son, a good brother, a good father, and an affectionate husband; yet, say his enemies, he was a monster of vice.' It could be said that Scottish self-rebuke, so far as the production of poetry and irony are concerned, excels itself in Burns:

> Had I to guid advice but harkit,
> I might, by this, hae led a market,
> Or strutted in a bank, and clarkit
>   My cash-account:
> While here, half-mad, half-fed, half-sarkit,
>   Is a' th'amount.

Good advice was to urge both poets to keep away from poetry.

For all the opportunities afforded by his magazine for going on about missing commas and errant negatives, it is easy to respond to Hogg's subsequent view of it: 'It has, doubtless, but little merit; but yet I think that, all circumstances considered, it is rather wonderful.' One of its wonders is that it was done at all. Another is his ascent and descent of Ben More in 1811,[15] at a time when there was a scheme to have the prettiest girl in Edinburgh repair to the Trossachs, during the summer months, to 'personate' the Lady of the Lake. Hogg felt that Scott's 'delightful' poem lacked the appearance of truth, its 'greatest fault'; nor was it possible to care about its characters.

Best to climb with a flask of spirits, he advises; he'd once been initially disappointed with a Nithsdale rock, but, with the help of provisions and 'repeated applications to a bottle full of whisky', the rock had improved, and 'continued to improve'. In the Grampians, at the top of Ben More, he drank the health of His Majesty, and looked down at the haunts of the Lady of the Lake, and at all Scotland. 'Where the body is, there must the mind be also; will any man then venture to deny that mind to be elevated, which is 4,000 feet above the level of the sea?' He then, significantly enough, doubts the assertion, mentioning an Edinburgh debating society to whose eloquence he contributed: 'This is only a specimen of Forum reasoning Sir; you must not mind it, but try if you can for a moment conceive the sublimity of my situation.' With that, he plummets down Ben More on his bottom – a quarter-of-a-minute mile. 'My staff of which I lost the hold when I fell, quite outrun me, my clean shirt, which was tied neatly up in a red handkerchief, came hopping down the hill, sometimes behind and sometimes before me, but my hat took a direction quite different.' He is not 'a farthing the worse' for this descent, emblematic of a careering and divided Hogg, who was not the whole Hogg.

CHAPTER SEVEN

Come down, Kilmeny

Every week for a year, his magazine 'flew abroad', said Hogg, 'like the sibyl's papers'. This friendless man had friends who wrote for it, and who kept him from starving. For his first six months in the city he lodged with John Grieve, owner of a red gig, and of a hat shop on the North Bridge, which seems to have enabled Hogg to give a hat to his minister in the country. Grieve and his associate, Henry Scott, 'would not suffer me to be obliged to any one but themselves for the value of a farthing'. 'Neither misfortune nor imprudence' could shake Grieve's affection for Hogg, Hogg's memoir affirms. James Gray and his second wife Mary, who had been a friend of Burns's flame 'Clarinda', gave the magazine their strong support. Hogg and Gray had met in 1808 as fellow travellers on a coach to Dumfries who struck up a conversation about the Ettrick Shepherd, who then unmasked himself. Gray, who moved in Whig circles, was both poet and pedagogue, and Hogg lobbied on his behalf for the rectorship of the High School. The imposing Gray is among the bards who compete with one another, and with Hogg, for the favour of Mary Queen of Scots in the most popular of Hogg's books of poetry, *The Queen's Wake*, published in 1813:

> His eye an intellectual lance,
> No heart could bear its searching glance.[1]

Hogg, with his eye for eyes, was pricked by Gray's intellectual lance when a company came to tea at Stockbridge, where Hogg was then living, and a dispute arose over a word in the *Wake*, then in manuscript; and a further meeting, held in Buccleuch Place, where the Grays lived, was broken up when, with Gray no further than page three of Hogg's long poem, one of nature's 'itinerant bards', 'a poor crazy beggar', began reciting his nonsense, his 'miserable stuff'. The boarders in the tenement were fascinated by this new bard, and Gray joined them. Hogg pocketed his manuscript and jogged home in a huff. In telling his story, he is both hurt and amused. Gray told Hogg's brother William, at this time, that he watched his friend's progress with no 'impartial eye'. The memoir says that Hogg never read any more of his poems to Gray, but the two of them kept up until Gray disappeared, a decade later, to Belfast and then to Bombay.

In 1813, Gray received two letters about Hogg from Hogg's shepherd brother William.[2] These forthright letters refer to a prehensile speed of thought consistent with careless raptures and a short attention span. There is talk of a dysfunction, one which could be seen as the defect of a dynamic strength, and as less descriptive of his prose than of much of his verse, with its aesthetic of the never-was, the ethereal, the fanciful, at the expense of the everyday. William remembered his brother as a boy 'distinguished by something vivid in his observations', imparted with 'an immediate fervour of spirit', and as a man whose actions could be uncertain. His mind is

> of an imperfect structure. His imagination is quite an overpoise for his judgment. Sanguine in his hopes, the world hath once and again disappointed him and ruined him, because he formed his opinions of men and the world rather from what they should be than from what they really are; hence he is disappointed whenever he steps out to transact business with them. The vivacity of his imagination disqualified him also from study and research. Present any intricate question to him for solution, his mind grasps it and pervades it with the rapidity of thought, as it really is; but if it miss solution, he cannot return to it again. The powers of his mind are so disordered by the rapidity of their first application, that they cannot for a long time be again collected to reconsider the subject. His judgment once baffled and overpowered, can hardly be brought again to renew the attack, or if it does, it is with diminished force, and more uncertain action.

The passage seems that of someone intent on saying just what he feels it is necessary for him to say. It makes you think both of James's intellectual development and of William's, of cottage vyings and debates, of the shared constraints of their first environment, and of the mystery of Hogg's fecund and fortunate imperfections, of his gift. He was a man, beyond admonition, beyond the calculus of good works, who could do what merit and method might fail to do, and who knew of a theology which prescribed in its own way for cases of this kind.

Gray's first wife had a sister, Margaret Phillips, introduced to his readers by Mr Spy as 'a charming young lady from the country', as distinct from a rosy ewe-milker. His magazine carried two songs written, Hogg said, with Margaret in mind, one of them among those set to music by Beethoven, 'Could this ill warld ...' Margaret, a girl with a cheerful smile, dark hair and black eyes, was twenty years younger than him, and was to prove no incarnation of 'mischievous woman', no witch-like enchantress.

With his gentleman friend, Robert Sym, a Writer to the Signet (or solicitor), and a man of wide learning, Hogg became bonded, tied together by heart-string and fiddle-string. Sym was a subscriber and a contributor to the *Spy* whose identity was made known to him by Andrew Aikman. Hogg gathered that when 'fine madams pointed out to him a few inadvertences, or more properly absurdities, which had occurred in the papers,' Sym had seen the bluestockings off: 'O, I don't deny that; but I like them the better for these, as they show me at once the character of the writer. I believe him to be a very great blockhead; still I maintain, that there is some smeddum in him.' Smeddum is spirit, spunk. Sym in his stateliness had it too, and so did Hogg's mother.

The fateful meetings with the young Turks, Wilson and Lockhart, belong to the same epoch of his life as the introduction to Sym. Hand in hand with these three, he would presently pass into the dark and dazzling wood of the 'Noctes Ambrosianae', with its spells and transformations.

When Hogg met the old Turk Sym, it was after the publication in 1812 of a book of poems, *The Isle of Palms*, by Sym's nephew, John Wilson, and it was at Sym's house, in George Square, where Scott had lived as a boy – to the south of the Old Town, but an inaugural element in the New Town's northward system of rectangles and circuses. He had imagined him to be 'some very little man about Leith'. 'Judge of my astonishment, when I was admitted by a triple-bolted door' into a splendid mansion, and introduced to its lord. There before him was a handsome old man, seven feet high and 'as straight as an arrow'. White hair, fresh face, full of benevolence when he stooped to talk to you. His good humour boundless, save in recoil from Whig or Radical principles. His soirées led to reels and Strathspeys, from the fiddles of Hogg and Sym, removed from their cases with the turn of a small gold key. When Sym, lifting the choicer of the two instruments, rosined his bow, 'there was a twist of the lip, and an upward beam of the eye, that were truly sublime.' When the sessions were marred by the laughter and jokes of their friends, 'if Sym's eye chanced at all to fall on them, it instantly retreated upwards again in mild indignation.' The memoir adds that Sym intends to bequeath Hogg his 'inestimable violin'.[3]

Hogg was once likened to some buoyant Irishman. The likeness did not protect him from Ireland's Maginn, the least equivocal – and yet not wholly unequivocal either – of his detractors in and around *Blackwood's*. William Maginn, an alcoholic and a liar, said the same of Hogg; he spoke of the *Spy's* 'dolorous and dram-drinking history'. Hogg had 'lost character' because of it.[4] If this was so, *The Queen's Wake* was soon to restore him to favour, or rather, to the chronic vicissitudes of his good name and stardom.

At this point in Walter Scott's 'watch over the struggling fortunes of the wayward and imprudent Shepherd', as Lockhart put it, which proved to be the eve of his greatest commercial success, his friend grew sceptical about his chances. This was the time when, in 1811, presenting to Harriet, Lady Dalkeith, a copy of *The Forest Minstrel*, he feared that the 'poor fellow', of whose friendship with her ladyship he may seem to have been a little jealous, was a spoilt farmer who hadn't the talent to support himself by writing. The following year, Harriet became Duchess of Buccleuch, and he wrote to her fearing that the 'poor bard' was 'a person whom it will indeed be difficult to serve to any essential purpose yet nature has been liberal to him in many respects and it is perhaps hard for those born under better auspices to censure his deficiencies very severely.' Two months later, Scott spoke of her 'kindness and munificence' when ten guineas – one of many such doles from those interested in his fate – went to 'poor Mr Hogg', who, a year later still, in 1813, in another of Scott's letters to the duchess, was termed, perhaps with a pinch of irony, his 'brother minstrel'. In another of Scott's letters of the period, to another brother minstrel, Byron, Hogg was carefully characterised:[5]

The author of the Queen's Wake will be delighted with your approbation. He is a wonderful creature for his opportunities, which were far inferior to those of the generality of Scottish peasants. Burns for instance – (not that their extent of talents is to be compared for an instant) – had an education not much worse than the sons of many gentlemen in Scotland. But poor Hogg literally could neither read nor write till a very late period of his life; and when he first distinguished himself by his poetical talent, could neither spell nor write grammar. When I first knew him, he used to send me his poetry, and was both indignant and horrified when I pointed out to him parallel passages in authors whom he had never read, but whom all the world would have sworn he had copied. An evil fate has hitherto attended him, and baffled every attempt that has been made to place him in a road to independence. But I trust he may be more fortunate in future.

This was the year of his mother's death, about which he wrote in his letter, mentioned earlier, to Bernard Barton in Suffolk. The letter contains a bulletin of Hogg's writer's news, in which Grieve, who gave a banquet for *The Queen's Wake*, features as a kind of literary agent. *The Mountain Bard* is called an 'uncultivated' work. Hogg is thinking of preserving some of the best of his *Spy* stories, and he lists the contributors to the magazine, now 'quite out of print'.

Never backward in coming forward, as journalists were to say of him, he approached Byron and began corresponding with him. He also met the members of the Lake school. Wilson was a part-time Laker, with his estate at Elleray in Cumbria, where he wrestled with dalesmen, strolled with Wordsworth the seventeen miles to Keswick, and kept a ten-oared barge in his long drawing-room. Wilson of the many talents and Norse God hyperpresence was styled the Admiral of the Lakes, and might also have been styled the Admirable Crichton of the Lakes.

Hogg spent five years in Edinburgh lodgings. *The Queen's Wake* was assembled in a 'weather-beaten, rather ghostly, solitary' place, like an old farmhouse, where the landlord drank and beat his wife.[6] By 1814, he was living in Ann Street, or St Ann Street, a 'den under the North Bridge'. Thereafter he moved to Gabriel's Road at the east end of Princes Street, adjacent to Oman's Hotel and Ambrose's Tavern. Gabriel was a murderous zealot, a tutor who had stabbed his charges. Wilson, who was to set up house in another Ann Street, then a secluded artists' quarter at the west end of the New Town, recalled a first meeting with Hogg under the North Bridge – up a spiral stone staircase in a room with a view of the Castle, where they shared a cod's head and shoulders. Gillies remembers him in this den, with his old shepherd's slate before him, to jot down his drafts, dreaming of a new journal that would be a 'bold, uncompromising, out-spoken work, having on all points originality, freedom and freshness of style to recommend it'.[7] Hogg's memory of meeting Wilson was different. Having read his 'visionary' poem, *The Isle of Palms*, he was anxious to get to know this fabulous hippogryphic creature, 'with hair like eagles' feathers, and nails like birds' claws; a red beard and an uncommon degree of wildness in his looks'.[8] He wrote asking him to dine at four in the Road of Gabriel – 'and if not, he might stay at home,' he adds, in the 1821 text of his memoir. There were times when those he wished to please he would first feign to insult.

Wilson gave access to the Lake school, and Scott to Byron and to royalty. Scott saw to it that *The Mountain Bard* obtained a subscriber in the Princess of Wales, Caroline, and a grand copy of *The Queen's Wake* was dedicated and dispatched, without acknowledgement, to her daughter, Charlotte. When he found the fifth Duke of Buccleuch 'literally covered with gold over the whole body with epaulettes and star', he felt for a moment that he himself looked 'very like a sheep'.[9] But he was a sheep who lay down with lions, and became one. It was thought to belong to his stardom that he made everything and everyone equal, that he was no respecter of persons. A man was a man. On his debut appearance in the 'Noctes' he was awarded a joke about the uses of error which indicates how he could be perceived, and could sometimes want to be perceived: 'Ae thing's just as good as anither' – 'ill things' as good as good things.[10] As if to say: all men are equal, and their mistakes may be equal to their best things.

After his own magazine folded, he remained in the public eye by serving as secretary of the Forum debating society, for the three years of its flourishing. The crowds were 'beyond all bounds', he said – audiences of a thousand paid sixpence to attend. But his salary of twenty pounds a year went unpaid, 'though I gave away hundreds in charity'.

The town jail was handed a sum which released petty debtors; poor families were helped. Friends advised him not to speak, but he flowed like the Grey Mare's Tail. 'Though I sometimes incurred pointed disapprobation', he was 'a prodigious favourite'. He 'came off with flying colours' – thanks to his 'unbounded' self-confidence. The debates were a continuation of his 'dear little meetings' in the hills, as Thomas Thomson referred to his shepherd discussions of twenty years earlier, and they were an education. 'I may safely say I never was in a school before. I might and would have written the "Queen's Wake" had the Forum never existed, but without the weekly lessons that I got there I could not have succeeded as I did.' His taste was improved by it, he felt. He learnt at the Forum how to satisfy, and avoid offending, an audience, learnt what they would 'swallow'.

The Forum did well, in 1812, to donate £20 to the Lunatic Asylum, which was about to replace the old City Bedlam, under the guidance of Dr Andrew Duncan, whom Hogg met through the Forum, and who did much to humanise the treatment of the mentally ill. Madness was thereafter to be a concern of Hogg's writings.

From any orator then, according to Thomson, Doric utterance such as Hogg's drew 'peals of ungovernable laughter': 'no public speech could pass muster unless it was in classical English.' This was not invariably so. The advocate Harry Cockburn pled in Scots, using the words and music of the speech to which 'the ears around him had been taught to thrill in infancy', wrote Lockhart, thinking this a ploy to distract juries. No doubt, however, there were those who would laugh when a Scots tongue was heard addressing such topics as 'whether the hope of Reward or the fear of Punishment tends most to the preservation of good order in Society'. Hogg, too, laughed, a little, at the Forum. He wrote a farce of that name, 'a Tragedy for Cold Weather', which he says he never showed anyone.[11]

There were those, predictably, who claimed that he made a fool of himself at the Forum and had his hand in the till. His enemy James Browne alleged as much. But there is something touching about the Forum and its till, its charitable and perhaps vulnerable till. 'He has no more command of language than a Highlander had of breeches before the Forty-Five,' said the great orator Wilson of Hogg's speeches, which were often hissed and greeted with 'shouts of derisive applause'.[12] The attempts to lower Hogg's flying colours in the Forum make him sound like the Dundee poet McGonagall, whose declamations were assailed in pubs by mockery and a wet towel in the face, and who walked to Balmoral, without appointment and without avail, for an audience with Queen Victoria. Both men drew a philistine derision, for their ill things, for getting above themselves, aspiring to be writers.

Another club was founded – Gillies as president, Hogg as croupier. This was the Right and Wrong Club: 'whatever any of its members should assert, the whole were bound to support the same, whether *right or wrong*.' A club for lawyers, it might seem, and for dualistic thinkers. The members met for drinking sessions that lasted for days. Some became 'deranged', and Hogg went down with a fever that almost did for him, he says. Members' visits to his bedside obliged him to replace the knockers and bell handles of his neighbours on the stair. In their derangement, members wrote love letters which resulted, according to Hogg, in happy marriages. But his fever dampened the general ardour and the club thought it right to disband. It was replaced late in 1814 by the Dilettanti Club, Wilson presiding, which was to hold anniversary dinners in honour of Burns.

George Goldie, a young Princes Street publisher, volunteered to bring out *The Queen's Wake*. He was to quarrel with Hogg over this, and his subsequent recriminations hark back to the Forum, where they may have met, with the charge that none of the office-bearers except Hogg 'had one farthing' and that not one farthing went to charity. Hogg's 'propensity to falsehood' and 'meanness of soul' were 'quite inexplicable'.[13]

When, in 1813, Hogg saw a format for the sequence of poems which became the *Wake*, he laid the plan before Constable, who was chilly. Hogg gave him a piece of his mind: 'What skill have you about the merits of a book?' 'I know as well how to sell a book as any man, which should be some concern of yours; and I know how to buy one, too, by God!' Constable relented to the extent of expecting him to find two hundred subscribers and of offering him £100 towards the printing of a thousand copies. Goldie, 'a lad of some taste', in Hogg's initial view, promised him the same sum, plus the subscription revenue. So the poem passed to him. Constable, who was having trouble with Scott at the time, cursed the ingratitude of literary men.

When the poem took off, Hogg, scenting Goldie's impending collapse, moved to place a further edition with Constable, who sent it to James Ballantyne to be printed. Goldie felt himself ill-used and induced Constable to cancel the deal. 'Nothing could be more cruel,' writes Hogg. Goldie was to challenge his suggestion in the memoir that in going bankrupt and stopping payment Goldie had sold or given away half the copies. Constable's rival Blackwood was one of the trustees who inspected Goldie's estate. Hogg recalled waiting on the head trustee, Samuel Aitken of 'the grey stiff eye': 'It is all over with me here,' thought Hogg. But Aitken ruled that creditors be denied the remaining copies: Blackwood sold them on commission and obtained for Hogg double what he'd have got from Goldie. The book was now in the possession of Blackwood, and his London associate, John Murray.[14]

The book made Hogg's name, though not his fortune. He was wandering up and down the High Street, afraid to enter the bookshops in case sales were bad, when a wine merchant, William Dunlop, a man with 'a great deal of rough common sense', accosted him with that species of Scottish praise which parades itself as blame:[15]

'Ye useless poetical bitch that ye're!' said he, 'what hae ye been doing a' this time?' – 'What doing, Willie! what do you mean?' – 'Damn your stupid head, ye hae been pestering us wi' fourpenny papers an' daft shilly-shally sangs, an' bletherin' an' speakin' i' the Forum, an' yet had stuff in ye to produce a thing like this!' – 'Ay, Willie,' said I; 'have you seen my new beuk?' – 'Ay, faith, that I have, man; and it has lickit me out o' a night's sleep. Ye hae hit the right nail on the head now. Yon's the very thing, sir.' – 'I'm very glad to hear you say sae, Willie; but what do ye ken about poems?' – 'Never ye mind how I ken; I gi'e you my word for it, yon's the thing that will do. If ye hadna made a fool o' yoursel' afore, man, yon wad hae sold better than ever a book sold. Od, wha wad hae thought there was as muckle in that sheep's-head o' yours? – damned stupid poetical bitch that ye're!' And with that he went away, laughing and miscalling me over his shoulder.

The poem imagines the arrival of Mary Queen of Scots at Holyrood, come to occupy her shaky throne, and a royal command performance, in the shape of a competition. Various bards, led off by the 'lady form' of her simpering Italian secretary Rizzio, take to their harps in pursuit of the palm, over three Christmas nights in 1561. Among the bards are contemporaries of Hogg, and Hogg himself. 'Each glen was sought for tales of old,' to be decked out and sung to native airs; exotic Rizzio studies a lay about Malcolm of Lorn. The field of reference is Celtic, Catholic and chivalric; synods and presbyteries go unsung. James Gray's contribution has Edward I dying on the Solway during an attack on Scotland, his last word 'Subdue!' Gray's harp is strung too high and too loud, and his lay appears to break down. In the poem that follows, 'Drumlanrig', meant to be by Allan Cunningham, young Morison of Locherben is slain resisting the Southron, and in defence of his sister, who marries the Scottish leader.

> O, stay, brave Morison! O, stay!
> Guard but that pass till break of day.

A memory here of the scene in romance, the shieling *à trois*, at Locherben? The thought enhances the effect of carnival created by the slaughter.

The runner-up in the competition is the bard from Ettrick, in whose glens, in modern times, spirits are seldom seen; witches are another matter, adds a note,[16] the one with the trick played by Lucky Hogg. The modern barefoot maid, of 'rosy hue', dares

> till midnight stay
> Among the coils of fragrant hay.

In this contribution old David Laidlaw stumbles on a fairy business which translates into a bandit abduction of local girls. The winner of the competition is the Highlander Gardyn.

> No merits can the courtier sway,
> 'Twas then, it seems, as at this day.

To this day indeed. These awards seem familiar. Holyrood looks fairly like Holywood on this occasion – the awards, Ossianically enough, like Oscars.

The project, the competition idea, is in certain respects similar to the game played in the *Spy* where the muses of contemporary Scotland, including those of Scott and Hogg, tread a kind of catwalk. Both projects involve a degree of impersonation, and are a first step towards Hogg's parodies in *The Poetic Mirror*. Nature's poet was at times a great impersonator. He could impersonate himself, and was the cause of impersonation in others. But his triumph in this capacity was yet to come.

Hogg's opinion of his poem was that 'it is a very imperfect and unequal production': three of the ballads are 'rather of a redeeming quality, some of the rest are little better than trash. But, somehow or other, the plan proved extremely happy' – 'though it was contrived solely for the purpose of stringing my miscellaneous ballads into a regular poem'. David Groves has endowed the whole with unifying themes. Hogg's main theme, he thinks, is adversity, symbolised by storms; and there's the suggestion in the poem that 'to be dominated by former times, or to try to ignore the past altogether, are equally wrong.'[17] These are, of course, themes that might as easily belong to a bad poem as a good. This is the book of a man on the move towards, in Thomson's phrase, 'the bettering of his condition',[18] towards an audience-pleasing poetry of the period, a flowing, floating poetry of dubious visibility, in which distance and confusion lend enchantment, in which it is easy to lose your place, in which one thing can seem very like another, and ill things loom through the obscurity.

Of the three 'redeeming' ballads one must be 'Kilmeny', which is not really a ballad at all, and another 'The Witch of Fife', which is an excellent one. 'Kilmeny' is a romance.[19] Here is a virgin, a more than nun, who flies up to the spirit world, and returns, but finally goes back to it for ever. In 'the land of thought', more fairyland than heaven, she is granted an overview of Scotland and a vision of its future. The opening contains the poem's best work, Wordsworth believed; John Buchan believed that the end was all right too, but that the intermediate passages were a blunder. These passages presage the girning malfeasance of John Knox and the depredations and defeat of Napoleon.

'Free frae stain', Kilmeny is brought to 'the light of a sunless day', where the sky is 'a dome of crystal light' and flowers bloom everlastingly. This is a language and landscape of the time. Three years later, Coleridge's 'Kubla Khan' had a 'sunless sea' and a dome. Ten years later, Shelley's Platonic elegy for Keats, 'Adonais', has

> Life, like a dome of many-coloured glass,
> Stains the white radiance of eternity.

Shelley's millennium dome went down badly with the *Blackwood's* wits. Maginn thought 'Adonais' 'unintelligible', the canoniser 'worthy of the saint': 'Locke says that the most resolute liar cannot lie more than once in every three sentences. Folly is more engrossing; for we could prove, from the present Elegy, that it is possible to write two sentences of pure nonsense out of every three.'[20] Hogg's dome, however, went unrebuked.

The poem opens:

> Bonny Kilmeny gaed up the glen;
> But it wasna to meet Duneira's men,
> Nor the rosy monk of the isle to see,
> For Kilmeny was pure as pure could be.

This was to risk offence to his growing audience, with the very idea that there might be Scotswomen ready for an evening with a licentious soldier or a flushed cleric. Having gone up the glen, Kilmeny has vanished, and it's a long, long time ere she is seen again. But then:

> The reek o' the cot hung over the plain,
> Like a little wee cloud in the world its lane;
> When the ingle lowed with an eiry leme,
> Late, late in the gloaming Kilmeny came hame!

A famous evocation, by which his audience was entreated and entranced.

How had she come to be snatched? Hogg used his antique Scots for the poem, and even in the modern-spelling versions of it which became usual there are words which disconcert, and elude the dictionaries. The scene of her disappearance is described:

> In yon green-wood there is a waik.
> And in that waik there is a wene,
> And in that wene there is a maike ...

Some of these words have multiple meanings; it might seem that we're being told that in that place there was a place and in that place a maike –

a man, a mate, a shape or image? At all events, 'in that green wene' Kilmeny
lay down and was taken up to heaven.

The man is an angel, who explains the reason for her translation.
Kilmeny is a kind of scholarship girl. The angel has been one of a
commission engaged for over a thousand years in keeping an eye on
womankind, and Kilmeny has passed the exam like no one else:

> But sinless virgin, free of stain
> In mind and body, fand I nane.
> Never, since the banquet of time,
> Found I virgin in her prime,
> Till late this bonny maiden I saw
> As spotless as the morning snaw.

Banquet of time? I notice that admirers of the poem tend to say little
about its propositional content, about the message that chastity is a
passage to immortality, that sex is a stain, human life a stain, and that you
are better-off dead – the message, admittedly, of more than one
eighteenth-century poem.

Hogg's translations to fairyland agree with and differ from the
snatches that occur in the Border Ballads, where Thomas the Rhymer
gets to kiss the Fairy Queen's 'rosy lips'. These lips are an effect easier to
associate with the hand of Scott, or Hogg, than with the diction of some
antecedent minstrel or minstrel collective, and rosiness was to become
an erotic signal frequent in Hogg's poetry. Kilmeny's lips seem deathly
pale and still. But in the 'Noctes' of January 1831, where Hogg's poem is
both celebrated and sent up, the Shepherd tells how, long before he
wrote down on his slate his magic words about the prime of her virginity,
and its heavenly reward, he had been visited by a seductive Kilmeny in
'the dream o' dreams'. 'Some other cretur nor me' had composed the
poem – Kilmeny had whispered the words to him. Ever since, he had
carried her about 'in the arms o' my heart', kissing her shut eyes, and her
lips 'as cawm as the lips o' death, but as sweet as them o' an undying
angel'. Christopher North responds: 'And such was the origin of the
finest Pastoral Lyric in our tongue' – Eros and Thanatos its inspiration.

Uneven and nonsensical as 'Kilmeny' is, it represented the fulfilment
of a purpose. It gave his readers what they wanted and continued to

want. It was what Barton of Woodbridge wanted at the time.[21] A poem of his offers commendation and admonition. 'O Heaven-taught Shepherd,' he asks,

> Say, hast thou, like Kilmeny, been
> Transported to the land of thought?

Hogg must no more distrust the Gift of God. He must follow his inspiration out of this world.

There are rosy monks elsewhere in *The Queen's Wake*. Abbot McKinnon of the Christian community founded by Saint Columba and based on the island of Iona consorts night and day with a girlish person in a cowl. Hogg was in years to come to be aware of a scandalous woman of the same name, the abbess of an Edinburgh brothel, so to speak, Lucky McKinnon. Women are, in general, suspected in this community of monks, as they often are in Hogg's verse. A note of his observes that Columba put the community's nuns and cows on a separate island, on the grounds that 'where there are cows, there must be women; and where there are women there must be mischief.' Cloisters were apt to excite Hogg. These monks are overtaken by stormy weather, and a mermaid predicts a watery death for the Abbot, who goes down with his ship, a herald's voice having spoken his doom from Ben More, which Hogg had gone down a little earlier. It may be that some of his first readers may have felt able to blame the Pope for the indelicacies of this risky tale.

The collection contains a poem in which the land of thought fails to eclipse the shire of Fife. Well might Scott and Wordsworth like 'The Witch of Fife', a true ballad in its abrupt, dynamic storytelling. An old fellow with dear wee bairns catches his wife in the practice of night-riding. She confesses what she has been up to – her visits to a world where a wee man with a wan cauliflower face pipes music to which the world swings.

> 'And the troutis laup out of the Leven Louch,
> Charmit with the melodye.'

The old man reproaches her, but she won't be told off and resumes her tale of travel by sea and air:

> 'And the bauld windis blew, and the fire-flauchtis flew,
>   And the sea ran to the skie;
> And the thunner it growlit, and the sea-dogs howlit,
>   As we gaed scouryng bye.'

Scotland, Lapland – all one to these witches, who are Scotswomen with altitude, in that sense Kilmenies, but with a quite different attitude to sex:

> 'Then soft in the armis of the warlock men,
>   We laid us dune to sleep.'

The old man has told his old woman that the worst-looking Fife wife is comely compared with her. But when he hears that they got drunk on the Bishop's wine over the Border in merry Carlisle, he wants to join the night flights:

> 'Beshrew my heart, I'll fly with thee,
>   If the deil shulde fly behynde.'

He won't go by sea or ride her hellish horse, but he can fly. She warns him off: the world would be turned upside down if everyone did it. But the auld man is a cunning auld man. One night he hides in Maisry's cot. 'The fearless haggs cam in,' and 'out at the lum they flew.' But he knows their password, places his foot on the hook which hangs pots over the fire, and goes after them up the chimney and all the way to merry Carlisle.

There are two endings. The poem is a duality. There is Hogg's original ending, and the one Scott wished him to write. The first has the old man burnt by the English, to whom he explains:

> 'I cam fra Fife,' the auld man cryit,
>   'And I cam on the mydnychte wynde.'

A warning is given about wine and the ill women that lead poor men astray. The second ending has him plucked from the burning when his wife murmurs the word of escape. He is swept up into the sky, leaving the English with 'a lang and a loud gaffa'. This time, the moral of the poem mentions drink as before, but also cautions against cursing your poor old wife, right wicked though she may be. It can be said of both versions that they have the residue of an ancient misogyny, that women and mischief go together here, as freedom and whisky do in Burns, but that both the ill woman and her old man enjoy an abundant life, a run for their money. It is not an ill poem.

CHAPTER EIGHT

Lies

To lie is human. Hogg, Scott, Wilson, Lockhart and Maginn all told lies. But Hogg was the most harshly stigmatised for this, though it's true that the matter has arisen with each one of them, and that Lockhart's biography of Scott has been, in certain respects, an object of suspicion. The biography lets drop that one of the Ballantyne brothers bore the name of 'Leein' Johnny', and it's a name which some people soon felt like applying to the author of the book. Half-joking, Hogg said of Lockhart: 'that callant never tauld me the truth a' his days but aince, an' that was merely by chance, an' without the least intention on his part.'

Scott's concealment of the Waverley authorship, which has its place in the period commitment to hoaxing and masquerade, has been treated as a white lie. To Louisa Stuart he wrote in 1817: 'I hope there is no great harm in the lies I am obliged to tell in self defence since my secret would otherwise be at the mercy of every one who chose to ask a blunt question.'[1] Of Scott's enabling secret, which made him fancy-free, and rich, while removing the cavalier from the stain of commerce, Hogg said that 'in all the common affairs of life' his friend was 'unimpeachable', but that, in view of his thousands of lies about his anonymous novels, it was 'needless to brag' about his truth.[2] He was speaking up here for veracity, as became a man from Ettrick Forest, a place with an ancient reputation for speaking the truth. 'True Thomas' of Ercildoune (Earlston), Thomas the Rhymer, refused to do so all the time, however, and Hogg felt the same way. 'Cheating an' leeing are nae sin,' he wrote in a poem for an angling competition.[3] This was a joke, as were many of his lies. A joke and no joke. But the joker Maginn was not joking when he claimed that Scott thought Hogg 'a man of genius, but destitute of a regard for truth – of no fixed principles, and so vulgar and intrusive, as to render it necessary to keep him at arm's length'.[4] Another lie, with its grain of truth.

Mendacity was an issue in more than one of Hogg's quarrels and huffs with Scott. In the autumn of 1814 Scott fell out with him over a project of Hogg's: a miscellany in the manner of the annuals that became popular, initially entitled *The Repository*, in which he intended to anthologise pieces by famous authors. Some of the authors defaulted, and some of the pieces he then wrote himself, as anonymous parodies. Whether or not this counts as mendacity, it hardly resembles plain dealing. He was a man, after all, who could ask Scott to present himself as the author of a piece of his, Hogg's, autobiography, and propose that Lockhart write his life of Scott in Hogg's name and style. On this occasion Scott, having promised to be in if Byron were in, dropped out, as did Byron, having offered *Lara*. A deeper resentment appears to have been caused by some strictures from Scott on the dramatic writings he'd taken to, and, before that, by a view of his work published by Scott in Edinburgh's *Annual Register*. One thing can turn into another with Hogg – one quarrel into another, as it did during the years that followed the *Spy*.

He wrote to Byron in October 1814 to say that 'I have differed with Scott, actually and seriously I fear, for I hear he has informed some of his friends of it. I have often heard poets in general blamed for want of common sense, yet I know that Scott has a great deal of it; but I fear he has had to do with one who had little or none at all.' Hogg had written Scott a letter of reproach, one of the 'terrible' letters of his to which he and his family would refer. Byron was told: 'I have quite forgot what in my wrath I said; but I believe I went so far as to say everything which I knew to be the reverse of truth . . . and I fear I expressed the utmost contempt for both himself and his poetry!' On another occasion, undated, Scott demanded his authority for certain statements – calumnies concerning the publisher George Goldie, whose bankruptcy was to change Hogg's life by introducing him to Blackwood – and was told: 'Deil o' any shirra they're jist a' lees.' 'Wicked lees,' said Scott. 'Eh, sirs, sae they may be, but I'd have tell'd 'em o' mysel.'[5]

His rejoinder suggests that lies may be a confession of human weakness: but it also suggests that, for him, they could be more than that. They were deception and error. They were the Devil's work. But then again they could be invention, imagination – poetry indeed, long known as a form of feigning. If Ettrick at large was unequivocally averse to them, its shepherd was not. And his interest in them – for all that he could not help it, at times – forms part of his developing interest in dual identity.

A lie may in itself represent a division of the self and some of his are utterances of his own divided condition. He was, in some degree, a self-belier, in ways which by this stage of his life had become more pronounced. His discrepancies increased when Ettrick and Edinburgh became his two different places. He could be seen as a strange compound of roughness and refinement, his conversation a perpetual contradiction of the delicacy of 'Kilmeny'. He was a poet of carnage and valour who in *The Pilgrims of the Sun* exclaimed:[6]

> What is a soldier but an abject fool!
> A king's, a tyrant's, or a statesman's tool!

He disliked the appearance of 'blackamoors', a 'hideous clan', one poem complains, with 'lips like puddings in a pan',[7] but he hired a black servant, and in *The Pilgrims of the Sun* evoked a solidarity of

> men of all creeds,
> Features, and hues!

The virgin in that poem rises above race and class:

> 'Child that I was, ah! could my stinted mind
> Harbour the thought, that the Almighty's love,
> Life, and salvation, could to a single sect
> Of creatures be confined, all his alike!'

And his poem 'Cary O'Kean' accepts miscegenation and feels for a South Seas belle who kills herself on losing her sailor spouse. He was a man who showed a hereditary regard for the Covenanters while writing in reproof of ultra-Calvinist tenets and of the exclusiveness of such brethren. These discrepancies are something to which his readers become accustomed, and to which they may be accustomed in themselves – *De te fabula* ... In Hogg's case, they are, in the main, something other than the falsehood to which they occasionally give rise. They are, indeed, inseparable from the truth he has to tell.

In January 1815, the fourth Duke of Buccleuch leased him rent-free the farm of Altrive, where he gradually installed himself, minding his farm, minding his poems, bottling whisky, shooting and fishing, then up to town to regale the literati at their symposia and to fiddle at soirées. The Duke allowed him to fish the Yarrow and to see people off that well-known water. In March 1813, Duke Charles's wife Harriet had been approached at Dalkeith Palace by Hogg, in search of a shieling. It was her countenance, rather than her money, that he was after, he informed her. 'I know you will be thinking that this long prelude is to end with a request: No, madam! I have taken the resolution of never making another request. I will however tell you a story . . .' There is 'a small farm at the head of a water', 'possessed by a mean fellow' by the name of Wilson, and 'there is a certain poor bard, who has two old parents, each of them upwards of eighty-four years of age; and that bard has no house nor home to shelter those poor parents in, or cheer the evening of their lives.' A certain beautiful lady had not moved to grant the favour. He added roguishly: 'I appeal to your Grace if she is not a very bad lady that?'

Harriet took an interest and told Scott that she was 'really sorry to appear "a very bad Lady"'. She replied through him to Hogg's request, on account of her 'fear of appearing some day in print'. The mean fellow was not dispossessed, but Hogg received a Buccleuch farm. Harriet died in 1814, shortly after the birth of a daughter, and Hogg wote an elegy on the passing of this 'fairest flower' of 'old Scotland's topmost tree'.[8]

In building himself a new stone cottage at Altrive Lake, at his own expense, Hogg insisted on a single chimney, to prevent passers-by from knowing whether the master was at home. The one lum, however, failed to stem a flow of visitors – spongers, gawpers, 'great skemps' most of them, he reckoned. He would talk of escaping to Edinburgh for a bit of peace. He contrasted his situation with that of William Blackwood, who sat 'at the fountain-head of literature' in Princes Street, while Hogg was a 'solitary hermit amid wastes'[9]: but his was a gregarious solitude.

A visit to Wordsworth in the Lakes, a month after Harriet's death, earned him a rebuff of uncertain proportions. 'No joke,' according to Hogg. Having met Wordsworth in August, in Edinburgh, he went to stay with John Wilson, no mean fellow, at Elleray, above Lake Windermere, and paid a visit to Rydal Mount. That night, a gleaming arch, rainbow-like or like the Aurora Borealis, stretched from horizon to horizon, and the company – Hogg, Wordsworth and his sister Dorothy,

Wilson and De Quincey – went outside to view the 'splendid stranger' (a comet had been, for the poet James Thomson, a 'glorious stranger'). Dorothy, squired by Hogg, who thought her 'a pure, ingenuous child of nature', her conversation 'a true mental treat', mused that the stranger might prove ominous, in the manner of some comets. Thereupon

> I, by ill luck, blundered out the following remark, thinking that I was saying a good thing: – 'Hout, me'em! it is neither mair nor less than joost a treeumphal airch raised in honour of the meeting of the poets.'
> 'That's not amiss. – Eh? Eh? – that's very good,' said the Professor, laughing. But Wordsworth, who had De Quincey's arm, gave a grunt, and turned on his heel, and leading the little opium-chewer aside, he addressed him in these disdainful and venomous words: – 'Poets? Poets? – What does the fellow mean? Where are they?'
> Who could forgive this?

'I have always some hopes that De Quincey was leeing,' wrote Hogg. And De Quincey, who thought that sentimentality was Wilson's fatal weakness, and that Hogg was vulgar and quotidian, insufficiently spiritual and intellectual, 'insufferable in conversation', always on about salmon, may possibly have made the most of Wordsworth's snubbing words. As reported, they bring to mind Allan Cunningham's remark that the great poet had a heart, 'for any manly purpose, as cold as a December snail'.[10]

A version of the snub appeared in the 'Noctes' of November 1824. The imaginary Mordecai Mullion prompts the Shepherd with a sly request for the story, which Mullion affects never to have heard. 'Toots! a'body has heard it – I never made ony concealment of his cauld, dirty-like behaviour ... just clean envy.' At the mention of a gathering of poets, 'Wordsworth turned up his nose, as if we had been a' carrion, and then he gied a kind of a smile, that I thought was the bitterest, most contemptible, despicable, abominable, wauf, narrow-minded, envious, sneezablest kind of an attitude that I ever saw a human form assume.' There were no real poets for Wordsworth save himself, his sister and Coleridge: 'would ony mortal believe there was sic a donneration of arrogance in this warld?' Lockhart reported that Wordsworth 'spoke kindly', on the whole, of Hogg the following year, despite having taken 'mighty offense' at the blabbing of the story in the magazine.[11]

Other poets also spoke kindly of Hogg, on the whole. Byron told Tom Moore in 1814: 'The said Hogg is a strange being, but of great, though uncouth, powers. I think very highly of him, as a poet; but he, and half of these Scotch and Lake troubadours, are spoilt by living in little circles and petty societies.' Having heard that Scott had been bothered by gales while coasting the Orkneys, he suggested that 'these home-keeping minstrels' should try the Atlantic, or the Bay of Biscay, 'to say nothing of an illicit amour or two upon shore' – 'beginning with simple adultery, and compounding it as they went along'. Two years later he told Hogg that London, though 'a damned place', was the only place in the world 'for fun', the English world at least, under the impression that the home-keeping minstrel fancied going there.[12]

Southey thought Hogg 'an extraordinary being'. Hogg listened to Wordsworth, when they first met, as to a 'superior being', while Gillies once heard Wordsworth say that Hogg was 'too illiterate to write in any measure or style that does not savour of balladism'. Wordsworth's 'egalitarian' views concerning the language of poets are not evident on this occasion: but they are plain enough in his complaint about the 'false finery' that disfigured the 'intermediate parts', or link passages, of *The Queen's Wake*, a poem which Maginn claimed was rather more admired than read. Wordsworth read it, felt it unduly dependent on Scott, and liked 'much the best', of the tales, 'The Witch of Fife', the 'former part' of 'Kilmeny', and the one about Abbot McKinnon.[13]

When Wilson's scientific brother James, 'The Entomologist', offered, in the late summer of 1814, to introduce Mr Wordsworth to Hogg, who had just returned from a northern progress, on which a Highland lady, Mrs Izett, had, he said, applied him to *Mador of the Moor*, a poem in celebration of the River Tay, and, one might feel, of Scott's *Lady of the Lake*, Hogg had expected to meet a 'celebrated horse-dealer of the same name', and had 'entertained some shrewd misgivings, how he should chance to be a guest in a house where only the first people in Edinburgh were wont to be invited'. 'Although he proses a little,' explained James Wilson, 'he is exceedingly intelligent.' 'I dare say he is,' rejoined Hogg: 'at all events, he is allowed to be a good judge of horse-flesh.' When the two poets then went off in a party on a Border tour, calling on 'noblemen and gentlemen' and examining the source of the Yarrow, 'several gentlemen', struck by Wordsworth's 'original' way of dressing, grey russet jacket and pantaloons, 'fell into the same error, expressing themselves at a loss why I should be travelling the country with a *horse-couper*'. Here is Hogg on the grand side of the fence which prevented Border farmers from spending an evening with their admired but drover-looking Burns. On the way south, the party called on Hogg's father in his cot; Wordsworth's sister-in-law, Sara Hutchinson, judged him 'a fine Creature', as if he were a Clydesdale. Out there in the Forest, where nobody goes, a fine creature had begotten a strange being.[14]

Having arrived at the Lakes, Hogg administered a snub of a different calibre from the one he received from Wordsworth at this point. Coleridge's son Hartley recalled, with detectable sympathy, that when Wordsworth was showing his visitor the lakes, he was told: 'I dinna want to see ony mair dubs. Let's step in to the public and hev a wee drap o' whusky, and then we'll hame!' 'Dubs' is Scots for puddles. This time, Wordsworth was amused.

Staying with Wilson at Elleray, Hogg entered into a poetry competition with his host. On wet days each man would sit in his room composing a rival poem, with Wilson sounding and chanting his lines as they met the page. He showed 'all the energy of a fine foxhound on a hot trail'. When Hogg heard the other's chant swelling in triumph, he would tell himself: 'Gude faith! it's a' ower wi' me this day.' If Mrs Wilson cast her vote in favour of the visitor, Wilson would that evening be 'desperate sulky'. Hogg's parody of Wordsworth, 'The Stranger', belongs to these sessions at Elleray.[15]

Wordsworth wrote poems about Yarrow and its poet, whom he esteemed and looked down on. 'Yarrow Unvisited' has a teasing reluctance to go near the place on an earlier tour:

> What's Yarrow but a river bare,
> That glides the dark hills under.

Yarrow could wait – let it go on being bare, and yet green and sweet, let

> The swan on still St Mary's Lake
> Float double, swan and shadow!

In 1814, 'Yarrow Visited' made amends. The valley blooms. 'Yon cottage seems a bower of bliss.'

Wordsworth floats double on the subject of Hogg (and his stream), and his mixed feelings were reciprocated. Hogg was bored by *The Excursion*, which came out in the course of the year, and in which, in the poem's pedlar, lineaments of the Ettrick Shepherd were to be surmised in Scotland, and he thought his superior being pompous and monstrously vain. This ambivalence issued in his parodies of Wordsworth, some sections of which could without extravagance be imagined as having been shared with Wilson, if only in his capacity as rival and monitor: Wilson was an idolator and calumniator of Wordsworth, and a writer whose talent honed itself to precision, and to its best efforts, under the impetus of a satirical derision. But it seems right to class the parodies, linked in his own mind with the Rydal Mount affront, with Hogg's best efforts as a poet, whether or not assisted. They were brought into play when his projected miscellany turned from *The Repository* into *The Thistle and the Rose* and then into *The Poetic Mirror*.

Earlier that year, in June 1814, he'd written as a stranger to Byron asking for any odd thing he might happen to have lying about. Byron promised to appear in the book 'in his best breeks', but *Lara*, as I have said, was withheld. There were other disappointments – not least Scott's dragged feet. So he sat down and wrote the bulk of the book himself in the space of three weeks, as he remembered it. John Ballantyne did so well in reading the 'Byron' aloud in public that it was taken for the real thing, and Hogg believed that had the Wordsworth imitations been less of a caricature, the whole work would have been deemed authentic. His memoir attributes a supernumerary secret to the *Mirror*, and Maginn alleged in *Fraser's* (May 1832) that the secret was that Wilson wrote the parody of himself. But then, two years on, Maginn said there that 'everything worth a farthing in *The Poetic Mirror* was written by Professor Wilson.' Some of these secrets remain intact: but it seems clear that the lies told in Hogg's Advertisement for the collection were no more wicked than Scott's statements about the authorship of the Waverley novels, which were now about to commence publication.

'I suspected that you were a dour ill-natured chiel but I am beginning to think I was quite mistaken': Hogg's letters to Byron are at times joshing, presuming, mock-insulting.[16] Byron bore with the leaking by Hogg of remarks of his about the Lakers. In October 1814, however, Hogg sailed close to the wind, when he quizzed him about his approaching marriage to the heiress Annabella Milbanke – 'assuring him that he was going to get himself into a confounded scrape', while wishing 'she might prove both a good *mill* and a *bank* to him'[17] – and received 'rather a satirical, biting letter' in reply. The following year, he fancied an heiress for himself. He wrote to Byron's, and his own, London publisher, John Murray, inviting him to come up and have 'fine fun' in Selkirkshire – to catch and eat hill-trout, drink whisky, sing songs, and to look out for a good wife for him in the South: 'I dare say there is many a romantic girl about London who would think it a fine ploy to become a Yarrow Shepherdess!' He may now have believed himself to be in a position to stop burning, and to marry above, or indeed below, his station. 'All unsolicited', Murray was informed, the Duke of Buccleuch had been so kind as to give him a farm rent-free for life.[18]

The letters to Byron and to Murray are among Hogg's most interesting. He remarked to Byron[19] that Wilson's poem *The City of the Plague* was 'a perfect anomaly in literature. Wilson is a man of great genius and fancy but he is intoxicated with Wordsworth and a perfect dreamer of moons ships seas and solitudes were it not for his antihydrophobia (forgive my mangling of that long Greek word) I do not know what he might not be capable of.' This describes some of the poetry which he himself was now writing. That poetry did not enable him to get through all of Wilson's, with its 'tendency to divest me occasionally of all worldly feelings'. It is doubtful, though, whether, in the course of their lifelong rivalry and bittersweet bonding, Hogg ever swerved from the view that Wilson the water-lover was the best periodical writer of the age.

He had planned to do a book of poems to be entitled 'Midsummer Night Dreams' and to contain 'The Pilgrims of the Sun' and 'Connel of Dee'. James Park of Greenock advised that the four-part 'Pilgrims' would do better on its own. When it appeared with the poem 'Superstition' it did not do well. *Mador of the Moor*, with its tale of the Tay and of a king disguised as a minstrel who impregnates and then marries a 'rural belle', to the distress of Thomas Thomson and of some of the people of

Edinburgh, did not do well either. 'Midsummer Night Dreams'[20] was dedicated in a verse epistle to Byron. The homage to the noble lord is paid, not for his lineage, or his radical politics ('thy crabbed state-creed, wayward wight'), or his 'virtues high' – but for his energy.

> Thy soul that dares each bound to overfly,
> Ranging thro' Nature on erratic wing.

Byron's mantle, he hopes, will descend on his plaid.

Hogg's verse of this period is aerial and antihydrophobic, with a decided stress on abduction by aliens and on a consequent overflight. *The Pilgrims of the Sun* is among his more signal abductions, in which Mary Lee of Carterhaugh is a more overtly erotic Kilmeny. 'There came a wight to Mary's knee,' an angel-faced wight, and 'up she rose a naked form.' She dons a nightie for a further ascent: 'Upward her being seemed to bound.' 'Bound' was to become, in Hogg, a word for romantic flight which can signify both the thing itself and the state it escapes. Hogg is responding to traditional conceptions of the way in which the old Adam, and the old Eve, may be shed in flight, while holding out hope that salvation and sexuality may remain acquainted. Mary climbs to a place where there is no up or down, no gravity, guided by her mentor, the 'beauteous stranger' eventually named Cela, whose whispered prayer corrects the precepts of her Catholic priests, proving that half the beadsmen said 'was neither true nor ever could be'. True religion is against soldiers and in favour of people of all colours.

David Groves has read the runes of the poem, where he identifies notions that relate to the meeting and mingling of opposites and to the meaning of rings and circles.[21] He observes that Mary and Cela are themselves readers; the second of the four parts, with its move from a ballad metre to rhyming pentameters, and its Miltonic airs, is a response to the English poetry of the seventeenth and eighteenth centuries. Part four places Mary in an Ettrick grave, where a robber priest tries to take her ring. But she rises from the grave and rejoins her family, doing so in the language of 'Kilmeny': ' 'Twas late, late on a Sabbath night!' Unlike Kilmeny, she does not opt for the land of thought and is joined in Ettrick by Cela, in the guise of a minstrel by the name of Hugo of Norroway, an alias of Hogg's.

Hogg is not mocked, any more – rarely mocked, at any rate, since his twentieth-century accession to an academic respectability. And it may seem wrong to make fun of him when he writes like this. In my view, it would be wrong not to do so. He does so himself on many occasions; his absurdities are offered both as a joke and as no joke. But it's also the case that some of the messages they send are a serious matter. The deathliness and heavenliness, the dialect of purity and retreat, which preceded and invaded Hogg's verse was to outlast it by a hundred years and more. The idea of a better world persisted long after the point by which salvation had been widely recognised as a lie and a poisoning of the wells of speech.

'Connel of Dee' has its merits, though. This is an erratic, dactylic, aquatic poem, in which the hero is restored to the pastoral decencies after a nightmare exposure to the vices of affluence and privilege. It catches the note of all that was helter-skelter, accident-prone, schlemiel, equivocal and uncertain, in the life of James Hogg. It is more verbally adventurous than the other poem, and more Scots, though sparing with his antique spellings. 'For love he was just gaun to die': Connel tries to take the woman he loves in his native gloaming, in a nook, but she insists on marriage and they repair to, as it were, Edinburgh. Connel is somehow wounded as he passes into transports of joy in her mansion or castle, but he reassures himself:

> Thy spirits once broke on electerick wheel,
> Cool reason her empire shall gain.

The word 'electric' was to be an important one for Hogg. His use of it on this occasion might be felt to unite Ettrick and erotic, and perhaps galvanic, and to look forward to an occasion in the 1960s when the Incredible String Band arrived in the Borders asking, spiering, the whereabouts of the Electric Shepherd. This shepherd is electrified by his wife, but she tires of him. She is an ill woman.

He is now in distress, and in debt: 'old debts coming due every day'. This is the dark night of Edinburgh, where he revels away among a scum 'who laughed at their god and their friend' – their Hogg, so to speak. He thinks of his Grampian paradise, very like Hogg's Nithsdale one – 'of his cake, and his cheese, and his lair on the lea!' When he finds his wife in the arms of a paramour, she laughs at him the heartless laugh of Edinburgh, *belle dame* turned beldame:

> 'Why that was the fashion! – no sensible man
> Could e'er of such freedom complain.'

Some freedoms are damnable, some mandatory, the poem indicates. When the ill woman shows Connel the guillotined head of a discarded paramour, he is off to the hills: 'he rose, and he ran! and he ran!' But 'it may not be said that he ran for he flew.' 'Poor Connel,' sighs the narrator, in Hogg's words at Elleray, ' 'tis over with thee!!' 'Tho' heels-o'er-head whirled again and again', he keeps on with his flight from the enchantress through an explosion of sounds and strange words. 'At chirk of the pyat or bee's passing boomb': a bomb is fashioned from a bumble-bee's boom. Finally he dives into the Dee and is molested by fishes. Eels are the worst. Dead and not dead, he is bored, warped, his loins guddled. Oh their cold noses!

This hot pursuit and watery grave prove to be a dream. He awakes in his Highland lair, visited by a sister. He is never again to sicken of his wilderness. He is subject to fits of fear at kirk or market, but he has learnt like the Ancient Mariner to cherish 'each thing that had life' – 'with two small exceptions, an eel, and a wife'.

Hogg was drawn in mid-life to the aesthetic of twilight, tumult and deliquescence, distance and obscurity, which had taken hold throughout the arts. *The Pilgrims of the Sun* is a less appealing poem than 'Connel of Dee': Thomas Thomson thought the first of these premature, out-of-period, in the sense that its Teutonic taste for wonders, water spirits, 'mesmeric trances and dual individualities', had been cast before an unattuned, hard-headed Edinburgh.[22] But it may be that the two poems go together, and that, as David Groves argues, the journeys performed there, respectively an ascent and a descent, contrast a spiritual exaltation with a momentum of the unconscious and the prospect of a watery death. The poems form a ring or a cycle; a similar configuration in *Mador of the Moor* signifies a fusion of 'opposite aspects of human life'.[23]

The poem 'Superstition', written at Elleray and designed as a third and last item in the 'Midsummer Night Dreams', is remarkable for its onslaught on contemporary religious infidelity. 'True Devotion', according to its solemn and orotund Spenserian stanzas, has waned in tandem with superstition, 'sole empress of the twilight', who ordered ghosts to walk and ordained flights, shudders and deliriums, who persuaded peasants to march into battle in the hope of heaven, knowing 'that there was one well able and inclined' to guard them from all hazards. An obscenely different view of the soldiery from the one taken up in *Pilgrims of the Sun* and in his *Lay Sermons*. Bring back the Stuarts! This coat-trailing, coat-turning poem says that witches are dead and not dead, and looks back in some tenderness at the 'days of marvel' when the King stood around in a ring with his priests and nobles, 'searching old beldame for the mark of hell'. When Hogg hears a spiteful hag

> Blight youth and beauty with a burning stain,
> I wish for these old times and Stuarts back again.

Chaste Mary Lee of Carterhaugh, in *Pilgrims of the Sun*, was to remind her maker of a striptease artist, of 'a beautiful country girl turned into an assembly in dishabille, "half naked, for a warld's wonder", whose beauties might be gazed at, but were sure to be derided'. She was not welcomed, in their stalls, by the bookselling fraternity. When he called on Constable to discuss the poem, the author of the star system in publishing, of large sums for the right, heavily advertised writers, went on scribbling at his desk without lifting an eye, and then, as his visitor recalled, burst into praise: 'By God, Hogg, you are a very extraordinary fellow! You are a man of very great genius, sir! I don't know if ever there was such another man born.' Hogg looked down and brushed his hat with his elbow. Constable raved on: 'I am told that, since the publication of the "Queen's Wake" last year, you have three new poems, all as long, and greatly superior to that, ready for publication. By God, sir, you will write Scott, and Byron, and every one of them, off the field.'

This was clearly a no. Constable did not think that 'the work would be best in my hands,' as publishers have been telling people ever since. What about Mr Miller, with Constable offering support and security for any deal that might be made? Mr Miller took receipt of the poem and showed it to his bluestockings, who thought it 'extravagant nonsense'. Blackwood discussed it with Murray in London, whose advisers concurred with Edinburgh's bluestockings. They nevertheless brought it out, and the *Eclectic Review*, a Dissenting journal, 'gave it the highest commendation I ever saw bestowed on a work of genius', remembered Hogg, and it sold ten thousand copies in America.[24]

The year that saw the battle of Waterloo also saw, on 4 December, the battle of Carterhaugh, near Selkirk, where Hogg and Scott appeared together in public, their quarrel resolved. Having fired up at a letter of Scott's containing criticism of one of his 'Dramatic Tales', and dashed off his 'terrible' letter in remonstrance, Hogg had fallen ill, and Scott had secretly offered to pay his medical expenses. 'I would fain have called,' Hogg said that Scott told Grieve, 'but knew not how I would be received.' Scott had called on Grieve instead, on his way home from the Court of Session, to enquire about 'poor Hogg'. Lockhart's 'worthy hatter' Grieve, and Willie Laidlaw, persuaded Hogg that he'd misread Scott's letter and he wrote to him in some emotion to apologise.[25]

By December 1815 the dudgeon was over. Hogg and Scott got together to stage their battle – the first sporting event of its kind in the Borders for a long time, apparently. Hogg had been living a sporting life since boyhood. Will o' Phaup's grandson had run races against himself with nothing on, and became a Flying Shepherd whose interest in flight was at once aesthetic and athletic. At the end of his life he recalled, like some shorn Samson:[26]

> Mysell for speed had not my marrow
> Through Teviot, Ettrick, Tweed, and Yarrow,
> Strang, straight, and swift like winged arrow,
>   At market, tryst, or fair,
> But now I'm turn'd a hirplin' carle,
> My back it's ta'en the cobbler's swirl,
> And deil a bodle I need birl
>   For cuttin' o' my hair.

The Carterhaugh event was a football match between the men of Yarrow and of Selkirk (the Sutors or Shoemakers), under the aegis of Duke Charles, of Buccleuch. The field of play was a meadow on the opposite bank of the Yarrow from Philiphaugh, where Montrose, whose buttons embellished the hunting coat of Johnny Ballantyne, sustained his Waterloo. Hogg served as the Earl of Home's aide-de-camp and as

Yarrow's assistant manager. Each team had over a hundred players, some of them no doubt fresh from the playing-field of the real Waterloo, and there were six thousand spectators. Bad light stopped play, and the result was a diplomatic draw. Scott informed Washington Irving that clan feeling still smouldered sufficiently to make such matches dangerous; but the *Kelso Mail* reported that these two teams 'maintained the most perfect good humour, and shewed how unnecessary it is to discourage manly and athletic exercises among the common people, under pretext of maintaining subordination and good order.' Chivalry was coming into vogue in Britain, and the event could be imagined as a salute to the heraldic and bloody past. Scott's son Walter, the future Fifth Hussar, 'suitably mounted and armed', said the press, rode on the field displaying the ancient grey banner of the Buccleuchs, their war cry 'Bellenden'. He 'became the old banner well', said Scott. He was dressed like the Robin Hood of pantomime, in 'forest green and buff', on his head a green bonnet with an eagle's feather, round his neck 'a large gold chain with a medal'. Earls and countesses were there, and famous Border names: Pringles, Mr Chisholm of Chisholm, Mr Elliot Lockhart, member for the county. Major Pott of Todrig was there, and Mr Boyd of Broadmeadows (where I once on a school holiday cuddled a lamb on the hillside of a Samuel Palmerscape, stirred to be in the classic dens of Yarrow). 'And many other gentlemen and ladies.'[27]

Hogg and Scott wrote poems to commemorate Carterhaugh.[28] Hogg's homage to the banner of the Buccleuchs, 'The Ettrick Garland', proposed that

> Valour and constancy alone
> Can purchase peace and happiness.

Then a softer note:

> May thy grey pennon never wave
> On sterner field than Carterhaugh!

Scott's poem is Caledonia-stern:

> There are worse things in life than a tumble on heather,
> And life is itself but a game at foot-ball.

The only known occasion on which the last word has served as a spondee.

All ranks enjoyed the tournament. The players were awarded refreshments, but the banquet and ball were reserved for nobles and notables. Niel Gow, youngest of the dynasty of musicians, who set to music Hogg's Jacobite song 'Cam' ye by Athol', played the fiddle all night long for the reels, and James Hogg played the Ettrick Shepherd. His *Familiar Anecdotes of Sir Walter Scott* describes the banquet, at which, according to Lockhart, who was not present and had yet to meet him, Hogg made another of his mistakes. Hogg wrote that at a certain table 'all were noble' – save for the disturber of the Amsterdam synagogue and Keeper of the King's regalia, Adam Ferguson, 'whose everlasting good humour insures him a passport into every company. But I having had some chat with the ladies before dinner and always rather a flattered pet with them imagined they could not possibly live without me and placed myself among them. But I had a friend at the cross table at the head of the room who saw better.' The friend was Scott, who intervened to put him at the second of the two tables, between himself and Scott of Harden, whom Hogg mistook for an English clergyman, thereby forfeiting the chance to talk feudal shop with his liege lord, 'my forefathers having been vassals under that house on the lands of Fauldshope for more than two centuries'.[29]

Lockhart's version of the placement issue cites Hogg's, which he attributes to his memoir, rather than to the *Familiar Anecdotes* – a work thought jealous of Scott, and sharply disliked, by Lockhart, in years to come. Lockhart claimed that Hogg had minded being placed next to the Laird of Harden, 'the first gentleman of the clan Scott'. Words are placed in Hogg's mouth: 'I am convinced he' – Scott – 'was sore afraid of my getting to be too great a favourite among the young ladies of Buccleuch.' A further agile use of quotation-marks comes about when Lockhart suggests that Hogg had moved to seat himself at a side-table for children and 'his friend probably whispered that it was reserved for the "*little* lords and ladies, and their playmates"'.[30]

Scott, thought Hogg, would worry what his friend might say or do next when loose among ladies and gentlemen. On this occasion, however, Lockhart overplays Hogg's vanity, jealousy and helplessness.

Hogg's version of what happened was meant to be funny, and to illustrate 'my ruling passion of egotism'. The rival versions put in perspective the importance for him of feudality. It mattered, and it did not. For the first forty-five years of his life he had never clapped eyes on the first gentleman of the clan Scott. After 'playing a great part' in this 'grand drama of football', wrote Scott to Byron, Hogg has 'returned to his cottage among the hills, and is there, again, I suppose, smoored up with snow and living beneath the wreaths like an Esquimaux'.[31]

Earlier in the year he found floridly romantic words for 'ancient Hebrew melodies', gathered in German synagogues. A few months after this he began work on an epic, as he hoped it would be, *Queen Hynde*, which is more of a mock-epic or burlesque, for all its foundational account of Scotland's Celtic origins.

CHAPTER NINE

Parodies

Hogg said on more than one occasion that to observe and imitate someone may be to control them. Part of him knew that this might be a devil's game which he himself was inclined to play. Other people might more obscurely feel that to observe and imitate someone may be to consume them and become them, as some cannibals are thought to have believed that they became the enemies they ate; and that for one writer to copy, parody, rewrite, ghost-write, even edit, another may be to take on, and so to take, that other writer's identity. Parody happens when one person seeks to behave as another, and it can hardly happen without intimations of assault, possession, ingestion and control. Meanwhile the influence that one writer has on another may result in imitation, and in a resemblance to parody, with the element of control vested primarily in the influential writer. The mutuality of imitation, in one or other of its many forms, is a tricky business.

Parody is a function of personality, and takes part in its enigmas. And it is also an aspect of community. It stood at the heart of Hogg's literary and other activities, and of those of his *Blackwood's* cronies. He studied to become like them, and he remained his own man. Knowingly and otherwise, he imitated the writings of others, and other writers imitated *him*. Here is a jamboree which conveys that parody and pastiche are at once convivial and critical, collaborative and original, and that they have much in common with modes of writing ostensibly different, in which imitation and influence are nevertheless perceptible. When Hogg wrote poems in Wilson's manner, and Wilson tried to write down Hogg's manner of speaking, while ascribing to him, at times, his own opinions, they were doing what all kinds of writers, taking and adding, taking and adding, have always done. Wilson, however, did more of it than most.

When the contributions to his *Miscellany* proved hard to get, Hogg fancied he could do better than the stuff he'd been sent, and could do so in a manner that might be mistaken for the work of the writers who had failed his feast. *The Poetic Mirror* was published anonymously, in 1816, but Hogg's hand was detected. His words about the project indicate that it carried a strain of aggression and revenge. His parodies could be considered a hoax. But it is doubtful whether they were more of a hoax than the Waverley novels. And they contain some of his most interesting poetry.

Hogg attributed the 'Epistle to R.S.' to Thomas Pringle, who explained that the piece was meant as a contribution to the *Miscellany*, and not as a parody of Robert Southey; nor was it, Hogg says, a parody of Scott. The parodies or burlesques of Southey elsewhere in the collection are apparently by Hogg. The secret of the collection which he said in his memoir he was not at liberty to divulge was discussed in 1832, by Maginn, in *Fraser's*, on the occasion when he claimed that Wilson wrote the parody of himself (there are, in fact, three Wilson parodies, the weakest bits of the book): 'as Croker very well guessed in his review of that work in the *Quarterly*'. So it was absurd of Hogg to speak of a secret, in Maginn's view. Alan Strout denies that the *Quarterly* review makes that guess, but there's a hint of it in Croker's suggestion that a particular passage could scarcely have been regarded by Wilson as 'a disparaging imitation of his style'. Two years later, again in *Fraser's*, Maginn went further, with his claim that everything worth a farthing in the book was Wilson's. Wilson himself had earlier asserted that 'two of the imitations of Wordsworth are admirable. But Hogg never wrote one syllable of them. They were written by Lord Byron.'[1] Well, it would not be strange if more in the way of collusion took place than the anonymous author gave out. Poets of the day, among others, were given to participating in round robins, centos, seamless collaborative efforts. They were a pastime.

If the collection keeps a secret of any moment, it relates to the contrast between Hogg's fairy ballad 'The Gude Grey Katte', an imitation of himself, and the blank verse which purports to be extracts from Wordsworth's *Recluse*. Hogg was more at home with the balladism Wordsworth may have deplored in him than with philosophical poetry or blank-verse meditation. And yet the Wordsworth pieces are outstandingly successful.

His memoir says that the 'Katte' was written as 'a caricature' of *The Pilgrims of the Sun* and of 'The Witch of Fife'. It's a caricature of neither; nor is it an imitation of the latter, but more of the same thing, a further flight. The Laird of Blain has a talking cat who is also a beautiful woman and a fairy queen, and whom he invites to dinner:[2]

> 'I haif a feste in hall to nychte,
> Sueite pussye, be you there.'

A bishop gropes the beauty for marks of hell – the sort of inspection that used to occur in the golden days commended in 'Superstition'. The cat seizes the bishop by the ears and jaunts him through the Milky Way, singing the while, a music of the spheres. A Border hind, stood at his door, spies the unhappy priest throbbing through the night sky and eclipsing the Moon: the hind runs inside to blow on a coal and be shocked to read by its glow that no eclipse has been listed in the *Belfast Almanake*. To the sound of some 'great bom-be', or bumblebee, he is dropped to Hell like a bomb down the 'ausom hole' of volcanic Mount Etna, where a 'greate filossifere', a mute Empedocles, is on the watch. Of the groping bishop only his gown remains, flapping above the crater. The ballad misleadingly concludes that where there's neither sin nor shame, no sorrow can there be, while registering a triumph for pagan superstition over the sin and shame of pre-Reformation Christendom.

The Wordsworth poems in the collection – for all that Wilson may have assisted with them, from the standpoint of a man obsessed with Wordsworth, whose medallioned features he bore about with him on a snuffbox – are an overmatch for Wilson's own poems. The Stranger, in the poem of that name, has the tanned and shaggy look of one of the cartoon descriptions of Hogg by his *Blackwood's* friends. He arrives at a tarn, where a mountain boy holds his horse, which snorts

> Like blustering cannon, or the noise that bursts
> From heaven in thunder through the summer rain.
> The boy was stunned – for on similitude
> In dissimilitude, man's sole delight,
> And all the sexual intercourse of things,
> Do most supremely hang.

This passage is one which Wordsworth helped to write. 'Similitude in dissimilitude' is an iambic pentameter line which comes, in fact, from the prose of his Preface to the *Lyrical Ballads*, where the pleasure of perceiving likenesses is seen as 'the great spring of the activity of our minds': sameness in difference is a principle on which poetry depends and in which 'the direction of the sexual appetite' originates. His argument, set to music in the parody, is mentioned, by someone other than Hogg, in the pre-'Noctes' piece 'Christopher in the Tent II', carried in the *Blackwood's* of September 1819. Wordsworth's power and interest – in particular, his discovery of portents in the everday – can often be inferred from these imitations, together with his primness, the faint praise conferred by his prudent negatives ('not inept'), and his bathos.

The Stranger vanishes, and it was noted afterwards that one of the locals had acquired a novel by the infidel Voltaire for his window-sill, and had

> Appeared at church with a much better hat
> Than he was wont. For it was made of down
> That by the broad Ontario's shore had grown
> On the sleek beaver ...

The speaker of the poem, 'Wordsworth', goes on to say that he has since visited the region, not unaccompanied by Hogg, and by Southey ('the laureate') and Wilson.

> Late did I journey there with bard obscure
> From Scotland's barren wastes – barren alike
> Of verdure, intellect, and moral sense –
> To view that lonely tarn.

The visitors talk:

> Not inept,
> Our conversation ran on books and men.

The Border bard obscure praises another Border bard obscure, Scott, and 'Wordsworth' has to intervene to set right the matter of Scott's deserts, and those of his companions at the tarn. The poem could be read both as a version of the Rydal Mount snub and as a revenge for that.

The companions discover, beneath the waters of the tarn, a human skeleton, which is pored over.

> The laureate, sighing, uttered some few words
> Of most sublime and solemn tendency.
> The shepherd spoke most incoherent stuff
> About the bones of sheep, that on the hills
> Perish unseen, holding their stations so.
> And he, the tented angler of the lakes,
> Alias the man of palms, said nothing meet;
> He was o'ercome with feeling: it is known
> To many, and not quite to me unknown,
> That the youth's heart is better than his head.

Who is to be quite certain that Hogg's host at Elleray, man of palms and fisherman of feeling, might not have inserted an oar here, or, indeed, there? Hogg's revenge against Wordsworth ends with the moving towards the poets through the pool of a portentous shape which turns out to be a tadpole.

'The Flying Tailor' is better still. Hugh Thwaites of Grasmere is a tailor who is also a gymnast and a romantic poet who can see a 'symbol of the soul' in a simple pair of breeches. He is 'a perfect whirligig' of feeling. His leaps are like those of Will o' Phaup, and like those of Will's grandson, which were both mental and physical. The narrator, 'Wordsworth' again, observes that tailors are highly sedentary. The circulation of Hugh's blood has been impeded by having to sit cross-legged on a board all day – with catapult consequences. A principle is elaborated:

> That all excessive action by the law
> Of nature tends unto repose. This granted,
> All action not excessive must partake
> The nature of excessive action – so
> That in all human beings who keep moving,
> Unconscious cultivation of repose
> Is going on in silence. Be it so.
> Apply to men of sedentary lives

This leading principle, and we behold
That, active in their inactivity,
And unreposing in their long repose,
They are, in fact, the sole depositaries
Of all the energies by others wasted,
And come at last to teem with impulses
Of muscular motion, not to be withstood,
And either giving vent unto themselves
In numerous feats of wild agility,
Or terminating in despair and death.

This is a good poem in its own right, I think, and a very funny hit at the manner of the philosophical poet (the line break 'so / That' enrols itself in the joke).

Hogg seems to be alluding to a passage in Wordsworth's verse play *The Borderers* – where 'Action is transitory,' and to be contrasted with suffering – which was used, in supplemented form, as a motto for a later edition of his 'The White Doe of Rylstone', a poem which first appeared when the parodies were being written and which Scott liked. Wordsworth disliked the suggestion that this tale of Elizabethan times, of recusant suffering and solace, was an excursion into Scott country. Scott, said Wordsworth, who plainly did not want to be associated with adventure stories, conducts an action which proceeds to a termination, whereas this poem of his tells the story of a 'female patience winning firm repose'. So 'the comparison is inconsiderate.'[3]

'Repose' was a favourite word of the eighteenth-century meditative poetry transformed by Wordsworth (whose pedlar in *The Excursion* sought repose from intellectual activity), and can often, in that context, appear to signify death. Hogg's parody takes up Wordsworth's concern with action and suffering, and, perhaps, with part of what is sometimes meant in modern times by the state or process of entropy. His 'unconscious cultivation of repose', with its hint of inertia and of thanatos, is worthy of Wordsworth and of a Freudian futurity. These principles of flight may be aeronautically unsound, but good poetry can stand a certain amount of nonsense. 'The White Doe of Rylstone' has some: 'Lie silent in your graves, ye dead!'

'The Flying Tailor' ends, as Shelley's 'Adonais' was soon to do, with a starry triumph over the anthropophagy of critics. Wordsworth's name will shine 'conspicuous like a star', amid a galaxy of choice spirits

> Who, laughed at constantly whene'er they published,
> Survived the impotent scorn of base Reviews.

Of these, the *Edinburgh Review* seems to be the worst. It is 'accursed'. It lives 'on tears, and sighs, and groans, and brains, and blood'.

'Wordsworth' alludes in the 'James Rigg' parody to

> men before the flood,
> And therefore in the Scriptures rightly called
> Antediluvians!

Parodic humour has to struggle here with the knowledge that James has lost his sight when a spark ignited gunpowder he'd been handling. Hogg more or less succeeds in avoiding offence, though his partiality for bodily harm put him at risk. James Rigg almost finds 'a charm in blindness', and James Hogg assigns him a smiling dignity grounded in patience and suffering. A comic riff might appear related to the notion of internality which Wordsworth, distancing himself from the active Walter Scott, wanted for 'The White Doe'. The soul does not depend on the sustenance of the external world, Hogg suggests on this occasion. Without eyes, she sees. 'Without the vestige of an ear', she listens.

> And in despite of nose abbreviate
> Smells like a wolf.

Peter of Barnet, in the poem of that name, adopts an 'unfathered' child and has to have Burns's merits explained to him: he then wishes to spare a daisy, looking around for a stone to throw at a ploughman indifferent to the merits of the flower. All this is at the expense of the recently laurelled Southey, who is also taken off in 'The Curse of the Laureate'. The curse has to do with Southey's preposterous tyrant poem about Kehama, Raja of the World, who goes to Hell. Hogg's laureate mentions the fiend critic Jeffrey: the 'bane of genius – party's sordid slave'. This is a Carmen Judiciale, a confused Vision of Judgment, which was followed by Southey's poem of that name and by Byron's riposte of the same name.

The *Mirror* versions of Scott and Byron are approximate and blood-boltered. Two lame poets are launched into berserker frenzies. Heads roll. 'Byron's' Spanish warrior Alayni's betrothed is raped by Gauls, and he takes his revenge by murdering her for her pains, and her pollution. He becomes what the hero of the Scott poem is, 'God's adversary' (like the old reiving Scott known as 'Flagellum Dei'). The Walter Scott hero is Wat o' the Cleuch, the giant Border baron reincarnated in Hogg's novel *The Three Perils of Man*.

The two Coleridge poems in the collection mimic the obscurity of which Byron complained ('I wish he would explain his explanation'), and were said by a reviewer of the day to have caught 'the soft unmeaningness of what Mr Coleridge terms a conclusion'. Here is what can appear to have been a word of the day: Hogg's 'large, grey unmeaning eye' was spied by Wilson, writing in *Blackwood's*.[4]

The Wilson imitations are antihydrophobically redolent of Wilson. 'The Morning Star' is, indeed, largely a transcription of his work. The Moon is both aerial and aqueous. The Morning Star patrols the sky with a 'sinless paramour', as Mary Lee does.

'A New Poetic Mirror' was published a decade later in the *Edinburgh Literary Journal*,[5] and several pieces in it, or linked with it, are likely to be Hogg's. The series also has James Park's Catullus imitation, reprinted from the *Spy*. Hogg's 'Andrew the Packman', 'after the manner of Wordsworth', is a long way after – a less disciplined affair than the earlier efforts, and a poor validation of Hogg's authorship of these.[6] Interesting, nevertheless. The poem makes him look, at times, like some sentimental Calvinist. Andrew appreciates 'the prime regard that's due to pence and farthings'. And he is a sceptic who is taxed on his deathbed with his future prospects. God's grace is lacking: no light can be expected from 'thy good works'. The Earl of Lonsdale's pyramidal hatrack stands for the good order of things threatened by the packman, and championed, runs the ironic suggestion, by Wordsworth, who has recourse to one of his guarded negatives:

> Not unapplausive
> Have I beheld it cover'd o'er with hats.
> Apt simile in dissimilitude

> Of that most noble fabric, which I have
> In majesty of matter and of voice
> Aroused me to defend.

Hogg's appetite for simile may be thought to have fastened over the years on the sexual intercourse of things and on the good order of things. This Earl of Lonsdale was a patron of Wordsworth's and a cousin of the nightmare vote-faking Earl who employed Boswell.

In 1817, four *Dramatic Tales* were published in two volumes by Longman in London and John Ballantyne in Edinburgh: *All-Hallow Eve*, *Sir Anthony Moore*, *The Profligate Princes* (the subject of Scott's resented strictures, and a modification of his first play, *The Hunting of Badlewe*, which had sunk in 1814 amid the flotsam of Goldie's crash), and *The Haunted Glen*. These plays have been treated as errors, and Hogg himself was not enthused by them, though he retained a feeling for *Sir Anthony Moore*, which was submitted to the stage and then withdrawn from possible travesty at the hands of 'bungling and absurd' actors.

There is travesty in the plays themselves, with their borrowed tales and titbits from Shakespeare. Scott, who thought that his friend Joanna Baillie was his country's highest genius, told correspondents that these plays were 'a great failure' and 'sadly vulgar'. They are also zestful and suspenseful and playable. *Sir Anthony Moore* lifts from *Romeo and Juliet* and *Othello*, and even manages to steal a designation of Othello's: 'The man who speaks of union with the Moore ...' This Moore weds Caroline, of an enemy house, and is Iago'd for it by two friends. He asks:

> Faucet, think'st thou that hell had ever been
> Unless for women?

Potions miscarry. Restored by Moore's burning kiss, Caroline sits up in her coffin.

The Profligate Princes features a good king and bad nobles. Knights take to the woods in disguise and 'in frolic', on the hunt for deer and girls. There's talk of 'the slim virtue of his facile dame'. The noble Badenoch is really Robert III's brother and Robert is among the guisers, but he behaves well and marries a local lady, Annabel, for all the world an English gentlewoman doing her best in the Scottish greenwood. The play has its diverting touches. One lady says, as did Hogg elsewhere, and as many Scots have said since: 'Dreams are often contrary.' In Hogg's proleptic fashion, the Earl of Crawford owns to a 'slow-motion'd soul'. Hogg was drawn to the similitude of replication and anticipation: in 'Andrew the Packman', human life on earth is 'proleptical' of everlasting life.

He reckoned that *The Haunted Glen* was anticipated by the ballad of Tam Lin, but it also derives from a play that spoke to his condition, *A Midsummer Night's Dream*, with its fairy folk and poor folk and its courtiers. A prince, Lu, one of the Ayrshire Lus, it seems, is snatched by the fairies and made their monarch. Field sports are manfully condemned by this sportsman, and equated with the seduction of virgins, one of whom is required for Lu's coronation. Lula, a princess in concealment, is pursued by an evil knight and by simple Simon, a rustic, whose family affairs introduce a welcome sub-plot (omitted in Thomson's *Collected Works*) of Scots badinage and protest. Simon is like to die for love. He says what Hogg liked to say: 'It's a' owre wi' me now!' He wants to 'worry' Lula – in English, make love to her – while his father worries that she may be a gypsy, for all her 'thrimble-thrumbling at the harp'. An author's note explains that 'the great length of this Pastoral rendered its full insertion here inconvenient.' But since these tales were written 'merely as exercises in dramatic composition', the author 'deemed that a part of any of them, and of this last in particular', was 'as amusing as the whole'. Now read on.

There is bungling in *All-Hallow Eve*, which has been critically shunned. And yet it has real if intermittent power, and is predictive of what he went on to write. A Hogg-to-be is present in the play, together with Allan Ramsay, and Shakespeare. There is even a Father Lawrence, and there are cordials of the sort Shakespeare's was cunning in. Gelon Graeme has a swain in the shepherd Gemel, and another in the laird Hindlee. Two weird sisters, Nora and Grimald, bode and curse. Once again, there flickers a language of the future: 'How art thou outed, witch!', 'prying, low-lifed thing'. Hindlee goes about on the brink of paranoid dementia:

O I had such a dream –
I would meet hell in countertime before
I braved again a vision of such woe.

The weird sister Grimald worships a god, 'the bomb of the sky', Moules
or Gil-Moules: the demon of Hogg's *Confessions*, six years later, is Gil-
Martin. 'Mouly, Gil-Mouly, sly mouse of the mill,' she conjures. She is
duped by her partner Nora, a mere robber, into thinking herself
prophetic, though Nora admits: 'Some strange events by her have been
forespoke.' Hindlee is at the centre of the play, and is the character most
resembling of its writer:

I possess a heart
To kindness prone, but it has vehemencies
For which I'm not accountable.

Hindlee can't help himself, but he believes himself to be God's
commissioner:

O what a glory to be sent abroad,
A mighty minister to do, do, do!
And never to do wrong.

Gemel, remembered in childhood by his mother as her 'little chubby
snowball, sound asleep', is dispatched by this justified sinner, who dies
in the delusion of his predestined role. In his hands 'was squeez'd the
snowball leaven'd with his blood' – the echo is far from inept.

The verse of these dramas seems indebted to Wordsworth's
Borderers, and this play can also, at moments, look like a precursor of
the *Confessions*. Both works are about prophecy, about what is decreed
and what is dark, about confusion, about piety and its perversion, the
crimes of the unco gude, the very holy. There is a moving speech which
bears on this proleptic resemblance:

O that this night were past, and a new day
Would ope its eye on this deranged world,
Where human beings, and beings without mould
Or earthly quality, together blent,
Move in confusion!

126

This is a derangement which fascinated Hogg. Human beings, and spirits, together blent, moving in confusion – this is what happens in the *Confessions*, and in other works of his.

His dramatic tales have the interest of their anticipations. The uncertainties pictured there look forward to the *Confessions*, which looks forward in turn to a modern world whose arts and sciences take an interest in uncertainty, and from which uncertainty has yet to be eliminated. They also look back at the ancient world – by means of the quasi-feudal one of *A Midsummer Night's Dream*, which he went to see when he was young, and in which he might have seen his own face. He was entering a wood in which someone may turn into someone else, or be mistaken for someone else. He was acquainted with nobles and rude mechanicals, and with spirits, and with translations from one sphere to another.

His bewilderments are apt to involve likeness, similitude, doubtful or disguised identity, change of rank. The year after the *Confessions* was published, in 1825, there appeared in *Blackwood's* 'Some Passages in the Life of Colonel Cloud', a domestic tale of contemporary Scotland which turns on imposture and social mobility. The narrator meets a man he thinks he knows but can't really remember, but who remembers *him*. His 'illustrious friend' is revealed to be a 'common weaver', like Bottom, instead of Assistant Deputy Adjutant-General to the Emperor of Austria, and skilled sportsman. Call me McDevil, says Colonel Cloud, at one point. The story seems to allude to the demonic Gil-Martin, and has a resonance which makes it more than the account of a confidence trick. The narrator suffers a hallucination, a derangement. It's almost as if he is the person who is deceiving him.

CHAPTER TEN

Two Fine Friends

In the *Blackwood's* menagerie Lockhart played the scorpion, and Hogg the pig and the Ettrick boar.[1] Wilson was a beautiful leopard at times, and an eagle. But he was mostly a lion. And he must certainly have been a Leo. There's a painting for which Central Casting might have dressed him up as Leo the Byronic Brigand: he is all mane, fierce face, bewhiskered jaw and banging gun. Wilson was an inordinately colourful man who was not of entirely sound mind.

He was a poet and a writer of fiction. He was a 'splendid declaimer', as his daughter Mary Gordon puts it in her biography of him. From 1825 to 35 he was chiefly responsible for the 'Noctes Ambrosianae', that most brilliant of journalistic inventions in the periodical field. He was a star whose evil genius, according to De Quincey, was the sentimental.[2] According to a student in Glasgow, 'that man is a fool,' and 'if he was na sic a big fool, he would be laughed at.'[3] He was an admired panjandrum who might be called one of the wisest fools in Regency Edinburgh; a statue of him stands up straight at the dead centre of pivotal Princes Street. There is no statue of Hogg in Edinburgh.

This was an age of personality, and of physiognomy, and of Phrenology: the city had its Craniological adepts, led by George Combe, and its sceptics, such as Hogg and the Shepherd of the 'Noctes', who were agreed that Selkirk fair had more to offer in the line of interesting cranial bumps than Phrenology did. For the Shepherd, moreover, it was indelicate of adepts to feel young ladies' heads. Wilson was, as Hogg and Lockhart were, of physiognomic interest: they were marked men, whether or not their marks were any of them of the Devil. Mrs Gordon wrote that her father was 'long-maned and mighty', and light and agile too – 'lish'.[4] He was a jumper, with a short trunk, long legs and arched instep. William Ritson, a North Country wrestler, testified that he was 'a verra bad un to lick': 'as strang as a lion, an' as lish as a trout, an' he hed sic antics as nivver man hed.' Wilson sported flashing blue eyes, floating hair, yellow locks. De Quincey judged 'his eyes not good, having no apparent depth, but seeming mere surfaces'. Unmeaning eyes. These could be the eyes of the warrior seen in him by Lockhart, for whom he was like one of Attila's Huns, *bello gaudentes*.[5] He was a Teutonic knight who liked to cut people up in print, but who didn't like being cut up himself. In this, he was like Lockhart. Lockhart, wrote Wilson's daughter, 'was certainly no coward, but he liked to fight under cover, and keep himself unseen.'[6] When Wilson 'impaled a victim' he did so, 'not vindictively, but as if he loved him', in the manner of Walton's complete angler – which was also the manner, one might think, of the complete parodist.

The most penetrating descriptions of Wilson were given at various times by Thomas Carlyle, who called him 'an exuberant enough, leafy and tropical kind of tree rather exhaling himself in balmy odours than producing fruit'. He encircles himself, said Carlyle, 'with wild cloudy sportfulness, which to me often seems reckless and at bottom full of sharp sorrow'. A later writer, Donald Carswell, called him a bully and a coward, and, a little cryptically, 'in the worst sense of the term a man's man', while De Quincey rated him an Alcibiades who aspired to the Hellenic ideal – no taint here of Keatsian sensuality. A still later writer, the Ambrosian Moray McLaren, called him a 'cruel anonymist and *faux bonhomme*'.[7]

He was born in Paisley in 1785, the son of a gauze manufacturer, his mother a descendant of Montrose. He was what Lockhart was for Scott – 'perfectly a gentleman' – and he patrolled the drawing-room at Elleray debating with Coleridge's son Hartley whether or not Hamlet, too, was a perfect gentleman.[8] Wilson was a gentleman whose faults were not felt to threaten his excellent condition – a justified sinner of a kind. He was an Episcopalian, and a gregarious Tory who had slept in the cottages of hundreds of the poor and who felt that they did not want, and shouldn't be asked, to bother with politics.

He studied at the Universities of Glasgow and Oxford, and passed advocate at Edinburgh. Having lost much of his patrimony because of the actions of a dishonest uncle, he became a writer. An early love affair with an orphan maid in the countryside near Glasgow was frowned on

Calotype of John Wilson by Octavius Hill and Robert Adamson

by a strong mother, and he soon after took a bride who had, he certified, 'remained pure, as from her Maker's hands'.[9] He was, it would appear, an ardent and conscientious husband and father, very successful with children and pets.

His sentimental education may be glimpsed in 'The Lily of Liddesdale', one of a collection of stories entitled *Lights and Shadows of Scottish Life*. The shepherdess Amy is loved by noble George Elliot, whose liberal sister tells her: 'May God and my mother forgive me this, but my sister must thou be.' But Amy refuses him for a virtuous rustic, Walter Harden, to whom she had pledged herself. Another of these tales has three lovely daughters who succumb to consumption. With one of them, 'the disease assumed its most beautiful show.'[10] Hogg thought the tales suspect as a guide to rural Scotland.

Lockhart spoke of his intimate Wilson's 'total inconsistency' in matters of opinion, and of the 'sore places' in his nature.[11] This seems fundamental, and an aspect of Wilson's ambivalence in respect of Hogg – of his choosing to hurt so much someone he cared for. His daughter's biography, which conveys that Lockhart was haughty, habitually sarcastic, and distrusted by his friends, is severe with Hogg too: he had qualities which 'made it impossible to respect him', and his vanity became 'unendurable'.[12] In her biography of 1934, Elsie Swann dwells on Wilson's volatility and intermittent hostility towards Wordsworth: his alias Christopher North 'could abuse Wordsworth anonymously in an article, and, in a later number of the magazine, attack with scorn the author of his own article, and write a stern letter against himself for libelling so great a poet – then, in the following number, round off this Protean transaction with another vigorous onslaught on the Lake poet'.[13] One onslaught followed immediately after a festive visit by Wordsworth to the Admiral of the Lakes at Elleray.

In 1820, Wilson was elected Professor of Moral Philosophy at the University of Edinburgh. This was a political appointment; the Town Council were patrons of the Chair. And Scott backed him for the Tory he was and as if he were a Parliamentary candidate: Wilson had 'the fire of genius' and was less eccentric than Henry Brougham. He must suspend his 'wrath' for the duration of the canvass, 'must leave off sack, purge and live cleanly as a gentleman ought to do'. Scott assured the

Lord Provost, in contempt of the probabilities, that Wilson was 'altogether incapable' of 'composing parodies upon Scripture'. He assured Lockhart that all Wilson needed to make him the first man of the age was steadiness and consistency.[14]

The declaimer proceeded to go down well with the students, though the Irish among them heckled him for speaking disrespectfully of their nationalist leader Daniel O'Connell. He responded by speaking disrespectfully of 'modern Radicalism and its cant phrase, "March of Intellect"'. The phrase gained currency in the course of the later 1820s. Hogg was to write a jaunty poem entitled 'The March of Intellect', in which 'subscription' – joint-stock investment – is seen as fashionably advanced and as part of a phantasmagoric future, in which a bridge is built over the Forth to Kirkcaldy, phrenologists cast about for old perukes 'to cover their assinine bumps', and we 'dad out the wee stars wi' our shoon'. The 'Noctes' De Quincey held that the march of intellect must be accompanied by a flow of feeling.

There were occasions when Professor Wilson appeared to be addressing an audience of 'hard-browed, scowling Scotsmen, muttering over their knobsticks', who can't have judged him a metaphysician of equal worth to his friend and Whig rival for the Chair, Sir William Hamilton. The roll of papers on which his lectures were written was 'composed in large measure of portions of old letters', sent by Wilson's 'Wizard', an Englishman, Alexander Blair, whom he had consulted in distress, faced with the discussion of Plato, Socrates and whatever next: 'Could you write to me *at some length* on Beauty and Sublimity and power of Piety on all that is good in our minds? ... Who were the Sophists?' Wilson and Blair used to share a seat as they talked and studied, with Wilson 'playfully pulling the somewhat silvered locks' of his companion 'to draw his attention to something in the tome spread out on their knees'. Wilson read from his papers with fluency; only on 'dark and murky days' did declamation falter.

Carlyle sat at his feet, and published an exquisite reminiscence at the age of seventy-two of Wilson at the lectern:

> He stood erect like a tower; cloudy energy, determination, and even sincerity (or the visible wish to be sincere), looking out from every

Mr. Wilson, *alias* "The Leopard."

Drawing by J. G. Lockhart

feature of him; giving you, among his chaos of papers there, assurance of a man. One of the times, and one only, he had got some rather strictly scientific or metaphysical point to handle, or to tide over in some plausible way. His internal embarrassment, and yet determined outer onrush in this troublesome matter, I still remember well; and how with wild strokes he plunged about, like a whale among tubs, hither, thither, churning the ocean into foam, for a length of time, and at last in some good way got floated over into more genial waters. All the other times I found him dealing with human life in the concrete; and this in a style, and with a stormful opulence of faculty, great and peculiar. Glowing pictures dashed off in rapid powerful strokes, often of a fine poetic and emphatic quality, this, I could see, was his favourite mode of illustrating and teaching.

Carlyle's stomach for abstruse philosophy was no doubt stronger than Wilson's, but a paper of Sir William Hamilton's proved more than indigestible. He told Wilson: 'like Hogg's Fife warlock, "my head whirled roun', and ane thing I couldna mind."'

That head was also taxed by 'my Night with Wilson', described in another of Carlyle's memorials of this superman with the malice of a spoiled child and the health of an athlete. On this occasion, Wilson downed fourteen tumblers of whisky-punch, 'steadily, not in haste, but without rest, and as a business'. A lava of talk from him – Carlyle abstemious throughout – 'principally of Distinguished Persons whom Wilson knew; Wilson nothing loth of that unsafe theme'. In the small hours his talk grew a little sinister. It was 'as if here were a lion, wild monarch of the woods, licking all manner of pretended favourites, but with every stroke of the tongue bringing away *blood*'. From his Night with Wilson Carlyle got back to Comely Bank on the outskirts of Edinburgh to find his 'pure white Spirit, lovely and loving', sitting up for him, over a book.[15]

When Wilson's wife died, he wept in the lecture-room. 'Two big tears were seen rolling down his cheeks as he tried to proceed.' When he was an old man, a student came on him insensible in his gown, went to his aid and found himself pinned down by 'the Professor's massive head'. Another plucked a memorial hair from that head. Other hairs were plucked for its cage by the sparrow with which he shared his study for eleven years, which would nestle in the folds of his waistcoat, and was alleged to be turning into an eagle.[16]

Himself a lion, a leopard and an eagle, Wilson was all for animals and birds. He intervened to stop a carter beating his horse, and went off with the horse, and the whip. He was passionate for dogs – chiefly Bronte, his bounding purple-black Newfoundland beauty, poisoned, some said, by medical students in revenge for his deploring of the Burke and Hare dissection murders. And there was a cat who was subjected to a pioneer baptism: Thomas Pringle told the English journalist Cyrus Redding of a faintly Hellfire Club occasion when, as Redding put it, 'Wilson, Lockhart and a number of wild men were met' and Wilson 'proposed to christen a cat instanter, and went through the entire ceremony, as I presume in the Scotch mode'.[17]

The last years of his life took him into a depression, after an almost impossibly full life. Lockhart too came to a melancholic end. Both suffered bereavements; Wilson wore 'weepers' on his sleeve after his wife's death in 1837 till his own in 1854. He became reclusive. Cockburn, who had long since forgiven him his political trespasses, told the story, retailed by an informant of Mrs Gordon's,[18] of a time when friends invited him to a party where he failed to turn up, and they went round to beard him: 'They forced their way to his den, and, he being seated in the middle of the room, walked round and round him in solemn, silent, and weird-like procession, he equally silent and regardless of their presence, only showing, by a slight curl of the corner of his mouth, that he was internally enjoying the humor of the thing.' The wizard bewitched. The monster had become sacred.

John Gibson Lockhart was twenty-four years younger than Hogg, and nine years younger than Wilson. Hogg had made friends with two sophisticates who can sometimes seem older than their middle-aged man from the country. Lockhart was a minister's son from Lanarkshire. When they first met, Hogg saw in him 'a mischievous Oxford puppy', a tease, a quiz, a dancer after girls. He was handsome, stylish, a Regency dandy, the author of cool, capable, censorious letters. His watercolour likenesses and caricatures were an aspect of his vigilance and apartness. A degree of deafness seems to have held him back at the Bar. At one of

Hogg's jolly athletic tournaments in the Borders he was reported 'dark and silent as the night'.[19]

Hogg was frightened of him – certainly at first. He felt jumbled, jangled, by him. 'I dreaded his eye terribly,' he writes in his memoir, and the 'Noctes' of November 1826 has the Shepherd agreeing with him about this: 'an ee like an eagle's, and a sort o' lauch about the screwed-up mouth o' him, that fules ca'd no canny'. This is to make his illustrious friend look as a princely tempter might look, like the devil Gil-Martin in Hogg's *Confessions*. Hogg's life contained, in fact, or in fancy, two Gil-Martins. Wilson causes the Shepherd, in the 'Noctes', to accuse him of 'Mephistophiles tricks', and in 1825 Hogg informed Blackwood of the 'strange indefinable sensation' inspired in him by Wilson, which he then defined as 'made up of a mixture of terror, admiration and jealousy – just such a sentiment as one devil might be supposed to have for another'.[20]

Early in his association with *Blackwood's*, on 15 July 1818, Hogg wrote to the publisher from Altrive to complain of the treatment he'd been receiving from his three Edinburgh friends: 'I have been quizzed too much by you chaps already; I will not so easily take again. I am writing for another Magazine, with all my birr, and intend having most excellent sport with it, as the editors will not understand what one sentence of my celebrated allegories mean till they bring the whole terror of Edinburgh aristocracy on them.' There was an Edinburgh aristocracy of which Wilson and Lockhart were turning themselves into stalwart journalistic defenders; Hogg's aristocracy on this occasion would seem to include the Whig élite and academic élitism. Six days later he wrote again to Blackwood to speak of the pleasure the last number of the journal had given him, and to retract his complaint:

> I never accused you of quizzing me and I hope I never shall have occasion. As for the two devils the thing is implanted in their very natures and I must bear it though I believe they have banished me their too much loved society. It may make me angry for an hour or two at a time but shall never make me admire or love them the less. The thing that I hinted at was that I might publish John Paterson's Mare and some strange rubs on another party which would not in the least be understood until they came to Edin.

Hogg's language makes contact with that of Shakespeare's *Henry IV*, where the new king says, 'I banish thee', in snubbing, and in a sense betraying, a man who was not only witty in himself but the cause of wit in others. There's a likeness here which lends a sadness to a letter of his to Murray the following month, in which he seeks to review 'any light work' for Murray's *Quarterly* in London, then edited by sour William Gifford: 'I do not know how any man can have a prejudice against me.' Gifford may 'consider me an intruder in the walks of literature, but I am only a saunterer, and malign nobody who chooses to let me pass.'[21]

These important letters touch on a journalistic culture of insult, sport, clandestinity, indirection and exclusion. William Maginn held that you should never deny what you had *not* written and never acknowledge what you *had* written; and, in the early days of their friendship, Lockhart, cigar in mouth, one leg 'flung carelessly over the other', would bamboozle Hogg with fictitious attributions for unsigned pieces.[22] At a meeting of the Dilettanti Society Lockhart told him a story about authorship. 'I forget what it was; but I think it was about somebody reviewing his own book.' As well it might have been, given the magazine's subterfuge and puffing propensities (the work of friends, and their own work, were excerpted from books, saluted – and insulted). It was on this occasion that Hogg diverted Lockhart by declaring that he had never told Hogg the truth.

'I found him constantly in company with all the better rank of people with whom I associated, and consequently it was impossible for me not to meet with him,' wrote Hogg. Nor was it possible for him to be unaffected by Lockhart's shrewdness and panache, those of a gifted man of letters and of manners. He discovered six black servants waiting on six white gentlemen at Lockhart's table. 'Such a train of Blackamoors,' he remarked, was 'beyond my comprehension'. But there did seem to be an explanation for the exotic symmetry of it all: 'he found them very useful and obliging poor fellows,' and 'they did not look for much wages, beyond a mouthful of meat.' A young woman told Hogg later that Lockhart had only one black servant, who invited along his friends when his master entertained, to share in the pickings. Hogg, too, appears to have had a black servant, an ephemeral one, who goes unmentioned in his memoir, and who must have been difficult to squeeze in at Altrive.

He was not invariably attentive to servants. 'I never heed the maid servants much,' ran an unpropitious testimonial of his for Margaret Milne, 'but I never saw or heard ought to her but honesty and application while in our service.'[23]

When Scott was made a baronet in 1819, Hogg affected not to like, or really didn't like, 'such grinning honour as that of Sir Walter – Shakespeare, hem!' The words are indeed those of Hogg's *semblable*, the castaway Falstaff: 'I like not such grinning honour as Sir Walter hath' – a slain Sir Walter. Scott felt that he'd been an aristocrat all along: the Duke of Buccleuch and Scott of Harden were 'the heads of my clan and the source of my gentry'. Lockhart was more dispassionate politically than Scott, but he shared his keen consciousness of social distinction and his anxious distance from the best blood. The sarcasm and asperity with which he and Wilson behaved at times towards Hogg, over the eventful years of their comradeship, have fostered the view that their praise of him was a tongue-in-cheek pretence and a condescension. But there can be no doubt that both men felt, as Scott did, an affection for him. He kept offending his cavaliers, and they kept attacking him, in a magazine which, as John Galt also discovered at this time, specialised in biting its contributors. This caused Hogg pain, but it is possible that there was less of an intent to harm than meets the eye two hundred years later. '*O sus quando te aspiciam?*' asked Wilson, or perhaps Lockhart, in 1818.[24] When shall I see you, you swine? This is the voice of friendship.

Lockhart met Scott in 1818 and married his daughter Sophia two years later. In 1825, he went off to London to edit the *Quarterly*, having recently produced two novels: *Matthew Wald*, which shared the concern in Hogg's *Confessions* with religious fanaticism, and *Adam Blair*, in which a 'primitive' but 'kind' rural community is described, and a minister who commits adultery, after his wife's death, in a romantic Highland setting, is sentenced to a penitential spell among the lower orders in his Lowland parish, his dress 'the same with that of the people into whose rank he had descended'.[25]

Scott pushed for Lockhart's succession to the *Quarterly* chair, and seems to have been responsible for embarrassments over the canvass. Before that, around 1820, he urged him to cultivate the virtue – unavailingly aspired to by Boswell – of being *retenu*. He should be

John Gibson Lockhart and (a posthumous likeness) his wife Sophia,
by Robert Scott Lauder (after 1838)

reserved, contained: this to someone capable of seeming silent as the
night. Lockhart should not undertake the Scriptural parody of behaving
as 'the Boaz of the Maga', *Blackwood's*, a pillar of that dubious temple.
He was later to reflect on Lockhart's past satirical enormities and to fear

that he'd been lured back among 'the Ambrosians'. As a London editor, Lockhart wrote to his star journalist, Croker, calling for blood: 'I hope you will murder another Tennyson.'[26] Lockhart's respectability was never to be wholly respectable.

Having published, in 1828, his life of Burns, dedicated to Hogg and to Allan Cunningham, he settled down in the mid-1830s to his pious and copious monumental life of his father-in-law, in which Hogg stands rebuked. His early book about the state of Scotland, *Peter's Letters*, which appeared in 1819, and in which he disguises himself as a Welsh traveller of anti-liberal bent, has a youthful freedom from embarrassment, and the portrait of an ear-to-ear Hogg, all stringy hair and brown face. This Hogg has the air of a prosperous farmer whose eye is meaningful and whose forehead towers with 'a true poetic grandeur'.[27]

The perfect gentleman explained in his *Life of Scott* that Constable hated Blackwood with 'a perfect hatred' at the time of Blackwood's re-animation and re-titling of the magazine he had begun six months before, in April 1817.[28] Constable's responsibility as Scott's publisher had been trenched on for a while by Blackwood, whose emergent ambitions were seen as a threat to the Constable empire, which encompassed the quarterly *Edinburgh Review* and its downmarket companion, the *Scots Magazine*. Hogg had a hand in the launch of Blackwood's monthly, and was to sail in her, with spells ashore, during the years that lay ahead.

Ever since the *Spy*, he had wished for involvement with a bold and original magazine, and in 1814, under Gillies's roof, in conversation with John Pinkerton, a historian and antiquary, and a collector, and in his youth forger, of ballads, had enquired:

'D'ye ken, Maister Pinkerton, it's a grand principle o' mine, that the less a poet reads, it's a' the better for him?'

'*Ex nihilo nihil fit*,' retorted Pinkerton; 'that is to say –'

'Ow, I ken the Latin weel eneuch,' interposed the Shepherd; 'I had it yince in *The Spy*.'

'Well, but you are for reversing the old proposition. You maintain that the less a man puts into his head, the more will come out of it.'

'I ken weel,' replied Hogg, 'that if a man never reads a book, and never heeds what other folk says, it's no possible for him to be an imitator. That's my plan, Mr Pinkerton; and it follows that my poetry, if it be no that gude, yet it's pure original.'[29]

It is given to Mr Pinkerton to speak an authoritative English, but Hogg's demotic is allowed to make its point. Hogg was an imitator who disapproved of imitation, and now wanted a really new journal. His idea of originality was not that of the rising William Blackwood, who took possession two years later of his new premises, a stone's throw from stone-throwing Ambrose's Tavern. And yet he was among the originators of practices and liberties which were to make the magazine's name.

He had pulled strings which helped to obtain for two Borderers, Thomas Pringle and an agriculturalist, James Cleghorn, both of them crippled, the editorship of the magazine Blackwood was starting. It fell flat, and Blackwood fired his editors, who then joined Constable's *Scots Magazine*, leaving Hogg with the choice of writing, with all his birr, for one or the other. In October 1817 *Blackwood's Edinburgh Magazine* began, with Hogg on board. It can be said that the owner was the editor, and that his stars Lockhart and Wilson were the editors too. In their inaugural issue, 'The Chaldee Manuscript', with Hogg as its originator, was published to electric effect.

This was a lightsome and daring imitation of the language of the Old Testament, and of the Book of Daniel in particular. Hogg worried about the commotion it would cause, imploring William Laidlaw: 'For the love of God, open not your mouth about the Chaldee MS ... Deny all knowledge else they say I am ruined.'[30] Blackwood laughed at it and opposed it at first, and was led to publish by the mirth it was eliciting. 'The Chaldee Manuscript' deals with the struggle for mastery between the two Edinburgh bibliopoles. It was Hogg's idea and inception. But Lockhart and Wilson (with a little help from Sir William Hamilton) sat up over their punch adding to it – inserting what Hogg called 'devilry of their own'. He wrote to Blackwood: 'I have laughed at least as heartily at the continuation of Daniel as you did at the original.' A quarter of the published text, including the bulk of the early passages, is likely to be his, though he claimed more and was sneered at for contributing less. What was mine, as he recalled, 'consists of the first two chapters, part of the third, and part of the last. The rest was said to have been made up conjointly in full divan' – written in council, like much else in the journal. Determined efforts were subsequently made to dispossess him of what was his. 'We shall next have him claiming' the murder of Begbie, ran the talk at Ambrose's, 'but he is totally incapable of either.' The text may seem to show him plumping for Blackwood's rather than Constable's magazine, but he was still being eaten raw by the Witch Maga a few months later for alleged desertion, while also being summoned to her embrace: 'Bring the coy Shepherd unto me.' A fragment of Hogg's draft suggests a truckling to Constable, but Constable is the more sharply handled of the two publishers in the printed version.[31]

Whig and Tory barely enter into the bibliopolarity depicted. 'The Chaldee Manuscript' is about personalities rather than politics – featuring 'the man which is crafty', with his two beasts, Pringle and Cleghorn, and 'the man whose name was as ebony', with his beasts Lockhart and Wilson – and the journal which it ignited became, in another sense of the word, a haven for personalities.[32]

Blackwood shows up early in Chapter One, as a 'man clothed in plain apparel', standing at the door of his house (17 Princes Street). He is accosted by suppliants (Pringle and Cleghorn, who are seen skipping about on staves): 'And they said unto him, Give us of thy wealth, that we may eat and live, and thou shalt enjoy the fruits of our labors for a time, times, or half a time.' Journalism's immemorial brittle tenures. Half a time, as it proved. Constable, the unicorn whose horn is the *Edinburgh Review*, must bestir himself with the advent of this enemy journal: 'Lo! this Book shall become a devouring sword in the hand of mine adversary, and with it will he root up or loosen the horn that is in my forehead, and the hope of my gains shall perish from the face of the earth.'

In Chapter Two, Ebony sits down in his inner chamber, which 'looketh toward the street of Oman' – proprietor of an Edinburgh hotel – 'and the road of Gabriel, as thou goest up into the land of Ambrose' ('land', happily, is an Edinburgh word for tenement). He is approached by a veiled editor (Christopher North had yet to be invented). The unknown assures Ebony that no one will touch a hair of his head: 'Do thou as it seemeth good unto thee; as thou sayest even so will I do.' Ebony recruits writers, 'and whomsoever he asked, he came.' In the guise of a bestiary. Wilson steps up as 'the beautiful leopard, from the valley of the palm-trees, whose going forth was comely as the greyhound, and his eyes like the lightning of fiery flame.' Lockhart is 'the scorpion, which delighteth to sting the faces of men': he is expected to 'sting sorely the countenance of the man which is crafty, and of the two beasts'. A third Ebony beast is 'the great wild boar from the forest of Lebanon': 'I saw him whetting his dreadful tusks for the battle.'

Chapter Three describes the Crafty's visit to 'the great magician which hath his dwelling in the old fastness, hard by the river Jordan, which is by the Border', in exactly the same words as Ebony's visit there is described. Neither embassy bears fruit. Scott's hands are 'full of working'; his plate is full, and so are those of others, for 'each man openeth his mouth, and my hand filleth it with pleasant things.' Constable shakes the dust of the fastness from his feet: 'the man which is crafty saw that the magician loved him not ... and said, Behold, I have given this magician much money, yet see now, he hath utterly deserted me.'

This chapter includes an outlandish assault (on John Graham Dalyell) which stung Blackwood to the tune of £230 in an out-of-court settlement. The victim is portrayed as a menial lawyer whose face was 'like unto the face of an ape, and he chattered continually, and his nether parts were uncomely. Nevertheless, his thighs were hairy, and the hair was as the shining of a satin raiment, and he skipped with the branch of a tree in his hand, and he chewed a snail between his teeth.' In the next chapter another Whig is spoken of as a nibbler of the shoe-latchets of the mighty.

Chapter Four has Macvey Napier, Jeffrey's future successor as editor of the *Edinburgh Review*, 'hired to expound things which he knoweth not'. John Ballantyne is 'a man of low stature, and giveth out merry things, and is a lover of fables from his youth'. Hogg's friend James Gray is 'clad in gray garment whereof one-half his wife had weaved'. Mrs Gray was a bluestocking, and Edinburgh's 'notable blues', in Hogg's expression, are slapped here: 'There followed him many women which know not their right hand from the left, and also some cattle.' The last verse of all has the narrator hiding himself and hearing a 'great tumult, but I wist not what it was.'

It was soon to be known what it was. The reception of 'The Chaldee Manuscript' scared Blackwood into removing the text from a second edition of the number, and printing an apology. 'All is combustion,' wrote Hogg to the great magician in his fastness. The godly were offended. Whig dignitaries were offended. The fair or blue part of the reading public can't have been pleased. Laidlaw, who had been set up by Scott to produce a 'Chronicle' for the paper, was told by him: 'Blackwood is rather in a pickle just now – sent to Coventry by the trade.' But Ebony was able to cheer himself, in his pickle, with the discovery that the circulation had soared to ten thousand. They were well on the way to pulling abreast of Jeffrey's journal.[33]

The magician was observed laughing by the border at quotations from the piece, but he had his misgivings. Scott wrote to Blackwood in November to say that Edinburgh was too small a place for satire and its personalities, and that there were those who had reason to resent the rough treatment that was being meted out. To his friend, Charles Kirkpatrick Sharpe, for instance, whose voice is as the screeching of an unclean bird, to John Playfair, a founder of the science of geology, and to Scotland's great lexicographer, Jamieson. 'Did I conceive it likely that the Magazine could continue to be a receptacle for articles, however able, composed in the same tone, I could not, consistently with my feelings of what is due to the literary society of Edinburgh, continue my personal assistance.' Blackwood promised him that 'no personalities should disgrace the work in future.'[34] But personalities continued to flow. Outrage too. The delinquents became sensitive to their ill fame. They improved. Wilson would one day claim that the magazine had become the least personal in the world.

Scots and English are descended from the same language. They can be seen both to diverge and to come together in Hogg's prose and verse. It may be said of him, as of the modern novelist Irvine Welsh, that he can write a coincident Scots and English. But it can also be said of Hogg, as of Scott, that he was exalted and released by choosing to employ the words and rhythms of his native Scots speech, and that in much of what he wrote Scots and English can look like two different tongues. This is a difference which bore a class meaning. Wilson, who spoke with a Scots accent, endowed Christopher North with a predominantly English speech clamantly contrasted with the Shepherd's Scots.

The power of Hogg's Scots is evident in his novel *The Brownie of Bodsbeck*, which he was completing just before *Blackwood's* began, and which was published in 1818 as a two-volume Blackwood's book, together with his stories 'The Wool-Gatherer' and 'The Hunt of Eildon'. *The Brownie* is a fiction which favours the Covenanters, not uncritically, but in line with a surviving national piety. 'Poor Grahame,' wrote Scott once, mourning the death of the Whig poet James Grahame, 'his was really a hallowed harp, as he was himself an Israelite without guile' – a good man. 'How often have I teased him, but never out of his good-humour, by praising Dundee and laughing at the Covenanters!'[35] Hogg wrote against Covenanting traits and tenets, but would never have praised Graham of Claverhouse, Viscount Dundee.

Scott's contemporaneous *Old Mortality* is a fiction critical of the Covenanters. Both novels are set in 'the killing-time', after the battle of Bothwell Bridge, when the Royalist general was chasing the Covenant's blessed remnant through the southern wilderness. Hogg's makes use of the 'rural and traditionary' material broached in the *Spy*, and then proposed to Constable for book purposes, and of the bogle who haunted the Chapelhope region and was understood to have shrieked at Hogg's birth. Walter Laidlaw, a farmer, is no devotee of the Covenanting cause, but succours the faithful hiding on his land, 'Westland Whigs', fugitives from the battle, hanging on among an alien peasantry. His daughter Kate is suspected of witchcraft, of truck with the Brownie, who proves, however, to be a Cameronian, a 'strenuous and desperate reformer'. Walter is led to a cave whose entrance is so low you have to stoop to get in, and beholds a party of Covenanters: they appear, in their raggedness, 'to our amazed goodman', as 'so many blackamoors'. He congratulates his daughter for aiding her fugitives: 'Ye hae taen the side o' human nature: the suffering and the humble side, an' the side o' feeling, my woman, that bodes best in a young unexperienced thing to tak. It is better than to do like yon bits o' gillflirts about Edinburgh; poor shilly-shally milk-and-water things!'[36] Here is the good-will of the humanitarian Hogg; the appeal to sensibility is restrained by the touch of reproof from Walter, and by a smile at the expense of his city-shunning sternness.

At the start of the story the Laidlaw parents wonder why their daughter has been 'stravaiging i' the night-time'. The narrator intervenes with some fushionless English about girls who stay out at night, while ushering in a 'home remark' from Walter's 'yokefellow':[37]

'Ye ken fu' weel, goodman, ye courtit me always i' the howe o' the night yersel; an' there was never ony thing improper or undecent atween us – at least nought to speak o'; an' Him that kens the heart kens weel that I hae never had cause to rue our bits o' trysts i' the derk – Na, na! mony's the time an' aft that I hae blest them, an' thought o' them wi' pleasure! We had ae kind o' happiness then, Watie, we hae another now, an' we'll hae another yet.'

This is a better advertisement for human nature than Walter's speech at the close. Mistress Laidlaw's weighed words about no impropriety, to speak of, or to be spoken of, were cancelled, disgracefully, for publication, and restored by the modern editor. Her final 'yet' is like a fond memory of Burns's 'Auld Farmer's New-Year Salutation to his Auld Mare, Maggie':

> Yet here to crazy age we're brought,
> Wi' something yet.

The humour and vivacity of Hogg's Scots are nowhere richer than in the family prayer offered up here by Davie Tait, a burning and a shining light of practical, literally pastoral piety. Davie was fashioned in the likeness of a neighbour, Adam Scott of Upper Dalgliesh, whose orisons are remembered in Hogg's *Shepherd's Calendar*. Davie's prayer is, as it were, man-to-man, in the manner prescribed by the New Christianity of the 1960s:

Thou hast promised in thy Word to be our shepherd, our guider an' director; an' thy word's as gude as some men's aith, an' we'll haud thee at it. Therefore take thy plaid about thee, thy staff in thy hand, an' thy dog at thy fit, an' gather us a' in frae the cauld windy knowes o' self-conceit – the plashy bogs an' mires o' sensuality, an' the damp flows o' worldly-mindedness, and wyse us a' into the true bught o' life, made o' the flakes o' forgiveness and the door o' loving-kindness;

146

an' never do thou suffer us to be heftit e'ening or morning, but gie lashin' meals o' the milk of praise, the ream o' thankfulness, an' the butter o' good-works. An' do thou, in thy good time an' way, smear us ower the hale bouk wi' the tar o' adversity, weel mixed up wi' the meinging of repentance, that we may be kiver'd ower wi' gude bouzy shake-rough fleeces o' faith, a' run out on the hips, an' as brown as a tod. An' do thou, moreover, fauld us owernight, an' every night, in within the true sheep-fauld o' thy covenant, weel buggen wi' the stanes o' salvation, an' caped wi' the divots o' grace. An' then wi' sic a shepherd, an' sic a sheep-fauld, what hae we to be feared for? Na, na! we'll fear naething but sin! – We'll never mair scare at the poolly-woolly o' the whaup, nor swirl at the gelloch o' the ern; for if the arm of our Shepherd be about us for good, a' the imps, an' a' the powers o' darkness, canna wrang a hair o' our tails.

Davie's is a broad-church Calvinism (with 'good-works', as opposed to faith, hyphenated but not reprobated), delivered with an endearing wit, and a cogency nowhere excelled in Hogg's turns toward religious affirmation. It has something that could be thought to resemble, but avoid, the unction Blackwood felt was needed by latterday writers about the Covenanters. It was too much for the Rev. Thomas Thomson, whose collected edition of 1865 omits Davie's prayer. Adam Scott, his original, has this to say in Hogg's *Shepherd's Calendar* about a girl 'somewhat miraculously saved from drowning': 'We particularly thank thee for thy great goodness to Meg, and that ever it came into your head to take any thought of sic an useless baw-waw as her.'[38]

Was he, in *The Brownie*, with its predatory Claverhouse, attempting to copy, controvert, or ride on the coat-tails of, *Old Mortality*? The two novels are so different that the question becomes uninteresting. So far from his having imitated Scott, said Hogg, Scott could be called 'an imitator of me'. He asserted that his novel was written long before Scott's, but that he couldn't get Blackwood to bring it out. He was still transcribing and revising it, though, after the Scott novel had appeared, and he seems to have changed the name of his principal Covenanter, from that of the character in Scott's novel called John Balfour of Burley after the assassin of Archbishop Sharp. It has been persuasively argued that Hogg's novel effectively pre-dates Scott's.[39] But there is no evidence that Scott had read Hogg's manuscript and was ettling at an imitation.

When it appeared in print, Hogg visited his friend, and noticed that 'his shaggy eyebrows were hanging very sore down, a bad prelude, which I knew too well.'[40] What then ensued included a denial by Scott of the Waverley authorship – a secret his visitor had not taken long to penetrate. According to Hogg, Scott kept insisting that his friend's novel was an 'exhaggerated and unfair picture' of the times, 'a distorted a prejudiced and untrue picture of the Royal party'. Hogg replied: 'It is the picture I hae been bred up in the belief o' sin' ever I was born and I had it frae them whom I was most bound to honour and believe. An' mair nor that there is not one single incident in the tale – not one – which I cannot prove from history to be literally and positively true.' The Brownie was not, after all, presented as a real Brownie. 'I was obliged sometimes to change the situations to make one part coalesce with another but in no one instance have I related a story of a cruelty or a murder which is not literally true. An' that's a great deal mair than you can say for your tale o' Auld Mortality.'

Hogg made to depart in a huff, but Scott told him not to 'go and leave me again in bad humour'. Hogg told him that 'ane's beuks are like his bairns he disna like to hear them ill spoken o' especially when he is conscious that they dinna deserve it.' Scott's 'again' referred, presumably, to their late estrangement, among whose features was the sneer at Hogg's poetry in a survey published in the *Annual Register*, followed by a retaliation in the *Spy*. The survey article, thought by Hogg to be by Scott, mentioned a strange efflorescence of working-class verse, stirred by the example of Burns: Hogg was one of 'the poets who daily spring up among the lees of the people and find admirers to patronise them because they write "wonderfully well *considering*" '. This is worthy of Maginn, who thought that the *Spy* was too 'trumpery' an affair for Scott, tenacious as his memory was, to remember a quarrel over it years later; and worthy, too, of Lockhart, who remarked in the *Blackwood's* of August 1818 that, thanks to the success of Burns and Joanna Baillie, 'our very footmen compose tragedies.' There is good reason to believe that Scott did write the offending article. But the Great Unknown had equivocated: 'What right had you sir to suppose that I was the author?'

Hogg's recollected or reconstructed rejoinder can't be considered pointless: 'Nay what right had *you* to suppose that you were the author of it that you are taking it so keenly to yourself.' But now they were friends again, and on the way home from a dinner party in Castle Street where Scott had fallen ill, Hogg threatened to dash James Ballantyne to the pavement for betraying his fear that the illness might be serious. 'I never knew that you were so dear to me,' he wrote to Scott, 'till last night when I saw your seat taken by another.'[41]

The *Brownie* volumes bore a verse dedication to Lady Anne Scott, daughter of the fourth Duke of Buccleuch. Duke Charles let Hogg know that she would be 'proud of the honour you intend her' – provided there was nothing 'profane or irreligious' in store for her.[42] Her beauty, wrote Hogg,

> oft hath shed
> Joy round the peasant's lonely bed.

Had she lived, as Hogg had, 'amid the scenes where martyrs bled', she would have felt as he did about their service to 'the cause of liberty divine'. The Buccleuchs, his stratospheric neighbours, were Episcopalians. They were on the other side. But they too, he concedes, had bled for liberty's sake. The poem ends with talk of

> Bonds which the Heavens alone can rend,
> With Chief, with Father, and with Friend.

Then comes

> He little wist –
> Poor inmate of the cloud and mist!
> That ever he, as friend, should claim
> The proudest Caledonian name.

Whose side was he on here? He could speak of the Covenanters as virtuous, as freedom-lovers, while speaking of Parliamentary reformers as villains. Here he sings the praises of an Episcopalian noblewoman whose peasant and pal he says he is, while believing as he grew older that Scottish peasants were slaves. 'Bonds', used in the dedication for the nexus of clan, family and friends, was used by him elsewhere for God's promise to the good Christian and the Reformed Church. It was also used then, as now, for fiduciary transactions. Scott told the fifth Duke of Buccleuch, in asking him to cover his borrowing requirements when he was failing financially: 'Your Grace can bring down the Bond when you come to Scotland for the season.' In describing Scott's response when his London creditors Abud and Company – Jewish, he thought – held him to his bond, Lockhart referred mordantly to the firm as 'these Israelites without guile'.[43]

Politically, Hogg could often be observed on the side of hierarchic Toryism. 'Had Hogg taken the other side,' mused *Fraser's* in the year of the 'Jacobin Bill' to broaden the franchise, the side to which 'it might have been conjectured his humble origin would have inclined him', he might, given his 'song-making' talents, have done harm.[44] Minstrel dangerous.

The volumes of 1818 also had the ridiculous, as Scott thought it, 'Hunt of Eildon',[45] a tale of royalty and diablerie, shape-changing, gluttony and cannibalism – a self-disclosing carnival work of some gusto. The King has two ominous beagles, one of whom is called Mooly, the name of the dark god in one of Hogg's plays. Croudy the Shepherd is changed into a hog. A greedy victualler marks 'the poor boar' for slaughter, and there's nothing his good dog Mumps can do about it. 'No words,' growls the voluptuary: 'The hog is mine. Name your price.' The poor boar is dragged to the slaughterhouse, distressed by the knowledge that his bonds are the garters lent by the witch Pery, fancied by him when he was in human form. White magic saves him from the knife.

'The Wool-Gatherer' is the tale of a young laird who finds strangely interesting a single mother who arrives in the parish, and is mercifully revealed to be of gentle birth, and innocent of being the child's mother. A convincingly benevolent shepherd boy befriends her; she marries the laird. It's a tale in sentimental vein which Hogg declared in his memoir to have been a 'universal favourite' which Blackwood had wanted to exclude from these volumes. This was a reflection on the behaviour of booksellers, who 'never read works themselves, but give them to their minions, with whom there never fails to lurk a literary jealousy'. The minions Lockhart and Wilson were no doubt especially in mind. Hogg insisted that he had always been looked on by the learned part of the community as an intruder in the paths of literature, and every opprobrium has been thrown on me from that quarter. The truth is, that I am so. The walks of learning are occupied by a powerful aristocracy, who deem that province their own peculiar right; else, what would avail all their dear-bought collegiate honours and degrees? No wonder that they should view an intruder, from the humble and despised ranks of the community, with a jealous and indignant eye, and impede his progress by every means in their power.[46]

The most productive phase of his career had begun. Having moved in the main from verse to prose – though there were good poems still to come – he also busied himself at this point with the two volumes of his *Jacobite Relics of Scotland*, collected on a fee from the tight-fisted Highland Society of London and assisted by a network of correspondents, by lairds' bluestocking ladies and by the Jacobite minstreless Betty Cameron of Lochaber. The first series was published by Blackwood in 1819, the second two years later. Few can doubt that, of the two minstrelsies, the 'Jacks' had the better tunes, and the better words: Lady Nairne's, and the tradition's, 'Will ye no come back again?' must still be, for many, irresistibly moving. The Whig songs speak up in numbers for liberty and prosperity, for

> Court, country, and city, against a banditti,
> Lillibulero, bullen a la.

But most of the songs are for the Stuarts. The Government victory of Sheriffmuir in 1715 inspired a hymn to indeterminacy:

> There's some say that we wan,
> And some say that they wan,
> And some say that nane wan at a', man.

But there's a sense in which the Whigs lost the war of words, man.

Many of the pieces were 'versified by me', and by other modernisers, with Allan Cunningham responsible in that role for 'The Wee, Wee German Lairdie', a spite on the House of Hanover. Modernisers are now held, by some, to have been responsible for the material of greatest value in the tradition. Of the Highland songs which Hogg liked to write over the years, his faintly bowdlerised version of 'Charlie is my darling', 'Maclean's Welcome', his free translation from the Gaelic –

> Come o'er the stream, Charlie, dear Charlie, brave Charlie,
> Come o'er the stream, Charlie, and dine with Maclean

– 'The Piper o' Dundee', and 'Cam ye by Athol' ('one of my worst,' he said, in his *Songs* of 1831), are four of the best. 'Donald Macgillavry', portrait of a clansman, who is asked to come as a weaver, a tailor, and other sorts of Lowlander, to exact 'justice' and revenge, is one of his most vigorous. 'The best specimen of the true old Jacobite song' – Jeffrey hailed it as such, in an otherwise hostile review of the first series, and of the Jacobite rebellions, not knowing the song was Hogg's, 'put in to fill up a page,' said Hogg.[47] In saying so, or being made to say so by Lockhart, he exulted over Jeffrey's error, having hailed the specimen himself, in his notes, as 'one of the best songs that ever was made'.

Hogg has 'grubbed up a great deal of old poetry', Scott told the Buccleuchs, twenty years after he had grubbed up, with Hogg's help, the minstrelsy of the Scottish Border. 'I shall never forget with what sly and disdainful looks Donald would eye me, when I told him I was gathering up old songs,' Hogg told the readers of his memoir. Donald the proverbial Highlander is meant. The volumes were an achievement which did not gain the recognition they deserved. They 'established the Jacobite song canon', observes the editor of the *Collected Works* edition of the first series, who goes on to say: 'What we know as the Jacobite song (providing more is known than the odd lyric of Burns and Lady Nairne) is substantially Hogg's text.'[48] Both series carried editorial narratives and explanations, which drew on the writings of Smollett among others, and on a forward-looking passage of Horace Walpole's: 'Old Sarah, duchess of Marlborough, ever proud and ever malignant, was persuaded to offer her favourite granddaughter, Lady Diana Spencer ... to the Prince of Wales.'

The Jacobite rebellions were by no means ancient history, though their politics had subsided. Hogg's father was on the harvest field when the battle of Prestonpans was fought, but he remembered 'the Highlanders' raide' with, in his son's view, 'the utmost minuteness'.

Hogg's poem of dedication in the *Relics* suggests that Jacobitism divided him, complicating his bonds and loyalties:

> For his Whiggish heart, with its Covenant tie,
> Was knit to the Highlands, he could not tell why.

He could not tell why he was a Jacobite, and he was also to say that he did not know why he was a violent Tory. The symbiotic Covenant Whig – rather than Reform Whig – is frank here about the horrors of the Catholic religion professed by his 'unfortunate Prince', his poor pretender, and about those of absolutism. Sentiment attempts to reconcile the competing claims of the opposing sides: 'Much as every lover of his country must deprecate the arbitrary principles of that exiled house, an hereditary disease of which it expired, he must have a cold and selfish heart who sheds not a tear at its misfortunes.' Since the revolution of 1688, the power of the Whigs had 'predominated in the counsels of Scotland, and ultimately in the field, though the spirit of chivalry has been wholly displayed on the other side'.

He felt 'enthusiasm' for his 'disinterested', and interesting, Jacobites, whose soldiers were treated in a manner lacking in 'sentiment' during the hours that followed Culloden (a battle heinously mismanaged by the Jacobite leadership, with half their host absent and the other half – stood there in close order, intent on the Highland charge – cannonaded into the ground). The second series has Hogg's survivor:

> I'm puir, an' auld, an' pale, an' wan,
> I brak my shin, an' tint a han',
> Upon Culloden lee, man.

Relishing as he did the style of these coup attempts, he may not have known that only a minority of the clans was Jacobite at the time of the Forty-Five. The Highland Clearances are only fleetingly acknowledged in the modern material, and the working-class unrest which led to the 'radical war' of 1820 – an agent-provoked uprising of weavers, put down by cavalry attack at Bonnymuir – is visible only, and if then, in the reference to a weaver Donald bent on justice.

A 'curious Chaldee Manuscript' is quoted, 'The Chronicles of Charles the Young Man': Hogg's work, presumably, but a misapplication of the old satirical ploy. 'Now the young man was a great prince, and of a goodly countenance, and all they that saw him loved him, and they called his name Charles.' Hogg remarks that a previous Stuart king, Charles II, 'never could mould his deportment into that starched grimace which the Covenanters required as an infallible mark of conversion' – a mark of Heaven, as opposed to other marks he was to write about. This is to wear his Covenant tie with a distinct difference. He also cites the Covenanting minister's ecstatic cry when prisoners were being massacred after Montrose's defeat at Philiphaugh: 'O but the gude wark gangs bonnily on!'

Among the idiosyncrasies of Hogg's edition is a tendency to make light of Burns's contribution to the Jacobite musical museum. Of the urban contribution he seems to have been well aware, for all his talk of the Jacobite minstrelsy as 'the unmasked effusions of a bold and primitive race'. Stuart propaganda, with its Charlie songs and its toxic lampoons, came from the town rather than the glen; it did not come from an earlier world, or a heroic age; nor was the Jacobitical Allan Ramsay a shepherd. The clan fighter had by now enlisted in the British Army, and Hogg was aware of this too, in celebrating Highland valour, at a time when marriage and domesticity had overtaken him. He may possibly have felt that the Royal Georges had learnt to trust the honest Highland lad.

It is not surprising that, in order to impress the Royal Society of Literature in 1821, Lockhart should have advised Hogg to write 'another famous "Carle an the King Come"' for the Coronation festivities held in Edinburgh for George IV, and that Walter Scott should have greeted the monarch with an adaptation of the same Jacobite song when he arrived in the city the following year. A Hanoverian spin was in train. When the King came, he was found to be kilted, and hedged with Highland chiefs. Hogg took Lockhart's advice: he attended a loyal dinner in 1821, a private affair rather than the Lord Provost's banquet, and described it in Part Two of the August *Blackwood's*. In this unsigned article, once thought to be by Galt, he says things that he says in his contemporaneous *Memoir* – about the lies told him by Lockhart – and provides what is in effect a further item in the 'Noctes Ambrosianae' series. The *Blackwood's* stars shine in this description of the dinner, and Hogg is the 'country-looking man' who rises to sing the famous old several-handed song, one that had hardly been 'written' by Hogg, as Lockhart had perhaps slyly implied.

> Thou shalt dance, and I will sing,
> Carle, an the King come.

The version he sings is longer and richer ('We's gar a' our bagpipes bumm') than that printed in the *Relics*; shoulders are slapped at every return of the word 'carle', with its allusion to the Stuarts. George IV is toasted in the piece, for all that, and George III, 'our good auld man'. This is an article in which the less evolved, more bucolic Hogg of the earlier 'Noctes' is served up by none other than Hogg himself.

In the October 1820 number of *Blackwood's* there appeared two 'Letters from James Hogg to his Reviewer'. The reviewer was Jeffrey, whose discussion of the first series was trashed as so much 'balaam' – a *Blackwood's* word of disparagement. The second letter offers the first letter for publication. Alan Strout gives reasons for thinking that both were rewritten by Lockhart, who seems to have wished to make Hogg out to be more of a Tory than he was, and who conveys here that friendship unites with philanthropy, loyalty and religion to make his friend the Tory that he is. Hogg had his doubts about the divine right of kings, but, says the letter, 'principle, and established SENSE OF RIGHT', kept him from siding with the *Edinburgh Review*, though Mr Jeffrey, 'I shall always think and always say, is a GENTLEMAN'. At a later point Hogg was to say, or to be made to say, the very opposite.

From these manoeuvres one might infer that Lockhart respected Jeffrey, as did Wilson, and that Hogg and Jeffrey were two very different men. It's worth quoting what Jeffrey had to say in his review about armchair, 'speculative' Jacobites, such as Hogg and Scott. They were like the Jacobites themselves in that 'they hate the cause of popular principles; they dislike a free and rational government; they had rather see a king unfettered by a parliament; a judge unchecked by a jury; and a press free to praise only the stronger side.'[49]

The second of the letters, the covering letter, mentions Keats. In September, Lockhart had written to John Aitken of Dunbar, whom he seems to have looked down on: 'I have aready attempted to say something kind about Mr Keats, in *Blackwood's Magazine*, but been thwarted.' Lockhart hoped that his health would improve and that he would 'live to be a merry fellow'. In October, the second of the published letters mentions that Aitken had informed the writer that Keats 'is really a sweet-tempered inoffensive young creature, only just like to be ruined altogether, I suppose, by having forgathered, at that early and inexperienced period of life, with such a set of conceited reprobates'.[50]

Lockhart was trying to make amends for his attacks in *Blackwood's* (1817–8) on the inhabitants of 'Cockaigne', in which Leigh Hunt's verse 'resembles that of a man who has kept company with kept-mistresses', and milliners. Lockhart had a particular contempt for milliners, and no patience whatever with 'the odious and unnatural harlotry' of the subversive Hunt's 'polluted muse. We were the first to brand with a burning iron the false face of this kept-mistress of a demoralising incendiary. We tore off her gaudy veil and transparent drapery, and exhibited the painted cheeks and writhing limbs of the prostitute.' Readers were also told of 'the calm, settled, imperturbable drivelling idiocy' of Keats's 'Endymion': 'It is a better and a wiser thing to be a starved apothecary than a starved poet; so back to the shop Mr John, back to "plaisters, pills and ointment boxes". But, for Heaven's sake, young Sangrado, be a little more sparing of extenuatives and soporifics in your practice than you have been in your poetry.'

In 1820, *Winter Evening Tales* was published by Oliver and Boyd. The collection gathers up and refurbishes earlier material, such as Basil Lee's adventures, and it includes, published for the first time, the fine story 'John Gray o' Middleholm', a comedy of starvation, to which I shall return. A concern with aristocratic misalliance is shared by a well-turned ballad, 'King Gregory', in a mild version of Hogg's antique Scots, and 'The Bridal of Polmood', a Radcliffian romance and royal bedroom farce, in which an authentic mismating gets lost amid the carry-on. This story of the revenge visited on the inordinately leisured deer-destroying court of James IV by Norman Hunter (a name also used by Hogg's nephew Robert), of the castle of Polmood, unfolds in an English stately and operatic. There occurs the (barbaric) mock-hanging by the King of a certain cheeky Border minstrel, who is then excused his home truths and 'metamorphosed into Sir William'. The two plan to go off together in disguise to check on the condition of the poor. The shepherd bard is an embodiment of the 'blunt rusticity' prized by Hogg and felt by him to have been practised in these tales of yesteryear. At one point in this one, he chants an allegory which censures the King's adultery, and which incorporates memorable lines learnt by Hogg from his mother, concerning a Christ-like knight 'whose wounds did bleed both day and night'. An ingenious, tumultuous piece, this allegory, in which an old song, as it may be thought, lies somewhat awkwardly enclosed within a pastiche of the bygone Border minstrelsy.

The collection has the 'Shepherd's Calendar' pieces by him which had appeared in *Blackwood's*. They embody a narrative of the great storm of 1794, when the Entertrony debaters were thought to have raised the devil. The countryside was shocked by the news: 'lips grew white.' Hogg's mother feared that such a work might have been attempted; Hogg, absent from the debate on this occasion, was unsettled by the excitement, but manages to make superb comedy of his mother's interrogation of the pretty servant girl at the shieling, called, as if in commemoration of Locherben, Mary Beattie, who was to marry his brother William. The pieces also embody the self-portrait, in a bravura Scots, of a bravura fisherman and fighter, Peter Plash, an account of his Border Games of a wedding, and the reproving portrait of a Moderate minister: a very different man from Peter, and from Edie of Aberlosk, Hogg's friend, a 'great original', also present, together with his letter to George III on his tax problems. 'Welldean Hall' is an oddly involving work of Gothic comedy and detection, which features a scheming relative who dies a libertine's death ('It is a pity there should be gentlemen of such dispositions, but nobody can help it'), a poltergeist, and two kindly alcoholics described by the libertine as estranged from 'the world's law' (a phrase from *Romeo and Juliet* which Jane Austen's *Emma* employed in 1816).

CHAPTER ELEVEN

Personalities

The *Blackwood's* of its early days was a magazine of personalities, and of squabash, bam and balaam. The term 'personalities', in its application to the magazine, bears a complex meaning. It could mean a recourse to insult, derision and insinuation, at the expense of individual enemies, but it could also mean more than that. 'Squabash' meant putting people down or cutting them up. A 'bam' was a trick or a leg-pull. And 'balaam' meant rejected or unsolicited material ('slush' in modern parlance), or worthless material which a journal might find itself having to publish, or to which the writings of enemies could be compared. These were terms which might be politically intended, and could also be aids to social advancement. Reviewers could aspire to be thought gentlemen by detecting, rejecting and blackguarding their inferiors.

Christopher North, the John Wilson persona of the 'Noctes', enquires there in March 1822, with reference to reviewing: 'What can be done without personality?' He is speaking of personal hostility, and of the ad hominem approach. He does not mean what the real Hogg meant in 1806 when he said: 'Where there is no thing of self, there is seldom any interest.'[1] In April 1827 North contradicts what he'd said in 1822: 'I hate all personality, James.' In the previous month's 'Noctes' the Shepherd pays tribute to the magazine – it has created a new world – and speaks of the symposiasts' way of passing themselves off 'sometimes for real, and sometimes for fictious characters': a glamour ensues for the puzzled reader. But the Shepherd could also feel, when at the receiving end, that 'it's no decent to be aye meddling wi' folks' personalities. I'm sure by this time the whole set o' you might ha mair sense. Ye ken what ye hae gotten by your personalities.' Arresting, this. Even more arresting is a later cry from the Shepherd: intolerably, everyone is imitating 'ma style o' colloquial oratory, till a' that's specific and original about me's lost in universal plagiarism'.[2]

For these writers, 'personalities' figured as a pun in which insult and hostility co-existed with aspects and avatars of the individual personality. In January 1828 North reproaches, or affects to reproach, the Shepherd: 'O, man, Hogg, but you are a barefaced "eemetawtor" of me.' This is and is meant to be rich, coming from a man who has been writing the Shepherd's speeches in the symposium: but there is something in it too, given that Hogg's verse had been influenced by Wilson's. The Shepherd responds here with the view that imitation robs folks of their 'oreeginality', and with the question: 'What's a Noctes withouten the Shepherd?' North holds elsewhere (January 1831) that the faculty of imitation belongs in excess to original minds.

In December 1828 North springs this pun, when he talks once again of 'hating all personality', while also talking about 'personating myself'. The Ambrosians impersonated both other people and their own interesting selves. Hogg became – in a modern sense of the word, prophetically enough, a sense then in the process of formation – a personality, a Scottish star known throughout the English-speaking world. The same thing happened to Wilson: Personality Hogg and Personality Wilson became famous together – in part, by passing themselves off as one another. Wilson could be Hogg and Hogg Wilson in the course of Hogg's transition from shepherd to metropolitan writer, and of his suspension between the two states.

It was an 'age of personality', wrote Coleridge. Literary anonymity and its overthrow flourished in unison. Names were in, and persons were in. Signatures were in, but so were pseudonyms. For Coleridge on this occasion, personality was spite. His was an age 'of literary and political Gossiping, when the meanest insects are worshipped with a sort of Egyptian superstition, if only the brainless head be atoned for by the sting of *personal* malignity in the tail'. It was chiefly in the field of personality, broadly construed, that the *Blackwood's* writers could claim to have changed the world.[3]

The most distinguished appreciation of the *Blackwood's* of the day is one rarely mentioned by writers about Hogg, who can sometimes seem blind to the achievements of those opposed to the political outlook of Scott. This appreciation belongs to the *Memorials* of Henry Cockburn, bamfully known to the 'Noctes' Shepherd as Hairy Cobrun. His book, which was published in 1856, ends in 1830 with the imminence of the Reform Bill. Before *Blackwood's*, Cockburn explains, Edinburgh's only monthly periodical was the 'dotard' *Scots Magazine*, and Constable broke that magazine's 'last spell' by changing its structure and title.[4] This gave Blackwood the chance for a 'new adventure', which proved to be 'a work of violent personality' – a journal of insult. In the world at large, the war with France had been succeeded by the shock of confrontation between the perpetuators of old systems and those out to destroy or reform them. 'A war of opinion,' he writes, 'is a condition of which libel is one of the natural products.' Libel and, as it turned out, homicide.

From the Pantheon meeting of Reformers in 1820 to the Reform Bill of 1832, Edinburgh was, it has been felt, a Whig city. 'With the exception of Scott, I cannot recollect almost a single individual taking at this time a charge of public opinion and of personal weight, who was not a Whig,' Cockburn writes. This carries a suggestion of chauvinistic retrospect. The Tories were still in government, and it was possible for a Whig like Cockburn's friend Jeffrey to say in 1825 that in Edinburgh 'the young men are mostly Tories.'[5] The success of *Blackwood's*, a young man's paper, and a gentleman's paper, helped to give that impression. The gathering momentum of Scottish Reform, however, must have done much to qualify it.

Cockburn goes on to say that 'the vice of offensive personality, which was flagrant at first, is the more to be lamented, that in talent and originality this magazine has been, and is, the best that has been published in its day in Britain.' The exception of his own journal, the *Edinburgh Review*, is tacit here: he would have seen it as a different thing, a review rather than a magazine. He notes that William Laidlaw's 'Whig feelings' caused him to withdraw from the magazine, and that Scott – 'disapproving (though he chuckled over it)' the 'reckless extravagance of juvenile satire' to be found there, and 'having no kindness for Blackwood personally' – 'appears to have easily acquiesced in the propriety of Laidlaw's determination'. But Scott is unlikely to have yielded to Whig feelings in the matter. The *Edinburgh Review* was less offensive, less imaginative, altogether more *retenu*, than its rival, which Cockburn was right to commend for its originality – a version of the originality Hogg had hoped for. But it was in its own different way a superlative achievement. Carlyle was to smile at Jeffrey – infinitely and elegantly conversible, even at times Ambrosian, 'Noctes'-compatible – for telling him: 'You are so dreadfully in earnest!' But Jeffrey's journal had the importance of its earnestness and intellectual power. There was an awe of Jeffrey at *Blackwood's*, which caused them to make him make a fool of himself in a sham, bam appearance at a 'Noctes'.

Harry Cockburn's generosity towards the rival paper is a shame on its purveyors of personality, in the sense of insult and injury. Cockburn writes of the 'Noctes' as

> a series of scenes supposed to have occurred in a tavern in Register Street kept by one Ambrose. And no periodical publication that I know of can boast of so extraordinary a series of jovial dramatic fiction. Wilson, I believe, now professes to regret and condemn many things in these papers, and to deny his authorship of them; but substantially they are all his. I have not the slightest doubt that he wrote at least ninety per cent of them. I wish no man had anything worse to be timid about. There is not so curious and original a work in the English or Scotch languages. It is a most singular and delightful outpouring of criticism, politics, and descriptions of feeling, character, and scenery, of verse and prose, and maudlin eloquence, and especially of wild fun. It breathes the very essence of the Bacchanalian revel of clever men. And its Scotch is the best Scotch that has been written in modern times. I am really sorry for the poor one-tongued Englishman, by whom, because the Shepherd uses the sweetest and most expressive of living languages, the homely humour, the sensibility, the descriptive power, the eloquence, and the strong joyous hilarity of that animated rustic can never be felt. The characters are all well drawn, and well sustained, except that of the Opium Eater, who is heavy and prosy: but this is perhaps natural to opium. Few efforts could be more difficult than to keep up the bounding spirit of fresh boyish gaiety which is constantly made to break out amidst the serious discussions of these tavern philosophers and patriots. After all just deductions, these 'Noctes' are bright with genius.

Every word of this tribute – 'animated rustic' apart – strikes me as true. The Shepherd's 'joyous hilarity' was no invention of Wilson's. Gillies spoke of Hogg's 'accustomed mood of joyous contentment'. Robert Carruthers said that 'many years after this period' – 1817 – 'Hogg retained a careless brightness of conversation and joyous manner which were seen in no other man.' He at one time 'retained all his original simplicity of character'. There were those who felt that Hogg became spoilt, became worldly and crafty – with fame, perhaps, and the burdens of personality and poverty.[6]

How, then, did the 'Noctes Ambrosianae', in their originality, come to be born? In August and September 1819 the journal published two accounts of sporting expeditions, on the part of the cronies, which were also literary picnics, to coincide with the onset of the shooting season. Christopher North, a Wilson shown charismatically old and lame, holds sway, and forth, in his Deeside Tent. These accounts were a testing-ground for the idea that became the comic colloquy and camaraderie of the 'Noctes'. A version of Hogg is present but he did not otherwise contribute; he was made joyous by the fiasco of the enemy expedition to Kirk o' Shotts, in the West of Scotland. This set a pattern for the many 'Noctes' that lay ahead, though he did send in contributions to these, some passages of which reached the page. There was laughter, in the Tent, over 'his genius and infirmity'. Robert Macnish, a literary doctor, dualistic author and metempsychosist, or reincarnationist, spoke of him elsewhere as a phrenological curiosity (some organs well developed, others miserably), and, at a time of divided personalities, as a 'strange compound of genius and imbecility', or weakness: genius and its obverse became a convenient oxymoron for Hogg.[7] In 1822, the 'Noctes' began in earnest, so far as they were ever wholly in earnest.

Cockburn says that 90 per cent of them were Wilson's work. From 1825 till the demise of the feature ten years later, this seems to have been the case; and large amounts of the material were published in collections of his work. The idea, and much of the early writing, were mainly Lockhart's and Maginn's, with Maginn parading as Ensign Odoherty. The opening 'Noctes' was Maginn's; and Lockhart was to speak with relish some years later of how this demon had 'entered into the very core of Ambrose's'. After his move to the *Quarterly*, Lockhart ceased to contribute other than occasionally to the feature. The further contributing personnel were Robert Sym (as Timothy Tickler, a name also used by others), Thomas Hamilton, John Cay, James White, the advocate Douglas Cheape, D. M. Moir ('Delta'), another literary doctor. To Moir has been attributed 'The Canadian Boat Song', the unexpired sighing song of cleared Highlanders in exile, which was introduced by North in the 'Noctes' of September 1829, where it was said to have accompanied a letter from Galt, then a colonial ruler in Upper Canada, as the translation of a song heard there from 'strapping' Gaelic-speakers at their oars. The song has also been attributed to Lockhart (to whom the 'Noctes' has been credited) and to Hogg. North chants:

> From the lone shieling of the misty island
> Mountains divide us and the waste of seas –
> Yet still the blood is strong, the heart is Highland,
> And we in dreams behold the Hebrides.

Highland children, said the song, had been banished 'that a degenerate Lord might boast his sheep'. Hogg had earlier planned to bring sheep to the Hebrides, but is unlikely to have planned to be a usurper.[8]

The venue was a real place – William Ambrose's tavern, with a real landlord of that name in deferential attendance, and a tail of sprite-like waiters wonderfully named (such as Sir David Gam, and Tapitourie, a word for a crowning knob of pastry, or for a peak or high point). In 1826 Ambrose flitted from 1 Gabriel's Road, from the premises containing the Blue Parlour, next to a former flat of Hogg's and near Blackwood's shop at the East End of Princes Street. The show moved on a few hundred yards to 15 Picardy Place at the top of Leith Walk, near where Irvine Welsh's *Trainspotting* addicts were to live, less convivially. These feasts were barmecidal, ludic, over the top, but real too, in the sense that some of the contributors were hearty eaters and drinkers; the Victorian critic George Saintsbury insisted that there was realism here. A shorthand writer, Nathaniel Gurney, was written into the script, called after a Parliamentary practitioner of the art, and secreted in a cubby-hole entered by a mysterious Ear of Dionysus.

There were symposiasts who were visiting dignitaries, famous folk such as Byron, and local worthies. These and others were impersonations of real people: Kempferhausen was to the Germanist Gillies as the English Opium-Eater was to De Quincey. Some were more purely ideal.

But they were all 'Messieurs de l'Imagination', a term used by Shelton Mackenzie – all in varying degrees imaginary. They could later be referred to as 'eidolons', meaning images or spectres.

Opinions will always vary as to how close the impersonation of Hogg was to the man himself. The philosopher James Ferrier, Wilson's nephew and son-in-law, pronounced that 'James Hogg in the flesh was but a faint adumbration of the inspired Shepherd of the "Noctes".' He also pronounced: 'In wisdom the Shepherd equals the Socrates of Plato; in humour he surpasses the Falstaff of Shakespeare' – with whom, as we have seen, Hogg reveals an affinity. His daughter Mary Garden said, loyally and understandably, that 'the Shepherd of the "Noctes" is a myth.' But then Hogg was himself a myth, as well as a real man, and I have no doubt that the real man thoroughly resembled, while also being misrepresented by, the imaginary one. George Saintsbury was certain that the real man was the lesser literary talent: 'the Shepherd never did anything that exhibited half the power over thought and language which is shown in the best passages of his "Noctes" eidolon.' Elsewhere in the discussion, he makes the *Confessions* an exception to this claim.[9]

Hogg's contributions, never copious, came and went over the years, in step with estrangements that broke out. An account book lists payments and pages for the two 'Noctes' dated October 1828: Wilson, Maginn and James White are credited with over twenty and with seventeen and three pages respectively, and Hogg with one page.[10] 'I sent a complete "Noctes" once, which of course I never saw again,' Hogg complained to Blackwood in 1826. Lockhart thought of Wilson as the creator of Maga's Shepherd, while himself helping in his creation. 'We have of late had so much of Hogg's talk that I have made him say little this time,' he remarked at an early point. In December 1824, Blackwood blithely re-assured Hogg with one of the world's stranger sentences: 'You will laugh very heartily at your account of your interview with Byron at the Lakes.'[11]

Ferrier's praise, with its allusions to Socrates and Falstaff, now seems extravagant. But there is a great deal to praise here. Antecedents for the 'Noctes' mix of drama and discussion – in the Classical symposia, for instance, or the comedies of Shakespeare – make up a fairly narrow field, and the claim of originality is by no means far-fetched. The 'Noctes' have very much more of depth and intelligence than the long recoil from the

Wilsonian ethos has usually been able to admit, and it is philistine to deny their claims. In this tavern there were as many as two Falstaffs, North and the Shepherd, and a grand betrayal of the second, by his juniors, not unlike the one in Shakespeare's *Henry IV*.

The authority, sagacity and licence exercised by the Shepherd were a major source of the journal's international appeal. But if Hogg had reason to maintain that the 'Noctes' would be nothing without the Shepherd, there is reason, too, to state the obvious: that if Hogg was the Shepherd, Wilson (give or take an 'et al') wrote that Shepherd. Both he and Hogg were to be big in America, whose Shelton Mackenzie became a scholar of the magazine's ethos. Both Wilson and Hogg were responsible for what it was that led Isaac D'Israeli to say of himself that he 'rode triumphantly on Hogg's back through the pages of "Maga" ' (his son Benjamin, the 'Jew scamp' of Lockhart's letters, was to be instrumental in bringing Lockhart up to London to edit for Murray).[12]

In her in-house account of William Blackwood and his firm, Margaret Oliphant credits Wilson and Lockhart with the lion's share of the Maga triumph. When it comes to Hogg's fallings-out with the other three men – inevitable in what has to be seen as in some respects an unstable, unequal and unhealthy relationship – she is often mean and censorious towards the quartet's peasant: a trait of many pronouncers on Hogg until recent years. About the success of their adventure she is very definite, and as a shrewd ex-Edinburgh Victorian writer, she can well be believed: the 'Noctes' had 'a large, unacknowledged, perhaps uncomprehended, share in the mental training of our fathers'.[13]

The magazine's personalities were deployed in the Tory interest. 'The *Blackwood* tomahawk' – Mrs Garden's expression – flashed for King and Country. In 1827, Blackwood declared that 'my Magazine' is 'the only journal which has espoused the cause of the High Tories, and for years attacked the Liberals and Free Trade political economists'. Ebony also felt that in the protracted Reform debate 'ma Maga' had gone its own way, 'cutting up both sides when they deserved it'. The Edinburgh mob saw the paper differently: its windows were smashed when those within failed to light candles for the Reform Bill illuminations. The Bill was a violation of Lady Maga, said her journalists. In 1833, he felt that it had ruined the country with its revolutionary measures. It was bad for business. But he thought that Maga had received from it 'a stimulus as the great organ of the Conservative party'.[14]

In 1826 the journal carried a preface which reviewed its record in politics and letters.[15] It had 'diffused a healthy and manly tone throughout the empire' – the empire on which, as Wilson seems to have been the first to say, the sun never set. Its secret had been that 'we wrote like Britons.' The writer, Wilson presumably, is firm that the Scots are Britons, and that 'the first of nations' is England. 'We have not erred in company with the infidel and revolutionist, with the enemies of God and man.'

As for literature, the journal had done well there too. They had lost no time in putting a stop to criticism. 'Men of genius were insulted by tenth-rate scribblers, without head or heart ... We put an end to this in six months.' The journal which had insulted the apothecary Keats was not to blame for his death. He was killed by the Cockneys he ran with. The journal's critics had put a stop to criticism by dealing in enthusiasm and fancy. Their vein of 'prose panegyric', they said, was 'itself a poem'. But it can also be said that, so far from putting a stop to criticism, the journal gave it a shove, that it helped to transmit a mental training – grounded in sensibility, proclaimed morality and practical criticism, in a perusal of quotation and a ranking of authors – which was still prominent in the middle years of the twentieth century. The *Edinburgh Review* – more head than heart, as it might be represented – also served in this respect.

The attacks on Cockney poets, on elderly and decent Whig professors, and on so many others, brought disrepute as well as celebrity to Lockhart and Wilson. The former explained to the painter Benjamin Haydon, once bitten, that it was not his fault: that the scorpion had been a 'raw boy' at the time, that he'd felt no malice towards the people he had attacked, that 'the lordly Whigs' had no prescriptive right to persiflage, but that 'I now think with deep sadness of the pain my jibes and jokes inflicted on better men than myself,' while also having come round to the belief that 'the only individuals whom *Blackwood* ever really and essentially injured were myself and Wilson.' He'd been held back at the Bar and denied political countenance. He had been reduced to the 'intolerably grievous fate of the dependent on literature'.[16] Poor Lockhart.

Their politics mattered in the land. And so did their romantics. These High Tories were, in certain respects, as writers, distinctly radical, for all that they opposed, as some Edinburgh Reviewers did, romantic initiatives of the age. 'I can thole a hantle o' nonsense,' says the 'Noctes' Shepherd in January 1827 – put up with a lot of nonsense. 'I can believe ony thing,' he says. 'There never was a baseless fiction.' 'Nae truth like fiction,' he says. There is a beauty of the incomprehensible. According to the Shepherd, 'there maun aye be left something unexplained in every subject, sir.'[17] Dreams are not to be despised; nothing is, it sometimes seems. All men are mad. These extreme statements can look like Hogg-Wilson convolutes, joint communiqués. They were meant to shock the Scotland which spoke in the accents of Hogg's cousin, auld James Laidlaw, who said that 'Hogg, poor man, has spent much of his time coining lies,'[18] and that liars are destined for the lake that burns with fire and brimstone. This is a reference to literature. To men such as James Laidlaw Hogg's eidolon declared that truth and lies are the same, and that error can be a good thing.

Some of these statements are untrue in the sense of starkly untenable, some are exclamatory, some ironic, some a bam. There are those of them which can't be squared with opinions expressed by a James Hogg let loose from vicarious participation in the Ambrosian seminar on romantic indeterminacy and indifferentism, by the James Hogg capable of his best fiction. Each of his literary associates – Walter Scott was renowned for it – reached an accommodation with the rival categories of Scotch sense and Scotch romance. Hogg did this too. But his *Confessions* may be thought to transcend these categories. Meanwhile his life could be viewed, by more than one of Scotland's 'men of sense', as a scandal and a warning.

'They say I cannot reason,' volunteers North in August 1834, shortly after the Shepherd's return to the fold after a bad quarrel. 'That's a lee,' cries the prodigal son. 'There lies your glory; for you deal oot intuitive truths, ane after anither, till the tenor o' your speech is like a string o' diamonds.' The real Hogg was nevertheless aware that Wilson's intuitive truths and illimitable flights did not always ensure a readable poem. One flight was 'most splendid', he owned to William Blackwood, 'but I have never been able to get straight through it, and I don't think any man ever will.'[19]

Hogg wrote for the magazine, with intermissions, for the rest of his life, and he took part by proxy in the seventy-one 'Noctes' which ran from March 1822 until February 1835. J. H. Alexander distinguishes between the presence there of Hogg and that of the Shepherd, with the historical James Hogg as a *tertium quid*.[20] Hogg the figment arrives in December 1822, in the sixth (by Maginn, in the main) of the symposia, and

continues to appear as an interlocutor in numbers 7 and 8 (by Lockhart), and 9 (by Maginn). In numbers 12 and 14, by Wilson, he is replaced by the Shepherd; in 15 and 16 (by Lockhart), and 18 (chiefly by Maginn), Hogg reappears; in Wilson's 19 it is again the Shepherd; in those sections of 20 and 21 by Maginn, Hogg; and finally in 22 Wilson establishes the Shepherd on a permanent basis as in effect the centre of gravity of his series of 'Noctes' stretching into the mid-Thirties: in 'Noctes' 42 North agrees with the Shepherd that without the Shepherd the 'Noctes' would be 'a world without a sun'.

Alexander adds that 'there is little radical disjunction between the Shepherd and the figure of Hogg in the earlier "Noctes", apart from the Shepherd's much greater imaginative eloquence.' The imaginary Hogg starts the series as a simpleton, who has to have long words explained to him, and then moves to inhabit the psychological depth, and the lyricism and sentiment, proceeding from Wilson. Some of the early idiotising of the historical Hogg can be laid at the door of his latent and not so latent enemy, and admirer, Maginn. Alexander is right to insist 'that (certain obvious comic buffoonery apart)' the Hogg/Shepherd amalgam is 'a good deal closer to certain central aspects of James Hogg than has generally been recognised', and to endorse, in effect, Cockburn's claim as to the expressiveness of the language or languages of the series – of its double tongue. He quotes some words of Romantic (and Shakespearian) purport, from the Shepherd to North, in the especially rewarding 53rd number of January 1831, words which go to show how much Wilson could make of the new things that were being voiced – not all of them brand-new – by high-mettled literary people of the time:

I dinna remember ae single syllable o' what was said, either by you or me, at the last 'Noctes' – nor, indeed, at ony o' the half hunder

'Nocteses' celebrated in Gabriel's Road and Picardy since the Great Year o' the Chaldee. I never remembers naething – but a' that ever occurs to my mind has the appearance o' bein' imagination. An' thae Fifty-Two 'Noctes' – what are they noo but dreams aboot dreams! Sometimes when I read the record o' ane o' them in the Maggazin, I wonner wha's that Shepherd that speaks about the Forest – till a' at ance I begin to jaloose that he's my verra ain sell, and that I really maun hae been carrying on the war bravely that nicht at Ambrose's . . .

But enough of that, he concludes. 'Let's cut up Sir Walter' – criticise his demonology book. The real Hogg, who would hardly have come out with that Wilsonism about Sir Walter, was only occasionally responsible for the record of these conversations. But he was more than a little responsible for the inspired Shepherd of the 'Noctes'.

The year 1817 saw the start of his work with the magazine's leading lights, and of the most eventful period of his life. The journalist who contributes from a distance to a paper he badly needs to please is often anxious, and this was Hogg's case. He was a friend of theirs, a member of the 'dear Divan', of the council of Wilson's intimates, and yet far as well as near, rather as Ettrick was, as he put it, a 'trivial' distance from Edinburgh and yet a wilderness. He was a lavish contributor to the journal, a sham byline at times, but a true and frequent one nonetheless, and he was also a character in their play, and indeed their creature, as some of them must sometimes have felt, a creature like James Scott. This deutero-Hogg was a small, bald, simple soul, a bluff dentist, whose verse was written by Lockhart, whose works were advertised in the paper as impending, 'in the press', and who was fêted in Liverpool as Ebony's talented Odontist.

Mrs Oliphant's *Annals of a Publishing-House* refers to Hogg as if he did not belong to this 'brotherhood'.[21] He is said to have contributed only 'scraps' to 'The Chaldee Manuscript'; he occasionally 'had, or was allowed to suppose that he had, a large share' in the 'Noctes'; he was left to 'fill up', as he chose, the character of the Shepherd. He 'never was in the least the half-inspired delightful talker which he appears' in the 'Noctes'. He 'never forgave (yet was always forgiving) the brotherhood for attributing all their most poetical ideas to him'. He acquired 'a fictitious importance in that brilliant record'. She writes as if he should have been quietly grateful.

A series of letters to Blackwood made clear, from 1818 onwards, his sense of the way they were treating him. These were preceded by a letter to Hogg, in the magazine, from 'Timothy Tickler' – the work of Wilson, with or without Lockhart – which mocks three gravely affirmative articles on Hogg by his friend James Gray, and perhaps by Hogg as well.

Gray's eulogy came out in three parts in Constable's *Edinburgh Magazine and Literary Miscellany*, a continuation of the *Scots Magazine* (January, February and March 1818). It reflects Hogg's Wilsonian view, at this point, of his own talent. Gray notes that Burns, whose friend he had been, was a poet of manners and of pathos. Hogg's line was fancy. He was a 'student of nature' who could mould every object into 'a thousand combinations that never existed but in his own mind'. The 'interesting valleys' of the Esk and Yarrow had helped to make him this fanciful poet. The *Mountain Bard* poems are 'never uninteresting'. Lack of interest is 'the mortal sin of poetry' (there's no thought that fancy can fail to be interesting). He grew to manhood in 'a state of servitude' and ignorance, but 'would have been a poet if no one had ever existed before him'. 'No writer, perhaps, ever blotted fewer lines.' But he 'could not write at all' when he arrived at manhood. Gray points out that Hogg began publishing when Scotland was swarming with poets of the lower orders, but 'no man so circumstanced ever composed poems of such merit.' Anguish is reported after his financial failure: he'd been suspected by some of having deserted his flocks. The *Spy* sometimes sank into grossness, wounding people with its descriptions of vice. *The Queen's Wake* is 'a triumph of genius over misconception'. A new edition is coming out – 'only one guinea'. Such was Gray's mid-term report on his friend, who is both natural and fanciful, who flies off peerlessly into 'regions of pure fancy' but never gets 'out of nature', and who, as his early history permits one to understand, is sometimes vulgar.

Gray, 'the old gentleman', has overrated his friend's work, 'Tickler' writes in March 1818. The stuff before the *Wake* was not 'any great shakes'. The letter presents Hogg as a comet and as a comic turn:

You, it seems, are 'the new animal' which the old gentleman singles out to lecture upon, – your inspiration is the gas which he is to analyse – you, James, are the rough diamond whose angles he proposes to describe with mathematical exactness. Really, I felt, during this solemn note of preparation, much as one feels in a drawing-room, when, the stupid servant having forgotten to announce the name, the door slowly moves on its hinges, and some splendid stranger is expected to appear; but when, to the pleased surprise of the assembled company, in bounces you yourself, the worthy and most ingenious Shepherd, rubbing your ungloved hands ('would that I were a glove on that hand!') as if you were washing them, with a good-humoured smile on your honest face enough to win every heart, and with a pair of top boots that would do honour to St Crispin himself, and by the associating principle of contrast, instantly recalling the shining imagery of Day and Martin's patent blacking.

Gray's account 'brings your name into connection, not only with Scott, Byron and Campbell, but (*mirabile dictu*) (get Mr Gray to explain that), places the name of Hogg (*O sus quando te aspiciam!*) along with that of Shakespeare!!' The *O sus*, mentioned earlier, might suggest an interpolation by the Germanist Lockhart: *sus* alludes to the German word for sweet, as well as being the Latin for pig. Throughout the 'Noctes' there's an amorous turn towards Hogg, with his 'buck-like teeth and lips of red': 'Give the Shepherd to my arms,' commands Maga. Here also, in the 'Tickler' epistle, are the intimacy and spite of colleagues. A tavern 'not altogether unfrequented' by Hogg crops up, as does a Scots word Hogg liked – 'oxter' for armpit.[22]

All his friends, Hogg told Blackwood in October 1819, 'think that the editors have dealt cavalierly with me in "The Tent" verses', put into Hogg's mouth. 'I might pretend to be angry – I could easily do that – but the truth is I am not.' 'What a hound of me these Magazine rascals are making,' he wrote, however, to John Aitken, a year later. He proposed, in Chaldeespeak, 'being at Wilson's opening lectures with a dozen men with plaids about them and great staves in their hands' – to drive off enemies, presumably. But his cavalier friends had shown him that theirs was a rough love. 'I begin to feel a cold side to a work which holds such an avowed one to me.'[23] The coldness that set in was to last for two years.

At this point in his *Life of Scott* Lockhart made a pig of him, in telling of an Abbotsford hare-coursing.[24] A small black pig, which had formed 'a most sentimental attachment to Scott', is seen frisking at the heel of the hunt, and bringing a blush to his master's cheek. 'Poor piggy soon found a strap round its neck, and was dragged into the background.' Scott repeats an old pastoral song, 'What will I do gin my hoggie die?' This little pig, and the song, and, perhaps, the hints of subjection and a pathetic death, cause Lockhart to refer in a footnote to the Ettrick Shepherd, while explaining that, in Scots, a hog is an unshorn sheep. The chase was followed, on a pony, by the aged and precarious 'Man of Feeling', Henry Mackenzie, and his black servant. Lockhart tells, not long afterwards, how, after a bumper of mountain dew, the mountain bard bet that 'he would leap over his wall-eyed pony' and broke his nose in this 'experiment of "o'er-vaulting ambition" '.

A similar association of ideas occurred, in 1828, in Scott's *Journal*.[25] Scott had received the picture of a dog accidentally shot by its master: 'It was a very fine thing. I askd the Duke about poor Hogg.'

A profusion of animal analogies poured from the magazine in August 1821. The 'Familiar Epistle to Christopher North: From an Old Friend with a New Face', whose dispossessions of Hogg were looked at earlier, has been attributed to Wilson; it also has a hint of the special venom and irritated class-consciousness of the mobile Maginn. The writer is concerned with the first version of Hogg's memoir, prefacing the third edition of *The Mountain Bard*, which Hogg had riled Blackwood by handing to Oliver and Boyd. The memoir suggests 'the image of an unclean thing', which has made the writer forswear pork. 'Pray, who wishes to know anything about his life? Who, indeed, cares a single farthing whether he be at this blessed moment dead or alive?' Gray's pieces are recalled. Hogg could not write, says Gray, till he was upwards of twenty-three years of age. 'This I deny. He cannot write now.'

'Jamie has no ideas.' His life has been 'one continued bungle'. He is 'the greatest boar on earth'. He has these 'large, grey, unmeaning eyes'. Hogg's effect on the decorum of Edinburgh's bookshops is that of a bull in a china shop, or worse. 'Only picture to yourself a stout country lout, with a bushel of hair on his shoulders that had not been raked for months, enveloped in a coarse plaid impregnated with tobacco, with a prodigious mouthful of immeasurable tusks, and a dialect that set all conjecture at defiance, lumbering suddenly in upon the elegant retirement of Mr Miller's back-shop, or the dim seclusion of Mr John Ogle.' There are also allusions to a 'large surly brown bear' and a 'huge baboon'.

The writer imparts that Hogg did not write the Wordsworth parodies. Byron did. Nor did Hogg write 'The Chaldee Manuscript'. The murderer of Begbie did that. A North note is appended, saying that Hogg may have written the epistle himself in order to raise 'a cool few hundreds' on the third edition of his poems.

Not long before this, Hogg's crowning glory had been examined in Lockhart's *Peter's Letters* – as that of a thriving farmer in his picturesque sports jacket, and of a favourite of the ladies who played the fiddle well for all his horny fingers.

His very hair has a coarse stringiness about it, which proves beyond dispute its utter ignorance of all the arts of the friseur; and hangs in playful whips and cords about his ears, in a style of the most perfect innocence imaginable. His mouth, which, when he smiles, nearly cuts the totality of his face in twain, is an object that would make the Chevalier Ruspini die with indignation; for his teeth have been allowed to grow where they listed, and as they listed ...

But at least his eye is not unmeaning: it illuminates his features 'with the genuine lightnings of genius'. Maginn, too, spoke up for it, in his 'Memoir of Morgan Odoherty':[26]

> When fancy kindles in the eye,
> The good grey eye of Hogg.

North and the Shepherd box in the 'Noctes', where violent tricks are played on one crony by another, and where a source of interest is Wilson's way of dramatising his fraught relations with Hogg. In the fullness of time, the Shepherd told Hogg's truth, or some of it, to North, with Wilson, of course, writing it all down. Shepherd: 'You're jealous o' me, sir ... and you wish that I was dead.' North: 'Pardon me, James, I merely wish that you had never been born.'[27]

The early stages of the drama of his involvement with these men are caught in a momentous post-marital letter of Hogg's to Scott from Altrive, dated 3 October 1821:[28] 'Like every other vassal whose situation with his chief is perfectly understood though never once mentioned, I always sit wisely still unless either called out by you to some great weapon show or when I find marauders and freebooters encroaching on my own privileges ... I allude to the beastly usage of me by Blackwood and some beggarly new cronies of his.' He'd had

> a written promise, 19 months back, that 'my name should never be mentioned without my consent.' But you see how I am again misrepresented to the world. I am neither a drunkard nor an idiot nor a monster of nature – Nor am I so imbecile as never to have written a word of grammar in my life. I would not mind their vulgar injurious ribaldry so much on my own account but there are other feelings now that I am bound to regard above my own where the wounds inflicted by such assassins rankle with so keen a smart that I am unable to allay them ... I must do something for I am told there never was a man as ill used in Britain and truly I do not think there ever was. The most despicable thing of all in Blackwood is his having frankly promised me a little pecuniary assistance if I needed it and he thinks I dare not move for fear of losing this.

He says that 'for the late obnoxious article' – the assassination of August 1821 – he asked no satisfaction but the name and address of the correspondent. It is striking that he did not then know them. The letter adds that measles had kept him from seeing Scott and Laidlaw in the course of the past week. Scott replied by advising calm. No need for a duel. To take such a piece seriously would be like fighting a shadow.

On 4 September Hogg had written to Blackwood asking for the name and address, and on 17 October he wrote to him again to argue over sums of money, to deny that he was a swindler, and to vow that he would never forgive whoever it was that had written the piece. He did seem to have some idea, saying that he deserved to have had a 'frank avowal of the friend's name who in his rash and thoughtless manner wrote it'. Wilson – known and trusted for some while – appears to be meant, rather than the newcomer to Edinburgh, Maginn, with his 'Irish fudge'.

Blackwood replied by saying: 'You are so utterly ignorant of business that it is quite unnecessary for me to show you how completely you have misunderstood everything.'[29]

No doubt, as has been suggested, he was glad of the publicity brought by the Maga mentions. But there's no mistaking the earnestness and anguish of the letter to Scott of 3 October, which was followed by a confession of bewilderment: 'I am grown to have no confidence whatever in my own taste or discernment in what is to be well or ill taken by the world or individuals. Indeed it appears that were I to make my calculations by inverse proportion I would be oftener right than I am.'[30] It was as if one thing was as good as another.

This admission of a shaken confidence comes to mind when he is found, two years later, changing his tune, once more, about his chums.[31] The publisher is informed, with reference to Wilson, that 'he's my own dear John and you may tell him so and that I admire him more than I ever did. You may assure him that

I like my Jacky's grey breeks
For a' the ill he's done me yet.'

Here again is the erotic shepherd, in the part of the melting female who can't help loving that man of hers.

In the autumn of 1818 an anonymous pamphlet, 'Hypocrisy Unveiled, and Calumny Detected', attacked the paper for its scurrilous attacks. Lockhart and Maginn went, respectively, for two pioneering scientists and Whig professors, John Playfair and John Leslie, each the author of an *Elements of Geometry*. Lockhart and Wilson were made nervous by the pamphlet and by the prospect of duels and law suits. Leslie did indeed sue, and was awarded a farthing's damages. Playfair died in 1819. While warning Blackwood that he would divorce himself from the paper if such personalities persisted, Scott informed Lockhart, not yet his son-in-law: 'I did not approve of the personal and severe attack on Playfair though extremely well written.' He remarked of the pamphleteer that 'men of inferior literary consideration endeavour to distinguish themselves in an alleged vindication of others when in fact they only seek to gratify their own envy and malignity or to enhance their no-importance.' The pamphlet also reproved Wilson for making fun of Hogg, who told

Constable that he was glad to be away in the country, and able to avoid having his 'simple snout' thrust into the quarrel, and told Blackwood that it was 'absurd' of the paper to praise the free-thinking Madame de Staël and attack Playfair for religious infidelity. The following year, Keats wrote of the 'scandalous heresy' of the Blackwood Reviewers, who have been 'putting up Hogg, the Ettrick Shepherd, against Burns: the senseless villains'.[32]

Scotch reviewers had begun to review each other even unto death. For several years the kingdom had witnessed a vogue for duels, for 'satisfaction' on the field of honour. Politicians and journalists joined in. Manliness and gentle birth obliged. The inaugural occasion in a series of Northern encounters was referred to by Hogg as the 'Douglas Cause' – a play on the name of the previous century's most celebrated law suit, over the succession to the Douglas estates of Archibald, Lord Douglas, who was to marry Louisa Stuart's friend Frances Scott, a Buccleuch connection. Hogg's Douglas was the editor of the *Glasgow Chronicle*, revoltingly insulted in *Blackwood's* as the Glasgow Gander. On the morning of 11 May 1818, according to the *Glasgow Chronicle*, the Gander, John Douglas, 'horsewhipped' Blackwood, opposite the publisher's Princes Street shop. Later that day, as Douglas was boarding the Glasgow coach, Blackwood showed up, 'armed with a bludgeon, and apparently somewhat intoxicated, accompanied by a man having the appearance of a shop porter' – or, as Hogg's calumniator James Browne was to put it, by 'a trembling dastard' in 'the capacity of a gillie'. This man was, as Blackwood put it, his 'much respected friend Mr Hogg'. Blackwood spoke of inflicting blows with a hazel sapling, with Hogg stepping in to prevent interference. 'Now, you cowardly scoundrel, you have got what will make you remember me,' Blackwood remembered saying. Hogg wrote to the *Chronicle* about its editor: 'I can tell this same *gentleman* that I am a frequent and welcome guest in companies where he would not be admitted as a waiter.'[33]

The damage done by the two principal dastards varies according to which dastard tells the tale, just as Blackwood's weapon varied from wand to bludgeon. His lip may have been bloodied by Douglas's whip, and his writers made a meal of the beating handed out to 'the grim Douglas', in Scott's expression. On 23 May, a hot Saturday afternoon,

Douglas came out of the West once more, accompanied by two friends. Having turned from second to principal in the affair, Hogg was to be challenged to a duel by this ogre from a fairy-tale.

Scott passed the news to Duke Charles:

> Our poor friend Hogg has had an *affair of honour* a something tending that way which is too whimsical to suppress & yet I am vexd at it while I cannot help laughing for the soul of me ... Two mornings ago about seven in the morning my servant announced while I was shaving in my dressing room that Mr Hogg wishd earnestly to speak with me. He was usherd in & I cannot describe the half startled half humourous air with which he said scratching his head most vehemently 'Odd Scott here's twae fo'k's come frae Glasgow to provoke *mey* to fight a duel' – 'A duel' answerd I in great astonishment 'And what do you intend to do?' 'Odd I lockd them up in my room & sent the lassie for twa o' the police & just gied the men ower to their charge – and I thought I wad come & ask you what I should do wi' Douglas for he's at the Turf coffee house.'

Scott assumed that Hogg meant to decline the challenge, and advised him to go off to the Sheriff Court and press a charge, which he was said to have bungled. He then, Scott writes, 'took the wings of the morning and fled to his cottage at Altrive not deeming himself altogether safe in the streets of Edinburgh. Now although I do not hold valour to be an essential article in the composition of a man like Hogg yet I heartily wish he could have prevaild on himself to swagger a little.'

Hogg was not cut out, apparently, to be brave (in meeting a challenge which was rather more Blackwood's business than his). Scott was to report to the Duke that Hogg did not darken the streets of Edinburgh till the end of the year. In December Scott reported that 'the jacobite songs it is thought by his friends may balance the argument of his running away' before the grim Douglas. Running away is what the Whigs did at Prestonpans: Scott felt that Hogg was not knight enough to fight, but should have done better than he did. The affair led to a newspaper war in the city, while John Murray was addressed by a pamphleteer as 'the London publisher of a horsewhipped bookseller in Edinburgh'. Murray was presently to sever his connection with the magazine.[34]

The Douglas episode was the farcical prelude to a series of tragic events. Libels, duels, concealed authorship, and other stealths, were aspects of a time of political high tension, not least in North Britain, a time of radical uprisings, enraging to Walter Scott, and of pressure for an enlarged franchise, enraging to Scott and enlivening to Cockburn. This was a politicised Scotland, an awakened Scotland, with the lies and scandals to show for it, and the good causes and rearguard actions to show for it.

The people had arisen, or were about to arise, Cockburn believed. The Pantheon meeting of December 1820 was seen by him as a challenge by the respectable to entrenched Tory rule ('my coat was said to be the worst there'). Some weeks later two rival feasts and boastings were convened: Pittites versus Foxites. The Pittites were 'almost all born gentlemen', said Scott, who was present at their feast, where Hogg sang songs; the town's Whigs were, save for a few friends of Scott's, 'sad scamps', born gentlemen included. (The townees and tourists who pestered Hogg at Altrive, where he would portray himself as conversing only with the elements, were, he told Blackwood, what 'you Edinburgh people would call great skemps'.) Enemies claimed that Boswell's son Alexander behaved obscenely at the Pittite feast, an annual occasion. Cockburn claimed that even his friend Scott made a slightly smutty joke. A Polish visitor, Krystyn Lach-Szyrma, recorded that Scott took the chair – in due order, the Marquis of Huntly vacating – and called on Hogg for a song. Hogg dried at the fourth or fifth verse, and Scott helped him out, as on other occasions: 'The Ettrick Shepherd, our esteemed friend, is unaccustomed to sing to someone else's lute, he has his own!' The visitor said of Hogg that *The Queen's Wake* 'is romantic to the highest degree, as are all of his other works'.[35]

Ephemeral Tory papers sprang up to do their bit in the war of personalities. The *Beacon* began in January 1821, and after it came the *Sentinel*, with the same covert backing, which included Law Officers of the Crown. Scott was a bondsman and secret backer of the *Beacon*, but Lockhart works hard in his biography to dissociate him from the contents of the journal. He states that he never even saw it. But he does appear to have read it.[36] And he was threatened with involvement in a duel because of it. James Stuart of Dunearn, having been insulted in the

Sentinel, caned the printer in the street, and refused, on class grounds, to accept his challenge to a duel. Alexander Boswell, having published some anonymous verse which impugned Stuart's, his relative's, manhood, was killed, in 1822, in a duel with Stuart at Auchtertool in Fife, hours after an outstandingly convivial meal with Scott and Lockhart at Castle Street. Scott was saddened by this death: he liked sprightly and comical people, like John Ballantyne, Adam Ferguson, James Hogg.

Just before this, a comparable disaster had befallen an enemy. A Lockhart lookalike, with the same surname as Scott, a dark, handsome, Hispano-Celtic Regency beau, was slain on Lockhart's behalf, by Lockhart's lawyer, as the result of a proxy arrangement hardly compatible with the code of honour professed by duellists. A year before the birth of *Blackwood's*, Hogg had written incoherently to this man, John Scott, a Scottish journalist and editor who had taken his talents to London, as Lockhart was to do: 'The truth is that you are the only editor of newspapers whom I love in Britain for though I am myself rather a violent tory why I never know but you are the only independent one that I ever met with.'[37]

John Scott published, in his *London Magazine*, denunciations of *Blackwood's* in which Keats and the Cockneys were defended and the journal's treatment of Hogg was decried. Hogg was their Zany, said John Scott. In January 1821, Lockhart told his lawyer and friend Jonathan Christie that Hogg's 'chief pride, and the very breath of his nostrils, are such jokes as this knave makes such a pother about' – and it is certainly true that Hogg's truth did not inhibit jokes. Nevertheless, the denunciations came far too close for comfort. Walter Scott was blamed in the *London Magazine* for 'the excessive zeal of his late endeavours' to secure a professorship for Wilson. The Edinburgh magazine was 'a spectacle of outrage, hypocrisy and fraud'. 'Long impunity, or at least insufficient exposure', had 'converted what was at first but a system of provocation into a downright system of terror'. Lockhart and Wilson were poisoners-in-jest. Two men 'whose habits of life are notoriously free' and whose 'real opinions are known to be loose and sceptical' had started a magazine in which 'the most licentious personal abuse was to be the lure for one class of readers, and the veriest hypocritical whine, on matters of religion and politics, the bait for another.'[38] Spoken like an editor.

Misled by the magazine's cloud of aliases, and by Wilson's recent accession to his professorial chair, John Scott had treated Lockhart as editor of the magazine, and he now called on him to disclose himself as such. Lockhart was 'the Emperor of the Mohawks', a name for the magazine's scalping braves, its cutters-up, with their tortures and their hoaxes and masquerades, and with Hogg, one might add, their darling Cherokee and Zany. Walter Scott, 'the unprofaned', as Lockhart called him at this point, was embroiled in the quarrel, in the role of godfather to the *Blackwood's* gang. Coleridge also made an appearance. Lockhart told Blackwood: 'Coleridge is evidently mad and unintelligible, but I venture to say you will never repent giving him sixteen pages a month.' He had also written Coleridge a letter identifying himself as the editor of the paper: would this letter be produced? Professor Leslie, moreover, had named Lockhart as editor in the libel action he had brought against the journal in Edinburgh. John Scott called Lockhart a coward. De Quincey burned for vengeance on Scott, this impudent hypocrite. Walter Scott seems to have assumed that his son-in-law would have to fight a duel, and spoke despisingly of his opponent, no true Scott but 'some mongrel from about Aberdeen', while privately cognisant that certain of his objections to *Blackwood's* were justified. Lockhart was advised to 'post' – publicly insult – his opponent in order to get him to issue a challenge. So Lockhart pronounced him 'a liar and a scoundrel'.[39]

At one point he stated in London that 'he was in no sense of the word editor or conductor' of the journal: he had never had 'any emolument whatever from any management of it'. It seems clear that management was what Blackwood did, while also, though not single-handedly, editing his journal; Lockhart had been essential to its editorial team and been paid for his contributions. Blackwood made use of an alibi which has long been familiar in journalism, among owners and managers: 'The Editor took his own way, and I cannot interfere with him.'[40]

Lockhart's wife faced a taxing first pregnancy. He was in a plight. The passage of disavowal was not sent to John Scott, perhaps by an oversight, though it was later made public, and the affair became ever darker, and ever more Ambrosian. Charles Lamb, a contributor to the *London Magazine*, remarked that their rivals were such a nest of impostors that James Hogg might have come down to London to impersonate Lockhart 'and take pot luck – or shot luck – for his friend'.[41] That would indeed have been in the style of *Blackwood's Magazine*.

John Scott took the field. But Lockhart did not. He had gone back to Edinburgh to be with his wife, and his second, a friend from Oxford days, Jonathan Christie, may be said to have impersonated him. If the preliminaries to the duel, the sleights, claims and counter-claims, the displays of punctilio and patrician disdain, are confusing, so was the duel itself. It was fought at a customary spot, Chalk Farm in London, on 16 February 1821, on a foggy winter's evening – ideal for marksmanship. The Chalk Farm Tavern was employed as a field ambulance station. It was here, in 1806, that the police had frustrated an attempt by Francis Jeffrey – 'no owl more wise, no lark more aerial', in Cockburn's encomium[42] – to confront the no less aerial Tom Moore, whose odes he had reviewed. They lived to become old friends.

Christie fired his first shot in the air. Their seconds intervened, fussed, encouraged, said later that they had misunderstood each other. Christie's second shot struck his adversary in the stomach, and he went to reassure him: 'I would rather that I was in your situation and that you were in mine.' The wounded man wished all of them to 'bear in remembrance that every thing has been fair and honourable.' Walter Scott, who had described John Scott as 'absolute dunghill', said, on learning of his death: 'So much for being slow to take the field.' He was 'that dangerous animal a coward made desperate'.[43]

Duels were for gentlemen, Walter Scott and others felt, and it's possible to feel that for some literary men they were a passage to the higher respectability. Walter Scott pressed Lockhart to restrain his satirical contributions to the journal, 'the Mother of Mischief', and by the time Lockhart went to edit the *Quarterly* in London would point to his son-in-law's 'very slight connection' with *Blackwood's*. Christie retired to France after his opponent's death, and was declared not guilty at a trial on his return.

'Poor Scott,' sighed the painter Haydon as he took his last look at the coffin. John Scott was a bold and a good journalist and his death was mourned. Charles Lamb subscribed for his widow and children and Wordsworth very nearly did. Poor Keats, sighed Maginn to Blackwood in April of that year: 'I have just this moment heard of poor Keats's death. We are unlucky in our butts.' Poor Maginn. But 'if the threatened life of Scott comes forth, then indeed, if anything impertinent appears we may draw the sword again.'[44]

In the April number of the magazine a Homeric-dactylic berserker salute to Christopher North has 'Gruff-looking Z is there, wet with the blood of the Cockneys.' Z was a pseudonym of Lockhart's. Falchion-wielding North, 'Star of Edina', sits on his hilltop throne 'in thine own most romantic of cities', spreading 'jollity all through the nations'. Arthur has been thrust from his seat by Christopher.

More blood was shed in the August number of that year, 1821, which contained the blackguarding of Hogg's memoir. It was this article which moved the magazine's printer, James Ballantyne, to a remonstrance which deserved to be seen – at a time when respect for hereditary nobility fought fiercely with the thought that a man was a man, whatever his rank – as an action truly noble. The history of journalism can hardly supply many letters as creditable as this, to Blackwood:

> Do you really mean to insert that most clever but most indecently scurrilous attack upon Hogg? For my own part, I do not stand up for Hogg's conduct; but such language as is applied to him appears to me absolutely unwarrantable, and *in your Magazine* peculiarly and shockingly offensive.
>
> You will do as you think best certainly; but I must at once say that if it goes in I must withdraw, in all subsequent numbers, from the concern. How much I shall regret this on many accounts I need not say; but I cannot allow such an article to appear with even my implied approbation attached to it. It is hard, you may think, that an editor should be fettered by his printer; but I cannot help this. The printer must not be made to encounter what he considers to be disgrace.

Blackwood replied that there were to be alterations to the article, but that 'I cannot submit to be told what *I must not insert* in the Magazine.' Mrs Oliphant, in her history of the firm, sympathises with Blackwood here. James Ballantyne's diplomatic reply is termed an 'ill-judged attempt to have the last word' which brought down a 'thunderbolt' on his head.[45]

This was the year of his brother John's death. The brothers were known to Scott, their Kelso friend of early days, by the pet names he gave them, lifted from an eighteenth-century stage burlesque: Rigdumfunnidos (for 'Jocund Johnny') and Aldoborontiphoscophornio (for solemn James). They were implicated in Scott's crash, but they served him loyally and affectionately, and James may be regarded as the chief editor of the Waverley Novels. His long intimacy with Scott survived the crash, but was impaired by a late-developing religious zeal and by his support for the Reform Bill, by the belief of Scotland's favourite Scotsman that most Scots were unfit to vote.

John Ballantyne, publisher and auctioneer, was quizzed in the Ur-'Noctes' of the early *Blackwood's* numbers, but is also identified there as 'the most entertaining of all human beings'. He was among the imitators of the time, like Vattermare and the actor Charles Mathews, and like Walter Scott and James Hogg, both of them noted mimics.

By John's graveside Scott whispered to Lockhart, 'I feel as if there would be less sunshine for me from this day forth,' and he told his son Walter that he had taken 'a great loss in poor John Ballantyne'.[46] Lockhart bent himself to the task, in his *Life of Scott*, of blaming the Ballantynes, together with Constable and rather more than Scott himself, for the losses he was presently to take in the financial market. The account of poor John's raffish and other effronteries has a Gallic brilliance well suited to his Parisian hankerings. It is a prime example of Lockhart's scorpion gift for personalities. John Ballantyne's insecure gains were invested in the construction, hard by the Firth of Forth, of an overweening villa named by 'the little man' Harmony Hall. It is made to look like a brothel:[47]

His house was surrounded by gardens so contrived as to seem of considerable extent, having many a shady tuft, trellised alley, and mysterious alcove, interspersed among their bright parterres. It was a fairy-like labyrinth, and there was no want of pretty Armidas, such as they might be, to glide half-seen among its mazes. The sitting-rooms opened upon gay and perfumed conservatories, and John's professional excursions to Paris and Brussels in quest of objects of *virtu*, had supplied both the temptation and the means to set forth the interior in a fashion that might have satisfied the most fastidious *petite maîtresse* of Norwood or St Denis. John too was a married man; he had, however, erected for himself a private wing, the accesses to which, whether from the main building or the bosquet, were so narrow that it was physically impossible for the handsome and portly lady who bore his name to force her person through any one of them.

In 1837, the portly lady, whose marriage to this husband of the tight squeeze had known its passages of arms, wrote to the *Kelso Mail* from the Border town of Jedburgh (where Scott's carriage had been stoned by a mob of Reformers) to say that Lockhart's biography had calumniated John Ballantyne. Another vigorous remonstrance.[48] Hermione Ballantyne knew from bitter experience that John had been extravagant:

> But Mr Lockhart, in the extreme altitude of authorship, has only condescended to make vague or general remarks on the subject of my poor husband's extravagance: he should have told us that, at the christening of his (Lockhart's) eldest child, my husband actually purchased and presented him with Golden Spoons!! So flagrant, so glaring an instance of my husband being occasionally in the habit of throwing away his money, should by no means have been omitted; and this anecdote, being strictly *true*, might have amused Mr Lockhart's readers better than many others which are false and defamatory. In the hideously ugly, hopping, wry-faced, squeaking, croaking, 'scarecrow' portrait, given of my husband, by Mr Lockhart, neither I nor any unprejudiced person can perceive the most remote resemblance.

Is Lockhart suggesting that the Ballantynes robbed Sir Walter Scott? Hermione asks. What Lockhart mainly meant was that they were inept businessmen, that they were Scott's entanglement in commerce, and that 'Leein' Johnny', a nickname he was careful to repeat, was only imperfectly a gentleman.

CHAPTER TWELVE

Marriage

Hogg got married in 1820, and so did Lockhart. In the sense espoused by Edward Waverley when he settles down after the hurly-burly of the Forty-Five, the romance of Hogg's life was ended. The previous year, he had told his future wife about his children, and had worried: 'I am not yet convinced of the prudence of our marriage, considering my years and the uncertain state in which I hang as it were between poverty and riches.' For several years before that he had been on the look-out for a bride, conducting tender friendships with middle-class Edinburgh women – such as the bluestocking poet Janet ('Adeline') Stuart, whose work ('The Druid') he published in the *Spy*, and to whom he wrote a blue *billet doux* about 'knowing Miss Stuart!!' – and sounding out John Murray in the hope of an English heiress who might be interested in an Ettrick shepherd. In 1818, a smiling Scott wrote to Duke Charles – as if to Duke Theseus in *A Midsummer Night's Dream* – with the latest rumours about Hogg: 'Pray tell Lady Isabella it is thought Mr Hogg intends to propose (having faild in the affair of Miss Kitty Hert Redding) for one of the *rich* Miss Scotts – first however he is to try one of the rich Miss Brodies of Inverleithen.' Is Scott suggesting that his own Miss Scotts – no brides there for the shepherd – were poor?

At about this time Hogg wrote to Blackwood, from the house made by his own hand, to decline a trip to Edinburgh: 'Can I leave my fine house, my greyhounds, my curling-stones, my silver punch-bowl and mug, my country friends, my leister and my sweetheart, to come and plunge into general dissipation?' The sweetheart paired here with his leister or salmon spear may have been a composite, a manner of speaking.[1]

Two years after Scott's news bulletin, Hogg succeeded in marrying. In December 1819 he told Blackwood: 'I believe I could get Miss Phillips and I believe also that she is much too good for me and that is all I know about the matter.' A poem in the paper for January 1820, by the pseudonymous Wastle (Lockhart presumably, who has him in *Peter's Letters*), had expressed foreboding, or affected to do so:

> I fear the change will spoil a world of sport,
> Half-banishing the Bard from our Divan.

Scott's advice to Hogg not to choose 'a *very* religious' wife went, in the end, unheeded. Margaret Phillips, whom Hogg had known for ten years, was a pious woman from a prosperous Nithsdale farming family whose Mouswald Place made him feel ill-at-ease. Her mother was an invalid with lineage, and she was the sister of James Gray's first wife. She besought Hogg not to ask too many friends to the wedding, and Maginn gave out that Hogg's 'better half' had induced him to purge his tales of indelicacies. Early in the marriage she enquired of her husband, whose writings advise against anger: 'Why do you lose your temper so much?'[2] She was a loyal and supportive wife, who loathed the 'Noctes' Shepherd and didn't want his utterance in the house. There were spells when she felt that she'd forgotten what money looked like. But the lady who had come to the horn spoons, hardship and overcrowding of Altrive did well there.

'I am going into Dumfriesshire, and of course return to the forest a Benedick,' said the seasoned bachelor.[3] Shakespeare's plays were often in his head, and the title of another of these may have occurred to him at this point. All's well that ends well, he must have hoped. The wedding took place on 28 April, the day before Lockhart's. Lockhart would have been responsible for the 'Extracts from Mr Wastle's Diary' which appeared in the magazine in June, where the marriage is discussed and regret is expressed that the writer's friend Peter Morris, the narrator of *Peter's Letters*, had to leave Scotland before this 'interesting ceremony' took place. The marriage was conducted at the house of the bride's father, and the couple repaired to Ettrick the following day in a procession of four gigs, one of them, relayed the diary, 'filled by the two Messrs Brydon', Hogg's neighbours. 'In the fourth sat the Shepherd's faithful black servant, in a new suit of the Hogg livery.' The livery may be a *Blackwood's* quiz; Hogg's great-granddaughter, Norah Parr, vouches for the existence of the servant. The party dined at Altrive cottage.

Another ceremony, a solemn 'kirking', was held at Yarrow church, with the minister, Robert Russell it would appear, speaking to the text: 'Blessed is the man whom thou honourest and causeth to approach unto thee.' Absent from Nithsdale, he received from Hogg the present of a hat. Wastle says that the bride has been accounted amiable, prudent and intelligent. Mention is made of 'the silent but sure progress' of Hogg's fame, and of 'the late enormous puffing' of the Northamptonshire peasant, John Clare.

In the previous number of the paper Hogg had received the wedding present of a largely effusive review of the two volumes of his *Winter Evening Tales*. These adventures, 'not a few' of which 'we have heard him tell in nearly the same words', were 'commonly narrated', on such occasions, 'as having befallen no less a person than the Ettrick Shepherd himself'. Here is a way of life 'entirely inaccessible to any author moving in a higher order of society'. The tales show 'an occasional coarseness – we had almost said grossness'. Now and then he betrays 'what we shall at once call, vulgarity'.

Margaret was of a higher order of society. It was recalled in the family that Hogg rarely visited her old home, and it may be that, initially at least, he felt unworthy. He had told her, when the marriage was hanging in the balance, that if he thought she was being influenced against him, 'I am off in a moment,' and that he had previously declined a fortune in another quarter. Norah Parr is judicious about the threat posed by the journal to the domestic life of the Hogg family amid the hardships, and happy home, of their convivial fastness: 'These men liked James, but they *used* him, up to the limit of what he would stand, and sometimes they misjudged the limit.'[4]

The Altrive house had begun as a clay bigging. He added stone and made extensions, 'at his own expense'. But it was still a tight ship – like a pair of ship's cabins, indeed. Stowed there, family apart, were two maids and two male hands; a niece and old father; in three rooms plus closets and outbuildings.[5] Hogg was also to build a barn, and a school, at nearby Mount Benger. A few weeks before his wedding, William Laidlaw wrote to Scott to say that if the new young Duke of Buccleuch did not think of supplementing his nominal rent with an allowance, then the district might lose him. Since Duke Charles's death, the Buccleuch factors had been

Altrive (engraving credited to Octavius Hill and W. Richardson)

prejudiced against Hogg, according to his friend. 'One of them said to me, when I mentioned Hogg's genius and amiable character, *Cui bono?* I, too, say, *Cui bono?* What is the use of all his poetry, and the rest?'[6]

In October Hogg reported his father very ill and his house 'full of our friends'. His father was 'posting on I fear to his long home', and he died on the 22nd. On the 25th he spoke of 'the hound of me' the magazine was making. The house was presently to accommodate new guests, with Hogg moving to Mount Benger. His father-in-law had gone bankrupt, and Hogg now had to support the man on whose backing he had been expecting to rely. Phillips had lost five thousand pounds 'by the failure of one of his sons'. To the doctor who saw to the delivery of Hogg's first child, the following year, he said that he found 'the ready run so low with me that I cannot send you what you so well merit but which I will remit in a few weeks. Mrs Hogg does not know else she would be very angry.' The doctor recorded: 'Frae Hogg ye can get nought but grumph.'[7] There is a joke here, where no one would look for one. 'Grumphy' was a Scots word for pig.

His letters home are those of an attentive parent. His only son, James, born in March 1821, went to India as an accountant in a bank, lost his health, then moved on to Australia, and returned to live as a maternal relative's legatee in his country of origin. Four daughters were born: Jessie, Margaret, Harriet, and Mary, who wrote as Mary Garden about her parents. Harriet, called after Hogg's patron, suffered from a damaged foot. 'How is my poor Harriet,' he was to ask his wife, 'and what are they doing with her? I can hardly think of my darling being put into steel boots like the ancient Covenanters.'[8] His thoughtful brother William became a sheep farmer. Two brothers emigrated to America; their offspring settled at Mount Ettrick, near Binghampton, New York. His brother Robert, also a shepherd, became the Abbotsford butcher. A nephew, another Robert Hogg, William's son, died at thirty-two. He was a writer and a Classical scholar who chose not to be a minister. He helped his uncle with the second series of the *Jacobite Relics*, and went over his work with an eye, enlisted by Blackwood, for breaches of taste. He was said to have been 'invaluable to Lockhart in London in 1826', writes Norah Parr, and he took dictation from Scott, who 'conversed with me as if I had been on a level of perfect equality with himself'.[9]

In May 1821, James Hogg diversified by seeking and receiving a nine-year lease of Mount Benger farm from Lord Montagu, uncle and guardian to the fifth Duke of Buccleuch. This was a time of agricultural depression, and the farm had brought down two farmers over the previous six years. But Hogg went ahead and took on the responsibility – both pastoral and arable – for Mount Benger, which stood on the rising ground above the cross-roads where the Gordon Arms still stands, beside the road north to Traquair and Innerleithen. He took possession in May, but remained in residence at Altrive for the time being. In June 1824 he moved into 'my old thatched house of Mount Benger', while Mr and Mrs Phillips continued, in low spirits, to occupy 'my elegant cottage' of Altrive.

The dowry of £1000 which Hogg had anticipated at his marriage had fallen through. His memoir calculates that he had the same amount due from his various publishers – Murray, Blackwood, Oliver and Boyd, Longman – and says that he obtained this and devoted it to stocking his new farm: but it wasn't enough for the necessary 'one thousand sheep, twenty cows, five horses, farming utensils of all sorts, crop, manure, and, moreover, draining, fencing and building'. He 'got into difficulties at the very first, out of which I could never redeem myself till the end of the lease'.[10]

Lockhart reckoned that the arable part of the business – where Hogg was least experienced – was 'sadly mismanaged'. Scott was sure that the large and dear property of Mount Benger, where Hogg was engaged in ploughing the tops of hills in order to grow corn, would be his ruin. From this point on, Scott's own financial misfortunes would keep pace with his friend's.

In July 1821, he suggested that Hogg attend him at the Coronation of George IV in London; a post or pension might come of it. Hogg excused himself by saying that as an agriculturalist he ought to be present at the St Boswell's Border Fair. Scott was pleased by the refusal. 'The fair carried it,' he said. He imagined his man 'up', as it then was, in London, equipped with plaid, kent (crook) and collie, and lionised by bluestockings. He was thinking that Hogg, who had applied to him for a loan, might be assisted by the newly-formed Royal Literary Fund. Its panjandrums were not to Scott's taste, but they might help. They were to include a later acquaintance of Hogg's, the journalist William Jerdan. Pensions of a hundred guineas were to be paid to a small company of Royal Associates. Lockhart wrote Hogg a kindly letter holding out hope.[11]

In October he approached John Grieve for money, and an old Border farmer and his wife were to be quoted as remarking: 'when he took

Mount Benger he wrote to his generous friend Mr Grieve, of Ettrick, and desired him to send him £350 to stock the farm, which Mr Grieve refused, because he knew that the scheme was a ruinous one; on which he wrote *him* a very abusive letter, and would not speak to him for years.' Hogg's enemy James Browne was later to publish a letter from Grieve to the publisher Goldie, written on 4 September 1823, in which he said that he did not wish to be an informer against his friend, but that Hogg had acted towards himself 'in a most selfish and ungrateful way'. He complained of his 'contemptible vanity'. This had caused him to try, in print, to rob Goldie of his good name, 'which, to a commercial man, is every thing'. On 26 September Hogg made overtures to Grieve for a reconciliation: 'I find that once one has taken the pet it is not easy to get over it with any grace.'[12]

The husband and father had plunged into difficult times. Shortage of money was compounded by his impersonation and comedification, and indeed commodification, in the magazine, which intensified with the debut, in 1822, of his 'Noctes' eidolon. 'Terrible' letters were dispatched to the metropolis of Edinburgh, to his bibliopole Blackwood, with his wits about him, in more ways than one. The correspondence of the 1820s between Hogg and Blackwood, which has been presented with great diligence by Alan Strout, gives access to the domestic repercussions for Hogg of his dealings with the metropolitan wits. There is more to be said about these repercussions.

In the August after his marriage the two men were cordial enough with one another. Blackwood wants to know if 'your Romance', *The Three Perils of Man*, has been abandoned. 'My Romance has been stationary,' replies Hogg. It was said of him that he was never backward in coming forward, and in October he was quite forward with Blackwood: 'The Yarrow Library has given up the Edin. Review in utter disgust' – perhaps because of Jeffrey's review of the *Jacobite Relics* – 'and the members have ordered me as Secry to testify this to Constable in the strongest terms and pay up the arrears.' Would Blackwood 'be so kind as to send over some clerk or other' to help with the accounting? At this point Oliver and Boyd wrote to tell him that the *Winter Evening Tales* – thought by Byron to be 'rough, but racy, and welcome' – were 'nearly all sold off'.[13]

Late in October 1820 there was a clash over Hogg's award of the new edition of *The Mountain Bard* to Oliver and Boyd. How could Blackwood say that he'd never raised the project with him: 'I pressed till I was ashamed.' The letter refers to the epistolary attack on Jeffrey which had appeared in the magazine: 'My letter seems to me exceedingly strong but too much of the braggadocio in it.' This boastful disowning of a boast implies that the letter was by someone else. Three days later he writes to John Aitken about the treatment he is receiving from the 'Magazine rascals' who are making a hound of him: 'What strange fellows they are.' Two days after that he tells Blackwood, with kind remembrances from Mrs Hogg, that the latest number of the magazine is by far the best that has appeared and will give it 'a tremendous lift far beyond the Chaldee'. He claims that 'the unconscionable Christopher' has so far been inflating its circulation figures ('somewhere below 17,000'), and commends his nephew Robert's handwriting, 'as plain as any print'.[14]

Blackwood then assured him that he had 'always felt as your friend and brother, and never as a mere bookseller'. 'If you are really my friend,' rejoined Hogg on 20 November, with reference to a disparagement of his book, 'will you not allow me this, that if Oliver and Boyd sell more of "The Mountain Bard" "that exploded work the publication of which will do me more ill now than all the good I can reap from the trivial profits" I say if they sell more of it in one year than you and your London friends shall do of "The Queen's Wake" in seven, will you not allow that I do right in letting them have such editions as suit their sale?' He finds it 'confoundedly hard that I should be made a tennis-ball between contending parties'.

> I am almost ruing the day that I ever saw you. I have had letters, newspapers and magazines poured in upon me from every part of the country. The country is full of impatience. No one has any right to publish aught in my name without consulting me.

'Impatience' misreads Hogg's 'impertinence'. After that, a piece of optimism: 'This is a time of much anxiety to me and will be for a fortnight.'

In June of the following year, 1821, he growls at Blackwood: 'What signifies snapping at me in your letters as you were going to take me by the nose?' Very soon the magazine was to take him by the throat with its trashing of his memoir.

On 26 June he applied in desperation to Scott, 'my pattern and master in literature', for a loan of £200, explaining that his new book, presumably *The Three Perils of Man*, had been turned down by 'my Bookseller', Blackwood, on the grounds that it would invite invidious comparison with the romances of the author of Waverley. 'You warned me of the risk I run ere you asked the farm for me, but I am not to blame.' His father-in-law had urged him on with the stocking of Mount Benger but had then been unable to support him because of his son's failure. Strout believes that 'the summer of 1821 marks the climax of his life.' From a financial point of view. From a literary point of view, the climax had yet to come, and would show courage and resilience on Hogg's feckless part.

'What is Lockhart doing? When Wilson and he are quiet the world appears to me to stand still.' Hogg had become an asker of questions, and this one says a good deal about what had been happening to him. It was put to Scott on 8 July, on the eve of his departure for George IV's Coronation. What Lockhart was about to do was to write encouragingly to Hogg about the Royal Society of Literature, to report that 'Wilson is quite mad with idleness and champagne ever since his lectures were done,' and to make light of the pamphlet by the publisher Goldie in which Hogg's memoir account of his dealings with him was accused of being mendacious. Blackwood is 'in great feather but how he gets on with his magazine God in heaven knows. He won't tell me the name of the author of a single paper now-a-days.' He himself hasn't written a line there for eight or ten months, or so he chooses to say. The derision of Hogg's memoir in the magazine is only a month away.

The fatal entrance of Maginn, at this point, into the lives of the Edinburgh 'callans' or lads is described in the letter. Wilson 'has got his man who wrote against Leslie living under his roof these some days past. He is the queerest devil you ever saw, drinks like a fish – & tells stories worthy of Sir Dan Donelly. Buonaparte's death has not made half such a noise as Johnny Ballantyne's.' The queer fish Maginn made a noise in Edinburgh for two years, before leaving for London. He heaped humiliation on Hogg, and may also have liked him. 'Hogg every inch a man, full of fun and feeling, without the heaviness of Scott,' he said many years later.[15] 'In his simplicity consisted his excellence. Had he attempted anything great, he would have made himself ridiculous. What he did say never failed to be entertaining.'

In early August Lockhart paid a visit to his 'affectionate friend' at Altrive. On the 19th Hogg wrote to Blackwood about an agent or accountant by the name of Craig, 'a most honourable and disinterested man', but 'stubborn' too. 'I cannot help thinking with Mr Craig that you have made a great deal of unnecessary fuss about this bill of £50.' There seems for ever to have been a bill of £50 to trouble Hogg's head. The next day he wrote to say that Craig had informed him that 'he does not understand your business and mine and he declines further correspondence' on the subject. Hogg's business with Blackwood is certainly hard to understand. The first of these two letters asks Blackwood to 'recollect that I have a written promise from you most absolutely given that my name should never once be mentioned nor alluded to in your work without my own consent.'[16] This was not a promise that was kept, and it could not have been more violently broken than it was in the August number of the paper, with its attack on the memoir.

On 4 September he wrote his bitterly angry letter to Blackwood demanding to know the name and address of his attacker. 'Well sir,' he writes,

> you have now put the crown on all the injurious abuse that I have suffered from you for these three years and a half, and that in despite of your word of honour which no miserable pretext can justify. If I have ever done aught to you or your correspondents to deserve this it was unintentional. For my own part I would have regarded this wanton attack as I did all the rest of the ribaldry and mockery that has been so liberally vomited forth on me from your shop, but there are other feelings now beside my own that I am bound to respect ... If you really had it in your power to have repressed this piece of beastly depravity and did not do it I must consider you as worse than the worst assassin out of hell.[17]

Wilson was later to note that it could be disagreeable to have children and servants reading attacks on one in the morning papers.

Soon after this, on 3 October, ill in bed with measles, he made his appeal to Scott, with its disclaimers of drunkenness, imbecility and illiteracy. This was a protest as strong, in its different way, as the one to Blackwood. On the same day, however, he wrote to Grieve equivocating over the attack, and once again citing the letters of sympathy he'd been getting: 'There is surely something in it worse than I can see for it appears to me to be a joke an even down quiz without much ill meaning but written in a beastly stile.' He mentions that he'd been sent by Robert Cadell an invitation to support 'old Maggy' – Constable's *Edinburgh Magazine*, a continuation of the *Scots Magazine*. Cadell was promising 'equal if not better pay than Blackwood and an assurance of better treatment. He says after establishing their Mag (by the Chaldee I suppose) they have done all in their power to ruin me.' So 'there is an old door re-opened for me should another shut.' But that other door remained open. Mrs Hogg wrote to Blackwood to say that she had nothing to do with literary disputes, and that she grieved for 'all misunderstandings between old friends'.[18] This may have helped to make the uneasy peace that broke out. Once more there could be jollifications. Songs could be sung, trout taken. The Ambrosian Gaudeamus was resumed.

He should never have leased Mount Benger. Should he have quit *Blackwood's*? He had thrown in his lot with his 'madcap Tories', with the romantic Right of Scotland, which was also, at moments, the divine right of kings. There were misgivings and contrarieties, and he wasn't even sure that he knew why he was a violent Tory. But he had a living to make. And *Blackwood's* had become a very good place for a writer to be. Its sage-green cover sported the head of the republican Renaissance sage, George Buchanan, after whom Christopher North named his 'Noctes'-harbouring lodge by the Firth of Forth at Granton. Perhaps there was a suitable dissonance here? Blackwood's wits were both for and against the people, while preferring them to live in country cottages.

Those who used to stress that Hogg was a trial to Blackwood would have done well to compare his case with that of John Galt. Hogg was not alone in experiencing Blackwood as a trial. The ill-starred, faintly sinister and uncanny Galt was backed by Blackwood, and bullied by him. They fell out for a season, more than once. Having produced some of the best novels ever to come from the firm, or from Scotland, he was allowed to stagnate for lengthy periods in poverty and potboiling; he became, twice, one of the many insolvents of the time. Blackwood interfered dogmatically with his work, demanding big plots and romantic diversion, and marring, in particular, Volume III of *The Entail*. He was charged with indelicacy, and the Shepherd was set on, in the 'Noctes', to call him (and by implication himself) 'unco coorse'. Coarse, and at times low. 'People in the humble condition of Mr Galt,' wrote Wilson when Galt's recollections of Byron were published, 'are not, by the rules of society, permitted to approach nobility but in a deferential attitude' – for all Galt's 'extraordinary powers'. Galt joined Scott both in bankruptcy and in receipt of a concocted deathbed piety. A minister had observed him silent when the serious subjects of religion were raised during his last days: then, when Galt was speechless and paralysed, he managed to hear him 'confess himself a lost and hopeless sinner'. Authoritarian religion, by then resurgent, was sometimes to move in mysterious ways, and in the shadows of Scottish life, its wonders to perform.

'It is a strange thing that you will let *men of true genius* slip through your fingers for a few blemishes that are rather properties in the main,' wrote Hogg to Blackwood in 1821, with Galt in mind, and a certain crucial similitude in mind. He had been moved by the 'simplicity and extraordinary resemblances to truth' discovered in *Annals of the Parish*.[19]

The distraught Hogg of these letters to Blackwood is occasionally visible among the faces shown by Hogg in Scott's correspondence and in his journal. The figure he cuts there does not greatly change, over the years. He is the Great Caledonian Boar whose grunts are numbered there, the desperate fellow who comes over the hill to knock on the door of Abbotsford, the good shepherd who fails to mind his flock and ploughs the tops of hills. He is a minstrel of the Scottish Border. He is *Ivanhoe's* Gurth the swineherd, with his matted hair and amber face, and Wamba, with his 'privileges as a fool'. These creatures appeared in the world during the last year of Hogg's bachelor state, together with the novel's Jews. And what a novel this has been, with its ambivalence towards a poor injured 'nation' in whom 'there was much, to say the least, mean and unamiable'. 'A race that had been the wonder of the world' – this further description of the Jews belongs to Hogg's intrigued response to Scott's novel: the jolting Brechtian 'Adventures of Captain Lochy', which inhabits a Europe-wide turmoil of slaughter and survival, and which has its greedy old Jew and lovely Jewess, who elopes with the goys. John Lochy is a mercenary who goes to war with Marlborough and sundry other commanders. He is 'the tennis-ball of fortune', as Hogg once saw himself. He takes up with a shape-changing, war-profiteering devotee, who may be the Devil: neither can live without the other.[20]

There is, perhaps, a deepest of all the mutualities affecting Scott and Hogg. Scott was moved to the quick by the exasperating shepherd. He loved Hogg, and helped him time and time again. And he *was* Hogg. Both harpers, minstrels, poets turned novelists. Both Borderers. Both suffered financial troubles which lasted until their respective deaths, only a few months apart. For some, they looked alike, like brothers. Low and improvident, Hogg was nevertheless to Scott what Laidlaw also was – bedrock. He was the Scottish peasantry raised to genius by the power of the imagination. He was Scotland. And so was Scott.

Hogg's songs are more palpably Scottish than are those many poems of his which were not meant to be sung. Walter Scott, who could suggest that he was not a fan of his own poetry, wrote less of it in his later years, while Hogg, whose *Poetical Works* were issued in four volumes by Constable in 1822, went on writing songs, ballads, occasional poems, farcical, satirical and discursive poems – some of which harked back to the pastorals of his apprenticeship – for the rest of his life.

Following on the efforts of Burns, Alexander Boswell and others, efforts were being made to recover the heritage of Scottish song. George Thomson's *Select Collection of Original Scottish Airs* began life in 1793, and in 1822 the same man's *Select Melodies of Scotland* appeared. From 1821 to 1824 R. A. Smith's *Scottish Minstrel* appeared. At this point Hogg was the owner of a Cremona violin worth £100, and at this point, too, Beethoven published his *Schottische Lieder*, with its settings of poems by Hogg: 'The Highland Watch' and 'Could this ill world have been contriv'd'.[21] 'O had they no been made sae bonnie', in the second of these, was translated as *So wunder süss und appetitlich. O sus!* Ambrosia's word for the toothsome Hogg. Beethoven's setting incorporates the Scots tune 'Mischievous Women'.

Female mischief also enters into a group of lyrics which came out as *A Border Garland* in 1819. This collection has his plaid poem 'I'll no wake wi' Annie', an 'uncanny' Annie, and his celebrated 'Skylark':

> Bird of the wilderness,
> Blithesome and cumberless,
> Sweet be thy matin o'er moorland and lea.

As if on cue came, in 1820, Shelley's ode 'To a Skylark': 'Hail to thee, blithe spirit.' Another very popular poem by Hogg, 'The Boy's Song' (1831), was still being learnt by heart in Scottish schools well on into the twentieth century:

> Where the pools are bright and deep,
> Where the gray trout lies asleep,
> Up the river and o'er the lea,
> That's the way for Billy and me.

I remember that last line being chanted with glee by a Midlothian uncle.

'When the kye comes hame', one of his gloaming love lyrics, occurs in his novel *The Three Perils of Man* ('comes' became 'come' eventually, though a tailor at a wedding objected to the change as affectedly grammatical). This is a version of pastoral which has a melodious truth to life.

> See yonder pawky shepherd, that lingers on the hill,
>   His ewes are in the fauld, and his lambs are lying still;
> Yet he downa gang to bed, for his heart is in a flame,
>   To meet his bonny lassie when the kye comes hame.

Requested and rejected by George Thomson, 'My love she's but a lassie yet' is a poem in which pubescence is threatened with neither outrage nor perpetual chastity. These two delightful poems are quite free from the kind of sentimentality that was to be deplored in the Kailyard poets and assigned to precursors earlier in the century. And 'Good night an' joy be wi' you a'' is a convivial poem which shares that freedom: 'We'll maybe meet again the morn' is what people might say to one another on such an occasion. This is Hogg's 'Auld Lang Syne'. The extravert or adrenalin performances include a piece of reiver rodomontade which looks like his challenge to Scott's metrical roar about Bonnie Dundee. Hogg's roar was another of his pieces with a long classroom life:

> Lock the door, Lariston, lion of Liddesdale,
> Lock the door, Lariston, Lowther comes on.

His martial songs are torn between the Highland contribution to the British Empire and the magic of the unfortunate Prince. 'Donald McDonald' celebrates the first, while the Jeffrey-deceiving 'Donald Macgillavry' is idiosyncratically Jacobitical. 'Come like the deevil, Donald Macgillavry,' beckons Hogg, who made it possible to find in Donald, with his Lowland job skills, a rebel of more than one kind:

> Donald's the callant that bruiks nae tangleness,
> Whigging an' prigging an' a' newfangleness;
> They maun be gane, he winna be baukit, man,
> He maun hae justice, or rarely he'll tak it, man.

Among the good poems which escaped or post-dated the corral of Constable's four volumes are his piece of 1830 about ageing and ailing, 'The Cutting o' my Hair ('the souplest knee at length will crack,' and the famous locks that once 'cost many a hizzie sair' no longer need much shearing), the retrospective winter poem 'The Monitors', which appeared in a 'Noctes' of 1831, 'The Great Muckle Village of Balmaquhapple', from a 'Noctes' of 1826, and 'St Mary of the Lows' of 1829, which portrays Ettrick's beauty and history. Bowmen, bandits, balladeers, Covenanters lie buried in its graveyard, and this critic of the soldiery pays tribute to battles long ago:

> Yes, many a chief of ancient days
>   Sleeps in thy cold and hallow'd soil,
> Hearts that would thread the forest maze
>   Alike for spousal or for spoil,
>   That wist not, ween'd not, to recoil
> Before the might of mortal foe,
>   But thirsted for the border-broil,
> The shout, the clang, the overthrow.

The poem about the Fife village of Balmaquhapple, 'steep'd in iniquity up to the thrapple', seems barely singable, but has its music, an adaptation of the song 'Soldier Laddie'. This is a village where Johnny the elder prays every hour: 'But aye at a hole where he watches the lasses'. A Jamie the elder was created a few years after the poem was published in 1826.

In the pastoral 'Ringan and May', published, with antique spellings, in 1825,[22] then modernised for incorporation in *A Queer Book*, May struggles to withstand her swain, and the lubricious song of a lark. The poem has been linked with Robert Henryson's courtship poem, 'Robin and Makene', the sardonic account of a pastoral rebuff; and Hogg has been linked with the contemporary revival of interest in Medieval Scottish verse. He perceived a 'notable bard', with a measure of responsibility for the Border ballads, in the 'Ettrick' poet mourned in Dunbar's 'Lament for the Makars'.

CHAPTER THIRTEEN

Castle Cannibal

Having declined to attend the Coronation of George IV, in favour of St Boswell's Fair, Hogg could scarcely have failed the feast arranged and inspired by Sir Walter Scott to greet the arrival of the monarch in Edinburgh, a venturing north which was never repeated. Lockhart's *Life of Scott* offers a lingering but forthright account of the royal visit of 1822, for which Hogg wrote a masque, for which he was never paid. The September *Blackwood's* ran extracts from the masque, or 'Royal Jubilee', and supplied an ironic commentary. This work is like one of Hogg's *Dramatic Tales*. It has a Queen of the Fairies, the Genius of the Gael, of the Ocean, of the West, of Holyrood, Covenanters' ghosts (Third Ghost: 'I'm ready to lay down my life'). It suggests that the 'honours of the Gael' may be renewed with the coming of King George.

The masque was preceded, in the August number, by a loyal welcome which breathes a demented monarchism – as does the masque, conveyed Wilson and company: 'He is evidently slightly insane through the whole poem, as in duty bound on such an occasion; for it would have been most monstrous and unnatural for a pastoral poet from Ettrick Forest to have kept his wits when writing a Scottish Masque, *on the spot*, to celebrate the King's visit to the metropolis of his native land.' Hogg had been glimpsed at the festivities, 'his mind in the highest heaven of invention'. 'His keen grey eyes met ours.' When he saw the King, 'we verily thought he would have leapt off the platform into the coach.' Then he vanished, 'like one of his own fairies'.

'With all respect and admiration for the noble and generous qualities which our countrymen of the Highland clans have so often exhibited, it was difficult to forget that they had always constituted a small, and almost always an unimportant part of the Scottish population; and when one reflected how miserably their numbers had of late years been reduced in consequence of the selfish and hard-hearted policy of their landlords, it almost seemed as if there was a cruel mockery in giving so much prominence to their pretensions.' Scarcely very son-in-law of Lockhart to say this, and to say it so well, about Scott's Ossianic orchestration of these ceremonies. The monarch was placed in Royal Stuart tartan for his first levee, and was taken aback to be followed about by a plump knight in unearned Stuart regalia, with a dirk in his garter: George was 'grievously shaken by this heroical *doppel-ganger*'. 'Towering and blazing among and above the genuine Glengarries, MacLeods and MacGregors,' writes Lockhart, 'this portentous apparition cast an air of ridicule and caricature over the whole of Sir Walter's Celtified pageantry.'

The poet George Crabbe was there, known to the *Blackwood's* crew as 'the Old Driveller', and to Scott, who valued his poetry, as a 'sly hound'. Crabbe's pensive face was trained on the Highland chiefs, creatures from another world: 'I thought it an honour that Glengarry even took notice of me.' Glengarry impressed Scott and Hogg too. This Highland hero, however, was among the villains of the Clearances. A modern historian, Rosalind Mitchison, writes: 'The Macdonnells of Glengarry treated their tenants with systematic unkindness and the glen is empty today.'[1]

Earlier that year, in March, following on the 'Tent' trial runs, the 'Noctes Ambrosianae' began in *Blackwood's*. The Editor, Christopher North, is glad to see Odoherty. North won't write any more that night. 'Ebony may jaw as he pleases.' If there isn't enough for the number, 'let him send his devil into the Balaam-box' – where some of Hogg's contributions would later lie. The first appearance in the series of the Hogg eidolon, or persona, was in December of that year.

The full-blown 'Noctes' form was devised by Lockhart and Maginn, and the self-proclaimed *splendida vitia* of Maga's corps of writers were soon displayed there. Hogg's eidolon evolved. In the early numbers he was buffoonish, far less of the romantic genius than he later became, and some distance from the centre of the stage. In the December 'Noctes' Odoherty/Maginn refers to his 'gaucy' – plump, jolly – 'under-quarter, which, by the way, I wish he would give over scratching'. He came into his own when Wilson came into his own, having assumed, as Maginn sourly noted, 'the office of *Noctes Ambrosianist* to Blackwood's Magazine'.[2] But the persona was arresting from the first, and the 'Noctes' of December 1822 contained one of his most memorable sayings: 'Ae thing's just as good as anither. It's nae matter what ane pits in a book; my warst things aye sell best, I think. I'm resolved, I'll try and write some awfu' ill thing this winter.'

Before long, his best thing, the *Confessions*, would be published, and sell poorly. In the March 'Noctes', earlier in 1822, Odoherty is told by North that 'your life would sell as well as Hogg's, or Haggart's.' The malefactor Haggart was to be a recurrent concern of the Ambrosians, and his ghosted confessions may have been, as I argued some years ago,[3] a source for Hogg's. In the same 'Noctes', 'the Editor' nods at Hogg's 'new romance', *The Three Perils of Man*, splitting it up in familiar style: 'I dare say 'twill be like all his things – a mixture of the admirable, the execrable and the tolerable.'

A year after the start of the series, in June 1823, the Shepherd, in this case 'Hogg', utters the important 'Noctes' double meaning, having been called surly for complaining that he is always being brought into their havers. He replies: 'It's no decent to be aye meddling wi' folks' personalities. I'm sure by this time the whole set o' you might ha' mair sense. Ye ken what ye hae gotten by your personalities.' Mockery and insult are allied here with multiple personality and with concealed and collusive authorship.

'Personality' is a word which appeared to be gaining a new sense. It could now mean the power and magnetism of individual idiosyncrasy. It was on its way to meaning 'star'. Hogg embodied concerns of his time while also bestriding his time, as an extraordinary individual, a sometimes unreliable and scandalous individual, a genius, whose looks were a part of that genius. This is to suggest once more that the age of personality was an age of physiognomy, as the many descriptions of him attest, and as the inspired portraiture, the *verum corpus*, of the comedy of Dickens and Carlyle also attests. The middle-aged Hogg was described as tall, hale and broad-chested (his chest a little less broad than Sir Walter's, though). His hair, worn long with a ribbon at the back when he was young, was now 'auburn, slightly tinged with a peculiar yellow – that yellow sometimes seen in the border of the rainbow'. These are the words of a fellow Border shepherd-poet, Henry Scott Riddell, who knew a rainbow when he saw one, and who reported him full of humour and of mimicry (good at Highlanders). His 'simplicity' and 'single-heartedness' made him hard to understand. Another observer, Charles Rogers, thought him 'entirely unselfish and thoroughly benevolent'. His face, marked by illness, had 'the peculiarity of a straight cheekbone'.[4] Hogg could be thought both singular and plural, aefauld and manifold. He was himself, while also like the performers and multiples Vattermare and Charles Mathews, who could be just like other people.

Hale, happy, hectic, poet, peasant, debtor, rising bourgeois notable, storyteller, fiddler, singer, credited with a warm heart and sparkling eye, 'the best lungs in Yarrow' but with 'nearly as little voice as ever man had'[5] – this, and more, was Hogg. He was a personality, and an aggregation of dualities. Among these was the contrast between the jolly fellow and the anxious and precarious one betrayed by his acquisition of Mount Benger, with its twenty-two acres of turnips and four of potatoes, betrayed by his landed desires, modest as these were. There was a period name for such longings – 'yird hunger', or land hunger. Scott admitted to such longings at this time, making use of the expression (quaintly glossed in Lockhart's *Life* with reference to Jamieson's Dictionary, which claimed it could mean 'that keen desire of food which is sometimes manifested by persons before death', a presage of the gaping grave). The condition to which Hogg's counterpart landed desires had brought him is reflected in a note of Scott's to James Ballantyne in October 1822: 'I fancy you must renew poor Hoggs bill for him. I suppose I shall have to pay it at last – but will not if I can help it having given him enough.'[6]

In February 1822, Hogg wrote to Constable about a 'very queer paper' which Maga, *Blackwood's*, 'will hardly dare publish'. This seems to be an allusion to 'John Paterson's Mare', a satire on Edinburgh's magazine wars which also figures, in the epistolary record, as 'No 1 of my Hints to Reviewers'.[7] Constable's *Edinburgh Magazine* ('Maggy', as opposed to Maga) turned the material down 'on the score of sheer terror', according to Hogg. A letter of his refers to the 'Mare', in the April of that year, in proposing to Blackwood that 'either of two friends whom you know by going over it could make glorious sport out of it.' This is the conspiratorial language of his earlier letter to him on the subject (15 July 1818), in which, having been 'quizzed too much by you chaps', he is 'writing for another magazine, with all my birr, and intend having most excellent sport with it, as the editors will not understand what one sentence of my celebrated allegories mean till they bring the whole terror of Edinburgh aristocracy on them.'

Sport is linked to terror on these occasions, and to plots. By 'celebrated allegories' he seems to mean the Chaldee style of Biblical parody, which brought terror on his sportive head, and the 'Mare' is allegorical too, in that dangerous sense, but not Chaldee-Biblical. It went on being revised and proposed (as 'No 1 of an allegorical history of our miscellaneous literature', which would stand next to the 'Chaldee Manuscript' in popularity), and was refused by Blackwood for a thousand reasons: his journal was now 'too serious a concern to be trifled with', was now 'quite above attacks and malignities'; Constable was ill and not to be dealt with in this fashion; and they'd had too much of Jeffrey in the paper anyway. The 'Mare' found a nest in the *Newcastle Magazine* of January 1825, where Hogg's 'True Art of Reviewing' also appeared, two years later.

The *Newcastle* began in 1820. Hogg was admired there, and it was held there that the 'Noctes' quizzing had been the bane of his life. The editor, Robert Story, was a poet (his *Border Ballads* was dedicated to Hogg), and a journalist of Ambrosian flair who invented a brother for Timothy Tickler. The 'Mare' translates the Pringle and Cleghorn *Blackwood's* ouster to a world of farms, mills, stables and horse-races, with the Ballantynes, made one, figuring as Sleek Cobby. The Mare is the *Edinburgh Review*, a blood horse, a racer, compared with Constable's other nag, the old *Scots Magazine*. Jeffrey's alias is jovial Beau Nardi, given to freaks and fancies, and, as is Sleek Cobby, to girls, a hater of all pretensions to greatness. The Lakers are sandpipers or water larks harassed by Beau Nardi. Tom Moore is Tickle Tommy, the singer of 'very unsuitable songs to an immense number of rosy unthinking damsels'. William Hazlitt shows a leg. Douglas the Glasgow Gander steps up. Pringle throws in his lot with Constable. The piece has a barely injurious bucolic spite: 'Mephibosheth, the jew, came over to Bishop Paterson and his friends, assembled in a hayloft, in order to procure some sly arrangement with his opponent.' But it's sharp enough to sense the importance to the *Edinburgh Review* of the economist Francis Horner, alias Frank the Tinker.

In 1822, wrote Hogg in his serial memoir, 'perceiving that I was likely to run short of money, I began and finished in the course of a few months, "The Three Perils of Man, viz. War, Women and Witchcraft".' It was followed by his *Three Perils of Woman*; both novels were published by Longman, in London. That summer, Wilson said of the first to Blackwood: 'I could write a page or two rather funny on Hogg's Romance, but will not, if Mr L is doing it or to do it. Though averse to being cut up myself, I like to abuse my friends. But this I would do with good-humour.'[8] The romance was cut up by various journalistic hands, when it appeared; it is headlong and slapdash; it isn't hard to believe that it was written for money (like *Rasselas*). But a rehabilitation has recently been undertaken, in the defensible conviction that the work, so far from being some crazy attempt at a Waverley novel, is a parody of the historical romance of Scott's invention. This forms part of post-modernism's answer to the question asked by the 'Noctes' Shepherd in January 1827: 'May na a man of genius write a byuck that's no verra gude? Read ye ever a romance ca'd the Three Perils o' Man?' A moment before, he has explained: 'I can thole a hantle o' nonsense.' So can post-modernism. And yet it's fair to say that, while the literary criticism of Hogg's work is bound to register an incidence of failure, post-modernism's post-critical readings have brought an enhanced appreciation of the carnival Hogg.

Hogg, who told Murray in 1815 that 'there is nothing I am so afraid of as teazing or pestering my superiors for favours,' told Blackwood in 1821 that he thought he could 'prevail on Sir Walter to go over it in proof'. The novel's giant warrior, Sir Ringan Redhough, a Warden of the Borders, was originally called Sir Walter Scott of Rankleburn, which drew a protest from the contemporary Sir Walter Scott, when Hogg apprehensively consulted him in November 1821 about this untoward account of the Buccleuchs. Was there no danger, Scott enquired, in making this ancestor the hero of so wild a tale? 'The devil a bit,' Hogg remembered answering back. The present chief, Scott reminded him, was Hogg's patron, friend and admirer. Caught among Scotts, Hogg struggled to free himself. He pointed out that the man is supposed to be a hero. 'Do you not think you have made him a rather too selfish character?' 'Oo ay but ye ken they were a' a little gi'en that gate else how could they hae gotten haud o' a' the South o' Scotland nae body kens how.' Scott laughed at this sound reply, at this 'all a bit like that', and said with lifted eyebrows: 'Well Hogg you appear to me just now like a man dancing upon a rope or wire at a great height. If he is successful and finishes his dance in safety he has accomplished no great matter but if he makes a slip he gets a devil of a fall.' The exchange ended in tears of gratitude, and a rechristening for the reiver.[9]

Both sets of *Perils* have been read in recent times as subversive, carnivalesque. Neither is always as beguiling as it is carnival-looking. But they both lay persuasive claim to the originality he prized. *The Three Perils of Man* has baffled even its admirers. But it has more of structure than meets the eye – a structure mediated, as elsewhere in Hogg's fiction, by means of verbal chains or concatenations. It may even be an allegory on the banks of the Tweed. And it contains some of his best stories.[10]

It also contains some of his favourite subjects: chastity, carnality, carnage and carnivorousness. Here once more is the Cannibal King of Scottish literature. It's a medieval extravaganza, interested in personality and animality, division and transformation, in war, diplomacy and disguise, and in the siege of Roxburgh Castle, held by the English and invested by the Scots, with Sir Ringan seeking reiver's advantage in relation to each of the two sides. Princess Margaret of Scotland and Lady Jane Howard of England are present as promised brides for the victorious. An embassy led by the knight Charlie Scott of Yardbire heads off for advice to Sir Michael Scott's wizard's castle of Aikwood, near the spot where Hogg's forebears had served as feudal retainers. The assorted persons of the embassy made an appearance earlier in this book. They are a friar who approximates to the philosopher Roger Bacon, reputed inventor of gunpowder, Gibby Jordan, Laird of Peatstacknowe, the Deil's Tam (alias Marion's Jock), the maid Delany, and a poet by the name of Carol who is enamoured of her. At Aikwood, this company, which has begun to go hungry, is made to enlist in a storytelling competition whereby the loser, the teller of the worst tale, is to be flayed and eaten. Men turn into beasts; and Charlie obtains from Michael Scott a hint which enables him to capture Roxburgh Castle by disguising himself and his troops as cattle. Making a beast of me – Hogg's treatment by his grand friends may be audible in the Aikwood saturnalia.

Aikwood (engraving credited to Octavius Hill and W. Richardson)

Passages of the novel read like a pre-run of the film *Braveheart*, or like a Scottish rugby international, whose Border stars, with the ancient names of Laidlaw and Chisholm, have turned into moss-troopers. Much of it is written in superlatives. But it is less barbaric and bombastic than it is a form of burlesque, with lots of comic cuts of the broadsword. It 'diverts' its readers with the 'feats' of 'predatory' barons, while also pulling the carpet from under them. The thirteenth-century philosopher Michael Scott, an enemy of magic, is translated here into a fairy-tale master of the black arts who is not all bad, and finally ready to confront the Devil. Each of the characters suffers a magical self-duplication at his hands, and even more radical metamorphoses ensue. One of the characters, Gibby, is consumed at a barmecidal feast: 'The dinner was made up of me. I supplied every dish, and then was forced to cook them all afterward.' In the 'darkening haze' of an infinite complexity and division 'two of each of the three friends' are 'so completely alike that no one knew who was who'. An infinite imitation, a universal plagiarism, has broken out. 'All spoke of themselves as the right and proper persons, and of the others as beings in their likenesses, and the most complete uncertainty prevailed.' The 'two Gibbies then both began to tell stories, which each claimed as originally his, so that the perplexity still increased'. Meanwhile Hogg has Michael Scott prophesy a 'puissant' future for the Scotts, who were always likely to escape the larder. Lockhart thought that the real hero of the novel is its stubborn mule, but the real hero is Charlie Scott, and his horse.[11] It seems that Charlie may have been meant as a version of Wat of Harden.

The two castles in the novel have something in common: the beleaguered English in Roxburgh Castle are rumoured to be feeding on each other, while in starving Aikwood self-duplication is allied to mutual consumption, rather as it was around the table at Ambrose's. In a chapter epigraph from an alleged old Bacchanalian song Hogg can be found to feast on himself: 'Pork's the king o' a' the table!' The doubling that occurs encompasses the ordinarily aefauld Charlie, who remonstrates with Master Michael Scott, divider and diviner: 'I solemnly protest against being parted into twa.' But then he smiles his broad smile: 'if you will assure me that baith o' us shall be as stout and as wight chaps as I am mysel e'en now, gude faith, I dinna care though ye mak me into twa, for my master the warden's sake. If you could double an army that gate, it wad be a great matter. I doubt sair I'll cast out wi' my tither half about something that I ken o', and that's Corby' – his beloved horse. Charlie's relation to his wizard is not remote from Hogg's to the Wizard of the North, whose castle of Abbotsford was not remote from Aikwood, which in turn was just down the glen from Altrive.

This doubling is among the spells cast by Michael Scott in rivalry with Roger Bacon, a show which also has him splitting the nearby Eildon Hills in three. Bacon, whose name alludes to the favourite food of Marion's Jock, responds with a gunpowder plot. Their respective masters are compared for might and majesty. Scott's master hardly bears naming. Bacon's master is very great: 'Who can be greater than he who builded the stories of heaven, and laid the foundations of this earth below, who lighted up the sun, sending him abroad in brightness and in glory, and placed the moon and the stars in the firmament on high?' This anticipates by a matter of months the sinner's speech in the *Confessions*: 'Hath he not builded his stories in the heavens...'[12]

It has been suggested that Michael Scott's is a traditional magic which Hogg prefers to Bacon's modern, more technological variety. But then all magic has an element of technology, and Hogg is at pains to make clear that since Michael Scott arrived from the colleges, 'the nature of demonology in the forest glades was altogether changed.' Necromancy has supplanted the old, more human magic, characterised here as 'sports and amorous revels in the retiring dells by the light of the moon', the tuneful mermaid and moping kelpie, the fleeting wraith, the stalking ghost who 'perambulated the walks of him that was lately living, or took up his nightly stand over the bones of the unhouseholded or murdered dead'. In those days, the Ettrick spirits in question, 'the aboriginal inhabitants of the country', were hostile to men, but men could deal with them, and defend themselves against them, with the holy help of God.[13] You knew where you were. Now no one knew where they were and who was who. A definition of modernity.

Hogg was attached to Michael Scott, and took pleasure in the authorial magic inventions he devised for him. The 'Warlock o' Aikwood', who preceded the Wizard of the North, holed up in nearby Abbotsford, is the hero of an affectionate aerodynamic ballad of that name, almost certainly by Hogg, which was published, in 1949, in a study of Scottish witchcraft by Thomas Davidson, *Rowan Tree and Red Thread*. Michael sits sadly in the gloaming by the stream at Aikwood, and is then commanded by the King of Scotland to deliver a packet to the King of France. Having cast spells, he bounds to Paris in no time on a black horse. Courtiers obstruct him. To prove that he and his mount are better than they seem, he has the horse stamp his foot and cause the city to implode. Gunboat diplomacy.

> The muckle bell in Notre Dame
>   Play'd jow, and burst in twain.
> And lofty tow'rs and pinnacles
>   Came tumbling down amain.

Horse and rider return to Scotland:

> And as they pass'd o'er Dover straits
> The horse to speak began,
> A pawky beast, and, as he pleas'd,
> Was horse, or deil, or man.

Michael's centaur mount, the dualistic talking horse Diabolus, lewdly enquires what old wives do when they go to bed at night. He retorts that they kneel and pray, to a power mightier than the Devil. The ambassador is himself a centaur, and a double agent, both divinely and devilishly-inclined. Back so soon, he waits on the startled Scottish king at Holyrood, carrying a packet, his errand or embassy accomplished: as with a good deal of diplomacy, its point does not emerge. 'The Warlock o' Aikwood' turns to comic effect the swift motions of the traditional ballad, and could be thought to reflect – if we suppose that Hogg may have known about them – the peregrinations and international consequence of the historical Michael Scott.

The tales told in the competition for the Michael Scott Aikwood Award are a mixed bag. They are largely tangential to the other business of the book, to its projection of a dark view of the romance of chivalry and war. But the two best are of great appeal. The story told by Gibby Jordan of Marion's Jock and his devoured ewe and murdered master, and of his escape, has already been discussed. Charlie Scott hails it as a fine thing. But the poet bewails this feeding on the lamb's 'lovely form', this eating her flesh and drinking her blood, and Michael Scott develops that response to the tale with a psycho-symbolic reading of a kind that would one day make the fortune of many a literary critic: 'The maid Delany is the favourite lamb, whom he' – the teller – 'wishes you to kill and feast on in the same delicious manner as did the hero of his tale; and I am the goodman whom you are to stick afterwards, and fairly make your escape.'[14]

Hogg picks up presently on the word 'stick', when Charlie, interrupted in mid-story, remarks: 'I maun get on wi' my tale; for if I stick it in the middle, ye ken it is a' ower wi' me' – an expression which appealed to the Hogg who was apt to get stuck. Later in the series of narratives there's one from Tam Craik, the Deil's Tam, a picaresque account of hunger and of a knife-wielding delinquency, which is prefaced with a confession: 'I am neither less nor mair a man than just Marion's Jock o' the Dod-Shiel, that sliced the fat bacon, ate the pet lamb, and killed the auld miser, Goodman Niddery.'[15]

The story of Tam's further exploits, after his escape from Niddery's farm, is capped by Charlie's account of his first reiving expedition over the Border, an account in which the local tale of Auld Wat of Harden's abduction and accidental drowning of an English child can be discovered. Hogg the countryman, the killer of birds and beasts, is also discernible in the story, to a degree that might lead one to forget that, so far as human beings were concerned, he was not a violent man, and could even be laughed at by gentlemen as a cowardly one. The cruelty of the old Border warfare is stated with some chauvinism, but with unusual candour. A strain of sentiment is also apparent. The man of feeling is not absent from the slaughter.

Charlie is the Ettrick Shepherd gone to Heaven, the ideal incarnation of an aspect of his author. He is easygoing, pawky, shrewd, simple, not angry, but a fierce fighter, with his long sword and dear horse. This is his first big fight. His father has lost to the wars all his men save Charlie, the callant, and auld Will Nichol. Off they go to serve their chief, and cousin, the Warden Sir Ringan, whose army is outnumbered six to one by Sir Richard Neville's. These are odds that inflame Charlie's father, Yardbire, who tells the Warden that 'art may do muckle' to overcome the disparity. Redhough remarks on the piquancy of listening to someone 'speaking sagely about art that never thought of ony other art in his life but hard hand nevel' – fist-fighting. They join battle. Charlie excels, but his father is killed, not at all surprisingly. Later,[16] a party plunges down into England to get their own back on Neville's undefended family, in their castle of Ravensworth.

Aweel, aff Habby and I set; he wi' his Elliots, and me wi' my hard-headed Olivers, my grimy Potts, my skrae-shankit Laidlaws, and auld Will Nichol, – that was my army, and a gay queer ane it was: I hadna a man o' my ain name but mysel; for the warden kept them a' about him: He wadna part wi' the Scotts at no rate. It was clear moonlight, sae we set off before sun-set and rade a' the night, keeping aye the height between Tyne and Reid; and at daylight we fand oursels at the place where the twa Tynes meet.

The skrae-shankit, or heron-legged, Laidlaws, good fighters, are famous in the novel for their delphic speech, for not letting on. Habby, though, is famously forthcoming. Hogg picks up the word 'stick' once more, to tell how Habby saw a passing Englishman and 'chappit aff his head – he wasna very sticking that way.' Not very backward.

Charlie is forward enough to burn and loot the castle. But he saves Lady Neville's infant boy. By throwing him out of a window.

> When he saw me, he held out baith his hands, and cried 'O daddy, daddy!' I could nae think tae leave him to be burnt, sae I rowed him in some blankets and tossed him out at the window; and when I lookit out after him to see if he wasna killed, I heard him crying louder than ever, 'Daddy's boy fa'en! Take ye up, take ye up! O daddy, daddy! Take ye up, take ye up!'

Will Laidlaw of Craik rescues the child from a man who is eager to chap aff his head ('I saw what kind o' chap he was that Oliver,' says Charlie the word-player), and wraps him in a blanket.

Charlie and Will carry the child back to Scotland. It is as if Jamie Hogg and the real Will Laidlaw are doing it. They are driving the richest prey of cattle that Charlie had ever seen lifted. 'We gae the banks o' the Teme and the Blackburn an unco singe afore we left them. I was rather against the burning, but Habby wadna be stayed. "Na, na; tit for tat, Charlie. That will stand for Hawick and Abbotrule."' Lady Neville's ghost visits the fighters as they lie on the moor, to plead for the safety of her child. They lose touch with the child in a skirmish, get him back, then lose him again to a convent and a titled witch. But he turns up at the end of the novel. He is the poet we know already. The story peters out. But it's an extraordinary description of what fighting can be like, and of what it can do to a man whom the writer loves, and whom he enables the reader to care about. There is a likeness to Hogg (rather than Wat), but no repellent sense of narcissism, in the portrait of Charlie Scott.

The Three Perils of Woman is a romance of a different colour. The novel was spoken of as imminent in the 'Noctes' of March 1823 (its predecessor went unreviewed in *Blackwood's*, as the Shepherd complains on this occasion). In the 'Noctes' of May that year, we learn that the Shepherd has come in from the country to witness the hanging of the brothel-keeper Lucky McKinnon: 'I cannot bide away from a hangin' . . . I like to be garred to grue.' He testifies in the Chaldee Chamber that her bonny face was the worse for the hanging. Kempferhausen, a representation of Gillies, calls this talk barbaric. The skull of the murderer Haggart is looked at phrenologically, and a tale told of a root vegetable passed off on the phrenologists as the skull of a Swedish professor Tornhippson, whose bumps were pronounced to be distinguished for 'Inhabitiveness, Constructiveness, Philoprogenitiveness, &c – nay, even for "Tune", "Ideality" and "Veneration"'. *The Three Perils of Woman* has much that Kempferhausen would have been inclined to call barbaric. For more than one Edinburgh citizen 1823 was the year of the skull, a Golgotha. It was a year when Hogg's friends tried to behead him in their paper, and when he wrote his cadaverous best book.

His *Perils of Woman* consists of two stories. In the first, Gatty and Cherry are cousins entangled with a Highlander by the name of M'Ion (an 'ancient' spelling of McEwen, perhaps). Gatty catches a glimpse of Walter Scott and thinks him 'exceedingly good-looking'. Deaths, near-deaths and comas afflict them, and Hogg pores like some galvanic witch over these corpse-like catatonias. Gatty in love is a monster of pointless sentimental scruple, while Cherry is 'the pure unsophisticated child of nature', artless and affectionate. Around them revolve the energies of two lairds from the southern hinterland: Gatty's father Daniel, who rarely talks of anything but sheep, and a confrontational Northumberland farmer. Both portraits are tribally vivid and funny. Weaning his mind from tups and dips, Daniel prays in adversity to a God who must be allowed 'his ain way o' things. He's no likely to gang far wrang.'

When Gatty takes lodgings in Edinburgh, she writes home to say that 'nobody minds religion here but the ministers and the ladies.' She lodges among prostitutes, as it happens, whom she fails to recognise as such – a problem of the time, in the eyes of Scottish moralists, who were distressed to note that such women could so easily be mistaken for ladies. Hogg's treatment of the mysterious illnesses of Gatty and Cherry may be hinting that M'Ion has passed on to them a venereal disease.

The Heroine, the novel by Eaton Stannard Barrett, an Irishman with politics similar to Walter Scott's, had appeared ten years before this. 'Immured in a farmhouse', the heroine, another Cherry, takes the name Cherubina de Willoughby, repudiates her father, enlists as an orphan and a child of nature, takes flight, falls prey to designing males, and is then returned by a suitable suitor to *Rasselas* and right thinking. The 'adventures of Cherubina' are those of the adolescent drop-out, her ecstasies those of an ephemeral self due to grow up. Hogg could well have known this anti-romantic romance and used it for this first story, in which satire and sentiment are uneasily related, and it gets to be a question how far its Gothic horrors are being sent up, as in *Northanger Abbey*. Hogg's book, with its two stories, has also been linked with other contemporary fictional modes, with female fictions and with historical and 'national' ones.

The second of the stories is the more obviously concerned with nationhood. It is set before and after the Culloden carnage and in the vicinity of the battlefield. The 'unfortunate' Prince and his Highland host put in a brief appearance: these brave hearts are dualistically regarded – had they not once been the killers of Covenanters? A lecherous old minister lives with a housekeeper – known as Sally, a no less exotic name than Cherry for a Scots lass – who shows a taste for sexual intercourse with the local Jacobite blacksmith. The house is caught in a turbulence of shootings, grave-diggings, peepings and pryings, and other palavers. After the battle, Sally is a different woman, practically a changeling, having taken to the hills with a husband, one of those feudally indigent Highland shentlemen to be found in the fiction of the period. She's no longer the lass who'd seen off the minister with 'Ye're aye sae feared for my virtue, I wonder what you are gaun to do wi't!' She's now 'pure and unsophisticated', 'free of stain', but that doesn't save her from perishing in the wilderness, with her two partners interred nearby. Shortly before, a gravedigger in whom Hogg has shown what might seem a disproportionate interest, and whose pleasure it is to carry bits of cadaver on his person as he wanders about looking for custom, has lost his lugs to an irritated doctor, who had 'whipped' those ears off with a knife and caused the blood to 'whiz' against the victim's hand. Old Mortality was never like this.

The claim has been made, in recent times, that the confusion and uncertainty with which the second of these romances has been charged are, properly considered, strengths, and that this is a subversive masterpiece which leaves a 'more direct' and 'more lasting impact' than the *Confessions*.[17] Neither of the romances can be accounted a finished or successful work of art. But they are neither of them freaks or errors or failures. They are genuinely adventurous works, with a quality of the impromptu, and a kind of luck, which rewarded him with some of the finest passages in his fiction.

Gatty's sickness and sleep are – as is Sally's translation to the wilderness – a focus for reflections on appearance and reality, identity and mutability. What happens when someone changes? What is it to survive? Body and soul, Highland and Lowland – one duality opens on to another in the motley and medley, the 'varieties', of this remarkable, absurd book. Both *Perils* are remarkable. Gibby's transformation and ingestion, his dubious redemption, are another such focus. Both books register Hogg's developing sense of the uncertainties of personality, and of the enigmas of likeness.

The subordination of Hogg on class grounds is a fact of literary history, and of literature too. A resentment of this has led to a desire to detect a subversion of Scott and Wilson in Hogg's writings: in doctrinaire terms, to detect the deflation of a potent literary precursor (Scott, for what it's worth, was a year younger, and Wilson fifteen years younger, than Hogg). Such a subversion can't be considered a mirage, and it's also possible to detect a reponse to it, on Scott's part, in his fit of indignation when, by mistake for those of *Quentin Durward*, he took from James Ballantyne's office a bundle of proofs of *The Three Perils of Woman*, and glanced through them. In March 1823 Scott wrote to Ballantyne:

> naturally looking at it I found my self introduced with singular vulgarity & bad taste. However it is needless to say any thing about it – As Spenser says / Let Grill be Grill, & have his *hoggish* mind / Or in an adage more appropriate for the occasion "The more you stir the more it will stink" / I shall be desirous to have my own sheet & as soon as that can be gotten a copy of the first Vol. as printed.[18]

216

Scott's power of learning adds a porcine insult from Spenser's *Faerie Queene* to his protest at figuring in the book. Here is his most engorged miscalling of his friend. He really seems to have disliked him for this. It may be that he just didn't like Hogg's novel, which has other grounds for offence besides the passage about a bare-legged, torn-breeked, tree-climbing Walter Scott and his discovery of 'a nest wi' gouden eggs at the last'. But it may be legitimate to infer a deeper ire, which failed to notice, or to be appeased by, the passage which calls him good-looking.

This awareness of a subversion is a further aspect of the post-modern revaluation of Hogg, which can sometimes appear to see all his writings as equally in need of rescue, each one as good as another. He has been re-invented and exalted there, as he has elsewhere. His mutinies have been embraced, with his subversion of Scott writ large. Great Scott, once so overshadowing of other nineteenth-century Scots writers, has been challenged, if not replaced, in the affections of some, by poor Hogg.

The second of the two romances is dedicated to Lockhart, who, in July 1823, at his house of Chiefswood, near Abbotsford, received a letter of flirtatious domesticity from Hogg telling him of the dedication, and saying that as soon as 'a chaiseful of friends' has left Altrive 'I will come straight to you as I would rather ride fifty miles ere I missed seeing that delightful creature that has so often tickled and pleased me. If you could bring her up here to see the Lakes and my wife I would still like it better,' these lakes being Hogg's native dubs. Norah Parr writes that Hogg and his wife 'would know to a day the age of the little Lockharts', but that the children of the two men were 'unlikely' to have met.[19] In April of that year the 'Jacky's gray breeks' coquetry concerning Wilson, 'my own dear John', had been conveyed in a letter to Blackwood. Fences are being mended in the correspondence with Blackwood. Wilson's novel *The Trials of Margaret Lyndsay* charms him, in the same letter, despite 'two or three trivial misnomers regarding the character of Scottish peasantry'. Two months later, Lockhart's *Reginald Dalton* is 'a masterly work upon the whole'. But 'it strikes me that so masterly an artichek might have made a far more imposing fabric on the whole.' And it has too many 'short classical and French quotations' – a gentleman-like fault of Lockhart's, one might agree, and of Hogg's at times. The spelling of 'architect' brings to mind those 'Noctes' spellings which seem intended

217

to show the Shepherd as rustic or dyslexic: Hogg may be joining here in the joke at his own expense. In August, he explained to Blackwood that, 'on account of company', he'd been unable to 'finish the "Noctes" which I well intended to have sent this week'.

In the same month of 1823 Scott wrote to a friend: 'The great Hogg found his lair at Abbotsford on Friday, Lockhart bringing him here like a pig in a string, for which the lady of the mansion sent him little thanks, she not thinking the hog's pearls (qu. Perils) an apology for his freedoms.' On the 20th of the following month Blackwood wrote to Wilson about his review of *The Three Perils of Woman*. When he'd first read this 'terrible scraping', he'd enjoyed it,

> but on seeing it in types, I began to feel a little for the poor monster, and above all, when I considered that it might perhaps so irritate the creature as to drive him to some beastly personal attack upon you, I thought it better to pause. I felt quite sure that if published in its present state, he would be in such a state of rage, he would at all events denounce you everywhere as the author. This would be most unpleasant to your feelings, for now that you can look at the article coolly, there are such coarseness and personal things in it as one would not like to hear it said that you are the author of . . . I sent it to Mr Lockhart, begging him to consider it . . .

The man of feeling links arms with the man of sense in this letter, where Wilson's feelings are worth more than Hogg's. Lockhart had written to a Blackwood busy with 'a chaiseful of friends' to say that 'he could not be art or part in the murder of his own dedicator.' The review was held over till the next number, so that Wilson could correct it himself. God knows what it can have been like before Blackwood's solicitude for Wilson's feelings and reputation was expressed. One of the most unsettling of the journal's assaults on Hogg's self-confidence came at a time when he was engaged in writing a book in which his relations with the journal are implicit. Here, to the life, was the book he was writing.[20]

Wilson's October 1823 review of this 'most agreeable and bamboozling production', *The Three Perils of Woman*, remembers 'the would-be author of the Chaldee Manuscript, and of the murder of Begbie', as in his youth an erotic and athletic marvel:

What with his genius, and what with his buck-teeth; what with his fiddle, and what with his love-locks, lolling over his shoulders, as he 'gaed up the kirk', tastily tied with a blue ribbon; what with his running for prize-hats up the old avenue of Traquair, 'with his hurdies like twa distant hills', to the distancing of all competitors; and what with his listering of fish and grewing of mawkins, a gentler and more irresistible shepherd was not to be found from Moffat to Mellerstain.

Hogg's rapid rear is being exclaimed about with reference to Burns's address to the haggis, a dish Wilson professed to despise. The review talks of the 'rare union of high imagination with homely truth that constitutes the peculiar character of his writings. In one page, we listen to the song of the nightingale, and in another, to the grunt of the boar. Now the wood is vocal with the feathered choir; and then the sty bubbles and squeaks with a farm-sow, and a litter of nineteen pigwiggens.' Addressing Hogg, Wilson refers to these 'coarse daubings', a term used of Hogg's prose by Scott. 'We have heard such vulgarity objected to even in Glasgow,' grins Wilson, who was from Glasgow. Hogg is informed: 'you know little or nothing of the real powers and capacities of James Hogg and would fain be the fine gentleman, the painter of manners, and the dissector of hearts. That will never do in this world.' Jeffrey had earlier caused a lasting commotion by ruling in the *Edinburgh Review* that Wordsworth's *Excursion* would 'never do'. Hogg may be coarse but he is also potent, went on Wilson, compared with the Cockney Hazlitt. He has a mouth to 'devour unutterable things'. 'Unutterable' is a word from the Byron thesaurus, from a poetry in which unnamed sins are remembered: *Fraser's Magazine* was to maintain that because of Byron, the country had become 'peopled with misanthropes, "looking unutterable things" – in foolscap'.[21] Here, the word is used by Wilson to hint that Hogg is some kind of cannibal.

From the exhilarating 'Noctes' of the same October issue readers learnt that North had been staying at delectable Altrive. North then greets the English Opium-Eater: 'I thought you had been in Constantinople.' Before discussing the English Lakers with the Opium-Eater, and telling him that they are 'great yegotists', the Shepherd imparts his own experience of drugs, of falling down into a dream from the effects of laudanum.

He compliments De Quincey, 'Hech, sirs, yon bit Opium Tract's a desperate interesting confession,' and evokes his dream:

> I tried that experiment mysel, after reading the wee wud wicked wark, wi' five hunner draps, and I couped ower, and continued in ae snore frae Monday night till Friday morning. But I had naething to confess; naething at least that wad gang into words; for it was a week-lang, dull, dim dwawm o' the mind, with a kind o' soun' bumming in my lugs, and clouds, clouds, clouds hovering round and round; and things o' sight, no made for the sight; and an awfu' smell, like the rotten sea; and a confusion between the right hand and the left; and events o' auld lang syne, like the torments o' the present hour, wi' naething to mark ony thing by; and doubts o' being quick or dead; and something rouch, rouch, like the fleece o' a ram, and motion as of everlasting earthquake . . .

Wilson's feeling for Hogg's language appears symbiotically sensitive in this marvellous passage. It's also possible to feel that some of these words ('bumming' for 'humming', for instance) may be Hogg's.

The English Opium-Eater is given to flinching, in the 'Noctes', from the Shepherd's coarseness. On this occasion he commends him for his imagination: 'Sir, *you have no common sense*, and that in this age is the highest praise that can be bestowed on the immortal soul of man.' North agrees, assuring the Shepherd: 'There is no common sense in your Kilmeny, in Coleridge's Ancient Mariner, in Wordsworth's Ruth, in our eloquent friend's "Confessions" ' – De Quincey's, that is. Imagination has prompted the Shepherd to affirm that 'if the lowest shepherd lad in a' Scotland were to compose poems just on purpose to seduce lasses, he would be kicked like a foot-ba' frae ae parish to anither.' At one point Tickler imagines that Byron may have experienced the taste of human flesh.

CHAPTER FOURTEEN

Likenesses

In 1823, James Hogg sat down to write the at first anonymous *Private Memoirs and Confessions of a Justified Sinner*: a work so moving, so funny, so impassioned, so exact, and so mysterious, that its emergence in the twentieth century from a long history of neglect came as a surprise which has yet to lose its resonance. There are readers to whom it has seemed oddly superior to his other writings, and there are those to whom it might suggest a version of the great good luck of salvation embraced by the sinner in the novel: 'The might of heaven prevailed, and not my might.' William Blake said much the same, about his poems. But when Hogg said that the novel should not be spoken of, in *Blackwood's*, '*as mine*', he was referring, not to the might of heaven, but to the freedom that anonymity would bring.[1]

Others have suggested that it may have been inspired, or saved, in another sense, that it was too good for Hogg (*vide* Robert Louis Stevenson's mother) or for Hogg alone. The sinner says that his adventures will 'puzzle the world', and this is what they have done. The Victorian sage George Saintsbury found Hogg's adventurous book a 'puzzle', and detected the hidden hand of a collaborator, Lockhart. Saintsbury was 'absolutely unable to believe that it is Hogg's unadulterated and unassisted work.'[2] There is no evidence – as distinct from reasons of a sort – for this hypothesis, shared for a time with another Victorian, Lockhart's biographer Andrew Lang.

Hogg was capable of proposing that writings of his be edited by Lockhart (as they sometimes were), that Walter Scott might like to transcribe and adapt a piece of Hogg's autobiography, 'putting He for I', and that Lockhart might like to employ Hogg's 'name and forthright egotistical stile' for his life of Scott, with the aid of a possible manuscript in Hogg's hand, and the prospect of 'ten times more freedom of expression'.[3]

William Bewick's drawing of Hogg, done at the time of the *Confessions*

Lockhart thought that jokes were the very breath of Hogg's nostrils, but that he had 'peculiar notions, or rather no notions, as to the proper limits of a joke'[4] – an objection to which Lockhart's own writings were not invulnerable. His writings were those of a man who co-scripted the conversation attributed to Hogg's Ettrick Shepherd persona in the 'Noctes Ambrosianae', the work of several hands, where impersonated real people mingle with figments, all of them in some sense Messieurs de l'Imagination, to form a collective consciousness, a narcissistic personality pool, a mutual imitation society. This was an ambience in which mysteries were likely to thrive, and were meant to. William Blackwood and his associates went for the power of mystery: the right hand, of his confederacy of star authors, did not always know what the left hand was writing, and the public loved it out there in the dark. None of this, however, is evidence, in the present case, of ghosting or collaboration; and it can't be an argument for denying the work to Hogg that he omitted to boast about it. Saintsbury points to his silence on the subject – which was not, in fact, unbroken. He mentions it in his autobiography, as 'a story replete with horrors', and in a letter of June 1824 he speaks of it as being as far above his other prose works as 'Kilmeny' was above his longer poems.[5]

The *Confessions* is a tall tale, but there is no nonsense in it – except for the postscript which follows its two narratives. These consist of an editor's version, followed by the sinner's version, of the sinner's life. The editorial postscript, which incorporates a letter of Hogg's printed in the magazine, describes the discovery of a suicide's grave on a hilltop near Hogg's house at Altrive. It gives details of a gruesome grave-robbing souvenir hunt involving a party which includes the editor and the Tory literatus Lockhart, and William Laidlaw – Hogg's friend and Scott's friend and factor, a poet, and a Whig sympathiser – and is itself a gruesome response to the period craze for corpses and interment. It has been read as intentionally discreditable to the editor.

In the manner of the literary duality of the time, and of other times, the novel implies that a person can be two persons or more. Another dualistic novel, E. T. A. Hoffmann's *The Devil's Elixirs*, appeared at this point, having been translated for Blackwood from the German by Hogg's friend R. P. Gillies, and is likely to have influenced him: the double of the time owed much to Allemagne. Hogg was a divided man, and the idea of the double stands here in allegorical relation to the opposites and self-belyings apparent in the story of his life, as in the lives of others. It's possible to plead authority, including Hogg's, for this generic claim. With Bunyan in mind, perhaps, he spoke of certain of his fictions as 'allegories', while also making use of Bunyan's (and Wordsworth's) word 'similitude'. Puritan election and predestination, puritan abhorrence of morals, merit, 'filthy works', in contradistinction to God's grace, belong to the dualistic 'involute' of the novel, to use an expression of De Quincey's, and have been seen in general, by Yvor Winters, as 'a long step towards the allegorisation of experience', as opposed to its patient exploration. The novel might possibly be seen, by those who think better of the allegorical than Winters did, as fighting fire with fire – as an allegory that confronts the allegory of justification by faith.[6]

Hogg was a poet and a peasant, a poor man who was also a personality, a star. A devotee both of war and of peace, of animals and of their destruction, of truth and of lies, openness and disguise, of reason and imagination, simplicity and sophistication, chastity and licence. Both a Tory and a Whig, a Cavalier and a Covenanter, a Jacobite and a Hanoverian. He was more than 'ostensibly' a Tory, as he is thought to have been in the *Collected Works* edition of the novel: he was a denouncer of radicals, liberals, Papists, deists. But he was also in certain respects an egalitarian and a Whig of sorts, while despising the Enlightenment beliefs held by the Whig intelligentsia grouped about the *Edinburgh Review*, by Francis Jeffrey and Henry Cockburn, neither of them enemies of religion, and by the economist Francis Horner, who made clear to Jeffrey that he would be sorry to betray, in an article, 'any of the scepticism, which is my real sentiment'.[7] Late in life Hogg characterised the condition of the rural labour force as 'slavery', and he was attached to the Covenanting heritage extant in Ettrick Forest, to the Whigs of old, known to the enlightened (and to Episcopalians) as the fanatics of old. His sinner is a Whig and a fanatic of old, and a serial killer: he feels for him, nevertheless. His editor has in modern times suffered the antipathy of critics who have construed him as a specimen of the enlightened upper-class Edinburgh which praised and victimised Hogg, and as something of a Tory, despite the fact that the enlightened

Edinburgh of that decade was predominantly Whig. Meanwhile, for all these complications, the novel could well be summarised as a bold exposure of ultra-Calvinism's antinomian excesses, of the conviction that God's chosen few are infallible, and will not be forsaken by their dualising maker, with his sheep and his goats.

Not every ultra-Calvinist subscribed to the heresy, but it had not gone. Forty years before this, Burns's Holy Willie prayed to a God whose pleasure it was to send one to heaven and ten to hell, regardless of merit. 'Vile self gets in,' Holy Willie must 'confess': but despite his lapses he is saved. His prayer rhymes 'place' with 'race'. His place is in Ayrshire, and his race is Ayrshire's one in eleven, elders especially (Hogg became an elder, having been shamed by the kirk when he was young, like Burns, for sexual lapses).

Earlier in the eighteenth century, justification by faith had been a bone of contention in Ettrick, when the Rev. Thomas Boston, whom Hogg admired and whose descendants he knew, came under investigation by the Church of Scotland. To James Hog of Fife, an expert on the grace of God, Boston had recommended a seventeenth-century treatise, *The Marrow of Modern Divinity*. Others took an interest in the treatise, and the Marrow men were accused, it seems harshly, of antinomianism. The controversy laid bare the difficulty of setting proper limits to – no joke – the permissiveness granted to the elect. The seventeenth-century Westminster Confession of Faith, on which Presbyterian doctrine depended, had stated, pragmatically, or politically, that faith 'alone' was sufficient to save, but could not stand alone, within the experience of the individual Christian, as evidence of salvation: good works would and should get out. Boston had to distance himself from extremist versions of the doctrine of election, and to remain for his pains in remote Ettrick, famous though this fierce Calvinist was to prove.

In March 1820, *Blackwood's* carried 'a letter from the Ettrick Shepherd' which enclosed a letter from America in which a cousin of his, James Laidlaw, who may well have been the same James Laidlaw who once blamed him for telling lies, reported that the 'Methidests' there were unsound: they supposed that 'a man may be Justified to day, and fall from it to-morrow.' In 1828 Lockhart's *Life of Burns* reported the view that Cameronians believe that 'the greatest sinner is the greatest favourite of heaven' – the Saviour loves those he loves because he loves them, and not for any 'lovely qualities' they may possess. From the oracles of ultra-Calvinism Scots people learned that they must repent and that most of them were incapable of repentance, that they must and could not improve, that repentance was, in some uncertain fashion, for the saved alone. Perhaps there will always be a need to be told, in one way or another, about the inefficacy of merit.[8]

Hogg's novel tells in its two different ways of a young man, Robert Wringhim, whose real father is a predestinarian divine, and whose nominal father, a jolly laird, has a son, handsome and chivalrous George, as the editor portrays him. Robert takes up with a princely tempter, Gil-Martin, who tells him what he already knows about the immunity of the elect. All hell breaks loose.

Robert follows George about as Gil-Martin follows Robert, whose dogging of George is compared by the editor to the behaviour of a demon who attends 'some devoted being that had sold himself to destruction'. The sinner confesses to the strange sense that he is two persons, and that one is his brother George and the other his princely companion, who may be Czar Peter of Russia incognito, and who has the knack of looking like whoever he pleases.

This, strikingly enough, was a knack which Hogg had attributed several years before to himself, to his incarnation as Mr Spy, editor of his periodical of that name. In the opening number of 1 September 1810, he spoke, somewhere between earnest and irony, of an 'abominable propensity' of his, to be intent on other people's behaviour regardless of his own: 'by contemplating a person's features minutely, modelling my own after the same manner as nearly as possible, and putting my body into the same posture which seems most familiar to them, I can ascertain the compass of their minds and thoughts.' In the novel, Gil-Martin speaks of a 'peculiarity in my nature': 'If I contemplate a man's features seriously, mine own gradually assume the very same appearance and character. And what is more, by contemplating a face minutely, I not only attain the same likeness, but, with the likeness, I attain the very same ideas as well as the same mode of arranging them, so that, you see, by looking at a person attentively, I by degrees assume his likeness, and by assuming his likeness I attain to the possession of his most secret thoughts.' He does not have 'full control' over this peculiarity, but it enables him to control others.

Hogg's re-use of his own words – from a time before he and Lockhart had met – does not suggest that someone else wrote the *Confessions*. It suggests a conscious participation in the Gil-Martin mimesis. It also suggests a wide span of authorial sympathy, and it relates to a working definition of personality and community. The eye that observes and possesses is itself possessed – in more ways than one, engrossed. The observer is consumed. The eye of the beholder is a we. The *Blackwood's* world of parody and mutuality, impersonation and usurpation, is apparent, together with the author's flair for mimicry, in these two passages. Eyes were important to Hogg, and to some of his associates. He knew about the green eye of the carnivore and the cannibal, and of critics and fellow writers, the keen eye of the spy. He could imagine an evil eye that sees through people and invades them.

There are many involutions to be found in the novel. But the heart of the matter is the energy, pathos and delusion of the human struggle, along with the ability to feel that those who are not with us, or like us, are against us (an ability soon to be displayed by the Church of Scotland in its treatment of the new race of Irish immigrants). The *Blackwood's* circle was preoccupied with delusion, with the power of human error. Hogg's novel, however, can be considered a comedy and tragedy of errors to which his associates would appear to have made the mistake, as did Scott, of being indifferent. Unless, of course, they helped to write it.

Robert's account of his admission to the elect is a pivotal scene in the bi-part novel. He now belongs to the society of the just made perfect. A made man, as the Mafia used to say. Away he bounds into the countryside, as if into the sky, his every nerve 'buoyant with new life'. These nerves are about to be electrified.

> As I thus wended my way, I beheld a young man of mysterious appearance coming towards me. I tried to shun him, being bent on my own contemplations; but he cast himself in my way, so that I could not well avoid him; and more than that, I felt a sort of invisible power that drew me towards him, something like the force of enchantment, which I could not resist. As we approached each other, our eyes met, and I

can never describe the strange sensations that thrilled through my whole frame at that impressive moment; a moment to me fraught with the most tremendous consequences; the beginning of a series of adventures which has puzzled myself, and will puzzle the world when I am no more in it. That time will now soon arrive, sooner than any one can devise who knows not the tumult of my thoughts, and the labour of my spirit, and when it hath come and passed over, – when my flesh and bones are decayed, and my soul has passed to its everlasting home, then shall the sons of men ponder on the events of my life; wonder and tremble, and tremble and wonder how such things should be.[9]

Hogg swore that he never revised, and Scott blamed him for carelessness, for being in a hurry. There is no need to think this of the twin narratives, which are closely co-ordinated and carefully worded. Bound, bond, bounding, buoyancy, bounty, nature and fantasy – these are notions which serve to hold the novel together. The murdered minister Blanchard has seen religion as 'the bond of society on earth', while the Wringhims despise 'the bonds of carnal nature' and think of 'the bonds and vows of the Lord' as a means to freedom. The hope of infallibility is a longing for boundlessness. A strategic pun on 'bound' is effected, which lends, to the novel's teeming dualities, a double meaning of freedom and constraint, rise and fall.

The vocabulary of the novel unites the language of the King James Bible and of the metrical Psalms, that of the Covenanting martyr and commemorator, a shrewd and humorous Scots vernacular, and the new words of romanticism. This is a Gothic novel, drawn to the 'unaccountable' and the 'singular', and to the alarming. Scott's friend, Mrs Hughes, busy wife of the Canon of St Paul's, was almost the only one of Hogg's contemporaries who is on record as having had a good word to say about it. Scott spoke of the social skills of its author, in a letter of 1828 to Lockhart: 'Hogg who roars or grunts in a good natured stile keeps Mother Hughes in play.' Hogg then informed Blackwood that 'Mrs Hughes insists on the Confessions of a Sinner being republished with my name as she says it is positively the best story of that frightful kind that was ever written.' Blackwood should buy up from Longman, in London, the remaining copies.[10]

The novel is enhanced by a series of deft linking touches, and of delicate ones comparable to the 'garnish' of dewdrops on George's hat as he climbs Arthur's Seat, soon to engage with his brother on the summit. When Gil-Martin greets Robert in a park and is observed to be reading a Bible queerly marked with red lines, 'a sensation resembling a stroke of electricity came over me.' Hogg's electrics are always of consequence, and this example is connected to another, which occurs when the congregation at Auchtermuchty is 'electrified' by a sermon delivered with hellish eloquence by the Devil in angelic guise.[11]

Hogg's technology encompassed electricity, the likenesses of pioneer photography, and the explanation and awed appreciation of natural wonders, tricks of the light, the *lusus naturae*. He was aware of the magic lantern, the camera obscura; his friend David Brewster invented the kaleidoscope, and helped in the 1840s to develop the calotype – 'sun pictures'. *Sol fecit*, they said of the pictures, and the sun did things for Hogg too. These interests are reflected here in the spectral summit scene on Arthur's Seat, where duality and meteorology meet, and George Colwan is greeted at dawn by a diabolic blow-up, a monstrously-enlarged projection of his brother's features. In his essay 'Nature's Magic Lantern', Hogg tells how, early one misty morning at the age of nineteen, a halo of glory invested him, and he went on to encounter his double: 'my eyes fell on a huge dark semblance of the human figure, which ... at first appeared to my affrighted imagination as the enemy of mankind.' The following morning the thing appeared to him again in the likeness of a giant blackamoor. He wants to rush home and hide behind the blankets with the Bible beneath his head. He takes off his bonnet and scratches that head. And lo, the apparition does the same.

> His arms and his fingers were like trees and branches without the leaves. I laughed at him till I actually fell down upon the sward; the de'il also fell down and laughed at me. I then noted for the first time that he had two collie dogs at his foot, bigger than buffaloes. I arose, and made him a most graceful bow, which he returned at the same moment – but such a bow for awkwardness I never saw! It was as if the Tron Kirk steeple had bowed to me.

Just such a bow is exchanged between the eighteen-year-old Robert and Gil-Martin. Such sights were mentioned to 'Sir D. Brewster', who claimed to account for them 'by some law of dioptrical refraction, which I did not understand'.[12]

The tale told in the *Confessions* of the electrified Auchtermuchty congregation was got by Robert's servant Samuel Scrape from an auld wife, Lucky Shaw. Crows are overheard conversing, as in Scott's colloquy of the two corbies: 'Whaten vile sounds are these that I hear coming bumming up the hill?' 'O these are the hymns and praises o' the auld wives and creeshy louns o' Auchtermuchty, wha are gaun crooning their way to heaven.' The saints of this place are then to be gulled with the introduction of a glamorous preacher, whose cloven hoof is mercifully detected. Lucky Shaw adds: 'Frae that day to this it is a hard matter to gar an Auchtermuchty man listen to a sermon at a', an' a harder ane still to gar him applaud ane, for he thinks aye that he sees the cloven foot peeping out frae aneath ilka sentence.' There's an infallible golden rule for spotting the cloven hoof – among lawyers, preachers, pious blue-bonneted Cameronians. But Samuel Scrape of Penpunt (where a policeman was convicted of rape not long ago) regrets to say: 'The auld witch didna gie me the rule, an' though I hae heard tell o't often an' often, shame fa' me an I ken what it is!' The golden rule is that you can't grasp it.

A delicate chiasmus occurs when Gil-Martin explains that his impersonations, his likenesses, are a gift from God, who knows, 'and so do I', whether it's a blessing or not, and then, five pages later, when he and Robert have started 'popping' people off, Robert admits that God only knows, 'for I do not', which of his guesses about his eminent friend is correct. These linking touches, few of them hard to detect, are worth mentioning because they are meaningful and blissful, and structural, and because they upset the sense of Hogg as the rough diamond whom Mrs Hughes had been expecting to meet in North Britain, and the sense of him as the rhapsodist and sentimentalist of later disapprovals.

'Likeness', likewise, is a main concern of the novel and a clue to the novel, and to Hogg's paradoxical shape-changing life. Arabella Logan's maid Bessy Gillies, a brilliant Scots-speaker, is questioned in court about her mistress, who had also been the old laird's mistress, and about her belongings. Was this gown hers, or like hers? '*Like* is an ill mark. Sae ill indeed, that I wad hardly swear to ony thing.' Gil-Martin's likenesses are certainly an ill mark, a bad sign (witches' bodies could be thought to bear the mark of the Devil), and Bessy's sceptical note is a suitable contribution to the polyphony of the novel. 'Very pertinent, Bessy,' as the prosecutor says here about another of her replies.[13]

The novel is a mystery which yields to enquiries as to influence and provenance. It tacks and quivers in response to a variety of recent events. Impersonation was a *Blackwood's* concern which reached a height in 1823. A few months before the *Confessions* was written, Personality Hogg was made to complain, as we have seen, to his 'Noctes' companions: 'It's no decent to be aye meddling wi' folks' personalities ... Ye ken what ye hae gotten by your personalities.' 'Maga' had disgraced herself with her insulting attacks on political opponents, and on rival writers, categorised as Cockneys, as low Londoners, counter-jumping city-dwellers. The Shepherd's play on words here, with its double meaning for 'person-alities', embodies a commendation of 'sense', a quality much favoured in Scotland, where 'you should have mair sense' had become a heart-cry. Hogg believed in sense, while sometimes lacking it, and being praised, in his Shepherd persona, by the 'Noctes' impersonation of De Quincey, for lacking it so richly. But Hogg also believed in meddling with folks' personalities, including his own, as in the imminent *Confessions*.

Precedents and sources are explored by those responsible for the recent accession of the novel to Hogg's *Collected Works*. Writing in the distant past about two such texts – each the purported autobiography of a repentant malefactor, saved by God's grace, *The Confession of Nicol Muschet of Boghall* and the *Life of David Haggart* – I underrated the significance of the second for the *Blackwood's* symposiasts, as revealed by the presence of Haggart's *Life* in the 'Noctes'. Edinburgh was keen on its great crimes. Others included Gabriel's murder near Ambrose's tavern of his tutorial charges, the work of a religious zealot; the unsolved murder of the bank messenger Begbie, with which Hogg was humorously linked in the 'Noctes'; the resurrectionist stiflings of Burke and Hare; and the murder of a young man in her brothel for which Mary ('Lucky') McKinnon was executed. The year before the personalities complaint, North had given his assurance to Odoherty that with vignettes by Cruikshank 'your life would sell as well as Hogg's, or Haggart's'

(Cruikshank illustrated 'The Adventures of Captain Lochy'). Haggart's life was editorially presented, and was an equivocal production. Cockburn, who defended him in court, declared that it was almost all lies. It showed 'a strange spirit of lying', which is what the Ambrosians thought of Hogg's autobiography.[14]

Lucky McKinnon's execution preceded Hogg's *Confessions* by a matter of months. She was hanged on 16 April before a crowd of twenty thousand. A client had been dispatched in her house, in the course of an affray at which she had arrived late. The case against her was weak, but the justiciary was after her blood, and advised a discounting of the female evidence. As we have seen, the Shepherd is supposed in the 'Noctes' to have witnessed her death – an 'easy' death, but afterwards her face was black: 'black, but comely,' puts in the imaginary Dr Mullion. Francis Jeffrey, editor and advocate, defended her, pleading that she was 'thrown into her situation rather by misfortune than misconduct'.[15] George Combe of the Phrenological Society, for whom Haggart's malefactor skull was greatly deficient in conscientiousness, examined Mrs McKinnon's and pronounced large the organs of combativeness and destructiveness; organs of similar shape might have been identified round the table at Ambrose's, in Gabriel's Road.

The editor of the *Collected Works* edition discusses the resemblances between the McKinnon crime and punishment and what happens in the novel, during George Colwan's visit to a brothel and subsequently. This interesting woman was understood to have been neglected and violated in her youth, while the novel's Bell Calvert had been, she says, forced by ill-treatment into prostitution, when she became a sight to be seen and 'there were few to be seen like me.' This woman, whose future had held the spectacle of a shameful death on the Grassmarket scaffold, becomes one of the book's two female detectives; the other is another Bell, Arabella Logan.

Bell Calvert is treated with humanity in Hogg's novel, while his fellow Ambrosians were to remember Lucky McKinnon as a 'murderous Jezebel' (a not entirely inconceivable reference back, by these attentive namers, to Hogg's fallen woman), and Scott's antiquarian friend Charles Kirkpatrick Sharpe wrote about her what the new edition calls a 'heartless lampoon'. Whigs befriended her, these Tories handled her as if she were a Whig, and Hogg turned her into Bell Calvert, thereby measuring his distance from such men as Sharpe. Hogg had assailed Sharpe's editorial treatment of a Covenanting narrative in a review of December 1817 in the nascent magazine which referred both to 'this refined, reasoning and deistical generation', abbreviable to 'Whigs', and to 'the waggish Tories of the present day', and to 'every social tie that binds man to man in the brotherhood of confidence'.

Harry Cockburn, one of the country's foremost historians and chroniclers, is barely consulted in the *Collected Works* edition. He wrote superbly about the 1820s and about Lucky McKinnon, as he did about the 'Noctes' – tholing the personalities, and loving the Shepherd's Scots. Of all Whigdom's princes, Cockburn and Jeffrey are probably the least excoriated in the magazine.

The new edition uses the text of the first edition, printed in Edinburgh by James Clarke, arguing that it can be judged exceptional, so far as Hogg's tormented publishing history is concerned, in conforming with the wishes of an author who seems to have successfully insisted, this time, on a printer to whom he had satisfactory access. This mysterious book, of which no manuscript has survived, is nevertheless a relatively uncontentious text. The strength of the edition lies in its supply of biographical, territorial and theological information, and in its suscept-ibility to what might be termed the new dynamic bibliography, whereby the material existence of a book is weighed in relation to its expressive and persuasive purpose and historical background. The approach is not without a faint likeness to the period interest in the body to which Hogg and many others responded, in bodies dead or alive, and in the physiognomy of authors. This is an interest which has lately been subject to resurrection. The body has risen again, in the academy.

The approach fits the novel very well, not least because the making of the sinner's share of the book in an actual Edinburgh printing-shop enters his narrative – a process abridged by the arrival of the Devil hot on the heels of the textual record of his subversions. The new edition has a quotation from *Autobiographical Notes* (1892) by William Bell Scott, an artist and poet, a first-rate Border Ballad pasticheur, and the son of an engraver whose studio overlooked Parliament Square. 'I was getting my Latin exercise overhauled,' he writes of his early life, 'when a publisher, one of my father's clients, brought in a short stoutish countryman in a light-coloured suit, who wanted an imitation of the writing of 1700 made as a frontispiece to a book.' Likeness is an ill mark, and the body is in the eye of the beholder: the likenesses bestowed on Hogg by the many describers of his appearance were protean, and he could be a lot taller than he is represented here. His taking the trouble to arrange for a holograph page to be forged, in the handwriting of the period when the novel is set, a page which duly appeared in the first edition and in others, is in line with Hogg's sometimes accident-prone flair for artifice, and with his ludic, tragic, earthly and uncanny, actual and allegorical, ideal and corporeal book. He dedicated it, fulsomely, to a virtuous Glasgow Lord Provost, and implored Blackwood, in a letter of 28 June 1824, to make it clear in the paper that it was 'written by a *Glasgow man*'.[16] He seems to have been looking for cover, fearing it might prove an allegory to enrage an aristocracy – the scholars and gentlemen of the Edinburgh élite – and to outrage the devout. Not presenting it *'as mine'* would give excellent 'scope and freedom' – boundlessness. The June 'Noctes' identified the work as Hogg's, with Odoherty informing the Shepherd, prophetically enough, that he would be 'dug up, no doubt, quite fresh and lovely, like this new hero of yours, one hundred summers hence'. But the following issue carried the statement that it was, 'as it professes to be, the performance of a Glasgow Literateur'.

The Cresset Library edition of 1947 – with its introduction by André Gide, who had three years before referred to the work, in his journal, as *'un des plus extraordinaires livres'* that he had read – was based on the first-edition text, as were the edition of 1895 (entitled *The Suicide's Grave*) and those of 1924 and 1969. The editions in question helped to bring about the book's escape from the shadow cast by the bowdlerising activities of Victorian editors. This has led to a justification by fame which must seem ironic to those acquainted with the depreciations of class-conscious associates and their nineteenth-century biographers. These depreciations lasted well into the twentieth century, when a latterday physiognomist was still able to find that Hogg had a slack jaw.

Gide helped to make Hogg respectable. In 1947 he went to Oxford for an honorary degree and attended a seminar where he mentioned this strange and remarkable book. The name of the author had slipped his mind. *'L'auteur, c'est...'* Douglas Johnson, then a postgraduate, supplied the name. Gide's 'Mr 'Og' was very different from that of his compatriot Lady Scott. He said that this was a book whose nature was a mystery. It was a mystery of another kind to the teachers of French at the seminar, who had heard neither of the novel nor of its author. Johnson felt that perhaps he would have done better not to have read it. Elsewhere, at this time, it began to be read as it can seldom have been read before.[17]

Ian Campbell's Afterword in the new edition tackles the question of who in the book is to be believed. He argues that 'Robert, like Gil-Martin, indeed like the Editor, is true up to a point. Recognising that point is the key to the novel.' He is well-disposed towards the 'increasingly post-modernist readings which the novel is currently attracting'. The teleology, or perfectibility, perhaps discernible in that 'increasingly' might be doubted, but it is not difficult to see why he endorses a description of it as 'a kind of premature post-modernist novel'.

There are grounds for supposing that a deconstruction takes place in the *Confessions* whereby each of the component narratives is undone by its neighbour, and that the novel undoes itself, that the enigma promised by its author has survived as an aporia for modern interpreters. But it is possible, too, in dualistic style, to suppose that the novel stands on its feet, and that it has an expoundable aim. If it were to be credited with a single or paramount meaning, it would have to relate to a dislike of intolerance and of exclusionist religion, to the 'be not angry' scoffed at in Hogg's morality by Carlyle.[18] The novel inhabits a space where Lockhart's novels of the time were also located. Lockhart believed that Gabriel's crime illustrated 'the effects of puritanical superstition in destroying the moral feelings', and his *Matthew Wald* contains a fanatic who invites the language of Hogg's sinner: 'he had been permitted to make a sore stumble.'[19]

The *Confessions* is a post-modern work which is also a pre-modern work, by a man who believed, not strongly but 'to some extent', said his daughter Mary Garden, in ghosts and in demonic possession,[20] and who produced a book with demons in it which is not, fundamentally, a superstitious book. It's about the effects of puritanical superstition. Hogg's novel is as complex as it is lucid and direct – a feat of ambivalence, from sophisticated Edinburgh's country cousin. If a suspicion of the editor, as a specimen of the exploiting literati, opens a door to multiple or indeterminate readings, such readers have to accept that he is editing a killer: but then Robert is the kind of killer whose personality can compel sympathy when exhibited in the nineteenth century's diaries of a madman.

Hogg's was a countryside in which shepherds wore the blue bonnet of the Covenant and a renowned Cameronian, Renwick, the Covenant's last martyr, preached his last sermon on his way to the Grassmarket scaffold, and in which the Episcopalian Wilson's ancestor the Royalist general Montrose went down to defeat; but Hogg was also a vassal, in some more than vestigial way, as was Scott in his grandness, of the Episcopalian House of Buccleuch. Scott's feudal loyalties and anti-Presbyterian bias made him in some sense an enemy of the people he lived among, many of whom admired his books while thinking his politics 'mistaken', 'imaginative', as Laidlaw did during the crisis over Parliamentary Reform.[21] Hogg's politics, so far as he was political, leant towards Scott's in a number of respects, and they are visible in his novel. To some extent. They are opposed there by its diary of a madman, which is in turn opposed by the affirmation of a benign piety.

The novel makes a virtue of its lifelike uncertainty. It's the work of a man who has met his double in the pages of a magazine, and been attacked by those in whom he had confided. It's a work expressive of the life of a man who has moved from one environment to another, country to city, Whig to Tory, and back again, a genial, glowing man, an 'unbounded laugher' in his youth, put to anguish by these changes but able to say what they might mean. Like Bottom the weaver, he was translated, and his translation forms part of his story of a suicide.

A further source for, and incitement to, the composition of the novel has been located in the *Blackwood's* of January 1823. This was a year in which carnivorousness featured prominently in the magazine, and in which gluttony and duality, meals and personalities, coincided there. The anonymous 'Confessions of an English Glutton' has been attributed to Thomas Colley Grattan, a travel writer, and David Groves has spotted resemblances to Hogg's *Confessions* in the Grattan parody of De Quincey's. The piece opens with the words: 'This is confessedly the age of confession, – the era of individuality – the triumphant reign of the first person singular.' Writers 'think only of number one. *Ego sum* is on the tip of every tongue and the nib of every pen.' An anti-democratic doom poem by Hogg was to concur: 'the lograthim o' number ane' commands us.[22]

The writer owns up to the 'invincible appetite' of bulimia, and grows anorexic thin, in a world of 'gastronomical literati', in an age, a vegetarian might add, which was keen on corpses and keen on eating them. Fancying himself a Jew, he is drawn to pork and repelled by it. A 'beautiful porker lay smoking in his rich brown symmetry of form and hue'. He flies to the sky astride a pig, and his prospective bride turns into a Pig-Lady in Canterbury Cathedral: 'her muslin robe became a piebald covering of ham-sandwiches.' She rejects him, worried that he may 'eat her up one night in bed'. Worse is to come. He meets his double in fat Mr Lambert, and I was intrigued to notice elsewhere that a Daniel Lambert died in 1809 at fifty-two and three-quarter stone – by no means a Monsieur de l'Imagination. 'The notion struck me that I had become his second-self – his ditto – his palpable echo – his substantial shadow.' His girth is now excessive. 'I, in short, was Lambert, and Lambert me.' The encounter is like 'an electric shock'. He heads for the river, seeking to shake off this 'horrible phantasm', to fight 'the foul fiend'.

There are more resemblances to Hogg's book than to De Quincey's. The eater explains that 'the earliest date which I am able to affix to the development of my propensity is the month of August 1764, at which period, being precisely two years and two months old', he was punished by an aunt for an excess of greed. The passage anticipates the dating by Hogg of the onset of Robert's sense of salvation. Perhaps inadvertently, Grattan's surreal piece directly implicates Hogg, the Great Boar of the Forest. Grattan writes that vulgar gluttons belong to the class *Epicuri de grege porcus* – a quotation from Horace, used here to classify connoisseurs of pig flesh, of the pig tribe or race – 'or may be compared rather to the *Porcus Trojanus* of the Ancients, a wild boar stuffed with the flesh of other animals – a savoury, punning parody upon the Trojan horse'. Such a man is no better than an animated sausage.

Among the sneering reviews of Hogg's novel was one in the *British Critic* whose author may have remembered the Grattan delirium in belittling that of Hogg. The journal spoke of 'a diseased and itching peculiarity of style, a *scabies et porrigo Porci*, which, under every disguise, is always sure to betray Mr Hogg'.[23] A tell-tale mange or dandruff or porridge had ruined Hogg's incognito.

The Shepherd maintains in the 'Noctes' (April 1830) that 'there never was a Scotch Lambert,' and that the English are gluttons: 'to the varra infants (what sookers!) that a' look as they were crammed – instead o' wee piggies – for the second coorse o' the denner o' the King o' the Cannibals'. The Shepherd's 'Mr De Quinshy', the English Opium-Eater, maintains that eating food is sensual (elsewhere he says that Keats is too), but that the Scottish notion that the English are gluttons is wrong; and the 'Noctes' certainly go to show that the Scots are gluttons, and the Ambrosians gastronomical literati. They were of the school Wilson laughed at, entitling it, in the *Blackwood's* of July 1823, 'The Gormandizing School of Eloquence'.

Such was the year 1823 that when Lockhart reports[24] that he has invited Hogg to dinner, to meet Maria Edgeworth, and that 'she has a great anxiety to see the Bore', we might half-imagine that she meant to eat him. In the October 'Noctes' of special sprightliness, the business of eating is sifted. Mullion is warned by Tickler about voracity. If he goes on like this he'll cut himself from ear to ear: 'For the sake of our common humanity, use your fork.' The Shepherd objects: 'I hae used my knife that way ever since I was fed upon flesh, and I never cut my mouth to any serious extent, above a score times in my life.' Hogg's mouth is made to seem like a cannibal's in the same issue, where, subjecting 'Hogg the Well-Beloved' to the gobblingly bad review discussed in the last chapter, Wilson calls it 'a mouth to devour unutterable things'.

The Opium-Eater now declares, in the October 'Noctes', that heavy suppers shorten life. The Shepherd suffers a slight loss of appetite at this point. The diets of writers are discussed. Tickler says of Byron, 'I never suspected, at least accused him, of cannibalism' – a connection prompted by the maritime feast in *Don Juan*. The Shepherd has been thinking that 'when Tam Muir was penning his Loves of the Angels', he 'fed upon calf-foot jeelies, stewed prunes, the dish they ca' curry, and oysters'. The Opium-Eater then confesses (aside to Tickler): 'I fear that Mr Mullion's excessive animation is owing to a slight mistake of mine. I carelessly allowed a few grains of opium to slide out of my box into the plate of kidneys which Mr Hogg sent for my delectation,' and the dish had been wafted over to Mullion.

Towards the end of the feast Tickler asks the editor to describe his visit to Altrive that autumn: 'Pray, North, tell us how you kissed the rosy hours at Hogg's?' Eating came into it. Gigots, gravies, potatoes, a moorfowl – and 'that old cock'. 'Frae neb to doup,' testifies the sensual Shepherd, 'did our editor devour him, as he had been a bit snipe – he crunched his very banes, Mr Tickler; and the very marrow o' the cretur's spine trickled down his chin frae ilk corner o' his mouth, and gied him, for the while being, a most terrible and truculent feesionomy.' The face, for all the world, of a nineteenth-century cannibal.

North suggests that he is being represented here as an eloquent Scots glutton, as a member of 'the Gormandizing School of Oratory'. The Shepherd replies with reference to North's appetite both for food and for personalities, for those persons he cared for and turned on, such as Hogg, whose duplicate or ditto, Wilson's dummy, ventriloquially responds:

> Oratory! Gude faith, ye never uttered a syllable till the cloth was drawn. To be sure, you were gran' company at the cheek o' the fire, out ower our toddy. I never heard you mair pleasant and satirical. You seemed to hate every body, and like every body, and abuse every body, and plaud every body; and yet, through a' your deevilry there ran sic a vein o' unendurable funniness, that, had you been the foul Fiend himsel, I maun hae made you welcome to every thing in the house.

It might therefore seem that Grattan's fiend and double were echoed later in the year by Wilson's fiend and double, by the demon and cannibal North. Wilson reared a second self for himself in the magazine, and another for Hogg, a self Hogg came both to love and to hate. The Shepherd complained (April 1829) about North's 'Mephistophiles tricks': 'I aften think you're an evil speerit in disguise, and that your greatest delight is in confounding truth and falsehood.' And Hogg told Blackwood that he felt for Wilson what one devil might feel for another: terror, admiration, jealousy. Fiends may be friends, and friends may be fiends. They can be the foul fiend who goes about seeking whom he may devour.

Meddling with Hogg's personality was wicked work, on the part of his friends. But not simply or singly so. It was hilarious and sagacious work too, a work of art, a homage to human nature. And Hogg's novelistic response to its early days is an even more wonderful work of art.

CHAPTER FIFTEEN

Flesh

———

The Shepherd says, in the 'Noctes' of October 1823, that he has been 'fed upon flesh'. For James Hogg, 'flesh' could mean both human flesh and animal meat. This was a double meaning which helped to express his keen interest, shared with his fellow Ambrosians, in eating and drinking, the slaughter of beasts, the catching of fish, in the raw and the cooked, and in anthropophagy – the eating of people. The critic Jeffrey was, for Byron, 'the great anthropophagus' of the North, so called in a prose postscript to 'English Bards and Scotch Reviewers', and there were others of that ilk.

Hogg's interest in the subject is of a piece with his re-invention of primordial concerns, and is freely confessed in *The Three Perils of Man*. Here was a mouth to devour unutterable things, and to utter them. When the Deil's Tam, alias Marion's Jock, tells the story of what happened to him when he ran from his master's farm, he speaks of the discovery that ill deeds thrive best, for the time being, and that liberty can lead to captivity, but that captives need not starve. This illicit ox-slayer makes a voracious prisoner:

> There were some square pieces of perfect, pure white fat, that I sliced down like cheese! They were from the flanks of fat beeves, the briskets of wedders, and the ribs of fatted hogs; and I could not but admire the want of good taste among the gentles who had left these savoury bits to their slaves and prisoners. I was so delighted that I could not sleep by night, but always awakened from my straw and fell a-munching. I wish we saw such a feast again; but, indeed I saw nothing, for our house was in utter darkness; but it was a good meat house, and I could have been content to have lived in it all my life.

Kafka's stories can be like this; a later contribution to the literature of the Gothic, they are as strange as they are true, and the same can be said

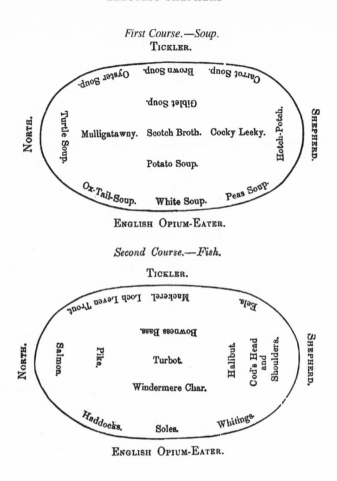

First Course.—Soup.
TICKLER.

Carrot Soup.   Brown Soup.   Oyster Soup.

Giblet Soup.

NORTH.

Turtle Soup.   Mulligatawny.   Scotch Broth.   Cocky Leeky.   Hotch-Potch.   SHEPHERD.

Potato Soup.

Ox-Tail-Soup.   White Soup.   Peas Soup.

ENGLISH OPIUM-EATER.

Second Course.—Fish.

TICKLER.

Mackerel.   Loch Leven Trout.   Eels.

Bowness Bass.

NORTH.

Salmon.   Pike.   Turbot.   Halibut.   Cod's Head and Shoulders.   SHEPHERD.

Windermere Char.

Haddocks.   Soles.   Whitings.

ENGLISH OPIUM-EATER.

of this story of Hogg's. During a pause in the narrative the listening Laird puts in: 'I wish ye wadna always turn your green een on me that gate when you speak about your fat flesh.' This is a response to Tam's wondering 'whether men's flesh is likest to beef, or mutton, or venison'. It's not for nothing that James Hogg was called Hogg. He is the laureate, not just of the mountain and the fairy, but of the nicely toasted rasher and of the fat that glistens there 'like small drops of honey'.[1]

It could be claimed of the Ambrosian gastronomy that the cronies devoured the impossible, that their plainly imaginary feasts were meant

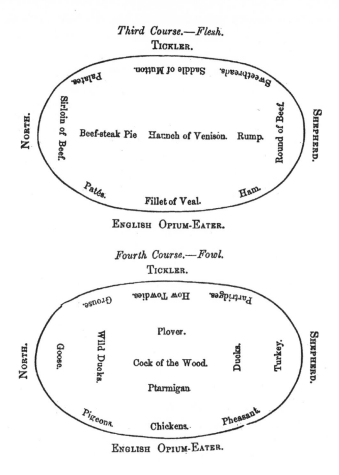

Third Course.—Flesh.
TICKLER.

Palate. Sweetbreads. Saddle of Mutton.

Sirloin of Beef. Round of Beef.

NORTH. SHEPHERD.

Beef-steak Pie   Haunch of Venison.   Rump.

Patés.   Fillet of Veal.   Ham.

ENGLISH OPIUM-EATER.

Fourth Course.—Fowl.
TICKLER.

Grouse. How Towdies. Partridges.

Goose. Wild Ducks. Ducks. Turkey.

NORTH. SHEPHERD.

Plover.

Cock of the Wood.

Ptarmigan

Pigeons.   Chickens.   Pheasant.

ENGLISH OPIUM-EATER.

to be read as a slave to excess, and a joke. This is not realism. No one eats so much, and so eagerly. The 'Noctes' – interleaved with menus and placements – depict Scotland as a land, not just of cakes, but of a full range of comestibles, with heartiness, rather than a gourmet French finesse, ruling the roost, but with a considerable scholarship in play. Wilson declared their suppers 'a mere Barmecide business'. But George Saintsbury declared that 'the Shepherd's consumption of oysters not by dozens but by fifties', the six kettlefuls of water for a night's toddy ration for three, North's bottle of old hock at dinner and the magnum of claret

243

afterwards, the dinners and suppers and 'whets' – that 'all these stop short of the actually incredible.' There were 'extremely convivial' nineteenth-century eaters – Saintsbury's Lord Alvanley for one, with his 'three hearty suppers', not to mention the 53-stone Daniel Lambert – who were equal to it.[2] But were the Scotch, who lacked a Lambert, equal to it? On this showing, they certainly did their best. Those who took part in the cannibal feast of a universal plagiarism were also pledged to a more conventional diet of festive proportions. Lionel Trilling's joke comes to mind – that to encounter the mere record of Dickens's conviviality is exhausting. The question of the Ambrosian gluttonies may repay further investigation.

Eating was what lords did, ladies less so. It was a way of being up, or of endeavouring to be –'upping', as it could be called – in a society where fat was more beautiful than it is now, where the poor could be very thin. Hogg's cries of hunger were something more than poor-mouth hyperbole: they had a history, shared with compatriots. He was 'fairly starved into' Edinburgh, he said of his arrival there in 1810, and but for Messrs Grieve and Scott would soon have been 'starved out of it again'. Twenty years later: 'You have starved me fairly out of my house and country,' he told Blackwood as he left on his visit to London.[3]

The diet of the poor was looking up, however, and they were well-acquainted, as their betters were, with strong drink. Cockburn, eventually a Lord of Session, dilated – or, as they used to say in Scotland, 'murmured' – the judges of his youth for nodding off and fuddlement on the bench. Scott's correspondence has adjacent letters of 1823 in the first of which he complains of it as 'a most pernicious thing' for the Edinburgh poor that whisky should be ninepence or tenpence a bottle, while in the second an Abbotsford gaudy has them 'all in the highest spirits flag flying and whiskey provided with plenty of stout brown ale'. 'Give our twa sonsie babbies a drap mother's milk,' he said once at table, his guests Constable and James Ballantyne. A famous exuberance, at a time of entrepreneurial triumph, and a far cry from starvation. But not, as it proved, from insolvency.[4]

'Serious devouring' forms part of a stage direction in the 'Noctes' of April 1829, which is preceded by North's encomium to the Shepherd's tongue: 'how deeply, darkly, beautifully red'. No scurf at all. A man of genius has a long tongue, proceeds North, the better to devour: he can 'shoot it out, with an easy grace, to the tip of his nose'. The Shepherd then suits the action to the word.

In the 'Noctes' of the following July a diner calls for a pig's ear, and the request introduces the story of an alderman who eats his way through a wild pig, raw, having been offered the services of his cook by a marquis. 'My cook only prepared it for the spit,' exclaims the marquis in dismay. The deferential alderman says that it was not too bad, though deucedly stringy. The scholar John Leyden, as we have seen, preferred his meat raw: 'meat can never be too little done.' And on one occasion the Witch Maga ate raw her own dear Shepherd. It may be said of Hogg that he was eaten by Maga and that he stuck in her throat. He was never an easy meal.

The concern of these cronies with cannibalism is many times displayed. Gillies tells of a sheriff who was made into a soup; and Scott voiced an old suspicion of Scotland's Dark Age nobility (in a *Quarterly* review, which was challenged on the point by his editor, Lockhart). When Byron was also suspected, the grounds for suspicion may have been, as I've suggested, the *Don Juan* shipwreck, in Canto II:

> The longings of the cannibal arise
> (Although they spoke not) in their wolfish eyes.

The cannibals of the time were apt to be portrayed as lustfully greedy predators, but Byron's castaways are forced into it: they draw lots as to 'who should die to be his fellow's food'. Tam's green eyes in *The Three Perils of Man*, one of the main dishes in the 'bothering repast' discovered by Wilson in Hogg's writings, shone in the wake of Byron's transgressive episode.[5] There's a poem of Hogg's, 'The Lord of Balloch', in which a captive chief becomes his own chef and main dish: 'on his own flesh he strove to dine.' 'Strove' is delicious.

In deploring the greed of the English in the April 1830 'Noctes', the Shepherd proclaims that the very infants look like a dish to set before the King of the Cannibals, while in the March issue of the previous year an evangelical lady craves a pig which is 'the very image of a human squeaker' of infant-school age. Edible bears' paws are mistaken by the diners for human hands. Intimations of anthropophagy, noticeable both in the symposia and in Hogg's writings, are inventive and wide-ranging. There are cannibals in Fife. There are cannibal crows. There are cannibal critics.

Cannibals may be both black and white. In the 'Noctes' of June 1826, the Shepherd evokes an officer possessed of 'mustaches about the mouth like a devourin' cannibal, and proud fierce een'. Hogg's uncertain view of the military life is mirrored here. The Shepherd scorns a cowardly soldier by the name of Fozie Tam, a poltroon at school who won a medal at Waterloo, and then Wilsonly declares that 'the British army, drawn up in order o' battle, seems to me an earthly image of the power of the right hand of God.' That this hand has put down foreign cannibals in its time is well understood.

A man-eating Scot, Sawney Bean, once inhabited an Ayrshire cave, and Hogg invented a similar ogre for a hole not far to the south, and not far from the hole he occupied himself on Queensberry Hill. The ogre in question is the Grousome Caryl, glanced at earlier. The ballad about him was collected in his *Queer Book* and is the first of its items in time, having been published originally in *Blackwood's*, in 1825. The antique spellings are an exotic dress for an exotic and troglodytic tale: his 'ancient stile' is at once perversely disobliging and, occasionally, to the point. 'Caryl' means man or chap, and was usually spelt 'carle' (it is a word favoured in the 'Noctes', where the Shepherd refers, in June 1826, to 'that Carle, Weber'). The ogre lives with his brood of dames and children at a spot still marked on the map as the Giant's Grave. Lord Annerdaille, chief of the Annandale Johnstones, heads a posse to put a stop to the disappearance down the hole of animals and a maiden. His men are killed, and the monster's wives and bairns run out and drink their blood.

> And aye they quaffit the reide warme tyde,
>   Their greide it wals so ryffe,
> Then trailit the bodies into the holle,
>   Though fleckerying still with lyffe.

The crack Border bowman gets his ogre, and the wives are strung up.

> Some saide those gyantis were brotal bestis,
>   And soulis they colde haif none ...

But a certain Peter of Bodsbeck, who sees what others can't, spies a flight of crows, each one with a giant's soul writhing in its beak. The souls are dropped on Galloway, from which they'd come: it was the 'worste helle' known to the birds.

This Grousome Caryl is both damnable and agreeable, and the ballad has a spring which is like that of the more ludic of the traditional ballads. The giant is kin to Maginn's Timothy Thady Mulligan, terror of Leith, the embodiment in verse of an Irish energy from an Irishman bent, like Burke, on joining the English élite. The giant also carries the image of his maker. Hogg's appearance was described and re-described for as long as it lasted. Late in the day, the *Blackwood's* De Quincey pontificates about the ethnic Scotchman as 'a being apparently human, with sandy hair – high cheek-bones – light blue eyes – wide mouth'. 'Aiblins wi' buck-teeth like mine,' puts in the Shepherd, seeing his own face in the portrait.[6] The body of this Narcissus, which fascinated his contemporaries, and has fascinated recent writers too, with the coming of a new theoretical interest in the corporeal, is a fusion of beauty and beast: it has in it the feral child, the folk hero, the romantic genius, it has a male and a female allure, and a shaggy, stringy-haired animal horror. The image of the Cannibal King sets a crown on this fascination.

The Shepherd is an object of desire in the 'Noctes'. Eaten there by the Witch Maga, he is also the Big Boar who rolls the Lady Maga in his plaid. His physical presence recurs eternally – his tongue, his teeth, his toes, each one a thought longer than the other. In 1827 North is still reverting to the 'fine animal' who entered, mane flying, the kirk at Ettrick. His might, mane, talent and disastrousness are embraced and stigmatised in the Shepherd eidolon, which crucially reflects, besides, qualities of his beholder. The sentimental Wilson was physical too, in life, none more so: a wrestler, walker, jumper, angler, an eater and a drinker and a lover – a Hogg. North purports to be old and lame, and free from stain; no books to his name either. But an author nevertheless, and one still vain of his athletic past.

A bold and perceptive account of Hogg's physicality has been offered by the American scholar Ian Duncan.[7] He argues that the Shepherd functions in the 'Noctes' as Wilson's body, that there occurs 'a jealous, bullying re-appropriation of the Other, who has become the Narcissistic image of a lost, pure, better self'. He thinks that the two men are a symbiosis, while tending to see Wilson the sentimentalist as spent, as needing, in the manner of Dracula, infusions of Hogg's vigour, that of the wild boy and creature of appetite. This phase of his argument is less than fully accommodating of the knowledge of how wild and subversive the living Wilson was, both in and out of the 'Noctes'. The living Hogg learnt to appear sentimental, aerial and genteel from a Wilson who was all of these things, but who also needed no lessons from his friend in how to be physical and Hoggish, in the sense of that word espoused by the *Blackwood's* coterie. What separated the two was more a matter of class than of corporeality. Each was divided between fine feeling and animal vigour: this constitutes their symbiosis, and served to promote a shared hypocrisy. Wilson, North, Hogg and the Shepherd persona tack, in unison, between the raunchy and the chastely fastidious. 'Are the "Noctes" indelicate?' asked a page heading in the issue of November 1828. They are and they aren't.

Ian Duncan ends his account by speaking of Hogg's admissibility to 'the convivial table of the Blackwoodian boys' club' only under 'strict conditions of patronage and supervision', while remarking that, 'even cast as Wilson's phantasmatic, alienated corporeal self', he 'continued to triumph over them all'. But then it could also be said that the exceptional energies of those about him at the board have their triumphs over the Shepherd and his original. Duncan's essay is nevertheless a welcome demonstration of the richness of the Hogg/Wilson duality so often scanted in the past – at one time, on the basis of a snobbery patterned on that of Wilson and Lockhart, and, latterly, on the basis of a repudiation, on more or less political grounds, of the magazine's entitlement to admiration and respect.

Both here and in other essays of his, Duncan writes about further aspects of the spell cast by Hogg on his associates and about the images of Hogg produced in his immediate circle and beyond it.[8] The Gurth and Wamba likenesses of 1819 are discussed; four years later in Scott's *Quentin Durward*, the Wild Boar of the Ardennes, of a countenance part human, part bestial, projects a revolutionary violence – a Hogg potentiality to which Scott would not consciously have responded. Sarah Green's novel, *Scotch Novel Reading*, is adduced, with its ringleted 'rosy cheek of poor Hogg', and a heroine who wants to be like Jeanie Deans and 'walk leagues, barefoot (*à l'Ecossaise*), to get only one sight of him'.

Maximum joviality took place at a thrice-described 'Noctes' supper of 1825, where Hogg presided and 'two grand Americans' of his were introduced, among other strangers or 'fresh men': such men, claimed Gillies, who was present, supplied, when sufficiently intelligent to appreciate their broad humour, one of the 'main charms' of these occasions. He also claimed that 'the greatest attraction of all consisted in the complete *sans gêne* and comfort of the place, contrasting with the humility of the apartments.'[9] On this occasion, Lockhart and Galt looked in later. Blackwood woke from sleep to demand an entire Finnan haddock. Hogg mixed jug after jug of Glenlivet punch, and remembered the scene – written up by Lockhart in the 19th 'Noctes', of March that year – as one in which a Whig-deriding song of his, the 'Noctes Song' as it became known, struck 'like electricity'. At his rendering of the song, Gillies fell screaming from his chair, bringing a grand American gentleman down with him, in his old-fashioned frills and hand-ruffles.

The song, said Hogg later,[10] had been composed during the day for delivery in the evening, but the Shepherd calls it an improvisation, and is lauded by North as a 'perfect Pistrucci', after an *improvisatore* of the time. It went to the air of 'Whistle and I'll come to ye, my lad', and supposes it to be all over with the cowardly Whigs – who were moving, in the real world, towards their Parliamentary triumph.

> For the Blue and the Yellow's forsaken, young man,
> The day is arrived that's nae joking, young man,
> 'Tis vain to be murmuring and mocking, young man;
> A Whig may be leal,
> But he'll never fight weel,
> As long as he dadds wi' a docken, young man.

These three witnesses, Gillies, Lockhart and Hogg, shed light on the 'Noctes' operation: not many of the times of Hogg's life can have elicited three separate imaginative re-enactments in print.

Lockhart's March 'Noctes' is interesting for the Shepherd's rebukes. He talks of writing a pastoral play which will be unlike Ramsay's *Gentle*

Shepherd in that the lads won't turn out to be sirs and lords, though he might perhaps write about rank there, in pursuit of a Wordsworthian 'similitude in dissimilitude'. He engages to immortalise North and Tickler 'in my yawtobeeography', while settling some old scores. North fixes him with a cannibal stare, and is told: 'Confound thae gray glittering eyne o' yours, you warlock that you are!' Tickler is told: 'You wadna shed a tear gin your Shepherd, as you ca' him, were dead, and in the moulds.' Tickler is 'evidently much affected': 'Have I not left you my fiddle in my will?' Sym had indeed done this.

Hogg's extravagant long poem *Queen Hynde*, started and shelved in 1817, was published in 1825. It was excerpted, and equivocally extolled, in the magazine. 'The words came out, helter skelter, ane after the other, head to doup, like bees frae a hive on the first glimpse o' a sunny summer morn,' explained the Shepherd in April 1824 to cronies one of whom, Odoherty, in a 'Noctes' swarming with these words (January 1825), responded in gala style: 'On he goes, splash, splash – by Jupiter, there's a real thundering energy about the affair.' Another friend, North, viewed it as his best poem. In the same 'Noctes', an anti-*Blackwood's* song by Bowring of the *Morning Chronicle* is chaunted and yawned at:

> When messan dog treats Jamie Hogg
> In fashion rather free.

Jamie bit back in March with his 'Noctes Song'.

Tempers were rising with the push for Reform – one reason, perhaps, for how tormentedly good were the 'Noctes' of 1825. The one for May opens with an old song, touched up by Burns:

> She's draiglet a' her petticoatie
> Coming through the rye.

Wilson was accused of singing, at a public banquet, a petticoat-lifting song, but was never as indelicate in his capacity as North. Here, the Shepherd's first words to the company are 'Leeze me on ye – ye're aye at the auld work, lads.' This invokes Burns ('Leeze me on drink' – blessings on the bottle), and employs a sometimes sinister phrase, 'the auld work', attributed by Cockburn to a weaver at the Pantheon meeting, as referring to the devilries, during the 1790s, of the Foxite Whigs.[11] It refers here to the talking and singing and drinking of these madcap Tory lads: a lighter work, but not empty of political intent.

William Blackwood has been made a baillie, and North deplores the Town Council's award (Blackwood dissenting) of the freedom of the city to the Tories' *bête noire*, Henry Brougham, destined to serve as Lord Chancellor in London, who was an ass to accept the civic honour. The affair had been 'a *bêtise*' throughout, and it was hard to say who was 'the greatest *bête* – Brougham or the baillies. The Shepherd asks: 'What's bait?' North pointedly replies: 'Beast, Hogg, beast.' 'A black-burning shame,' contributes the Shepherd to a fury that suggests none of them gives a damn. Tickler speaks of the dinner for the new freeman, where Cockburn, having called for a bumper to the King and the Duke of York, had also called 'for a raäl bumper', moans Tickler, to Squire Brougham of Brougham Hall (a Whig leader whom Cockburn called, in private, morally and intellectually mad). 'Weaver wit,' says Tickler of Cockburn's toast, and the Shepherd says: 'He was aye a very vulgar speaker that Hairy Cobren.' Cockburn was a master of Scottish-sounding forensic eloquence whose cousin had been Pitt's minister Henry Dundas. His place in the *Blackwood's* demonology was never secure.

The diners pass to the topic of Catholic emancipation, to which Scott, initially hostile, came round. North, for whom Odoherty was a 'sturdy Orangeman', was of the view that individual Catholics might be respectable, but that Catholicism was a bad religion, and that while the penal curbs on Ireland's Catholics were bad law, at least they drove the intelligent into the arms of the Protestant Church. Only the dregs were left. The Shepherd would hang Papists – 'I hate the very name of them.' Odoherty talks of Irish Catholicism as a savage beast, Tickler of 'the flood of envious innovation – that foul flood, that would fain be bloody too, if it could'. The attitude of Scott and his associates towards Ireland and Catholicism, however, was more complex than these anathemas would suggest. The Scott who wanted Louisa Stuart to know that his was an Episcopalian family was hostile to those sections of the Presbyterian Church where hatred of Catholics was a Christian duty, and in the magazine Orange marches were aspersed: 'Unhappy, ignorant men propose to walk in procession, assuming the vain and silly badges and decorations which they have been taught to love.'[12]

The May 1825 'Noctes' ends with discussion of an advertisement: 'Accommodation for four or five Sportsmen and their domestics'. With Hogg's parents-in-law dead, the Shepherd is seeking to let Altrive: now that he has a snug steading across the stream at Mount Benger, it is 'past a' telling the inconvenience' of having to go 'tramp, tramping' back to the old place, which is just right for a hunting-lodge. Altrive affords 'the mistress's chaumber, and the bairns' room, and the tway box-beds i' the drawing-room, and the lasses' laft, and the crib in the trance, and the laft ower the gig'. Mullion quizzes him about the advertised use of the library. It contains many a Hogg: 'the Confessions o' a Justified Sinner, achteen; Queen Hynde, nineteen, Hogg on Sheep ... and there's Gray's works – I mean James Gray, and the ither Gray too.' He calls it one of the 'best collections in the parish' – 'a braw library'.

The September 'Noctes' is notable for Tickler's disquisition on polygamy. A polygamist knows no bounds. Tickler has read Milton's treatise *De Doctrina Christiana* and feels

> disposed to agree with him in his doctrine of polygamy. For many years I lived very comfortably without a wife; and since the year 1820, I have been a monogamist. But I confess there is a sameness in that system. I should like much to try polygamy for a few years. I wish Milton had explained the duties of a polygamist; for it is possible that they may be of a very intricate, complicated, and unbounded nature, and that such an accumulation of private business might be thrown on one's hands, that it could not be in the power of an elderly gentleman to overtake it; occupied too, as he might be, as in my own case, in contributing to the Periodical Literature of the age.

North's case is different. He is no unbounded bachelor. He figures in the symposia as a sportive old man of feeling who becomes involved, in no lubricious way, with the perfection of sensibility, the widow Mrs Gentle, whose no less gentle daughter is in receipt of Hogg's gallantries. But his real wife is Maga.

North responds to Tickler on this occasion with an attack on Wordsworth, comparing him with the mischievous and rebellious Milton. Wordsworth 'often writes like an idiot' and 'is, in all things, the reverse of Milton – a good man, and a bad poet'. Tickler yells: 'What!

That Wordsworth whom Maga cries up as the Prince of Poets?' North affects to defer to his friend: 'Be it so,' he replies, using a phrase which appears, to argumentative-comical effect, in one of Hogg's possibly Wilson-assisted Wordsworth parodies. Soon North is saying, to boot, that 'Scott's poetry puzzles me – it is often very bad . . . Except when his martial soul is up.'

Tickler denounces the 'eternal talkers most men are' these days, especially in the country. Tickler talks on about this near-universal bavardise. They are all, or almost all, at it.

> The surgeon! The dominie! The old minister's assistant and suc-
> cessor! The president of the Speculative Society! Two landscape
> painters! The rejected contributor to Blackwood! The agricultural
> reporter of the county! The Surveyor! Captain Campbell! The Laird,
> his son! The stranger gentleman on a tour! The lecturer on an orrery!
> The poet about to publish by subscription! The parson from
> Pitkeathly! The man of the house himself! My God! his wife and
> daughters! and the widow, the widow! I can no more, the widow! the
> widow! the widow!
> (*Sinks back in his chair.*)

Mrs Gentle can scarcely be intended here, at the close of Tickler's expressive aria or outburst. This may be the quintessential voluble widow of bourgeois Scotland. North then says: 'I have heard Coleridge.' But Coleridge is 'entitled to speak on till Doomsday'. Towards the end of the session North commends the do-nothing state: 'The state goes on of itself. All that the ministry is expected to do, is not to stop the state.' Elsewhere in the series, North commends the principle of a divided Cabinet and is told by the Shepherd that this is not a principle which has governed North's editorship of the magazine.

In November of this year came another of Hogg's glorious social occasions, unreflected, this time, in the magazine. A traveller of feeling, on a tour of romantic Scotland, the Englishman Julian Charles Young, Rector of Ilmington, snob and aesthete, visited Abbotsford, and Chiefswood too, where he dined with 'Lockhart and his sweet wife': 'I was much struck with Lockhart's beauty.' In a memoir of his father Charles, a tragedian, a Haymarket Hamlet, a Macbeth, he noted Scott's indifference to music at Chiefswood, save when Sophia took up her harp and played 'Charlie is my darling'.[13] At another house, the great house of Bowood, Young heard Tom Moore's account of a supper at Ambrose's, where he'd found Scott, Lockhart, Jeffrey, Wilson, James Ballantyne, and two peeresses, who had begged to meet Moore. The ' "ladies of high degree" were in full evening costume, or, as Moore described it, "in shoulders" '. Between these pairs of peeress shoulders a place was left for Hogg, who livened things up, for all his stench. The Hogg topos of smears and smells unfolds:

> His approach was discernible before his person was visible; for he came straight from a cattle fair, and was reeking with the unsavoury odours of the sheep and pigs and oxen in whose company he had been for hours. Nevertheless he soon made himself at home with the fair ladies on each side of him: somewhat too much so; for, supper over, the cloth withdrawn, and the toddy introduced, the song going round, and his nextdoor neighbours being too languid in their manner of joining in the chorus to please him, he turned first to the right hand, then to the left, and slapped both of them on their backs with such good will as to make their blade bones ring again; and then, with the yell of an Ojibbaway Indian, shouted forth, 'Noo then, leddies, follow me! "Heigh tutti, tutti! Heigh tutti, tutti!" '
>
> Moore expressed himself as horrified at Scott's want of refinement in giving countenance to such people as Hogg, and taking part in such orgies as the 'Noctes Ambrosianae'.

Alan Strout tells a story which dates from 1825, or perhaps from the time of Hogg's descent on London in 1832, and in which Hogg might be thought to be settling some old scores with Tom Moore – known as Tammas Muir to the 'Noctes' Shepherd, just as 'Pop' was Shepherd for the poet Pope.[14] 'In a brilliant asemblage of wit and fashion, the simple Shepherd made crude allusion to his lowly origin, in the words, "You and me maun be friends, Maister Moore, for we're baith leerie pauets, and baith sprung frae the dregs of the people!" ' 'Leerie' can mean a cock, a chanticleer, or it can mean sly. These two cocks fell out over versions of Moore songs done by Hogg. Some, including Hogg's 'Minstrel Boy', had to be withdrawn, as he complains in the notes to his

Songs of 1831: 'It was manifestly because they saw mine was the best. Let them take that, as Gideon Laidlaw said when the man died who had cheated him.'

A few weeks after the slapping of the peeresses, on 12 December, Hogg called on Scott at his house in Castle Street with a friend, and with a tart opinion of Moore's verse. Scott told Lockhart:[15]

> the great Hogg of the mountains made a descent this morning and not thinking himself a sufficient boar or desirous of a foil or perhaps in order to make a Bardic convention 'of huzz tividale poets' brought with him Thompson the song making not psalm-singing weaver of Galashiels. This was rather cool on the said Hoggs part but Thompson is a good enough fellow so it all went off well the better that Lady S. did not know that the Boar of the forest had been the introducer of the poetical Thrums. Our Hogg gave one superior *grunt*. Talking of Moore or according to his mode of accentuation Muir he said his songs were written wi' owr muckle melody – they gied him a *staw of sweetness*.

A surfeit of sweetness. 'The porker' insisted that 'ma ain notes are just *right* strung,' and his 'are clean ower artificial'. Scott proceeds:

> Dont you think you hear this echoe of a pigstye passing his criticism on Moore. I thought Lady Anne would have spoken but thank God she gave a gulp and was silent. After all the Hogg is a kindly animal very grateful to you though I think he rather believes you honourd in the accession of the juvenile Squeaker to your train of emigration.

His journal, begun not long before this, gives a less ebullient account of the visit, adding that Hogg's 'just right' reminded him of Queen Bess's remark to a Scottish courtier who had informed her that Mary Queen of Scots was taller than her: 'Then your Queen is too tall for I am just the proper height.' Lady Anne was a family nickname for Scott's second daughter, while the 'juvenile Squeaker' was Hogg's nephew Robert, who worked for Lockhart in London, and who had not long to live. David Thompson, the weaver poet or 'poetical Thrums' of Galashiels (said to have adopted for a time Scott's fictional name for the town, Gandercleuch), was a talented if feudally obsequious bard. These weavers took to holding an annual procession: they would advance with banners, and with Scott's piper John of Skye at their head, to meet a carriage bearing the Scott family and Hogg, who wrote ballads for the occasion. Lady Scott, who would have minded Hogg's introduction of a Teviotdale poet into her drawing-room, rode in triumph with the introducer through Galashiels.

The Border towns of Hogg's youth were conspicuous for their loyalty to the Crown. But Galashiels was 'now a nest of Radicalism', said Lockhart of the year 1822.[16] In later years, after the passing of the Reform Bill, he met Thompson, who 'ran up to me, with the tears in his eyes, and exclaimed, "Eh, sir, it does me good to see you – for it puts me in mind of the grand days in our town, when Scott and Hogg were in their glory – and we were a' leal Tories!"' Border radicalism – *et in Arcadia ego* ... 'We hae the breed on the braes o' Yarrow,' gloomed the 'Noctes' Shepherd in July 1827. During the Reform contentions that followed, Scott encountered the turbulence of the breed in Jedburgh. 'Burke Sir Walter' went up the cry.

Queen Hynde, his last long lay, was a busy poem for a busy time in his life. It can look silly, even imbecile, at first; half-way through the last century it could look to admirers of his verse like his worst poem. But taste has changed since then, has moved towards an ability to perceive the poem as multivalent, indeterminate, undecidable, post-modern. It is not the epic which the poet called it ('the best epic poem that ever had been produced in Scotland'), and which its modern editors call it, at times. It is a mock-epic, a burlesque. Its affinities are with the *Dunciad* and with Byron's *Don Juan* rather more than with the Gaeldom of *Ossian* or with the narrative poetry of Scott, influential as both of them were on this occasion. *Buffa* rather than *seria*, it veers at times towards the slapdash sublime.

The poem is often inadvertently as well as deliberately funny, not least with reference to carnage and carnality, and it could well be said that the indeterminacy of the humour, as between accident and design, is among its fundamental features. ' "Tidings!" he bawled with tremulous cry' – this foretells the manner of McGonagall. Of the ancient city of Beregon he writes:[17]

And many a fair and comely breast
Heaved in that jewel of the west.

The sun is worshipped for sustaining the world and rearing 'the racy
pea', and there is this enterprising swipe:

Sheer to the belt he clove the sage;
To either side one half did bow,
His head and breast were cleft in two,
An eye was left on either cheek,
And half a tongue, to see, and speak.

Queen Hynde is set in a Dark Age Scotland of the mind, subject to the
wrath of the Norseman and ruled by this lovely and ineffectual monarch.
We are in the Albyn, or Caledonia, or Dalriada, which incorporated
present-day Argyllshire. Its capital city Beregon, or Beregonium, in
Ardmucknish Bay, with its Ossianic Selma towers, was founded by
Fergus, patriots have believed, on the day after the creation of the world
in 3640 BC. It may be that Beregon used to exist, and can be taken to
resemble Dunwich in East Anglia, once a Medieval emporium town of
world renown, now a scatter of stones. An independent Scotland may
one day require it to have been more than apocryphal, and may follow in
Zimbabwe's footsteps by renaming itself Selma.

A claymore Christianity invades this Early Scotland, in association
with a knockabout Saint Columba, and the poem melts into a whirlpool,
a Corryvreckan, of Highland games and single-combat sword fights. To
counter the Viking menace, the saint has been ferried from Ireland by
the strange warrior M, Houston (*sic*), who turns into King Aiden of
Albyn, who resembles James Hogg. Albyn and Erin are finally united.
The blood of Fingal will mingle in amity with that of Fergus, a prophecy
which the events of the past century in Ulster have failed to fulfil.

The poem is addressed to the virgin daughters of Caledonia, some
of whom have recently offended the poet by giving themselves to
Napoleonic-French prisoners-of-war – an intriguing historical point.
And it addresses 'the Maids of Dunedin', or Edinburgh. A collective
muse or patroness is thereby conjured up, in the style of epic invocation.
Hogg flirts with and reproves Edinburgh's gaggle of mincing belles,

257

some of whom have been shrinking from the bard's brown hand on dance floors. The Ettrick Shepherd flits though the poem. Of a certain peasant, or 'hind', who arrives plaided on the scene, a couplet, present in the manuscript but cancelled for the first edition, has this to say:

> Thro' every look and action ran
> The self-importance of the man.

But this 'motley clown' should not be blamed: 'Few are his paths that lead to fame!' One such path for the clown, as Hogg and McGonagall discovered in their respective ways, was to play the fool: a class-conscious Scotland expected that of the Ettrick Shepherd, one of its most gifted writers. M, Houston, too, comes on, elsewhere, in plaid and sandals, a 'rude uncourtly hind':

> Cunning and strength, combined with all
> The rudeness of the savage kern,
> Kithed in his heideous face altern.

'Some fiend of other sphere?' wonder Columba's monks.

> The youth advanced with giant pace;
> While his elf-locks, of dew to dry,
> He wildly shook above his eye;
> Folded his rude plaid o'er his knee;
> Looked at his leg of symmetry;
> Next at his sword that trailed behind,
> An oaken club without the rhynde ...

'Rude' means rural in Hogg. It also means actions that might frighten the maids of Dunedin.

Here, as in other places, he is capable of seeing both sides of the conflicts he describes, and of falling into the contradictions and inequalities sneered at by the prissier of his contemporaries. His poem has the negative capability of certain varieties of satire, in which everybody gets it, while his heart was big enough to find room for Highland and Lowland, pagan and Christian, patrician and popular sympathies – a breadth of response which is implied in the poem's strategic pun on 'hind', which can mean a farm hand, a female deer or a queen. It can find room for two views and more of women, for a gamut of conjoined hostility and concupiscence: here is a poet who ogles the bosoms of the fair while continually seeking to burn alive a consignment of virgins and send them to Valhalla. Searching the poem for doctrinal coherence, the *Collected Works* editors speak of a democratic, Covenanting strain, whose importance others might miss. It has recently been argued[18] that, while the poem can't be thought to 'promote democracy', its open-endedness and fluid identities are a 'reforging' of the epic in which Hogg 'demystifies, and subverts, the existing power structure and promotes social mobility'. But it may be that it is even more anarchic than carnival interpretation makes out.

There's no point in denying that all this sows confusion, or that the whole thing appears to have been written in a rush – or rather two rushes, separated by an interval of years. But Maginn was right to talk, not just of rushing and splashing, but of a thunderous energy. The poem is more of a satirical stew than it is a foundation myth, a Lowland pastoralist's Celt-centred Scots cosmogony, and it is, as such, as often as not very enjoyable.

Its composition was interrupted by that of three novels, the two *Perils* and the *Confessions*, and its start was accompanied by another poem in the same style and metre, the *Russiade*, a mock-epic which got no further than two books. It seems to represent a harking-back to the parodic work that went into *The Poetic Mirror*. One of Selkirk's traditionary 'sutors', or shoemakers, votaries of the Saints Crispin, tells the story of a Scottish hero, a giant womanising warrior pursued for his misdemeanours.

> His name was Russell; but in sport,
> Or else, because the name was short,
> Men called him Russ.

A Wordsworth-parody moment. Russ lays about him with a priest he snatches up:

> None ever wrought such dreadful doom
> As did this limb of papal Rome.

Venus descends from the sky and snatches Russ:

Clasped his huge fists around her bosom;
Bade him hold fast lest she should lose him.

She takes him up and then plunges him into the sea; he is due to pay a visit to Hell.

The main source here is Byron's *Don Juan*. Another source appears to be Virgil, who is mocked by Hogg in accordance with a period disposition in his disfavour: Aeneas, equivocally regarded in the literature of recent times, may have been reckoned a suitable escort, so to speak, for this Don Juan's descent into the Underworld. The poem is a contribution to Hogg's thematics of ups and downs, escapes and humiliations: but the shape of his life is better read elsewhere, and I am not sure that the poem is as interesting as Philip Cardinale's ingenious essay on its provenance and textual history.[19]

CHAPTER SIXTEEN

Sporting Life

'The place that once knew us will know us no more!' sings Master Ambrose in the 'Noctes' of February 1826. The Shepherd laments their flit from the cramped and cosy hostelry beside Register House to a grand hotel in nearby Picardy Place. The large letters facing down Leith Walk would catch the eye of passengers from the London steamboats and smacks, and the old place had become choked with custom because of the popularity of the 'Noctes'. But the Shepherd hadn't the heart for the move, and would miss the Blue Parlour. It did nothing, though, to stop the mouth of outrageous talk.

'I am noo the Yeditor o' Blackwood's Magazine,' confides the Shepherd in the February number. 'Angels and ministers of grace defend us!' responds Tickler. The Shepherd tells him all: 'they couldna do without me. North's gettin' verra auld, – and, between you and me, rather doited – crabbed to the contributors, and – come hither wi' your lug – no verra ceevil to Ebony himsel.' This catches the note of the journalistic politics of all time. Letters making unrefusable offers, asking him to name his terms, had been raining down on Yarrow, and to escape this embarrassment he had driven to town 'on the Saturday o' the hard frost, and that same night was installed into the Yeditorship in the Sanctum Sanctorum'. What a change is impending. 'Wha wad ha thocht it – that day when I first entered the Grass-Market, wi' a' my flock afore me, and Hector youf-youfin' round the Gallow-Stane – where, in days of yore, the saints –'

'Sire!' Tickler breaks in with a homage, only to be made aware that he must do better or will have to go – hardly, at his age, an early retirement: 'you maun compose in a mair classical style.' The Shepherd threatens to open the Balaam-box of spiked articles and unsolicited contributions. Tickler implores: 'James, as you love me, open not that box. Pandora's was a joke to it.' And there's a threat to make Tickler a sub: 'Ay, Sub. I create you Sub-yeditor of the Magazine.'

Ambrose produces the alarming Balaam-box. It is a safe, with a spider nesting in the lock. The Balaam-box might have been feared to contain some of the Shepherd's own pieces. It contains an 'Essay on Popular Education', which the new (and temporary) editor rejects. He is against providing for the poor by such means as Mechanic Institutions, favouring the trickledown from a general advance in wealth and knowledge. The view imputed to the Shepherd here squares with a denunciation, imputed to him later, of the Enlightenment educator Madame de Genlis, Tickler's 'absurd old beldame'. It does not square with Hogg's creation in 1828 of a local school in a hut by Mount Benger. A generous act by a man then 'liable to arrestment' for debt: 'Margaret was just saying she had forgot the time she had money in her pocket and I replied that I had just one shilling in my possession which I had kept alone since the Border games and it had remained so long a solitary residenter that I thought it would be a lucky one.'[1] The axis of resemblance between Scott and himself was fortified by the establishment of this school, which lasted until 1962. Scott (with Cockburn) had founded a school and, as Boswell's father said of Johnson, called it an academy. Edinburgh Academy began to teach its upper-class children in 1823.

The old work of anthropophagy went bonnily on in the magazine. Tickler utters a lewd desire to swallow 'a well-fed chaplain, or a delicate midshipman, or a young negro girl'. This may elucidate his taste for polygamy. The Shepherd, that fine animal, professes a great liking for wild beasts – 'Oh man, gin we had but wolves in Scotland' – and for chasing and eating them. He hotly defends fox-hunting, while condemning the wasp: 'There's nae sic thing as pleasin' him.' Lockhart's uncanny Gil-Martin laugh is evoked in a conversation sited in their new place, between the 'Tria Lumina Scotorum' – the Shepherd, North and Tickler. They like the new place: but the 'dear auld tenement', 'our ancient howf', in the Shepherd's expressions, will always be, for North, 'holy and haunted ground'. Previous old places are recalled. Hogg's Ann Street, by then knocked down, was where North first saw his Shepherd's honest face, and ate cod's head and shoulders in his company.[2]

Hogg became the impresario of a 'Scottish Olympics', a name conferred by a contemporary journalist. He became the master of sporting ceremonies which are barely mentioned in the 'Noctes', and yet are in some respects cognate with the ceremonies of conversation and consumption reported in the magazine, where he was a victor ludorum who was also a victim of the games that were played.

Grandson of the athlete Will o' Phaup, one of those Laidlaws boasted of for never having been beaten, Hogg had been a sportsman in the days when there was no competitor to beat. At seven, he was 'wont to strip off my clothes' – a prelude to the Shepherd nudities of the 'Noctes' – 'and run races against time, or rather against myself; and, in the course of these exploits, which I accomplished much to my own admiration, I first lost my plaid, then my bonnet, then my coat, and, finally, my hosen; for, as for shoes, I had none. In that naked state did I herd for several days, till a shepherd and maid-servant were sent to the hills to look for them, and found them all.' Shoeless, too, were some of the competitors in his Scottish Olympics: having walked the many country miles to the venue, they would run barefoot or in their stockinged feet. Hogg's 'Flying Tailor' Wordsworth parody carries the zeal of those trudgers to the point of take-off or ignition. A later poem of his, another 'Minstrel Boy', remembers his own 'conscious energy of soul' and 'high resolve not to be beat'.[3]

Energy and resolve took him into a range of sports. He does not seem to have been a football-player, though he served as a football manager at Carterhaugh in 1815. It was said of him that he was over sixty when he learnt to be an archer, and was given a bow and arrows by Adam Ferguson, a yew bow as tall as himself, which Achilles might have bent but Allan Cunningham could not. The Bowmen of the Border, captained by the Ettrick Shepherd, were responsible for the St Ronan's Games, which held its inaugural meeting at Innerleithen on 26 September 1827, in the glow of publicity that had come to the town from its picturing in Scott's spa novel *St Ronan's Well*. The Bowmen dressed themselves in Anglo-Scottish style – as Robin Hoods, in doublets of Lincoln green dashed with yellow or gold, and broad blue bonnets. It was at about this time that Hogg felt like a sheep compared with the entirely golden young Duke of Buccleuch: but he knew how to shed his sheep's clothing.

Tom Tait, 'the great oracle of Innerleithen', sang the praises of the prodigy of Mount Benger:[4]

> There's poiet Hogg in his green coat,
>   And it was faced wi' yallow,
> Wi' medals bright to crown the might
>   O' ilka gallant fellow.[4]

These medals were pinned for distribution to the chest of the master of the revels, which were rounded off with a banquet and with songs by, and sung by, the master.

The annual Games featured archery, running, jumping, wrestling, 'stone-heaving', hammer-throwing, hop-step-and-jump. And there were further events, the most important of which, the angling-matches, sometimes took place at Yarrow. The country pleasures of the Scots, not least their songs, were drying up, felt the singer of songs. So Hogg said: let there be games. He sought funding from landowners and farmers, helped to pay for the prizes (with what?), and saw to it that the winners' names were mentioned in the papers. The St Ronan's Border Club enjoyed middle-class and patrician sponsorship. It would have needed more than a hop, step and jump to remove the asperity of class difference in the restive new Scotland of rural poverty and urban squalor and overcrowding. But the Games must have helped to bring people together.

'The Meeting of Anglers, or The St Ronan's Muster-Roll', a poem thought to be Hogg's, is an adaptation, and excelling, of the Jacobite song 'The Chevalier's Muster-Roll', a relic of the Fifteen rebellion.[5]

> Little wat ye wha's comin' –
> Will o Powderha"'s comin',
> Jock is comin', Sandy's comin',
> Mr Nibbs an a"'s comin';
> Scougal's comin', Rose is comin',
> Robin Boyd, to blaw, 's comin',
> Philosophy and poetry,
> An' doctors' drugs, an a"'s comin'.

His Nibbs was an Englishman, and men came from far and wide to the various gatherings of the sportive. Powderhall is a stadium in Midlothian, where the twinkling of legs, many of them canine, has gone on into the present day. Mrs Hogg's nephew James Gray was among the winners, carrying off the Marchmont Arrow, as was Hogg's shot-putting farm hand William Goodfellow. His friend Henry Glassford Bell, who felt like shelling Britain's cities, did well at quoits, and was a sprinter. Hogg took a twenty-pound salmon from the Tweed below Innerleithen, and there was a time when he gave bystanders 'the terrible impression' that he'd 'become all at once insane': he'd been trying to land another salmon, from St Mary's Loch. The 'mystery' was cleared up when he was found displaying it in triumph at the porch of Tibbie Shiel's inn.

His magazine friends were present at these events. In 1831, John Harper skimmed the bar 'more like a bird than a man', and a flying tailor also flew. At six in the afternoon the ninety members of the club, broiled by the sun, gathered to drink punch and dine. 'Dark and silent as the night', Lockhart was there – it was as if Gil-Martin had shown up at Powderhall. There too were Wilson and Blackwood, Robert Sym (Tickler), the Earl of Traquair, Captain William Burns, son of the poet, Henry Glassford Bell. They dined on roast mutton, potatoes and gravy, green peas, small beer, cold punch.

At the dinner, a 'murder shout' was heard from the Ettrick Shepherd: 'an exclamation which, but that our friend has lately been elected a member of the kirk session, we should have interpreted into an oath'. A waiter had spilt a charger of gravy over Tickler's head. Up rose his giant form, 'the unctuous fluid hailing off from his redundant locks – the Shepherd standing with a rueful visage, exposed to the "minute drops from off the eaves"'. The day went on till midnight with speeches from Wilson, the silent Lockhart, and Bell, songs from Hogg. The episode might have come from the tented pre-'Noctes' 'Noctes', or indeed from the series proper.

On the second day of the 1831 Games an episode of deeper interest was noted by the same journalist.

We were examining his bow ... when a lady of high rank left her carriage, and addressed him. We stepped aside, and of course are ignorant of the nature of her address; but the Shepherd's plain response – he seldom speaks in an undertone – 'Ye're a gude leddy,' had in it such an utter want of factitious feeling, and withal such a plaintive earnestness in its tone, that it went to our heart more directly than any words we ever heard.[6]

A few months before, having been caught poaching on Buccleuch land, with the Mount Benger lease up for renewal, Hogg had been forced to give up this weary farm. He was back in Altrive. And by the end of 1831 he had withdrawn from *Blackwood's Magazine*. Baillie Blackwood's services, which had included the procurement of shooting licences, had been solicited earlier in the year. Intent on building an addition to Altrive, with a connecting passage, he thought it 'prudent' to do it in Blackwood's name: 'as if you had built the house'. Unless the Lord build the house, one might say – *Nisi Dominus frustra*, Edinburgh's motto – they labour in vain who build it. Hogg and his lord, however, were now to break off relations.[7]

The ballad 'Robyn Reidde', which may have been written about the time of the August Games, at Blackwood's bidding, to fill a hole in Hogg's *Queer Book*, has a gladiatorial content and a Hogg-like hero, 'ane strainge unchancye boye', an archer and a wrestler, who goes around incognito downing formidable opponents. Robin Reid (if I may) is in some degree a Border Robin Hood, and the ballad alludes to the Robin Hood corpus of ballads: but there's no word of robbing the rich to give to the poor. He enlists in the Border wars, and the road that runs from the hereditary reiver violence towards nineteenth-century sports, including soccer and rugby, is once more apparent. He goes over to the English chief Lord Scrope (Henry Scrope of Bolton was the English Warden of the West March from 1563), who claims Reid as a North of England name. He out-wrestles a French master, to whom Robin reveals his identity in these exciting words:

> 'Myne naime' sayit hee 'is Robyn Reidde
> I thynke no shaime to telle
> Myne fader wals dafte myne moder wals keude
> And I'm hardly richte myselle

But quhat is withhelde from mee in wytte
    In mychte of airm is giuen
For I will not yielde to ainy wychte
    That braithis aneathe the heuin

For I haif ane knolege at myne herte
    From quhare I cannot telle
That I am double – I'm Rob Reidde
    And I'm besyde myselle.'

By the foreign master he is seen at first as a clowne, a hynde; and Robin serves Lord Scrope both as a champion and as his 'motelye foole', his Wamba. Robin is a daftie, of daftie blood; just what is double about him is not made clear. Eventually he lays low the Scottish chief Lord Douglas, and James V, who banished the Douglas family, former perpetual holders of the Wardenship of the Scottish West and Middle Marches, is pleased. The King proposes to set Robin on to 'kille myne nobilis all', for being proud and oppressive. Robin also becomes a royal page.

'Most respectfully' dedicated, this 'motley work', to Christopher North and Timothy Tickler Esquires, *A Queer Book* of 1832 has several of his good poems. It consists of ballads, burlesques, pastorals and satires, and is both sped and retarded by its Chattertonian ancient style, which may have allowed him to write more raunchylye than elsewhere, and which can sometimes suggest the defensive posture of difficulty and obscurity adopted by Anglo-American poets of the twentieth century. The Scots of the pastorals, he thought, might also prove difficult for some. 'Thae Englishers,' he told Blackwood, who wanted them to read the books he published, 'winna understand a word of it': a prediction echoed in the 'this'll fox them' of modern writers. The antique and sometimes arbitrary spellings, and the bilingualism of his often convergent and coincident Scots and English, can have the effect of at once enlarging and unsettling the sense of what he writes:

And jollye mischieffe on his face
    Wals prentit stamphishlye.

The last word, Scots for 'robustly', is given the further meaning of 'stamped' by the word that precedes it. His poems imitate the ballads of the past, and they imitate the imitations of others. His venereal 'weicked damis' show the menace of Keats's Belle Dame. But his ballads are ballads in their own right, rather than pastiche. Hogg's was a large vocabulary, and the book has its share of his proleptic expressions. Rainwear occurs there. Someone is

> Als if all swaithit and furlit
> In Mackintoshis patent wairre,
> The merval of this worlde.

Here, too, is the 'full ignition' acclaimed earlier in this book.[8]

The 'Noctes' of 1827 were full of good things, including a summer celebration of Hogg's sporting prowess, at some remove from the Scottish Olympics. The January number has the Shepherd's maudlin and gloating evocation of Cockneys in the snow – of two bagmen, or commercial travellers, overcome by hypothermia north of the Highland Line. 'Pretty babes o' the wood', they sit down and cry, and freeze. 'They've gotten a sair Scotch starchin' – and the fierce North cares naething for their towsy hair a' smellin' wi' Kalydor and Macassar, no it indeed, but twirls it a' into ravelled hanks, till the frozen mops bear nae earthly resemblance to the ordinary heads o' Cockneys – and hoo indeed should they, lying in sic an unnatural and out-o'-the-way place for them, as the moors atween Dalnacardoch and Dalwhinnie.' Requiescat Leigh Hunt.

North, the other North, is moved by the pathetic picture intended by the Shepherd, which is also a derision of inferior city-dwellers caught out of their element. But he then visits a derision of his own on a cast of dodgy characters imprisoned in one of the snowstorms about which the real Hogg wrote so well. Tomintoul is a 'wild rendezvous' for 'the wildest spirits of the wildest clans, old soldiers, poachers, outlaws, bankrupt tradesmen from small towns, and bankrupt farmers from large farms, horse-coupers, cattle dealers, sticket ministers, schoolmasters without scholars, land-measurers, supervisors and excisemen, tinkers, trampers, sportsmen, stray poets, contributors to Magazines – perhaps an editor – people of no profession, and men literally without a name, except it be recorded in the Hue and Cry, all imprisoned in a snow-storm, James! What matter if the whole body of them were dug out dead in the morning from the drift, a hundred feet high?' One of Wilson's accesses of homicidal mania has here encompassed an inventory of Scottish jobs, several of them Hogg's. Wilson, in the flesh, took off his jacket once and thrashed a bully at Tomintoul, while an adjacent wild spirit ran off with his wallet.[9]

In July came the climactic indelicacy of a nude sally by Tickler and the Shepherd from their bathing-machines at Portobello. They swim out towards the islet of Inchkeith, basking and splashing and chatting in the waves of the Firth of Forth, along the bay from North's country place Buchanan Lodge. The piece opens in a welter of underclothes. The Shepherd never wears drawers, he cries (though Hogg did). His breeks are lined with flannel all the year round – a different thing. 'As for thae wee short corded under-shirts that clasp you like ivy, I never hae had ane o' them on syn last July, when I was forced to cut it aff my back and breast wi' a pair o' sheep-shears, after having tried in vain to get out o't every morning for twa month.' Tickler is startled to find the other so rough about the back: 'You are a perfect otter.' He is told: 'Nae personality, Mr Tickler, out at sea. I'll compare carcasses wi' you ony day o' the year.' The Shepherd goes on: 'I sud like to be a dolphin.' Tickler would like to be a shark, the better to eat the people he fancies. 'Oh! that I were a whale,' sighs the swimming Shepherd: 'Nae fish that swims enjoys so large a share of domestic happiness.' Tickler spouts that a whale is not a fish. 'Let him alane for that,' rejoins the Shepherd. 'He's ca'd a fish in the Bible, and that's better authority than Buffon.' Then he sighs: 'O that I had been a sailor!' The Shepherd of the 'Noctes' is often in optative mood.

This brilliant Portobello episode does not let up. Tickler has been seized with cramp, and his friend has to tow him by the locks, while suspecting that he may be malingering. Tales and allusions spill into the ether of a sparklingly clear day, so clear they can see a man and woman standing on the top of Arthur's Seat. It seems that the Shepherd learnt to swim by ploutering out from the shores of St Mary's Loch. Cramp threatens to return. The Shepherd: 'The cramp's just like the hiccup, sir – never think o't, and it's gane.' 'You would make a beautiful corpse, James,' enthuses Tickler, as James floats on his back mentioning mermaids. Thereby hangs the tale of his sexual intercourse with one.

'The fishiness o' that kiss!' He was in a cave on the Isle of Skye, at night, with nothing on. A colder sort of moonlight falls on his limbs. A 'plaintive wildness' is heard, a bit like the strain of an Aeolian harp. The next thing he is in the embrace of a mermaid, her hair green and slimy. 'What een! Like the boiled een o' a cod's head and shouthers!' It seems to be all over with him. He is enveloped in a whirl of hands, paws, fins, scales and maw. He starts to repeat the Lord's Prayer and the Creed, while sputtering out her fishy kisses. From ledge to slithery ledge, the pair go 'tapsalteerie', like the world turned upside down in Burns's love song. Like the knight in Keats's ballad, he has been subdued by an outlandish female.

Tickler has kept interrupting the romance with news of an approaching steamer. 'Ship ahoy!' Through a speaking trumpet, the captain keeps them posted on the political news: 'Lord Wellington's amendment on the bonding clause in the corn bill again carried against ministers by 133 to 122.' A young lady in a straw bonnet, with a green veil and a ruby sarsnet, has a spyglass at her eye: she seems to be known to the Shepherd, whose yoo-hoo risks ruining her reputation. North's Newfoundland dog Bronte – a big beast, but there are fears over the Shepherd's recent purchase of Bonassus the bull – joins them in the drink. Vociferations are transcribed in a veracious manner that had few precedents, even in *Tristram Shandy*, with Bronte's Bow-wow-wow antiphonal to Tickler's 'Whoo – whoo – whoof – whroo – whroo – whroof – proof – ptroof – sprtf', and to cries of female alarm from a passing pleasure boat, at the sight of the Odyssean pair. They then rise from the foam, to meet the Nausicaa of Mrs Gentle, on the strand at Portobello.

The Shepherd goes by coach to Edinburgh, with Mrs Gentle and her daughter Mary; tall old Tickler, spent from his swim, snoozes at their side. The Shepherd makes up to the daughter, takes her by the hand. The women vie with each other in displays of sensibility, and with the gallant Shepherd, who assures the daughter that a friend of hers, struck down with consumption, needs only the fresh air of Ettrick to restore the roses to her cheeks. Having, in the previous 'Noctes', blamed Wilson's naturalist brother for exposing Miss Gentle to a puma ('he may endanger his ain life wi' Pumas, or Crocodiles, or Krakens, or ony ither carnivorous cannibals, but he sha'na tak young leddies in wi him intil their dens'), he lectures these ladies on the flirtatiousness of phrenologists, who are handling girls' heads in the exercise of their mystery, hands not long from perusing the plaster-of-Paris skull of that murderous Jezebel, Mrs McKinnon, if not the very skull itself. The phrenologists are accused of finding that this 'she-devil' had 'a great organ o' veneration', as shown by the fact that she had been a Madame Butterfly, had once 'drapped on her knees on the Calton Hill, and imprecated furious curses on the vessel that was carryin' off an offisher, or some other profligate, with whom she had lived in sin and shame'.

The discussion turns to the septuagenarian North's powers as a satirist and to his bump of vilification. 'It's curious how many sumphs become satirists,' offers the Shepherd. North remarks: 'What a rare faculty 'tis, James, cutting-up.' The Shepherd suggests that there's no one now who can handle, as North can, the cat-o'-nine tails. But this is to forget, says North, that his favourite instrument is the knout. He also likes, though, the thrust direct: 'Give me a desperate lunge at the kidneys.' (The later critic, F. R. Leavis, was once praised by an associate for knowing 'where to jab'.) The Shepherd observes that North can refrain from the knout for a year at a time, but then he takes it up again, and the Cockney has to confess him

> the First Leevin' Satirist o' the age. I wud like to see you, sir, by way of vareeity, pented by John Watson Gordon, in the character o' Apollo flayin' Marsyas. Noo for the Roond. Thank ye, Mr Tickler – some udder. Awmrose, Dickson's mustard.

Watson Gordon did a portrait (herewith) of Hogg, whose eidolon sweeps at this point from flaying folk alive to the eating of udders. Marsyas was from the dregs of the people, a piper who had the rank-subverting temerity to challenge Apollo to a contest of musical skill; Titian painted his portrait, imagined his punishment. Throughout the 'Noctes' conversations, the Shepherd takes part in a sado-masochistic badinage which could turn on him and exact a punishment distressing to his original. Elsewhere in the series, he was said to be unable to swim, but he showed himself a Byronic bonny swimmer this July. He also showed, on this occasion as on others, a talent for being flayed alive.

James Hogg, by Sir John Watson Gordon (1830)

The 'Noctes' for July 1827 has a bright passage on the delivery of sermons. The Shepherd points out that the gentlemen of the press are wicked enough to go reviewing a minister's pulpit performance – his 'vice' (a piquant phonetic rendering) and 'his way o' managing the whites o' his een' in transports of piety.

CHAPTER SEVENTEEN

Personality Hogg

To Allan Cunningham, in October 1828, Hogg sent the cheeriest of bulletins about his welfare. Here is a brave face at a bad time, the face of a simple, struggling farmer rather than some Ambrosian man of letters. 'If you saw me you would think me younger like by a good deal than when you first saw me on Queensberry. I have a most amiable, virtuous and kind hearted young lady for my spouse' – a spouse apt to be unreasonably jealous of him, Blackwood had been told four years earlier. His 'one son and three daughters', he says here, are 'all blooming, healthy and happy creatures', though Harriet's foot was a worry – would she prove a 'lameter'? – and in the course of the year she was taken to Edinburgh for medical consultations. A fourth daughter, Mary, the memoirist, was born in August 1831. 'I have hitherto been uniformly happy in all circumstances and thankful and truly grateful for my lot. Embarassed I have been by the affairs and expenses of others but every one has behaved to me with the greatest lenity so that I have still been enabled to keep my head above water.'[1]

In Edinburgh, Hogg shone. A personality. Robert Chambers, bookseller, encyclopedist and evolutionist, has summoned up his celebrity and his conviviality.[2] He would stay at Watson's Selkirk and Peebles Inn in Candlemaker Row in the Old Town, and was constantly out and about, as lion and as good fellow. After breakfast, perhaps with Scott in Castle Street, other calls were paid, and there were sessions in the back-shops of booksellers, and at dinner with Blackwood's wits. Having set that table on a roar, he might foregather with lads of his acquaintance in the tenemented Old Town, telling them stories, singing them songs. Then back to the inn to round off the daylong gaudeamus.

On his last night in town, he'd throw a supper at the inn for 'twa-three' friends who would become some seventy.

Meal-dealers are there from the Grassmarket, genteel and slender young men from the Parliament House, printers from the Cowgate, and booksellers from the New Town. Between a couple of young advocates sits a decent grocer from Bristo Street; and amidst a host of shop-lads from the Luckenbooths, is perched a stiffish young probationer, who scarcely knows whether he should be here or not, and has much dread that the company will sit late. Jolly, honest-like bakers, in pepper-and-salt coats, give great uneasiness to squads of black coats in juxtaposition with them; and several dainty-looking youths, in white neck-cloths and black silk eye-glass ribbons, are evidently much discomposed by a rough tyke of a horse-dealer who has got in amongst them, and keeps calling out all kinds of coarse jokes to a crony about thirteen men off on the same side of the table. Many of Mr Hogg's Selkirkshire store-farming friends are there, with their well-oxygenated complexions and Dandie-Dinmont-like bulk of figure.

Such company would rush into Watson's inn, with the author of 'Kilmeny' borne along like a leaf on the tide. All company was deemed to be equally acceptable to Hogg, and all classes of the community were present, though not always in perfect accord. Loyal toast after loyal toast was drunk. Baillies and burgesses and commissioners of police served as chairmen and croupiers, the literati upstaged. On one of these markedly civic occasions, a toast goes to a High Constable's wife, delivered of a daughter. The captains and the chiefs depart, and Hogg takes the rest of them into the small hours, with songs and glee. What a singing Scotland, what a merry Scotland, he made of it in the course of his revels. Chambers, then a lad, remembered him as a 'prodigy', an underrated marvel: 'The time will probably come when this inspired rustic will be more justly appreciated.' He was a poor man who threw banquets, a happy family man who was also a star; he was civic and poetic, a wise man and a fool. Personality Hogg was a phenomenon, and a complex one.

The 'Noctes' for 1828 abound in statements about the sovereignty of the imagination which may in part reflect what Wilson sensed that his friend then needed to think. The Shepherd's ability 'to believe ony thing' may have owed something to an unwillingness of Hogg's to believe that he was broke. And the same might be said for the claims that 'there's nae truth like fiction,' and that 'there never was a baseless fiction.'

In October, the Shepherd performs an imaginary murderous assault on his editor. He blackens his sleeping friend's face, as an experiment, to induce him to dream various sorts of death – drowning, hanging, guillotining. He tightens the handkerchief round North's neck: 'in a moment you'll see him get blue in the face.' Ambrose objects to the experiment. He is from Yorkshire, and lacks imagination. North wakes, except that he has never been asleep. Not altogether a baseless fiction, this assault.

Other Ambrosian events include, in May, a poem, for Kit North's seventy-third birthday, which resents the role of Cockburn and Jeffrey as pleaders against magazines in actions for defamation, actions which grew fewer when juries were found to be awarding trivial damages.

> In Embro town they made a law,
>   In Embro at the Court o' Session,
> That Kit and his lads were fautours a'!
>   An' guilty o' a high transgression.
>   Decreet o' the Court o' Session;
>   Act Sederunt o' the Session;
>   Kit North and his crew were fautours a',
>   And guilty o' a high transgression.

The poem parodies one of Burns's in *The Merry Muses of Caledonia*. Hogg compares Kit and his merry men – whose transgression has been to trash the Whigs – with the 'standing pricks' indicted as fornicators, as fautours or offenders, in the Burns.

In November, another indelicacy appeared. North tells his friends that 'it was only last Saturday night, that I had rung the bell for Shoosy, that we might wind up the clock' – an allusion to the hero's begetting in *Tristram Shandy*. Shoosy is North's housekeeper – not, as the Shepherd misconstrues, his wife. She is in tears because the moths have been at North's 'devil's dozen pair of breeches, including one of doe, and two of buckskin!'

In December, Tickler sings a ballad more erotic than any poem by Hogg, about a lady wooed and won by an inferior ('Awa, awa, ye coal-black smith'). Change shape as she may, this lady can't escape the blacksmith.

> Then she became a duck, a duck,
> Upon a reedy lake;
> And the smith, wi' her to soom or dive,
> Became a rose-kamed drake.

Other shapes ensue:

> Then she became a het girdle,
> And he became a cake ...

The Shepherd attributes this ballad, 'The Twa Magicians', to a collection of ancient pieces put together by Peter Buchan of Peterhead. It was never likely to have figured in Scott's *Minstrelsy*, but the girdle and the cake are reminiscent of an excellent cannibal love poem of Scott's, addressed in adolescence to a girl trysted-with in her aunt's cupboard:[3]

> Come hither! You my closet are
> Where all my sweets are stored,
> Oh save me from your aunt's good things,
> And some of yours afford.

Strained relations between Hogg and the *Blackwood's* triumvirate are indicated by the exchange of April 1829 between North and the Shepherd, who says: 'You're jealous o' me, sir, that's the real truth, – and you wish that I was dead.' North says: 'I merely wish that you had never been born.' This leads to a discussion of *Othello* and to the Shepherd's complaint about the 'Mephistophiles tricks' played on him by his Iago friends, as they can occasionally seem. Tricks, rejections and financial need were to drive him to seek new journal outlets, principally *Fraser's* in London, run by Maginn, and the *Edinburgh Literary Journal*, run by Henry Glassford Bell and published by Constable; and he had already moved his fiction to London, for book publication there. 'When I found, sir,' he wrote to Bell, 'that I would now be at liberty to publish my free and unbiassed sentiments of all my literary contemporaries, I felt precisely like the Laird of McNab, when he had got with some difficulty up to the winning-post at Perth races – "By the Lord, but this is me now!" [4]

In December 1828, and in March of the following year, there appeared in the second of these journals a pair of 'Noctes Bengerianae', in which Hogg went it alone. In the first of the pieces there's a doppelgänger meeting with a patrician vagrant who advises him that his family, his hinds and his neighbours cheat him, that he thinks himself a little prince; he appears to be a prince given to kissing the maids and making them laugh at him. Might not Hogg, as the vagrant himself has done, and as Edgar Allan Poe was soon to speak of doing, 'soar away into the unutterable regions of delirium', with the spheres 'all dancing round you, and the elements subject to your control'? Hogg advises the vagrant against obloquy aimed at the King and his ministers, though 'I'm sure they canna hae done less for you than they hae done for me.' The cast of this meagre Bengerian material consists in the main of Hogg and his servants, among them Wat Nichol, whom six years before Hogg had been willing to retain, slow though the honest fellow was, paying him five pounds, 'ten sheeps' grass', peats and potatoes, and not 'a farthing more'. Wat is assigned a song about a merry fellow with whom 'a' gaed wrang that should hae gaen right,' who has been in trouble with the priest over a girl he then married, and who has lived happily ever after. [5]

The issue of 6 September 1829 carried 'A New Poetic Mirror by the Ettrick Shepherd No 1 – Mr W. W.': 'Ode to a Highland Bee'.

> I choose not say the wild emotion
> Of my moved soul, and its devotion,
> At thy astounding locomotion.

The poem ends:

> And thus shall I ambitious be,
> When inquest is perform'd on me,
> To rise above my grovelling race,
> Bounding, like thee, and one day trace
> My path on high like heavenly dove,
> Which none dare challenge or reprove,
> A path all human walks above!

277

Levitation is patterned on the bee's 'astounding locomotion', a word that belongs, as 'ignition' does, to the language of Hogg's proleptic technology. This is no parody of Wordsworth. If anyone or anything is being taken off it is Tom Moore's ecstatic 'Ode to the Flying Fish', which has the same four-stress line, and in which the gregarious Moore longs to leave the 'grosser throng' of human beings, to shed his stains, and calls on Virtue to raise him to heaven. Moore is parodied by name elsewhere in this series. Hogg's Ode is a poor piece which all but casts doubt on the unaided authenticity of his 'Flying Tailor' and other Wordworth parodies of earlier times, so little like the new piece in their calm crispness.

Wordsworth is parodied by him in the journal, and no mistake, in 'Andrew the Packman' (30 March 1830),[6] but once more disappointingly for any admirer of the earlier 'Wordsworths'. Hogg, the reprover of Calvinism, can seem at times like some sentimental Calvinist, and Wordsworth is turned into one in this poem, looked at earlier. Andrew is the sceptic who knows,

> better than any man
> In all the eighteen towns of Cumberland,
> The prime regard that's due to pence and farthings.

And who is warned that no light emanating from 'thy good works' can be expected on his deathbed. The Earl of Lonsdale's pyramidal hatrack is meant to symbolise order, the good order threatened by Andrew's scepticism and supported by Wordsworth – whose patron, in real life, the Earl was. This is a passage which does stand comparison with the poetry of the earlier parodies, where Wordsworth's 'similitude in dissimilitude' is a concern, as it is here, and which suggests that the properties of metaphor – which can find hierarchy in a hatrack – may have been perceived by Hogg as an aspect of his interest in likenesses and in a dualistic psychology. Robert Wringhim and Gil-Martin are a simile in dissimilitude.

The poem is in general an uninviting piece, however, which skids on its own ironies. A scarcely recognisable Wordsworth defeats the infidel, whereupon the infidel hitches his pack on his stooping shoulders, and then,

> with gait
> Of peddling uniformity, and ell
> In both his hands held firm across that part
> Of man's elongated and stately form
> In horses call'd the rump, he trudged him on,
> Whistling a measure most iniquitous.

There comes to mind the Edinburgh rumour that, in Wordsworth's *Excursion*, the Wanderer, an austere Scotsman reared in Ettrick-like natural surroundings, and infused with their virtues, showed an awareness of Hogg, who thought the poem 'ponderous' but whose Packman may perhaps show an awareness of *The Excursion's* Solitary, depressed by his lack of religious faith.

After several months of reluctance on Blackwood's part, *The Shepherd's Calendar* was published in February 1829. The stories and reminiscences which it contains had appeared in the magazine over a period of several years. Blackwood hired Hogg's nephew Robert, as a young man of 'much tact and good taste', to relieve the book of, in Robert's words, 'objectionable or superfluous' material. The *Collected Works* edition of the book restores the text to its magazine condition; the editions stress the harmful effects of the editorial attentions Hogg's writings so often received as civic standards, those of the public which came into being at a time of political and religious arousal, grew more demanding. Hogg could be told by the publisher of an annual, Thomas Pringle, that his rule was 'to admit not a single expression which would call up a blush in the Cheek of the most delicate female if reading aloud to a mixt Company'.[7]

The collection has his account of Will o' Phaup and some powerful stormscapes. A chapter on dogs precedes one on the lasses. Justice is done to the Hogg kennel – Sirrah, Hector and Lion, in line of descent. Intelligent collies and affectionate sheep find their own way home. One man's dog, not known to be pregnant, returns from hard work on the hill with a litter of puppies in her mouth: 'Her master's heart smote him.' Hogg had a heart-smitten love of animals, as Scott did: for both men, they were like men and women. This must register as a dimension of Scott's animalising of Hogg.

The stories are about storms, sheep, lairds, about farmers with designs on their servant girls, as in one of the most memorable, 'Tibby Hyslop's Dream', where a pious bonny lass, prophesied over by a second-sighted, 'unco parabolical' great-aunt, copes with such designs – and the farmer in this case comes to one of Hogg's suicidal ends. In *The Three Perils of Woman* he takes a more insouciant view of Border farmers, who, 'very properly, never style any of their servants maids'.[8] The version of pastoral apparent in his prose writings does not gloss over the facts of rural life, as his poems sometimes do. They depict a countryside in which 'pretty maids' are at risk of being harassed – 'jaumphed an' jurmummled'. Some lines of verse quoted in the tale of Tibby Hyslop ask who has ever seen, on a Monday morning, the grass growing green 'where a married man and a maid had been'.

Those familiar with the *Confessions* might be taken aback by 'The Prodigal Son'.[9] Old Isaac, a minister, disregards the protestations of a nagging daughter (women, he thinks, are 'rash', 'contrary') and sets out to save the soul of a delinquent youth, reckoned to be dying, the seducer of Isaac's granddaughter Euphemia, and a lapsed candidate for the ministry whose sermons had been 'mere cauldrife harangues'. Isaac holds that the saved are few in number: 'God knows who are reprobates, and who are not.' He asks his daughter: 'Do you not know that his grace aboundeth to the chief of sinners?' God's own, from before birth, may fall into sin, but repentance will earn them their heavenly reward. He reaches the cottage: 'A stroke like that of electricity seemed to have affected the nerves of all the rest of the family on the entrance of the good old man.' Euphemia implores him, 'Father forgive me, for I knew not what I did,' and is rebuked for an abuse of Scripture. The youth repents, recovers, and becomes Isaac's Helper. The banns are called. 'I have always considered the prayers of that good old man as having been peculiarly instrumental in saving a wretched victim, not only from immediate death, but from a despair of endless duration.' A tale Hogg's wife must surely have savoured.

'Mr Adamson of Laverhope', a *Calendar* story first published in the *Blackwood's* of June 1823, enacts a providential sheepfold electrocution. Lightning strikes a cruel master. Papists are 'a' the deil's bairns', avers an old shepherd. A cursing Catholic tramp is sympathetically seen: but there were those who believed 'it was the devil who had attended the folds that day in his likeness.' The story reveals a divided mind, or perhaps it could be said that the writer spread his bets.

Two superstitious murder mysteries of his share with the *Confessions* an inscrutable duel. 'This is of God,' says the teller of 'The Cameronian Preacher's Tale', a good old man who has 'a gift in sarcasm which the wildest dreaded', and who is led by a light to the spot where a man and his treasure lie buried. 'Adam Bell', first published in the *Spy*, has a surly hero, no sooner glimpsed than gone. But his wraith returns. A neighbour claims to have witnessed Adam's killing. But did he witness it? Did he do it? This mystery is called 'insolvable'. Most of Hogg's mysteries get solved, but in this case, he just won't say what the solution is. Both stories have presence, together with contrivance.[10]

Another duel, and a further resemblance to the *Confessions*, can be found in the *Calendar* story 'The Laird of Cassway'. The laird has two sons, Thomas the spark and Francis the scholar, who fight over a girl, and in order to intervene he is teleported from England by the spells of a class-conscious witch aunt, whose vehement Scots – 'afore I were a landless lady, I wad rather be a tailor's layboard, and hae the red-het goose gaun bizzing up my rumple' – required the editorial interventions of Robert Hogg when the story was admitted to the book.

Some of those tales of his which approximate in time or temper to the *Confessions* differ from it in one important respect. They have their duels and their demons and their indeterminacies. So far as they are religious, as opposed to superstitious, in feeling, however, their tendency is Cameronian. They look back to the faith of the martyrs, and, perhaps, some twenty years forward to that of the Free Kirk exodus from the General Assembly of the Church of Scotland.

In 1828, an excellent year for the storytelling Hogg, a curious approximation to certain aspects of the *Confessions* came about. In 'The Brownie of the Black Haggs', published in the October *Blackwood's*, a laird's witch wife forms a sado-masochistic bond with an 'audacious' servant, Merodach. A serving-maid has died: 'There was little doubt that she was taken off by poison,' a fate later to be attributed to a woman of Hogg's acquaintance. We have entered a 'delirium' of hate and 'delicious' revenge. Merodach is at once a child and an old man: a rare illness of accelerated ageing, Progeria, induces the 'elvish' look which he displays, and it seems possible that the illness contributed to the likenesses, the ethereal physiognomy, which Hogg took part in transmitting to the Victorian supernatural. The neighbours are puzzled by Merodach. Half-man, half-spirit? 'Some thought he was a mule, between a Jew and an ape.' A mule falls between a horse and an ass, and the word is used here to refer to the old idea of intermediate creatures – dualisers, as they have been called. But most people thought he was a brownie.

The laird's wife is a tormentor of Covenanters who is tormented by this creature, with whom she eventually elopes. 'Nipping an' scarting are Scots folk's wooing,' reflects a shepherd. The story has the electric mutuality of two abusers who can at times be seen as the one person. When the lady looks at her servant, 'it was not a look of love nor of hatred exclusively; neither was it of desire or disgust, but it was a combination of them all. It was such a look as one fiend would cast upon another, in whose everlasting destruction he rejoiced.' Hogg said that he felt for John Wilson 'just such a sentiment as one deil might be supposed to have of another': theirs was a not incomparable mutuality. This is a well-written grisly piece which trenches on the writer's essential concerns, and in which both a previous James Hogg and the subsequent Samuel Beckett are suggested.

Only in point of prestige and flourish can the poem about Kilmeny, who goes to heaven, be considered a superior work to the translation to another world effected in a *Blackwood's* tale of February 1828. 'Mary Burnet' is both humane and inhumane. It is meaningfully mysterious, coherent, deeply rooted in the countryside forsaken by this girl. A lad she knows, his heart 'a mere general slave to female charms', makes a 'delirious' attempt on Mary's, and is struck down with a burning fever. Mary vanishes, but returns in the guise of a series of teasing Greensleeves, culminating in a patrician superstar who inveigles and mangles the libertine. The bad man's father speaks of his son's doom in a passage that points to the life and legend of the author of the tale: 'On the night that he was born, there was a weeping and wailing of women all around our house, and even in the bed where his mother was confined; and as it was a brownie that brought the midwife, no one ever knew who she was, or whence she came.' Mary's father Andrew, a shepherd, tells a wizened old chap who appears to him that he, Andrew, is 'looking for that which he would never find' – his daughter. But the 'audacious shrimp', his 'shrivelled monitor', leads Andrew and his wife – an affectionate, sharp-tongued pair, affectionately portrayed – to an encounter in Moffat with their socially mobile Mary, who keeps the appointment as a beggar woman but immediately becomes a queen. She kneels before her parents, gives them rich gifts and introduces her two sons. At midnight she climbs into a gilded chariot and is gone, back to fairyland, or heaven. The parents are happy ever after. In Moffat they had passed a test, by showing that they would have been pleased to see their daughter even if she'd turned out to be poor.

No work of Hogg's shows a more dynamic affinity with the *Confessions* than 'John Gray o' Middleholm', published in 1820, three years before that book was written. This is a comedy of starvation, and of its ruses and expedients. A folk tale, an enhanced and very funny fabliau, intricately fashioned, yet charged with suspense. Poor John, a lazy weaver, goes in frantic search of treasure trove, of purses – 'poses', as he pronounces the word – which may lie hidden on battlefields and, by rich prelates, in the neighbourhood of monasteries, on the principle that 'he that hides kens best where to seek.' A crafty old fellow appears to him in dreams, and John then meets him in the beautiful town of Kelso, where John has arrived in order to dig near its ancient abbey. His new friend is a cobbler with an interest in treasure, and with dreams of his own, of being a monk and shrieving Kelso's bonny lasses: 'I'm sure I confessed Bess mair nor a hunder times i' my sleep, an' mony was the sin I pardoned till her.' John is an Anti-Burgher Presbyterian, but 'knows little more about the matter, save that his sect' – valiant against state intrusion – 'was right and all the rest of the world wrong'. His minister is another Anti-Burgher, one who knows more about the matter. This 'Calvinistical' man, so-called by a writer who wants him seen as something of an enemy of the folk, meddles greedily with the excavations.

The story has an interest in what can be known, or kent, and in who kens it. When they meet in Kelso, John and the complicit cobbler of his dreams conduct a dialogue of doubles, on the uncertainties of personhood. 'This is *me*,' says the cobbler, 'as sure as that is *you*; but wha either you or me is, I fancy me or you disna very weel ken.' The sceptic proceeds: 'you thought it was *me*, and I thought it was *you*, an' it seems it turns out to be neither the one nor the other.' John's digs and poses help to keep the wolf from the door, by means hidden from his partner, Tibby Stott. The cobbler had earlier advised him to get rid of her, but John had refused: his gillygawpie wife and weans are dear to him in an equivocal way which reaches for expression towards Burns's poem – 'Mony a sair darg we twa hae wrought' – about the auld farmer and his mare. Of Tibby, who insists she's a mare rather than a hare, and whose maiden name means heifer or ox, her husband observes: 'we maun just tak the gude wi' the ill, an' fight thegither as lang as our heads wag aboon the ground, though mony a sair heart an' hungry wame she has gart me dree.'

CHAPTER EIGHTEEN

Balloonist

———

'Aughteen Hunder an' Twenty-Nine' was addressed by Hogg in a poem of the time as 'Thou dour, unsonsy, Papish year'. He joined in the *Blackwood's* cry against Catholic Emancipation, while also uttering pleas for toleration. Another poem plays with a simile for the degenerate times he inhabits.[1] In their travels round the world, storks have stopped coming to Britain, which is going to the dogs. A last stork, derived from the Book of Jeremiah, flies to these shores and is shot by a 'sporting Bishop'. The last stork curses the kingdom, but offers forgiveness too:

> Forgive them all save the state botchers,
> Those piteous pedagogues and poachers,
> Praters oppress'd with proud proficiency,
> Sapience supreme, and self-sufficiency;
> Degrading with their yelping bills,
> The shepherds on a thousand hills.

'Poachers' here is metaphorical. It means reformers and emancipators, as do the other pejoratives in the passage. It does not mean poachers – those guilty of the offence of which Hogg had just been accused. He was a poacher who was also an elder, and who had long been a well-known public figure.

Blackwood published the poem in February 1830, while feeling that 'it wants something to make it more direct and applicable as a Satire on the late Papist measure.' He also published two pastorals of this time which have the smeddum of Hogg's first poetry. In one of these, Will and clamorous, Covenanting Sandy debate the Papist measure: ruin awaited its delay, argues Will. 'A Sunday Pastoral', a courtship piece, was sanctified at Blackwood's behest, with Hogg highly reluctant: 'the mixture of love and religion in it can only be objectionable to those who are ignorant of the pastoral life.'[2]

With the tide turning towards Parliamentary reform, Blackwood's writers set themselves to face it down. Hogg's biographer Thomson was persuaded, as Hogg was, that, as a publisher of books, Blackwood could feel inhibited by 'the popular bias of the period', [3] but his magazine fought hard against it. To see Hogg as travestied, Toryfied, by his gentlemen friends is far from imaginative: it is less permissible to see him as the sum of the liberal or egalitarian sentiments he expressed, having subtracted the hierarchical sentiments to which he was also inclined. His politics were, in part, a way of belonging to a set of people with whom he could be a genius and a success, while also, at times, a ludicrous failure. He was made to say in the 'Noctes' that most of the time he didn't think about religion, all-important though it was: so far as this was true of Hogg, it might lead one to wonder how much time he spent thinking about franchise reform. Charles Marshall, who taught the school Hogg founded, and lived for a time in his house, remarked that Hogg was a constitutionalist Tory, 'or affected to be'.[4]

He made judgments of a political kind, nevertheless, which mattered to him unequivocally. His slavery case concerning the rural poor, argued at this time in Blackwood's *Quarterly Journal of Agriculture*, is an example. He was a Scottish patriot but not a separatist: it was left to Tickler to declare, in September 1829, chez Ambrose, that 'in losing our independent Parliament we lost every thing that made this nation a nation, and we have been countyfying ever since.' Hogg is likely to have agreed with the Shepherd's statement in the same issue concerning the Clearances: 'Weel, if the gentry lose the land, the Highland anes at ony rate, it will only be the Lord's righteous judgment on them for having dispossessed the people before them.' The Shepherd moves to the pathos of the Duke of Hamilton's cleansing of cotters from the island of Arran, where the Shepherd had once watched the smoke rising from the shielings on a braw summer's evening. Whereupon North introduces and chants 'The Canadian Boat Song', 'from the Gaelic'.

Hogg and Scott were the same but different. There was a similitude in dissimilitude. There was also a similitude shared between Hogg and Burns and cultivated by Hogg. All three suffered financial ordeals, which denoted somewhat different types of exposure to the profession of writer and to the expanding market for literary goods. In the last days of 1827

Scott's *Journal* described his response to a letter he had been sent by

> James Hogg the Ettrick Shepherd asking me to intercede with the D.
> of Buccleuch about his farm. He took this burthen on himself without
> the advice of his best friends and certainly contrary to mine. From the
> badness of the times it would have been a poor speculation in any
> hands, especially in those of a man of letters whose occupations as
> well as the society in which it involves him [unfits him for such
> business]. But I hope this great family will be kind to them – if not,
> *cela ne tiendra pas a moi*. But I cannot and ought not to look for
> having the same interest with this gentleman which I exercized in the
> days of Duke Charles.

It was indeed not his fault that Hogg, who had now become for him a
man of letters rather than a farmer, had chosen, as Scott saw it, to plough
the top of Mount Benger ('I will do anything for him except becoming
myself one of the cuddies'); and this was a patient response, given the
size of the Scott cataclysm, the exactions of his programme of recovery.
A year later, Lockhart told his wife that the young Duke, though 'turning
out a stupid scrub' or miser, had commuted Hogg's arrears at Mount
Benger.[5] By April 1830, however, there were more. He informed
Blackwood that 'everything is to be taken from me even to my books,'
which he seems, in fact, to have retained. 'Do you not think that in
London I could be well employd in some literary capacity?' Scott, in his
capacity as Sheriff, signed the warrant for his dispossession.

'The confusion and the sale are over and here I am crept into my little
cot again,' he told Blackwood in late May. He and his family were back
at Altrive. The sale had been a good one, considering the times, and
things were looking up: 'after all, with young Buccleugh's lenience there
will be but little loss.' Altrive's four rooms had to accommodate himself
and his wife, four children, with a fifth on the way, servants, and a
lodger, 'a gentleman of weak mind' with a mother in Liverpool, a Mr
Brooks. 'We are all in good health and as happy as want of room will let
us be but we are actually just like a swarm of bees at the casting and can
scarcely all get within the door of our cell.'

The gentleman of weak mind had a turn for literature, and had written
poetry which he wanted to publish, but for which, as a gentleman, he did

not expect to be paid. When Hogg went to London, his wife assured him that their paying guest was 'really behaving well', and when Hogg wrote back, having been sorry to see the poetess Laetitia Landon, at a party, 'quite naked all above the apron strings', he nonetheless felt that his wife might 'tell Mr Brooks how very lovely she is'. His own clothes were still being bought for him, as a rule, by his wife.[6]

The 'Noctes' of these months carry escapes by the Shepherd, dealt with in a carnival spirit unsuited to the Ettrick travail but not irrelevant to it. In March 1829, he burst in on them with a 'Huzzaw', having skated to Edinburgh, keeping to the road and going by Traquair and Peebles. The grand game of curling, with its granite planet and frantic brushers of the ice, supplies a similitude. 'Hoo I snuved alang the snaw! Like a verra curlin' stane, when a dizzen besoms are soopin' the ice afore it, and the granite gangs groanin' gloriously alang, as if instinct wi' spirit, and the water-kelpie below strives in vain to keep up wi' the straightforrit planet, still accompanied as it spins wi' a sort o' spray, like the shiverin' atoms o' diamonds, and wi' a noise to which the hills far and near respond, like a water-quake, the verra ice itself seemin' at times to sink and swell, just as if the loch were a great wide glitterin' tin-plate, beaten out by that cunnin' whitesmith, Wunter.' On he snuves – over the hills and far away, like Marion's Jock, or like the Old Pretender in the Jacobite songbook. Or, as Tickler has it, 'helpless as Mazeppa'. Byron's noble hero is tied for adultery to a wild horse that bolts into the Ukraine. The Shepherd then takes a well-deserved bath.

Mazeppa is once more in mind, some months later, when the company settles to the Shepherd's tale of his nude ride to Moffat on the back of the bull Bonassus. This 'Noctes' of April 1830 opens with the Shepherd gazing up into the night sky and comparing himself with the Chaldean shepherds who were the first astronomers. Not that they could have written 'The Chaldee Manuscript', the Shepherd reflects. But then there are those who doubt whether the Ettrick Shepherd wrote it, as Mullion's 'Hymm!!!' conveys in August. The Shepherd continues to look up at the April sky: 'He's a grim chiel, yon Saturn. Nae wonder he devourite his weans – he has the coontenance o' a cannibal.'

After that, he falls out with his 'Mr De Quinshy', who thinks the Shepherd more imaginative than Burns but can't understand Scots. The

Shepherd bams the humourless scholar and gentleman with his amazing nude ride to Moffat. 'I felt, all in a moment, that I was a Mazeppa.' Here, too, is the Byron hero. Here, too, the water-kelpie is invoked. Here, too, as at Portobello, he frightens the ladies, and is recognised by one. On the way, he encounters 'three gigs-fu' o' gentlemen and leddies; and ane o' the latter – a bonny creatur – leuch as if she kent me, as I gaed by at full gallop – and I remembered haein' seen her afore, though where I couldna tell; but a' the lave shrieked as if at the visible superstition o' the Water-Kelpie on the Water Horse mistakin' day for nicht, in the delirium o' a fever ...' Mr De Quinshy alludes to one of Thomas De Quincey's technical terms, the 'involute': it is not possible, he opines, to avoid feeling that 'in the image of a naked man on horseback, there is an involution of the grotesque in the picturesque – of the truly ludicrous in the falsely sublime.'

Flights, trips, of a chemical nature were also discussed that April. 'Gie me an unce o' opium, Mr De Quinshy,' demands the Shepherd. But he is only joking. He's too old for the poppy: 'I'se een keep to the maut.' His earlier experience with laudanum had cowped him over, toppled him over, and sent him to sleep for days on end. In the 'Noctes' of June that year, 1830, a dog takes drugs, swallowing a box of the Opium-Eater's pills and going barmy. 'Oh! That he cou'd gie the warld his Confessions!' cries the Shepherd. The Opium-Eater takes offence: 'How am I to understand that insinuation, sir?' The two self-confessors might almost be proceeding towards a duel. The dog is O'Bronte, son of Bronte, whose bark, North sorrows, will no longer be heard. Bronte has been poisoned, whether by Gilmerton carters or by students of the surgeon Knox who had been supplied with corpses by Burke and Hare. 'Had the murder been perpetrated by ten detected Gilmerton carters, I would have smashed them like crockery!' rages North. The Shepherd outdoes him: '*En masse* or *seriawtim*, till the cart-ruts ran wi' their felon bluid, and a race o' slit noses gaed staggerin' through the stoure, and then like a heap o' bashed and birzed paddocks wallopped intill the ditch.' The Shepherd's bark is worse than Hogg's verse can be when it comes to carnage.

Knox's depredations were 'far worse than the Chaldean Manuscript', maintains North in the 'Noctes' of March 1829, which wallows in the crimes committed by the Irishmen Burke and Hare and Burke's friend Helen McDougal, who were tried at the High Court of Justiciary, with Cockburn appearing for McDougal and securing her acquittal. The philosopher James Ferrier, together with his uncle and father-in-law Wilson, visited Burke in jail as he awaited execution, and Wilson dons the black cap in *Blackwood's* to deplore the killings and commemorate the visit. Burke used to dance jigs at Innerleithen but was certainly a bad man. 'Except that he murdered,' wrote Cockburn, 'Burke was a sensible, and what might be called a respectable, man.'[7] The Shepherd says here that the actions of the two Irishmen

> were too monotonous to impress the imagination. First ae drunk auld wife, and then anither drunk auld wife – and then a third drunk auld wife – and then a drunk auld or sick man or twa. The confession got unco monotonous – the Lights and Shadows o' Scottish Death want relief – though, to be sure, poor Peggy Paterson, that Unfortunate, broke in a little on the uniformity; and sae did Daft Jamie; for whilk last murder, without ony impiety, ane may venture to say, the Devil is at this moment ruggin' that Burke out o' hell fire wi' a three-prong'd fork, and then in wi' him again, through the ribs – and then stirring up the coals wi' that eternal poker – and then wi' the great bellows blawin' up the furnace, till, like an Etna, or Mount Vesuvius, it vomits the murderer out again far ower into the very middle o' the floor o' the infernal regions.

O for a picturesque variety! he cries. To this misapplication of a romantic tenet Tickler cries a welcome 'Whisht!' But the Shepherd is not done. He says it's all right to denounce the doomed atheistic murderer, and he enters into this murderer's last sensations: 'that drawin' up o' the knees that tells death's doure – and the labor o' the lungs in agony, when you can breathe neither through mouth nor nostrils, and a' your inside is workin' like a barmy barrel'. But the real villain is the surgeon: with these serial killings, the talkers convey, Enlightenment science has much to answer for.

The most remarkable of the imaginary escapes associated with Hogg was performed, not by the Shepherd, but by Hogg himself, and it has seldom been discussed. It was meant for the 'Noctes', and is very like one of the more surreal or ludic of the Ambrosian episodes, sufficiently like to qualify the case for claiming a travesty of Hogg on the part of his co-conspirators and fellow carnivores. But it went elsewhere. In the *Edinburgh Literary Journal* of 23 January 1830 there appeared 'Dr David Dale's Account of a Grand Aerial Voyage', in which two very different Scotsmen fly to the moon.

Like the chapter of a Scott novel, the story has an epigraph – an 'old nursery rhyme', which looks like the work of Hogg. The rhyme is about a shepherd, Davie Dale, who tethers his dog, which escapes and lets the ewes into the corn. The Dr David Dale of the story is a scientist who speaks like an Englishman, while his friend Hogg speaks a superstitious Scots. Dale is introduced by a narrator who explains that this old man had once been entangled in law suits and financial losses, to the derangement of his intellect and reduction to a state of absolute credulity, a state that resembles the 'I can believe anything' of the 'Noctes' pronouncements. Did Dale ever know 'an old odd fellow, styled "The Ettrick Shepherd"'? Know him? Thirty years ago he'd shared an experience with him, which had the effect of separating them from 'our enemies'. The narrator is about to tell the story – of an adventure 'without a parallel'.

The Shepherd of the adventure is approaching sixty, and has the mane of a polar bear, 'white as snow, rugged and shaggy', says Dale. As for his poetry, adds Dale, 'God mend it!' Poets are liars nowadays – none worse than Jock (alias, later in the tale, James) Hogg. This from the man who can believe anything. There glimmers here the paradox and aporia of the Cretan liar, who said that he never spoke a word of truth.

The witty advocate Harry Erskine, the name of an actual and admirable inhabitant of Edinburgh who died a decade before the tale was written, is implicated in the adventure. He is appearing in a law suit involving Dale, on behalf of opponents who are thought liable to lose the case if Dale remains on the scene. Walking with Erskine in the Meadows, Dale is shown a wicker tent thing, said to be a self-moving machine. In it sits Hogg. A balloon appears to be towing it, and the pair, Dale and Hogg, are off to the moon. Balloons were just the vehicle for an age of bankruptcy.

'The last sight that I got of Edinburgh,' reports Dale, 'the Castle was not so large as a molehill.' His companion stares in terror at the dark clouds about him, 'braying out "Murder! murder!" in a voice so Stentorophonick, that I question but it was heard at the North Meadow Walk, which would have been glorious fun for our enemies'. Hogg fears they may be entering the country of the bogles, but Dale is scientific and so is his flight, which is fuelled by, and ascends through an atmosphere composed of, hydrogen gas. Hideous shapes are seen in the sky, which Dale explains in terms of 'the refraction of the rays of light upon a denser body. For example, the refraction which the rays of light suffer in slanting across the higher regions of the air, is greater than what calculation assigns to the corresponding density of the medium. But the supposed discrepancy would entirely disappear, were we to suppose these strata to consist of hydrogen gas, which is known to possess in a remarkable degree the power of refraction.'

The Hogg of the story wails that these shapes are the deil's artillerymen (but it's worth remembering that the real Hogg, the debating-society graduate, kept company with the scientist Brewster). Hogg fancies the idea of a thunderbolt's driving their enemies helter-skelter down there in the Meadows and leaving them 'lying wi' their banes as saft as roasted ingans'. A tremendous thunderclap obligingly resounds. But the thin air makes him feel hungry and thirsty, and takes away his 'relish for thae grand gangins-on o' nature'. Hunger causes him to imagine being consumed. 'Od, I wadna wonder gin we war found in some far polar keuntry, twa dried skeletons, like Egyptian mummies, an' eaten for hams by the Esquimaux or the Greenlanders!' Dale assures his friend that if their fuel gives out in these celestial regions, the attraction of gravity may get them back to Earth. 'The attraction of what? Od, ane can hardly keep their gravity, when hearing you speak.'

Would hunger drive him mad? wonders Dale. Whereupon, in the space between Hogg's knees and his own, a six-gallon keg which bears the 'thrilling name' of Glenlivet is discovered, flanked by a hamper of food – wines, biscuits, tongues, pies, eloquent of the privations of the life on earth from which they have come, and of the long journey intended for them by their persecutors. Dale presently remarks that the keg 'appears to have changed the nature of things with you, most elevated

Bard', which revisits the insight into the nature of perception experienced by Hogg on Ben More. Here, the elevated bard spies a mountain that looks like Ben Nevis and is accused of being drunk: 'for this is no earthly mountain that we are coming upon, but the moon herself, while yon immense pale globe that you see at such a distance is the earth.'

Towards the end of the trip, which provides one of Romanticism's not unapproximate foretastes and similitudes of the Apollo 11 mission, Dale tells Hogg: 'We have formed a great paracentrical parabola, and I think must come to the ground somewhere in the North Highlands. Do you know what a parabola is, James?' 'Ou, finely that, man. – Here's t'ye. – It is just a kind of representation o' things by similitude – and a very good way it is. It answers poetry unco weel.' Dale corrects him, and says he is speaking geometrically, of a conic section. Having spoken poetically, and imparted his own idea of how poetry works, Hogg then speaks as geometrically as it's possible to speak, and that without the help of an 'able book' which he hadn't liked to ask its publisher, Constable, to lend him (he'd already been given a *Marmion*): 'I understand the parabolic and the hyperbolic curves; the cycloid and the epicycloid; the catenary and the logarithmic; the magnetic curve, and the curve of tangents, an' what the mischief mair wad ye hae for the understanding the principles o' geometry?' Dale finds it in vain to reason with this 'thirsty and ravenous son of the mountains', with his curve of hyperbole.

They worry about the landing. Hogg worries about ballast, about shedding the remains of the alcohol. They tinker with the gas supply. They overfly the 'fine island of Skye' and the rest of his native land. Hogg was genuinely and, in the main, appealingly patriotic. 'Ah, auld Scotland, how my heart warms to thee! Wha could look on sic a scene, an' no turn a poet?' And he turns a poet at this point in the story. Some of the poems given are in English, of a pallor that contrasts with the Scots of Hogg's prose speeches on the voyage.

> On such a scene, so sweet, so wild,
> The radiant sunbeam never smiled.

He means that Scotland is the fairest of them all. He does not mean that it lacks sun. There is a letter to Blackwood of January 1830[8] which indicates that, having written some Balloon songs, including one carried in his *Songs* of 1831 as 'The Witch of Fife', he wrote 'the little tour to take them in'. In the *Literary Journal* of 8 May came a poem which shows how bright his verse can be at its most Border Scots, and most Burns, a fisherman's flyting, 'kipper'd' and 'Shepherd' its felicitous parting rhyme.

They hover above Glengarry. Hogg tries to get down by throwing strictly empty bottles at the balloon, and calls for the help of Macdonnell of Glengarry – elsewhere perceptible as the father and betrayer of his people: 'For the love of McDonnell's name an' the Jacobite Relics o' Scotland, bring us down!' The chief is equal to the task. 'Crack went Glengarry's rifle, and before one could have said Mahershallalhashbaz, we were plashing in Loch Garry.' Dale suggests that their host is a bandit chief who would think nothing of beheading two Sassenachs, two English-speakers. Hogg says in Scots that that's no lie: but 'a mair kind an' ceevileezed gentleman I never crossed the door threshold o'.' He is the very model of a Highland chief: 'Fient a ane o' them a' has the true an' proper feelings of a chief but Glengarry himsell.' Lady Glengarry and her misses have a good laugh at the plashers, Glengarry buys the balloon for £100 (half of what Hogg received for *The Three Perils of Man*), as an aid to shooting eagles, and he and Hogg sit up all night singing Jacobite songs. And for all Dale knows, as he departs for Edinburgh and his law suit, they are at it still.

Enlightenment science gets them to the moon and back, but their true fuel may have been Glenlivet. This is a dualistic extravaganza: a complex image – and involute – in which an escape from enemies is also a persecution, a trick played by these enemies, like the nude ride visited on Hogg by his cronies. It's an escape from your troubles which enables you to keep on living while also returning you to your troubles, a space trip which is also a drunken spree.

Five years later, Edgar Allan Poe told the same story. 'The Unparalleled Adventures of One Hans Pfaall' consists of a flight to the moon under the same auspices that governed the Meadows lift-off.[9] Both stories are, in Poe's words, a 'depart, yet live'. 'Unparalleled' and 'enemies' are words important to both. Hogg's arrival at 'the moon herself' is paralleled by Hans's at 'the moon itself in all its glory'. Hans, with failure written into his name, blasts himself off in flight from duns and creditors, on a more precisely calculated formula of hydrogen gas. He survives. And perhaps it was all a drunken spree.

This duplication may be seen as an example of the power of the Edinburgh writers of the day to reach out into the world, to contribute to an international Romanticism. Poe and the Brontë sisters and their brother Bramwell were readers of *Blackwood's*, in which North's dogs bear, inadvertently, the Brontë name, and it is difficult to believe that Poe had never read Hogg's story in the *Edinburgh Literary Journal* – to deny that, while balloons had held the keen interest of the aspiring since the 1780s, Hogg's lunar flight may have inspired a departure from hard times in Baltimore. Hydrogen had been replaced in balloons by coal gas before the stories were written. So Hogg may have steered Poe to an outdated fuel.

Another of his imaginary departures and returns belongs to his early days on the hill. His master defied him to bring home a certain wild ewe, with the aid of his sagacious coal-black sheepdog Sirrah: 'You may as well try to travel to yon sun.' Hogg explained, in 1818, that 'the man did not know that I was destined to do both the one and the other.'[10]

Hogg's falls, his highs and lows, wanderings and tightrope walks, went on happening, on and off the page, as old age drew near. There is a rhyme from the oral tradition, 'Fall of Man', in which one of Hogg's Hoggs might seem to be pictured – it's of the class of invented 'old rhymes' sometimes used to head a chapter of his or of Scott's.

> Bleat, bleat, bleat, bleat,
> Pipe up the sheep
> On Cheviot's utmost summit,
> Where if you slip
> 'Twixt dub and dip
> Down the hill you'll plummet.

Error is beautiful, they said during the rosy hours at the house of Ambrose. Can it be said that Hogg's writings made a romantic hyperbole come true? They can sometimes appear to do this. It is possible to find, in the *Confessions*, something fortunate, something accidental. But it can't be doubted that he meant what he wrote there, and shaped it. The novel was not a mistake. Error is its concern.

CHAPTER NINETEEN

Buffoon

Hogg's moon voyage portrays him as a hungry and thirsty wild man of the woods with a flair for metaphor and mathematics. Elders of the kirk (other than himself) may have felt that it also portrayed him as a 'boozing buffoon'. These two words were used by Lockhart in 1831 when he denied in his magazine the *Quarterly* that Hogg was any such man. Maginn said that Hogg sat for his imbiber portrait in the 'Noctes', that it was true to life. Lockhart wrote that 'no more sober and worthy man exists in his Majesty's dominions than this distinguished poet, whom some of his waggish friends have taken up the absurd fancy of exhibiting in print as a sort of boozing buffoon.'[1]

Lockhart was herewith seeking, with a straight face, to obtain support for Hogg from the Royal Society of Literature. He was later to write to Blackwood explaining his motive, apologising for any offence he might have given, and saying that, before writing the article, he had seen Hogg at Altrive looking 'wet, weary, and melancholy'. The article declared: 'His acquirements are now such, that the Royal Society of Literature, in patronising him, might be justly said to honour a laborious and successful student, as well as a masculine and fertile genius.' On 12 May 1827, Scott had written to Lockhart offering to serve Hogg 'in any way of doing so consistent with my personal resolution to steer clear of the society', which he saw as composed of stuffed shirts. He wanted to help in this quarter, and to do so 'by enabling him to follow his own plans and not by thrusting my opinion' on him.

In February of the same year, Lockhart wrote Hogg a letter which suggests that, exiled from Edinburgh, he may have acquired a better understanding of Hogg's predicament: 'I am of opinion that your name should no more appear in Blackwood's "Noctes" and have taken the liberty of saying so to the Baillie (than whom I do not think you have a warmer friend in this world).' The Baillie was Blackwood. A postscript reads: 'May I hint that you should never *allude* to the "Noctes"?' Hogg ought not to seem to 'fancy it possible that anybody shd have attached the slightest or most momentary importance to such things'. At this time Lockhart said that Hogg was sulky about the Royal Society of Literature bid, and 'I am not sure but he may be in the right.' He said this to Blackwood, who cared about the bid, as we have seen. Hogg received £50 from the Literary Fund, and in 1832 a further £40.[2]

A few weeks after Lockhart's counsel of an exit from the 'Noctes', Scott told his son-in-law that Hogg might make a go of Mount Benger, where he still was, if he would stop ploughing and let it lie in grass. In Ettrick, there were an auld farmer and his wife (as there often are in such cases) who were eager to denigrate Hogg's estate management after his death. 'He was more fitted for books than for farming,' said they: he was 'hand in glove with great men in Edinburgh, Professor Wilson, and Scott, and the like'. He called himself the Ettrick Shepherd 'as though there was never a shepherd in Ettrick besides himself'. He 'thought himself a very great man', and Mrs Hogg looked down on her neighbours. 'These poets think nothing is good enough for them.' Hogg 'paid the Duke no rent, but he caught his fish, and killed his game; he was a desperate fellow for fishing and shooting. If people did not do just what he wanted, he soon let them know his mind, and that without much ceremony.'

The auld farmer, this well-informed neighbourhood spy, in Jane Austen's expression, went on to say that Hogg abused Sir Walter because 'he would not give him a poem to print when he asked him,' and he abused Grieve too when he refused him Benger money. 'He failed and paid eighteen pence in the pound: and yet the duke, though he got no rent, allows the widow the rental of Altrive.' It appeared to William Howitt, whose informants these were, that Border farmers thought Hogg an 'aspiring man, and bad farmer'.[3]

The Blackwood cabal or divan or rump, sans Lockhart, minded the *Quarterly* defence of Hogg, by a wag who had had a hand in crafting the Shepherd eidolon: the tendency of these writers to bite their own hand by turning on their friends and on each other did not excuse what this friend had done. It was worse than waggish, though Lockhart remained a fine fellow. In the 'Noctes' of March 1831 North orchestrated a riposte in which the Shepherd's pipe was heard, and his 'Haw-haws'. The Shepherd can't believe it when told of the unsigned piece in his defence. 'That's bacon I canna bolt.' The author is abused by the company as a sad dog, with the Shepherd desiring there to be no 'personalities'. 'The wiseacre, James, has been pleased to inform the Royal Society of Literature, that, in spite of the Noctes, the Ettrick Shepherd is a sober man, and a loyal subject.' 'Patronage I never asked,' exaggerates the Shepherd.

North thinks, or affects to think, that Lockhart has been bamboozled by some anonymous Cockney. The Shepherd asks a rhetorical question: 'Ca' ye't a matter-o'-fact that a boozin' buffoon ever Glenlivetised at the Noctes?' North answers: 'It is a matter-of-fact lie, James – and that the Cockney knoweth right well; but he wished to do you a kindness, without in his dotage clearly comprehending how to set about it, and with the best intentions in the world, has accordingly committed one of the usual calumnies of the Cockneys, manifestly priding himself all the while in the idea of having essentially served the Ettrick Shepherd, and given him a shove up the hill of preferment.' The piece has also alleged that the talk at Ambrose's is entirely about party politics: 'an even-doon lie,' insists the Shepherd. Hogg once called his own 'Noctes' eidolon an even-down quiz without evil intent. The intention here is to defend the group against the slur of treating Hogg badly, while treating him as gullible and docile.

At the time of this riposte Scott wrote down in his *Journal* his opinion of Wilson.[4] He had himself been attacked in the magazine. Now it had been Lockhart's turn. His 'chief offence seems to have been explaining the humbug of shewing up Hogg as a fool and blackguard in what they call the "Noctes"'. Wilson has lowered himself to the trade of journalism, Scott writes. He is

> by inclination and habits what others are by education and necessity, a thoroughgoing gentleman of the press without shame or judgement. As a politician he puts one in mind of Barm Jock of other days, a kind of blustering idiot whom a mob carried upon their shoulders during a riot rather as their banner than banner-man. But Barm Jock proved before judge and Jury that he was mortal drunk the whole time.

Nothwithstanding his low propensities John Wilson is a clever feller
or more he is a man of genius or rather

A hare braind Hotspur guided by a whim

only it is not always an honorable one.

Scott told his journal that 'I have tried to be of use to him which piece of
folly may be a very good reason for attacking me.'

One rainy autumn Saturday at Mount Benger an unidentified close
friend sat with Hogg in the parlour watching out for the carrier –
Ebenezer Hogg, no doubt, who ran the mails. Zigzagging down the steep
hill from Innerleithen came the cart.

> After fifteen minutes' delay, which seemed fifty to us, the packages
> were landed and cut open ... the gleg eye of the Shepherd singled out
> *Blackwood*, just issued for the month. The Noctes were laid open in a
> moment, and presently Hogg's mirth exploded in a loud guffaw, as he
> exclaimed, slapping his thigh, 'Gad, he's a droll bitch, that Wulson!
> an' as wonderfu' as he's droll!' He had alighted upon one of Wilson's
> raciest personifications of himself, and could not restrain his
> appreciation of its skill and genius.

Both Hogg and Scott were torn by their dealings with the magazine, and
Hogg's experience of the dilemma has great poignancy. 'Some things in
"Maga" have operated singularly to my advantage, for the applications
for contributions from my "highly-gifted pen" have of late increased to a
most laughable and puzzling extent.' Other things had not.[5]

Hogg drank heavily from time to time, even unto delirium. When
late in life he developed water on the chest, he protested that he'd
never touched a drop of the stuff in all his days, and once declared
himself so full of alcohol as to be fit for customs seizure. But he
probably drank less than his jokes made out, and no more than many
males, including Wilson, who was observed to carouse (and to take
port with, rather than after, his dinner). Equally, it mattered to Hogg
that he be seen as a moderate drinker, and he might have been more
grateful to Lockhart here for recruiting him to the ranks of the
Temperance movement. 'Sociality,' he told William Crichton, a doctor,

a connection of Margaret Hogg's who befriended the family, 'is so completely interwoven in my nature that I have no power to resist indulging in it, but I have been blessed by providence with a constitutional forbearance which prevents me from ever indulging in any sinful excess.' Sociality and vanity were among his leading traits, he reckoned. In February 1803, in the *Scots Magazine*, he wrote that vanity had 'carried me through, when every other friend failed'. And he later wrote of his loyal friend William Laidlaw, and of himself: 'as long as I had his approbation and my own, which last never failed me, I continued to persevere.'[6]

Hogg came to fear the magazine's portrayal of him for the anxiety it gave to his wife and family, and had always disliked its ascription to him of opinions he did not hold or did not wish to be known for. In the November 1830 'Noctes' he must have been aghast to tear open the carter's parcel and come across one of the most dazzling riffs in the series, on the subject of yawning. 'Nae yawning,' orders the Shepherd: 'Better that at ance you should cowp owre in a dwawm o' sleep.' North: 'The truth is, that admiration soon makes me yawn – and I fear that Sir Walter, and Coleridge, and Wordsworth, and Bowles, and others, may sometimes have felt queer at the frequent, if not incessant, opening and shutting of the folding doors of my mouth, during their most amusing or instructive, reasoning or imaginative harangues.'

The Shepherd then enlarges on a deficiency in the man he 'loves and venerates' above all other living men 'except your sell, sir': 'There's Sir Walter wi' his everlastin' anecdotes, nine out o' ten meanin' naethin', and the tenth itsell as auld as the Eildon hills, but not, like them, cleft in three, which would be a great relief to the listener, and aiblins alloo a nap atween.' Fools 'swallow his stalest stories as if they were manna dropping fresh frae the heaven o' imagination'. Wilson and Hogg had their own anecdotes to tell, of course, some of them everlasting. Earlier in the same conversation North recalls that hundreds of people have been none the worse for being bitten by mad dogs, and the Shepherd says, 'But then they have swallowed anecdotes,' and North rejoins: 'Which is more than I have been able to do in such cases.'

The alarm in Ettrick when parcelled blackguardings of Scott came over the hill can be imagined, and Norah Parr can well imagine the embarrassment caused when the Shepherd spoke early on, in the Tent, of his dog Hector's 'yawning and muzzling as if he had been listening' to one of Mr Robert Russell of Yarrow's 'very wearisomest action-sermons'.[7] These were preached on two important sacramental occasions in the course of the Presbyterian year.

In April 1830, Hogg was still confiding his troubles to Blackwood, while also telling him that the magazine had ruined him as a writer, and in September 1831, on the eve of rupture, he told him a shaggy dog story about a lost mare which suggests that mutual trust had yet to break down entirely, and which reveals him, as his dealings with Blackwood were sometimes to do, as a kind of peremptory schlemiel.[8]

> I have a queer story to tell you. The other day I bought a capital mare from one of my neighbours. About 24 hours after I brought her home the mare vanished. I sought her through the whole district for two days and advertised her. On the third day I found her lying quietly and snugly drowned in Altrive Lake a small part of her broad side then appearing above. I was so chagrined at the loss of my mare that I half ran home seized my pen and resolved to make her price before I slept and not last night but this have finished the accompanying essay. You are to send the price of my mare for it for a horse I cannot want and am quite out of money.

Near where the mare lay had lain the ballad lad, Willie, sought east and west and then found 'deep drooned in Yarrow'.

Blackwood sent £10. But the quarrel between Hogg and his publisher was approaching its chief crisis. The quarrel barely reached the pages of the magazine (the freedom of the press is such that such quarrels rarely do), but it left its mark on a number of events and occasions. He wrote in September 1831 to another publisher to say: 'I have put *not* by the Shepherd as a sort of *russe de guerre* to make people guess who it is but you may retain the *not* or not as you please.' It was a ruse that might have been meant to enable him either to hide his head or to show his face.

The creature of retractable 'not's', and of knots, and of subterfuge and pseudonym, had once made known to his Athol friend Mrs Izett that 'my designation when in the country is literally "James Hogg Craig of

Douglas"' – after a place associated with his father. He had earlier enquired of Byron: 'By the by have you read my friend Mr Craig's *Hunting of Badlewe* published by Colburne?' There is a piece on this play of Hogg's, an accurate assessment, which is signed 'J. H. Craig Esqr'.[9] A year after the retractable 'not', he made his immodest proposal to Lockhart that 'you will write Sir Walter's life in my name.' The quarrel with Blackwood gave fresh scope for strategies of occlusion and escape.

The 'Noctes' of the November of that year supplies evidence of Hogg's predicament. One of the visionary ballads in his ancient style appeared in the magazine at this time. Lyttil Pynkie is an ominous fairy who arrives in Kilbogye to cast an enchantment, cause death and defend maidenheads. She is interrogated by a priest, Mass John, who is then translated, very ineffectually, to an alternative 'world of wonder'. In the November 'Noctes' North comments pertinently, and in the teeth of much of his own precept and practice, on the perils of literature, with its imaginative worlds and specious pleasures: 'We turn the dread reality of existence into a show for indolent delight.' 'That's beautifu' language, sir,' applauds the Shepherd. North's reflections are pertinent, not only to 'Lyttil Pynkie', but to what some called 'a poetical age', and to what Jeffrey called, in his review of *The Queen's Wake*, a 'poetical country', meaning Scotia. Jeffrey confessed to thinking that Hogg 'knows more about beings of another world than of this', and that his verse was best when it least resembled Scott's.[10]

At the end of this 'Noctes' there's a poem in which harsh realities are intermittently faced. Self-inflicted admonition is levelled in 'The Monitors'.[11]

> The lift looks cauldrife i' the west,
>   The wan leaf wavers frae the tree,
> The wind touts on the mountain's breast
>   A dirge o' waesome note to me.
>   It tells me that the days o' glee,
> When summer's thrilling sweets entwined,
>   An' love was blinkin' in the ee,
> Are a' gane by an' far behind.

The winter sky points him to the cares of age and the 'downfa's o' futuritye'. The weather delivers a shepherd's warning; its signs are 'Kind Monitors'. 'Sad experience, dearly bought',

> Tells me it was not what I ought,
> But what was in my power to do,
> That me behoved.

But then: 'I am a king!' And his dominion extends over Scotia's mountains and fairy vales. A pastoral supremacy. Better that than to be some mundane ruler, with political problems.

> Who would not choose the high renown,
> 'Mang Scotia's swains the chief to be,
> Than be a king, an' wear a crown,
> 'Mid perils, pain, an' treacherye.

The stanza utters a 'Hurra!' and closes with

> I'll blaw my reed of game an' glee,
> The Shepherd is himself again!

'Blaw' can mean boast as well as blow, and the Shepherd is boasting to keep his courage up. The poem seeks insurance of a kind for his family and himself:

> An' I think mair o' auld Scotland,
> Than to be fear'd for mine or me.

He blesses the Duke of Buccleuch for rearing for him a little home in the wild, and finishes with talk of the world's ups and downs, of 'douks in chill misfortune's wave'. He is determined to 'outbrave' all that. 'Kind winter Monitors, adieu!'

In November, too, on the 5th, there appeared in the *Westmorland Gazette* a preview of lectures in which Wilson was due to pay ambivalent tribute to his friend, whose height was stated to be five foot six. Others were more generous, entitling him to belong, as he did, to the athletic Six Feet High Club, of which Scott was an honorary member. Hogg was 'round, stout and fleshy'. On gala days grey trousers were exchanged for nankeen. Hair 'of a yellowish red'. 'He is one of the greatest poets of the age, an indifferent novelist, a worse practical farmer, a tolerable astronomer, as good an angler as a poet, a bad archer, though wishing to be thought a good one, a poor manager of the things of this world, an amiable man, a warm friend, a tender husband, too good a master, a fond father, beloved by his neighbours, a humble Christian, and a man who, if he has one, does not deserve an enemy.' His musicianship goes unlisted.

Wilson was reported here as claiming that 'there is no likeness in James Hogg to the Ettrick Shepherd in the "Noctes Ambrosianae".' He was aware that the impersonation was a source of continual uneasiness to his family and to Hogg, whose views were quoted or summarised: 'The using of my name in that manner vexes me very much. Particularly, ye see, because Margaret and her friends are aye complaining about it. Now Wilson wad na for the world do me ony ill; but when I tell him about it he just laughs at it.' Hogg goes on: 'As I say to him, he makes me say things that he durna say himsel. And though it is a' well enough for people who ken me; yet, sir, he has sae mony o' my phrases, and the form o' the expression is sae often mine, that I dinna wonder at the public believing me to be such a person as is represented. And it is chiefly through that, that the folk in London say I have plenty o' genius but I want taste.' A month later, on 6 December, Hogg wrote to Blackwood: 'Please let the old proud aristocrate know that the old Shepherd despises him as much as the dirt among his feet.'[12]

He was writing 'those TERRIBLE LETTERS' of his. His friends had starved him, denied him space in the paper, made a show of him, lied about him, smothered him in anecdotes, made him say things they wanted said but did not want attributed to themselves. Distressed by his wife's distress, he wrote: 'It is the forgeries that are published to the world that wound the peace of families.'

In December 1831, writes Norah Parr, he 'refused point-blank to have his name in the Magazine any longer'. On the 22nd, about to leave on his triumphal visit to London, he accused Blackwood of having starved him out of his house and country.[13] And he was presently to tell Wilson: 'rather than finger a farthing of your hard-earned money with such a lovely family to support I would rather work in a ditch for my own. Read my letter over again and you will surely see that it all relates to a generous and kind old stingy friend yclept Wm Blackwood.'[14] Ebony had indeed never been all black in his dealings with Hogg, but Hogg's vanity and vexation were felt to be an increasing threat by more than one member of the circle, and by Mrs Wilson.

The crisis in his affairs coincided with, but does not seem to have been aggravated by, the approach of the Jacobin Bill, and of the fall of the Ancien Régime, of Scott's Troy. *'Troja fuit,'* mourned Scott's journal. The old world was gone. The Whig ascendancy in the British Cabinet, which killed Sir Walter, as Hogg believed, did not kill Hogg. But it was the ravisher of Lady Maga. The Bill is 'just another nightmare as Fuseli saw, when he painted that "Moon-eyed herald of dismay" sitting on the breast of a matron – like Maga – flung wildly across her bed, and moaning under the weight of the monster', declares North in May 1831. Such was his 'Word to the Wise from Old Christopher'.

In the April 'Noctes' the Shepherd asks if there's to be a revolution. If a revolution does break out, it will be 'a bloody one', North assures him, shouldering his crutch. The Shepherd: 'The verra first thing the Radicals will do – will be to extinguish the Noctes Ambrosianae.' The Whigs (rather than the Radicals) were about to see to it that the country would be under the thumb of ten-pound householders (an urban property valuation), with the broadening of the franchise. In August Tickler states Tory principles – 'let weel bide,' 'respect the landmarks' – and predicts that 'under the coming "dynasty of the hucksters", the petty, griping, long-cowled, dingy-faced denizens of the ten-pound tenements in our third-rate towns' will take power. What exactly were these long cowls ('cowlies' bore the bye-meaning of a frequenter in disguise of prostitutes)? Jeffrey's July speech in the Commons – that of an oddly English-accented Scottish Lord Advocate – had bombed, crowed the Ambrosians. Cockburn's 'loud, but mellow brogue, his plausible, homely, easy singsong, would, I suspect, have had a better chance up yonder,' North supposes, as would his 'man-of-the-world tact'.

To these displays of indignation Hogg contributed such poems – rarely countenanced by twentieth-century critics and anthologists – as 'The Magic Mirror', a poem which, according to Lockhart, had 'much of good and much of abominable, like most of the pig's'.[15] Here, the lords of the forest, allies of the Lion, have been 'kicked by plebeian vulgar hoof'. The poem refers to 'ten-pound biggings', or buildings, and to the 'herds' that 'burrow' in them. A foxhound moves to disperse them by yowffing the war cry of the Scotts, 'A Belandine!' The poem offers a vision of misrule: 'Nothing in view but self! self! self!' The magazine was apt to go on as if there were no provision in the Bill for the rural vote, as if its writers belonged to a countryside alliance out to see off a jacquerie in the swelling towns of the time, or to deplore its triumph. Reform was linked in Hogg's mind, as his satirical verse now shows, with the newfangledness of joint-stock investment, crazy schemes, bills of credit, the fluttering of paper money. This was the snow in which men of sense had foundered, which had subdued the baronial and entrepreneurial Scott – who was both scribe and subscriber, novelist and capitalist, a signer of warrants whose own warrant had been signed. Even Hogg, whose capitalism mainly consisted of having to keep asking for doles and for fees he had earned, was at one point a little snowbound. An uplifting story was told of his dealings with a 'stupid bank' whose dodgy notes he held: he had paid his workmen with the notes and may have undertaken to pay them again with other money.[16]

He said that he could not help one of his 'indomitable rages' of the time. This helplessness and anger seem to have got worse as he entered his sixties, to be confronted with an unravelling of his literary arrangements, which must at times have felt like the erasure of his achievements, of his life's work. What had he written? Had he written the *Confessions*? He wrote to Cunningham about losing a piece of writing – 'so much for your poor old friend's accuracy' – saying that he hoped there was 'a braw time coming' when such things would no longer happen. Also to Cunningham: 'Every body blames me for not writing my pieces twice over but it is as sure as I am writing you this letter that I take about double the time to copy an article that I do to write it exclusive of the terrible bore that it is.' His 'once over' had more to answer for than his conviviality. But he had held fast to his integrity.[17]

When he reached London early in 1832, he let Blackwood know that he was embarrassed by being greeted as a *Blackwood's* author, in view of 'our eternal separation'. During the severance which had taken place, Blackwood was to reflect: 'What a fortunate escape we have made in not having anything more to do with Hogg, for he would have been an eternal torment.'[18] He spoke too soon, and ungenerously.

In the course of that past year Blackwood had brought out Hogg's *Songs*. It has been suggested that his notes are more interesting than the main text, as is sometimes the case with Hogg's writings, and the notes are certainly interesting and feisty. But then so are the songs, including 'Cam ye by Athol?', that memorable Jacobite hyperbole: had the poet ten sons, 'they would follow Glengarry'.

The early song 'Love is like a dizziness' appears here docked of a stanza in the *Forest Minstrel* version: were Peggy to save his heart from breaking, he'd dive into the whirlpool of Corryvreckan, or 'howk a grave at midnight dark',

> Or gang an' spier for Mungo Park
> Through Africa sae dreary, O.

The 'Noctes Song' is here: 'Beware o' the Blue and the Yellow'. Maids are invited to 'gang to the brackens wi' me', to be jurmummled or revered. The soutars of Selkirk are seen as a type of loyalty to the Crown. This 'Minstrel Boy' is among those of Hogg's songs which were challenged by Moore and are in some sense replies to the Irish swain. The collection re-affirms Hogg's desire to do as Burns did in writing and restoring the songs of Scotland, a desire which was fulfilled. Some months before this, in January 1829, Bell's *Edinburgh Literary Journal* had discussed *Select and Rare Scottish Melodies*, words by Hogg, music by Henry Bishop. The journal said that a poet like Burns or Hogg was 'the intellectual bagpipe of the land'. Hogg had written a good deal of mediocre stuff, but that is 'the prerogative of genius'.

When he prepared his memoir of Burns for the edition of the poet's work which was published a year after Hogg's death (the memoir was begun in 1832) and which was done together with the poet William Motherwell, he made sure that features of his own affinity with Burns were apparent. For both lads, a lass to work with and cuddle. For both, the cutty stool. They were brothers in misfortune. Burns possessed the 'electric motions' of a powerful mind, as did his memoirist. They rescued Scotland's songs. There are, however, differences between the two which the memoir is careful to stress.

The ballad collector Peter Buchan lent his assistance. Burns scholarship was mustering, and Lockhart's *Life* had appeared in 1828.

Conscious of Wilson on Burns, of his views on the literary superiority of pastoralists to agriculturalists like Burns, Hogg's essay spends too much time copying what other people had written. But it is at times very revealing of Hogg.[19]

Burns of the dark looks was proud and overbearing. 'Except among the glaiket hizzies, he was a verra ill likit lad,' Hogg was told by an old acquaintance of the poet, a weaver. 'It appears that the countenance of the great was highly agreeable to him,' writes Hogg, who also says what writers have been apt to say, that writers are classless. 'In the society of farmers, I am one of them, we are all as brothers; and among the first nobility of the land, I feel I am equally at my ease: so that really I feel I belong exclusively to no one class of society.' The 'child of nature', the 'free denizen of the realm of his people' – such descriptions are felt to apply to both poets.

Burns was drunk but also sober, like himself. He was unlike Hogg in falling into low company: 'but I never heard that Burns held any intercourse with any class below' the peasantry – which must have made it difficult, the reader might think, for him to write 'The Jolly Beggars'. Burns had this exorbitant libido: but we must remember – as Burns did – how much he had to resist. He attends to Burns's 'sociability', as he felt he had to attend to his own, and blames him for his clubs. 'Such clubs are generally productive of more harm than good.' How much harm did Hogg's do?

Hogg attacks Burns's attackers, in the matter of his notorious morals, as James Gray did, but blames him for hurting the pious with his satires against the shams of religion and the brutalities of the unco good. 'The Cotter's Saturday Night' shows 'what he could have done, had he surveyed with a calm and untroubled eye all the influences of our religion'. A most weaselly conditional clause, from someone who had himself written against the inhumanities of religion, though probably incapable of Burns's reference to the phenomenon of an 'enthusiastic idiot piety'.[20] A simple past tense was required here. 'The Cotter's Saturday Night' was what he *did*.

Piety relaxes in a note: 'Why should it have been suggested that man was made to mourn? I deny the position.' It revives with the story of a pious man's night with Burns, who proves overbearing during a discussion of Calvinist tenets. 'He set a' the folks in a roar of laughin' twenty times over at me an' my original sin, till I was blythe to hing down my head an' laugh like the rest, an' gie him a' the argument to himsel.' This man relates that he shared a bedroom with the poet and caught him unburdening himself afterwards in a prayer of contrition.

The memoir incorporates long extracts from an account of Burns by 'the ingenious Tom Carlisle'. The man in question, alias Thomas Carlyle, had published in the *Edinburgh Review* of October 1828 a long review – domineeringly cut and edited by Jeffrey – of Lockhart's life of Burns. The article made a deep impression, commemorated in an endearing folk rhyme:

> As I was walking on the green,
> A little book it chanced I seen.
> Carlyle's essay on Burns was the edition.
> I left it lying in the same position.

As enlisted by Hogg – in the style of secondary-sourcing, amounting to an anthropophagy of lavish quotation, which is employed in Lockhart's biographies – Carlyle's review is a strange compound of strength and weakness. Bleak in its dogmatism and inconsistency, contemptuous of its own insights, it nevertheless presents a clear view of one of the main attractions of Burns's scenes from Westland life. 'He never writes from hearsay, but from sight and experience: they are scenes which he has lived and laboured amidst which he describes.'

Having said as much, Carlyle asserts that Burns's poetry fails, that most of his poems are not poetic, that 'Tam o' Shanter' is not poetic. An exception is made for 'The Jolly Beggars' and the songs. The trouble, again, is religion. Carlyle compares Burns with Milton and Cervantes: 'The golden calf of self-love, however curiously carved, was not their deity; but the invisible goodness, which alone is man's reasonable service,' whereas Burns's morality was largely that of 'a mere worldly man'. Carlyle calls the satirical Burns 'the fighting-man of the New Light priesthood'. Was Auld Licht fundamentalism a service to the invisible goodness? Carlyle's stance is by no means sectarian: he is commending a piety, an awe, a wonder, which is independent of conventional forms.

Then and long after, many advanced people have been moved by his essential or residual piety.

The opposition which Carlyle projects between the observed and the invisible, or the visionary, suggests an aspect of the Wilson aesthetic by which Hogg was at times misled. But his essay is not taken in by Carlyle's: part of his philosophy, he writes, is 'at complete variance with other parts'. On the previous page, however, a footnote, probably Hogg's, might seem to dissent from what he is about to say: 'Hold, Mr Hogg; fair play, – Carlisle's sentiment is not that Burns accomplished nothing, far from it; but only that what he did accomplish was nothing to what he might have accomplished, had his capacious mind been under a purer influence, and his mighty powers been more worthily directed.' Here is another weaselly conditional clause. Burns should have done better, is the ignominious refrain.

The memoir has words to say about Tom Moore's 'palling' harmonies and about Shakespeare's *Titus Andronicus*. The boy Burns threatened to throw the play in the fire, for its horrors. 'Well done Robert,' writes Hogg, who once, on a Stornoway sloop, almost threw it in the sea for the same reason. The presence in the volume of *Macbeth*, *Lear* and *Coriolanus* rescued it.

'Poor-manning' was an expression used by Scott with reference to his troubles.[21] It meant the displays of pity he wanted to avoid. The word 'poor' could also be applied to other people in the Scotland of his time, as an offer or show of compassion, or as a contempt or condescension. It was used constantly of Hogg, as we have seen, and Carlyle was one of those who used it of him. Of all the descriptions of the kenspeckle Hogg, none are more engrossing than those of Carlyle, based on sightings and encounters in London. On 22 January 1832, he wrote to his mother: 'Poor Hogg the Ettrick Shepherd is walking about here; dining everywhere, everywhere laughed at; being indeed the veriest gomeril. He appears in public with a gray Scotch plaid, the like of which was never seen here before; it is supposed to be a trick of his Book seller (a hungry shark, on the verge of bankruptcy) who wishes to attract notice from the Cockney population, and thereby raise the wind a little.' His brother John was told that Hogg was a 'singing goose'. Then, in Froude's life of Carlyle, there is this account of the same time:

Hogg is a little red-skinned stiff sack of a body, with quite the common air of an Ettrick shepherd, except that he has a highish though sloping brow (among his yellow grizzled hair), and two clear little beads of blue or grey eyes that sparkle, if not with thought, yet with animation. Behaves himself quite easily and well; speaks Scotch, and mostly narrative absurdity (or even obscenity) therewith. Appears in the mingled character of zany and raree show. All bent on bantering him, especially Lockhart; Hogg walking through it as if unconscious, or almost flattered. His vanity seems to be immense, but also his good-nature. I felt interest for the poor 'herd body', wondered to see him blown hither from his sheepfolds, and how, quite friendless as he was, he went along cheerful, mirthful, and musical. I do not well understand the man; his significance is perhaps considerable. His poetic talent is authentic, yet his intellect seems of the weakest; his morality also limits itself to the precept 'be not angry.' Is the charm of this poor man chiefly to be found herein, that he *is* a real product of nature, and able to speak naturally, which not one in a thousand is? An 'unconscious talent', though of the smallest, emphatically *naïve*. Once or twice in singing (for he sung of his own) there was an emphasis in poor Hogg's look – expression of feeling, almost of enthusiasm. The man is a very curious *specimen*. Alas! he is a *man*; yet how few will so much as treat him like a *specimen*, and not like a mere wooden *Punch* or *Judy*.

With its class disdain and fellow-feeling, the passage has Carlyle's preternatural gift as a memoirist. It reveals a saving uncertainty in one of the most admonishing and Jehovah-like of Scots judges of the human condition, the compunction of one literatus from the peasantry inclined to look down on another, and the scorn for inferiors native to the man of sense.[22]

The passage relates to a supper given by the publisher James Fraser at which Galt, Lockhart and Allan Cunningham were among the guests. 'Stupidity, insipidity, even not a little obscenity (in which all save Galt, Fraser and myself seemed to join) was the only outcome of the night,' he wrote. 'Literary *men!* They are not worthy to be the valets of such.' There goes the gruesome Carlyle, the iconic prisoner of his loathings.

But then there are other Carlyles, not least of these the comic Carlyle. His *Reminiscences* describe, very beautifully, a youthful walk about the Borders in the company of his friend the charismatic, and eventually fashionable, half-mad Church of Scotland preacher, Edward Irving. Ettrick and Yarrow were visited.

> The region was without roads, often without foot-tracks, had no vestige of inn; so that there was a kind of knight-errantry in threading your way through it, not to mention the romance that naturally lay in its Ettricks and Yarrows and old melodious songs and traditions. We walked up Meggat Water to beyond the sources, emerged into Yarrow, not far above St Mary's Loch; a charming secluded shepherd country, with excellent shepherd population; nowhere setting up to be picturesque, but everywhere honest, comely, well done-to, peaceable and useful, nor anywhere without its solidly characteristic features, hills, mountains, clear rushing streams, cosy nooks and homesteads, all of a fine rustic type, and presented to you *in natura*, not as in a Drury Lane with Stage-lights and for a purpose.

Carlyle alludes here to 'Hogg (who was then a celebrity)'. And who should Hogg go to hear when he got to London but Edward Irving? Irving, too, was a celebrity. But his sermon, Hogg told his wife, was 'the ravings of enthusiastic madness', as distinct from an idiot piety. This was not the response of a goose.[23]

1831, said a poem of his, had exuded talk of 'Burking, Bill and Cholera'. It was a year of struggle for him and his family: this 'poor Hogg of Fauldshope' had had a stormy time of it. There was more of that in store. 'Poor me,' he sighed in the *Fraser's* of November 1832. And yet this was the year of his greatest social triumph.

CHAPTER TWENTY

Ben Nevis on Blackheath

—

Separate and desperate, eternally adrift from Blackwood's lunar module, and yet genial and conversible, he set off on a steamboat, the *Edinburgh Castle*, down the east coast to London, in the midwinter of 1831-2. He was to be received, in the Southern metropolis, as a personality, a cynosure, a lion. He could be treated there as a 'wild pet for the supercultivated', to enlist some disapproving words from T. S. Eliot's praise of Blake, having been, in his own words, the 'flattered pet' of high-born Border women. But there were those, too, for whom he was not wild at all, but a solid citizen, perfectly polite. He went to London to deal with publishers and editors, one of whom, S. C. Hall, compared the sensation he caused in literary circles to the 'temporary presence' of Ben Nevis on Blackheath. Mr and Mrs Hall were from Ireland. The wife, Anna Maria, a round-faced, ringleted beauty, was a novelist who became a founder of hospitals. She was against the struggle for women's rights, and she thought that Tom Moore sang just as a mermaid might be expected to do. Mrs Hall said of Hogg that he was 'more like a buoyant Irishman, than a sturdy son of the soil of the thistle'. Her husband Samuel was a lifelong enemy of William Maginn from their days together in Cork, a Temperance activist, a connoisseur of gravestones, and an alleged original of Dickens's Pecksniff.[1]

Touching letters were exchanged between Hogg and his wife. 'May the Almighty be with you,' he wrote. 'I hope you have got warm drawers,' wrote Margaret. He should get his mending done 'by the person who washes your clothes it is pitiful to think of you going about with great holes in your stockings.' He was advised to 'leave before you are threadbare I do not exactly mean your coat, but leave the Londoners something to guess at – by the bye the coat is no joke either for you are apt to wear it too long but take care don't do so, buy a good new one &

whatever articles of dress you may require by no means appear shabby.'[2] Hogg and his wardrobe were to be in London for nearly three months.

This strange teeming place amazed him. 'Mercy on us, what a roar o' life!' cried the 'Noctes' Shepherd. The visitor to roaring London would take someone's arm in order to cross the street: these streets may have had for him the nightmare quality caught in Wordsworth's *Prelude*. For poets from the country, cities had come to seem more than ever phantasmagoric. His senses were ignited by London, and may have been smouldering a little even before he arrived there, to encounter a species of upper-bourgeois sexual fluency, verging on the bohemian, which was deemed to be less common in Edinburgh. He had responded to Anna Maria Hall, who had turned down a superstitious children's story as unsuitable, with 'I wish I had you for a few days to wander with me through the romantic dells of Westmoreland and sleep in my bosom all the nights and as this is never likely to happen I have no hopes of ever pleasing you.'[3] Few authors can have taken a rejection slip in such good part. The bit about sleeping in his bosom – there is to be someone to do that for Bonny Prince Charlie in Hogg's song extending 'Maclean's Welcome' – has been inked out in the manuscript.

Hogg's visit was in some degree a book launch, and it foreshadowed the ways in which modern publishers display their more marketable authors, with readings, signings, interviews and receptions. 'Cockney literati and sentimental bluestockings' flocked, 'Shepherdites' flocked. There was a struggle to tell his stories in their original Doric. The sort of stories that were told was illustrated by William Jerdan, the London-based Scottish editor and hedonist who had co-founded the Royal Society of Literature, and who felt that Mrs Hogg's title to the 'sure reward for the faithful' which is spoken of, in Latin, on the title-page of the exhumed manuscript of the *Confessions* was stronger than her husband's. There was this duchess in her castle who enquired: 'Were you ever here before, Mr Hogg?' Hogg answered with his 'usual candour': 'Na ma Laddy, I have been at the yett wi' beasts that I was driving into England; but I never was inside o' the house before.'[4] Hogg's 'malicious deevil' Jerdan was a maker and breaker of writers' reputations who was liked but not respected, according to Hall. He was a friend of Canning's and he had a high opinion of Maginn. 'I have drained the Circe cup to the dregs!' he said. Hall hated that. Hall held that egotists, such as James Hogg, 'dwell on matters which constitute their "personality" '.

Samuel Hall witnessed Hogg's meeting with Laetitia Landon, whose decolletage shocked him so much. Laetitia's bare back and shoulders were those of a talented poet and literary belle whose young life was wrecked by sexual slanders. Mournful and tuneful, her 'Lines of Life' is an orphan poem which explores a matter of similitude:

> I live among the cold, the false,
>   And I must seem like them;
> And such I am, for I am false
>   As those I most condemn.
>
> I teach my lip its sweetest smile,
>   My tongue its softest tone;
> I borrow others' likeness, till
>   Almost I lose my own.

Jerdan and Maginn were friends of hers, and Mrs Maginn came across letters in which Laetitia's regard for her husband was evident. This annulled Laetitia's engagement to John Forster, Dickens's biographer. Soon afterwards, in 1838, she married a colonial soldier, a Governor of the Gold Coast whose African wife had to be sent into the interior on Laetitia's arrival. She was said to have been found dying with an empty bottle of prussic acid in her hand – Hall thought murder more likely than suicide or accident – and was buried beneath the parade-ground at Cape Coast Castle, where Irish Lady Blessington managed, over the Governor's dead body, to install a tablet. Jerdan passed out at the news of her death, and Maginn broke down. 'Poor child, poor girl, poor woman, poor wife, poor victim,' mourned Hall, whose wife had been told by Laetitia: 'Envy, malice, and all uncharitableness – these are the fruits of a successful literary career for a woman.' Aware of the slanders that had pursued her, Hogg had formerly added to them. Meeting her in London gave him the chance for a display of gallantry. Hall heard him informing her, in his rich and manly Scottish voice: 'I've said many hard things aboot ye. I'll do sae nae mair. I didna think ye'd been sae bonnie!'[5]

A likeness of Maginn has been detected (and disputed) in Captain Shandon of Thackeray's novel *Pendennis*. Could the Captain's name contain an allusion to Laetitia? London's Landon and Shandon were inhabitants of a fashionably-affiliated literary world well-supplied with social occasions and with expatriate Scots. For Hogg, it was to prove both familiar and exotic, and a shade Circean – if only in the sense that hospitality itself became a trial. They were a relatively sober lot, but he was glutted with their attentions, and would utter the lion's complaint about being exhausted by them. On 21 January he wrote home:

> I have no news save that I am very well. Indeed it is almost a miracle that I keep my health so well, considering the life that I lead, for I am out at parties every night until far in the morning ... You will see that a great literary dinner is to be given me on Wednesday, my birth-day, for though the name of Burns is necessarily coupled with mine, the dinner has been set on foot solely to bring me forward and give me *eclat* in the eyes of the public, thereby to inspire an extensive sale of my forthcoming work. It was mooted by Lockhart, Murray, Jerdan and Galt, who have managed the whole business, and will be such a meeting as was never in London ... But do not be afraid, for vain as I am, it will not turn my head; on the contrary, it has rather made me melancholy, and I wish it were fairly over. Sir John Malcolm has been chosen to the first chair, and Lord Leveson Gower to the second, and among the stewards there are upwards of twenty noblemen and baronets. And all this to do honour to a poor old shepherd.[6]

The dinner was to mark both Burns's birthday and Hogg's 'official' or assumptive birthday, the 25th. Two of Burns's sons sat by the President. Punch was brewed in Burns's bowl. But it was Hogg's night. A 'pretty general *fama clamosa*', that he should be feasted, arose 'among the better classes' of the London Scottish, recalled Jerdan, and he and Lockhart, among others, took charge of the occasion. What *Fraser's* called 'The Great and Celebrated Hogg Dinner' was held at the Freemason's Tavern in Holborn, an area where left-wing protest was often to raise its voice in later times. There were two hundred people there on the night, at 22 shillings a head. John Wilson struck up the stave, to the tune of 'Auld Lang Syne': 'Shall Jamie Hogg be e'er forgot?' When the toastmaster called for 'a bumper toast to the health of Mr Shepherd', there was mirth.[7]

'*I did not mount the table* to speak,' Hogg, in italics, assured his wife, who had written in alarm: 'I should have wished you had kept your seat what in all the World took you on top of the table.' 'Up up! Mount mount!' the multitude had roared. A lamp or chandelier was obscuring his face. So he'd stood on a chair in order to be seen.[8]

The English journalist Cyrus Redding was named as a steward, but retired in a sulk when he arrived to find that the occasion had been sewn up by notabilities. The poet Thomas Campbell had cried off. There was not enough to eat. The dinner was 'paltry', and Cyrus Redding's grapes were sour: the whole affair looked to him like a job, a fix. Redding's memoirs describe a meeting with the guest of honour, a much quieter man than had been made out, who had been 'reported to say things he was too well-informed to utter'.[9] Hogg complained to him 'that Wilson made a show of him in "Blackwood". This was coquetry, he did not really dislike it; he was eager for notoriety. I told him that but for Wilson' Southerners would 'scarcely have known anything about him'. 'Aye,' replied Hogg, 'but Wilson is too bad, for he makes me say things I could not dream of uttering.' Redding believed that Hogg's writings were 'eminently Scotch, and were not adapted to make a sensation in this country'.

Hogg saw Allan Cunningham in London, but not Allan's brother Tom, a former friend from whom he'd become estranged. The two Scots skulked on opposite sides of the Thames for the duration of the visit. Sir Robert Peel was accosted by Hogg in 'Noctes' mode, with reference to Peel's political fortunes: 'Faith! Sir Robert, I heard you praised by both sides the other night; I hope you are not going to rat.' He also came to know the Ruskin family. Though 'not very fond in general of precocity' – an opinion shared with Scott – he wrote of the young Ruskin: 'yon is the most extraordinary callan I ever met with.' The callan was invited to Altrive, but said that he had better remain with his father during the period before his departure for university, adding that his father had read the 'Noctes' to him over dessert, even the naughty words.[10]

The London publishers with whom Hogg was chiefly occupied were James Cochrane and his partner John McCrone. Both publishers were young and ambitious; one or the other was the hungry shark blamed by Carlyle for wrapping Hogg in the plaid of publicity; Hogg made McCrone – a singer, a source of glee at the St Ronan's Games, and a friend and publisher of Dickens – the leaving present of a plaid. Hogg stayed with Cochrane and his family at Waterloo Place in Pall Mall, and became friends with them. Cochrane had undertaken to produce a multi-volume edition of Hogg's fiction, in emulation of Robert Cadell's edition of the Waverley novels. The first volume appeared, as *Altrive Tales*, shortly after the writer's return to Scotland, but Cochrane went bankrupt and the project collapsed. Hogg wrote to him in May to say that 'it is for you & for your lovely family that I grieve far more than for myself. Because I know well you will join with my friends in securing the remaining 2000 copies for me . . .' If this be done, 'I shall stick by you in literature as long as I live.'[11] Cochrane was to rise again, and fall again, in the lists of publishing, having brought out, in the course of his vicissitudes, Hogg's *Tales of the Wars of Montrose*. In 1832, Blackwood brought out, grudgingly, Hogg's *Queer Book*. Fear of 'that great bugbear REFORM' had caused him, felt Hogg, to keep postponing it.

The *Altrive Tales* has in it Marion's Jock and Captain John Lochy, and a surprising third story, 'The Pongos: a letter from Southern Africa'. 'The Adventures of Captain Lochy', discussed previously, represents familiar ground for Hogg, this tale told by a military rogue who goes about with an infernal friend, learns that the Highlander is 'a being void of any moral principle, save an inviolable faith and attachment to a superior', and, having detached himself from the Pretender in the first Jacobite rebellion, proves kin to the Whig Duke of Argyll and a claimant to great estates in Scotland. 'The Pongos' breaks new ground and wanders far from Scotland's shores. It is a Tarzan tale of nature and romance. Pongos are baboons. A white man loses his little William to an orang-outang, 'the monster'. His wife Agnes is abducted and gives birth to his daughter among the apes, who 'would make the most docile, powerful and affectionate of all slaves'. In Britain, slavery was soon to be legally abolished.

Lockhart summarily remarks in his *Life of Scott*[12] that Hogg was 'in no respect improved' by his visit to London – spoilt by it, perhaps. He was certainly the fatter for it. He had not starved there, and was unable to resume his old clothes on his return. He claimed that 'the generality of mankind have always used me ill till I came to London,' and had gained the impression that he might be in danger of leaving the place with the prospect of becoming a fat knight, of joining Scott in a title. In March, still in the city, he wrote for advice to his wife:

> You must consult your own heart whether you would like to be Lady Hogg or remain the Ettrick Shepherdess because you may now have the former title if you please. The Queen is it seems intent on it and I got a letter the other day from Lord Montagu requesting me not to see his Majesty until he and I consulted together as he understood there was some risk of being knighted which would run me into the expense of at least £300 of fees. For my part I despise it in our present circumstances and can see no good that it could do to us. It might indeed introduce our family into the first ranks, but then where is £300 to come from. In short I want you to dissuade me from it but I'll not look near his Majesty till I hear from you so write me directly. Dr Brewster was knighted yesterday. The cholera is raging and spreading terribly here now but do not say a word about that to James else it will kill him.

Lord Montagu, uncle of the Duke of Buccleuch, had sought to dissuade him from wanting to see the King and Queen, with the words: 'and then there is always the danger of being knighted.' This has the air of a joke, or a quiz. A sword might accidentally light on his shoulder in the palace. Margaret Hogg, at all events, wrote back directly in admirable style to urge him to decline. The Ettrick Shepherdess liked not such grinning honour as might be in mind. 'From my heart,' she told him,

> I can say I like no such titles & if you value your own comfort & my peace of mind you will at once, if offered to you, refuse it, it is an honor you may be proud to refuse but not to accept I think a title to a poor man is a load scarcely bearable, I dare say there are many men born with one on their back who would be thankful if they could get rid of it, Her Majesty must be entirely ignorant of your circumstances if the thing has *really* ever been thought of ... Did I possess five thousand a year I should wish to be unencumbered with a title I want

no more than to be the wife of plain James Hogg, we ought to consult the happiness of our family & such a thing I should look upon in every respect would be to them in all probability great misery.

'Dear Papa,' wrote his eleven-year-old son at this point, 'I have not been well since you left us but I think I shall get well when you come home.' In London Hogg composed, and dispatched to Ettrick, prayers for his children – for Harriet, Jessie, Jamie and the rest. He was told, and seems to have cared, about his lodger: 'Mr Brooks is very anxious that you should get his poem published,' wrote his wife. In his letters home there are few words about Reform, then in the long agony of its Parliamentary crisis. No foresuffering of the Act eventually passed in June. Some months later: the 'cause of our good old aristocracy is not thriving'.[13]

If the lionised Hogg, with his thoughts of a descending sword, needed bringing down to earth, Dr James Browne was willing to do that, and more. His pamphlet on Hogg, and on the latest instalment of his memoir which prefaced the *Altrive Tales*, was an attempt to bury him. Browne spoke of Hogg's arrival 'in the Great Babel of the South, where every *lusus naturae* is welcome'. 'The "Life" of the Ettrick Shepherd Anatomised'[14] abounds in a degree of insult which most, though not all, of the *Blackwood's* defamers would have hesitated to apply to the worst Whig. 'Claptrap', 'libidinous' were its words for this freak. 'Swinish' too – chief of these defamers' insult-endearments for Hogg. 'Any thing will be believed of him, except what he says of himself.' Of the chaperoning of Hogg in Holborn, Browne writes, conflating Wilson with Lockhart in the one Mephisto: 'The man who, he says, never told him a word of truth but by chance, – in other words, who made him a continual butt for raillery and derision, cramming him with all manner of nonsense and absurdity, and literally laughing in the face of the poor gudgeon as he swallowed it, – now took him by the hand, doubtless sniggering in his sleeve at the idea of such a protégé.'

Hogg's view of crony misrepresentation is caricatured: 'I dinna care what they say o' me, as lang as they allow that I am a man o' genius.' Hogg's 'bulls' are such that he must have Irish blood in his veins. His old quarrel with the publisher Goldie, maligned by Hogg, who had thought he was dead, is rehearsed. Browne quotes Francis Bacon on evil fame deserved. Hogg is one of those who follow at the funerals of their own reputations. He is also guilty of using the 'slang' of vernacular Scots.

Hogg was now restored to Ettrick, having cast off his braw claes and crept back in with his wife and bairns. This was to be Scott's last summer. He went on an exhausting trip to Italy in the hope of better health, and came back to Abbotsford to greet the waiting William Laidlaw: 'O man, how often have I thought of you!'[15] Let go as a result of Scott's financial collapse, Laidlaw had been reinstated as factor and amanuensis, and still lived nearby. Hogg's connection with Abbotsford had been strengthened by the presence there of his brother Robert as butcher and as master of Scott's sheep (he was not the only Borderer to take the view that Hogg would have done well to have paid more attention to his flock and less to literature). But Hogg had not seen Scott for the past two years. He called twice at Abbotsford during Scott's terminal illness, but was not admitted to his chamber.

Their last meeting was described in the memoir of Scott which he wrote soon after Scott's death.[16] In the autumn of 1830, he got word that Scott, who had lately signed the warrant for his friend's insolvency, would be passing by on his way home to Abbotsford from the Buccleuchs' Drumlanrig Castle: 'he was sorry he could not call at Altrive to see Mrs Hogg and the bairns it being so far off the way.' So Hogg waited for him at the Gordon Arms, a few hundred yards from Altrive, handed him out of the carriage and walked with him the short distance to Mount Benger. 'He leaned on my shoulder all the way and did me the honour of saying that he never leaned on a firmer or a surer.' Hogg recalled that Scott's daughter Sophia waited at the inn; Lockhart says that she wasn't there and that he himself was there – another of Hogg's lies, we are to feel, as were the compliments directed by Scott at Hogg's work in Hogg's account of the scene. Scott told him, Hogg writes, that

a certain gamekeeper on whom he bestowed his maledictions without reserve had prejudiced my best friend the young Duke of Buccleuch against me by a story which though he himself knew it to be an invidious and malicious lie yet seeing his Grace so much irritated he durst not open his lips on the subject farther than by saying, 'But my lord Duke you must always remember that Hogg is no ordinary man although he may have shot a stray moorcock.' And then turning to me he said 'Before you had ventured to give any saucy language to a low scoundrel of an English gamekeeper you should have thought of Fielding's tale of Black George.'

'I never saw that tale' said I 'an' dinna ken ought about it. But never trouble your head about that matter Sir Walter for it is awthegither out o' nature for our young chief to entertain any animosity against me. The thing will never mair be heard of an' the chap that tauld the lees on me will gang to hell that's aye some comfort.'

Hogg's sprightliness – Hell awaits the wicked, thank God, and the nature of things is feudal – failed to bring a smile. Scott said, his face 'as gruff and demure as could be': 'You are still the old man Hogg careless and improvident as ever.' The comedy of their relations was not what it had been. But the ironies habitual to it, ironies both intended and involuntary, are still discernible in Hogg's self-interested version of what happened at the Gordon Arms. He would have known all about Fielding's *Tom Jones*, with its gamekeeper turned poacher, Black George. He was a reader of Fielding in his youth, that of a patron of Mr Elder's library in Peebles.[17]

Hogg mentioned the idea of having the volumes of his prose tales (Cochrane's project) edited by Lockhart. Scott's shaggy eyebrows must have descended. A bad idea. 'I would not for anything in the world that Lockhart should enter on such a responsibility for taking your ram-stam way of writing into account the responsibility would be a very heavy one,' Scott is paraphrased (with some candour) as saying in response. Hogg had written a great deal that might be 'made available with proper attention', but this was not the time: 'at present all things and literature in particular are going straight down hill to destruction and ruin.' With that, he mumbled what Hogg took to be an 'inward curse' against democracy: the insults he'd had from the populace of his own country had broken his heart.

Hogg's account then sinks into the terrible, into what might almost seem a parricidal grimness. He did not regret being excluded from Abbotsford, for Scott was then reduced to the very lowest state of degradation to which poor prostrate humanity could be subjected. He was described to me by one who saw him often as exactly in the same state with a man mortally drunk who could in nowise own or assist himself the pressure of the abscess on the brain having apparently had the same effect as the fumes of drunkenness. He could at short intervals distinguish individuals and pronounce a few intelligible words but these lucid glimpses were of short duration the sunken eye soon ceased from distinguishing objects and the powerless tongue became unable to utter a syllable though constantly attempting it which made the sound the most revolting that can be concieved.

The pious admonitions imagined by Lockhart for delivery by Scott on his deathbed tell a different story. Hogg went to the funeral and was, he says, the last man to linger by the grave.

On the way back from one of his unavailing attempts to see Scott he was thrown from a gig and badly bruised. He expected to be laid up for a while, as if in a last likeness to his friend. But then he had long been accident-prone, and his friend was dying a tormented death. The letter of the following day, 21 July 1832, in which he tells of the fall, a letter addressed to an official of the Royal Literary Fund, goes on to be eerily gruesome, in the manner of the memoir, about Scott's sufferings: 'The great and good Sir Walter is lying in a state so utterly deplorable and degraded that there is nothing in nature so painful to contemplate.' His letter acknowledges the grant of £40 which he has received from the Fund, and does so 'with the deepest gratitude it being the second time that fund has relieved me in very peculiar circumstances'. He quotes from a 'note which I had from Mr J. G. Lockhart some time ago about the scrape I had got into with my London publisher', Cochrane presumably. Lockhart's note explains with all solicitude that the Fund's forty pounds, remitted by means of subscriptions for a 'forthcoming' book by Hogg, have been incorporated in a sum due to be sent him by another London publisher, John Murray, who had been showing an interest in his *Queer Book* and in the *Songs*, and had been told by Hogg on 17 February that they'd receive a helping 'hitch' from journalists in his new-found London. The involution of his finances never failed him.

Scott was not long dead when McCrone paid two visits to Scotland in search of material for a book on the great man. He stayed at Altrive and was shown round Abbotsford. In March 1833, a parcel containing Hogg's anecdotes of Scott was sent to London, where McCrone and Cochrane had started a new firm. Hogg teased Blackwood about the dispatch of the manuscript, at a point when it had yet to be dispatched, saying it would have filled at least forty pages of Maga: 'What a pity' the anecdotes had gone to someone else, 'as you will see when they are published'. In February of the year before, he had written to him from London – where he was consorting with lords, 'all genuine Tories' – to warn him that he was going to be 'bitterly severe' on him in the new instalment of his autobiography which appeared with the *Altrive Tales*: and he was now denying Blackwood access to his memoir of Scott.[18] The manuscript, entitled 'Anecdotes of Sir W. Scott', was borne to New Zealand by descendants, and has recently been published in Hogg's *Collected Works*. It begins as by McCrone, the visitor to Scotland, but at once branches off into Hogg's own words.

He wrote to Lockhart on 20 March 1833 to say that he'd been misled – by Cochrane, apparently – into supposing Lockhart's approval of his conduct in supplying material for a book on Scott ('How was he in the parlour?' it would enquire). He now had to cope with Lockhart's anger: he had meant no harm and would be content to show his stuff to Scott's friends. 'I do assure you on the word of an honest man ("although a vulgar clown") that there is not one of the anecdotes which is not literally and positively true.' He would write to McCrone that very day to retrieve the MS – of which McCrone had taken a copy. 'I assure you,' he wrote, 'if Sir Walter despised me and held me in the lowest contempt his behaviour and his letters to me testified the reverse.'

Two days later Lockhart wrote him a tough and resourceful letter about a clash with McCrone, saying that he'd been shown the 'bundle' of Hogg's Scott papers, and had hated the sight of it, or of what he had seen of it, hated the sight, for instance, of statements about 'Lady Scott & *opium!*' and about Walter Scott and *leeing*. Lockhart despised McCrone and he despised Cochrane, but he says here that he wouldn't have said that Scott despised Hogg. What he had probably meant to tell McCrone was that it would be easy to gather scraps of writing which might suggest as much, taken out of context. But did Scott despise Hogg? 'No – he condemned some parts of his conduct and smiled at his vanity, but he admired his genious and knew his heart was in the right place and if I published *all* that I could of what he has left written *anent* Hogg *that* would be visible.' In his dealings with McCrone, Lockhart had been concerned, he said, to explain to him the law of copyright as it affected Scott's correspondence.[19]

Soon afterwards, in London, Lockhart met Blackwood, who pronounced him the same old fellow, 'just the old man, as friendly and satirical as ever'. Reporting to Edinburgh, Blackwood mentions Lockhart's encounter with McCrone on the letters question. McCrone's 'next interview, and this is the best joke of all, was to consult Mr L. with regard to a large MS which he had received from his friend Hogg, containing most interesting anecdotes of Sr W. – Mr L. knowing well what a bundle of lies the whole would be, at first declined to look at it, but McC. pressed him so much that he opened the scroll. The very page he glanced at contained such beastly & abominable things that he could not restrain his indignation, and poured out his indignation against Hogg in such unmeasured terms that his poor auditor was quite dumfoundered.'

It appears that the manuscript was returned to Hogg. In May 1833, he wrote to 'Mac' with the view that 'it would be better to suppress the work for a while till we see if the bowls will rowe right.' His shoulder would once more be required: 'if I set my old shoulder to it freely depend on it I'll give it a heeze in spite of the devil the world and the flesh.' He had received a tempting offer from some American place by the name of Albany. He goes on to ask:

> Why do you not tell me any thing about the Cochranes? You should remember that there is no family in England whom I love so much as the Cochranes. Kiss dear sweet Mary Anne for me and give her the old shepherd's blessing. I would like to kiss Mrs Cochrane myself but I wont depute you so all that you have to do is to give my kindest love to her.

He ends with the news that, while curling on Duddingston Loch, skated by the minister in the portrait attributed to Raeburn, he had fallen in over his head through the ice. 'I have never been well since and find that I never will be well again.' In more ways than one, an ominous letter.[20] On a stormy night, later that year, Margaret fell from a bridge into the Yarrow, and was rescued by her husband. Sore stumbles, both.

He produced a revised text for the American who had been in touch, De Witt Bloodgood, who added footnotes of a radical tinge and an account of Hogg's life and work. This version of the Scott memoir was published by Harper and Brothers in New York under the title *Familiar Anecdotes of Sir Walter Scott*. A consortium of Scottish and London publishers pirated this text, bringing it out, with a few adjustments, as *The Domestic Manners and Private Life of Walter Scott*. Jill Rubenstein's *Anecdotes of Scott* gives both the draft that went to New Zealand and the new version that originated in Albany.

In August 1834, Blackwood's last days, he heard from Lockhart, who had been studying the *Domestic Manners*:

> In Wilson's hands the Shepherd will always be delightful; but of the fellow himself I can scarcely express my contemptuous pity, now that his 'Life of Sir W. Scott' is before the world. I believe it will, however, do Hogg more serious and lasting mischief than any of those whose feelings he has done his brutal best to lacerate would wish to be the result. He has drawn his own character, not that of his benevolent *creator*, and handed himself down to posterity – for the subject will keep *this* from being forgotten – as a mean blasphemer against all magnanimity. Poor Laidlaw will be mortified to the heart by this sad display. The bitterness against me which peeps out in many parts of Hogg's narrative is, of course, the fruit of certain rather hasty words spoken by me to Cochrane and MacCrone when they showed me the original MS, but nevertheless Hogg has *omitted* the only two passages which I had read when I so expressed myself, – one of them being a most flagrant assault on Scott's veracity, and the other a statement about poor Lady Scott, such as must have afflicted for ever her children, and especially her surviving daughter. Dr Maginn has handled Hogg in his own way in 'Fraser's Mag'.

The *Life of Scott* states in lapidary style that it would have been better for Hogg's fame if he had died before he did, 'for he did not follow his best benefactor until he had insulted his dust.'[21]

Lockhart's rage is excessive but not incomprehensible. He had recently lost an esteemed friend and father-in-law and a beloved son, when Hogg's account appeared. And he was engaged in writing his own account of Scott, which seeks to praise and monumentalise. It richly reveals, but it also conceals. It cruelly arraigns Scott's partners. Hogg's book or books are too slight to serve as a full corrective, and they have prejudices of their own. The memoir says more about Hogg than it does about his *semblable* and opposite, and ostensible subject. But it confronts the important truth of Scott's obsession with class, an obsession with which the complicit Lockhart was ill-placed to come to terms. What was wrong with Scott, in this respect, was wrong with Lockhart too, and with many others. Hogg was prepared to say, or couldn't help saying, that Scott's 'halo of glory' was, in his own eyes, his antecedents rather than his art.

Hogg observes that 'with regard to my speeches when before people of high rank he seemed always dubious as if afraid of what was next to come out,' and it is one of the attractions of the memoir that things do come out there which are better out than in, and which Lockhart's challenge failed to suppress. Poor Lady Scott's mysterious birth as the possible daughter of a nobleman (a matter still to be settled), her recourse in ill health to drugs, her sourness and grand airs – these suggestions have not been without corroboration. And it is no lie to suggest that Scott told lies about his authorship of the Waverley novels. The story of Scott's turning away in real chagrin on learning that a man he liked was a man of God – 'a preacher, God damn it!' – is impossible to disbelieve. Scott's being told on for telling his child Sophia, the surviving daughter mentioned here by her husband, that she hadn't 'the clearest head in the world' is an example of the tactlessness of which Hogg was capable.[22]

Maginn's anonymous review of the *Domestic Manners*[23] was done, as Lockhart noted, in his own way – with all of what Carlyle saw as his all-too-Irish mad mirth. Perhaps the least of its inflamed extraordinariness is that it was visited on a frequent contributor to the journal, *Fraser's*. The review is a recital of lie-detecting lies and of class aspersions. There is scarcely a passage in Hogg's account 'which does not contain a falsehood or an exaggeration'. Scott thought him a man of genius but 'destitute of a regard for truth – of no fixed principles'. Hogg did not, could not, know what he was talking about, being one of 'the Herd': 'as well might we expect from a costermonger an adequate sketch of the manners of the clubs in St James's Street.' Scott was on no 'footing of intimacy' with the Shepherd. He took care not to expose him at Abbotsford to anyone who didn't know his foibles (which many people wanted to witness). He met no nobles there. Oh how Scott kept him at arm's length. 'There are not three persons living who knew him at all, that knew him worse than the Shepherd.'

Hogg regarded Scott 'as a peasant does a gentleman, though he seems to think, or actually does think, that he looks upon him as one literary man does upon another of no very superior pretensions.' Maginn's animus may have been kindled by a wish to please Lockhart, at the time of his recoil from Hogg's anecdotes of Scott: if so, there's an irony in Maginn's mention here of Lockhart's earlier defence of Hogg in the *Quarterly*. 'None of his waggish friends ever thought of setting him up as a boozing buffoon ... until he himself had set them the example.' Maginn conveys that Hogg was never the same man after the *Spy* fiasco of auld lang syne, while also conveying that he was subsequently to 'regain caste'. Wilson wrote all that was 'worth a farthing' in *The Poetic Mirror*. Maginn denies that Scott died of the Reform Bill, of 'the quackeries' and jacqueries of 1830.

In the previous *Fraser's*, that of July 1834, there is an unsigned review of Hogg's *Lay Sermons*. The review goes back twenty years to an occupation by this lay preacher of the stool of repentance, 'that bad eminence', in Ettrick kirk, and dwells lasciviously on the embarrassment of his co-felon, a blushing 'ewe-milker'. The writer recalls attending the kirk, twenty years before, to watch Hogg

> as he underwent (or, in his own beautiful Doric, *tholed*) the awful castigation of the reverend Boanerges who in those days ministered to the spiritual necessities of that primitive population. The bonny, blooming, little ewe-milker, whose charms had caused James to deflect from the path of moral rectitude, stood at his elbow, wrapped all over in her *maud*, but trembling manifestly beneath its folds; and what of her sweet countenance was visible, now – when the minister

was 'splairging brimstone' – deadly pale with terror – now, when the worthy saint was dwelling on the particular character of her offence, its undeniable blackness, indelicacy, indecorum, &c,&c,&c, suffused with scarlet blushes, such as dimmed even the splendour of her accomplice's whiskers. He, meantime, maintained a stern, dogged, sullen obduracy of aspect, which spoke him a hardened and unrepentant sinner; he now and then eyed the lecturer with a glance of cool contempt, which seemed to penetrate like lava into the haughty bosom of the Calvinist; and when all the horrors of holy rhetoric were at length exhausted, and the diatribe must needs come to a conclusion, nimbly and gaily did Jamie hop from his pedestal, and was received almost with plaudits among a goodly company of brother-swains ... At the kirk door Hogg drew the ewe-milker under his arm, and away the two glided together, with apparently as much *sang-froid* as if nothing particular had happened.

The passage quotes from Burns's 'Address to the Deil', who 'spairges about the brunstane cootie', splashes about with the brimstone ladle, in Hell. While finding 'cootie' incomprehensible, a mere rhyme word, Hogg said of this line that 'spairges' is 'the best Scots word in its place I ever saw'.[24] His own verse could have done with more splairging (which became the more familiar form) of Scots words than he allowed it.

The James Hogg who'd been appointed an elder of the kirk is now, says the review, 'a wiser and a better man'. His youth gone, he wears spectacles, teeth 'somewhat smitten'. 'Time has thinned that huge mane of reddish-brown hair that then dangled even to the skirts of his grey jacket.' Much is made of Hogg's unregenerate youth, in order to mock his *Lay Sermons* as inauthentic. Hogg has been trying to make an honest man of himself: the reviewer complains about this, and about his autobiographical tendency, and about the cannibal feast of his admirers' attentions, about the 'open house for lion-hunters' that Altrive has become: 'What a burning shame it is to the barbarous *literati* and *tae* of our time, that they devour the heritage of Hogg and his household at such a rate!'

Jill Rubenstein has attributed the review to Maginn, and another editor of the *Collected Works*, Gillian Hughes, has argued that the reviewer – resentful on Lockhart's behalf of Hogg's life of Scott – played fast and loose with the text in an effort to present the 'picture of a jolly convivial man trying to express himself in moral terms essentially foreign to his nature'. One might agree that the effort was made while thinking the picture not wholly implausible. The review has also been attributed to Allan Cunningham, who was in a position to have advised and assisted with its description of a mutinous penitence. But the review, which includes the suggestion that Mrs Hogg may have put her husband up to publishing his sermons, seems, in general, all-too-Maginn. At the time specified for the penitence Maginn was still in Ireland (and Hogg forty-four), and it is more than possible to think that the scene was dreamed up satirically twenty years later, in the office at *Fraser's*. Who was it who was known to find Mrs Hogg's rectitude amusing? Maginn. For the postscript on Hogg's edition of Burns, which is said to hold Burns in 'complete contempt', the avowed 'Shepherdite' Cunningham, who brought out his own moralistic life and works of Burns that same year, is unlikely to have been responsible.[25]

According to the *Monthly Magazine* in London, 'a not inconsiderable portion' of Hogg's public looked forward to his sermons in the hope of a laugh at his expense, but were cheated of this pleasure.[26] Hogg knew himself laughed at, as well as with; his vanity was a joke, and he was willing to make a joke of it; and he was aware of his reputation for making things up. He was both a writer and a tournament archer, and he could behave as the heaven-taught Aeolian-harp peasant-poet who drew the long bow. The preface to the *Sermons* makes out that they are those of a French monk of the last century, delivered to Hogg in error by a dilatory publisher engaged in rejecting a manuscript of his: a familiar self-protective Gothic trope. 'I have now given so many tales of *perfect truth* to the public, many of them with not one word of truth in them, that I know I shall not be believed in this, and that people will say, "Oho! This is a mere subterfuge of the Shepherd's to get off, in case of any unsound tenets or instances of bad taste."' The story is nevertheless 'literally true'.

In the sermons themselves he is less laid-back about lying. 'Why does one expose oneself to the danger of circulating a lie?' Liars are bound for the lake that burneth with fire and splairging brimstone. And the sermons, as distinct from the story of their provenance, are, it proves, no lie, in the sense that they are his, and are very like sermons, stocked with upbraidings and injunctions. Each has its Biblical text. Each has the unction of the Presbyterian pulpit. And the old Border lady to whom he presented a copy, and who declared it 'no for Sabbath-day's reading', was too severe. The sermons are more genial than theologically demanding, but they can't be thought inappropriate to the Sabbath of his day, or any day.

Hogg thinks in terms of a wise and benevolent Providence which arranges trials and catastrophes for people to deal with, hurdles for the probationary interval of the earthly life. Man has fallen, but there is ample hope. The main charge against Hogg's odious Deists is that they have nothing to offer that can compete with the Christian hereafter, Hogg's fairy-like, pure and chaste hereafter. The soul is an incomprehensible matter, he remarks, but he is able to grasp that its immortality 'is manifest, from that longing after immortality inherent in every bosom'. He is loth to set down anything here that might be deemed unorthodox. Even so, that old lady in Yarrow wisna a' that pleased.

His idiosyncrasies are muted, and there is no lack of house-trained humbug, on the part of a man who could still be considered bizarre, half-savage. The Polonius who appears here quotes from Shakespeare's wiseacre: friends must be grappled to you with hoops of steel. Be prudent, dear ladies, he writes. Don't read ladies' novels. Better marry than burn, he advises the young. Don't be ludicrous. Avoid oddity, he insists, in Johnsonian vein. Mind how you quote Lord Byron, he tells the girls who will be reading him and whom he seems especially keen on instructing. This above all (his 'first great injunction' for the young women of Scotland): 'KEEP THE SABBATH. Do not be seen flying about with gentlemen in gigs and carriages, nor walking and giggling in the fields; for such behaviour is lightsome, and highly disreputable. Attend Divine service every Sunday at least, even though your minister should be *a bore*.' It isn't hard to recall that Hogg himself had once been a flyer-about with young women, who are urged by this good old man to steer clear of the 'smart reply': 'That little degree of vanity which enters into the composition of every man of learning and genius, however modest, is more flattered by being distinctly understood than well answered.'

Young men are urged to steer clear of universities, and the philosophy taught there – by Wilson, as it happened, among others.

Carlyle thought that Hogg's philosophy could be enclosed in a nutshell: 'Be not angry.' And this is certainly what these sermons say. Carlyle's own philosophy could perhaps be reduced to a precept less endearing, and Hogg's kindness and humanity don't wither here in admonition. You feel a need to believe in his smiles no less than in his vanity. The fourth sermon, on soldiers, dislikes what they get up to. It takes its text from the New Testament: 'Sirs, ye are brethren; why do ye harm one to another?' It breathes a rational pacifism. 'After the campaigns of Bonaparte, and the slaughter of so many millions among the most civilised nations on the face of the earth, and which ended so completely in smoke, I really thought there would never be any more wars in Europe.'

Hogg's *Tales of the Wars of Montrose* strike the same note at one point: a Borderer speaks of 'brethren mangling an' butchering ane another in this quiet and peaceable wilderness'. But the tenor of the tales is mostly very different; the Montrose tales have in full measure the twin interest in carnage and carnivorousness that turns up in many of his writings. The meat-eating passages are done with a gusto that might suggest long incarceration in an unlardered Grampian cave. 'An immense roasted side of ox' is slashed and cut to the jingling of gullies. A strange aroma as of some roasting human body is detected.

He expressly favours neither side in Montrose's royalist campaigns of the mid-seventeenth century, though he cheers on his great victory of Inverlochy. He admires Montrose, he declares, but the general is barely a presence in the tales; at one stage he is shown in disguise, but there's next to nothing behind the domino. Montrose's ragamuffin Highlanders stagger back to their glens for the holidays, 'loaden with spoil', while the ministers of the Covenant are hot for the slaughter of prisoners. An aphasic squire, 'quite a character', goes about killing peasants suspected of not being 'for the King' and ends up astride a carthorse. This is a joke, which may in part be a pacifist joke. On one occasion, cleaving close to his historical source while doing nothing to make it plausible, Hogg tells how a suspected royalist spy 'expressed himself against the king with so much rancour' that his inquisitor 'knew he was a true man'. The tales are intended, in the opinion of some, to project a less aristocratic view than Scott's of the Waverley material.

The last and most substantial of the five tales (in Cochrane's three volumes) is 'Wat Pringle o' the Yair'. This pursues the idea of witnessing the battle of Philiphaugh, Montrose's Waterloo, from the standpoint of Selkirkshire farm folk, some of whom betray his escaping 'kerns', waylay stragglers, despoil the dead and finish off the wounded. These witnesses are not for the King, but not for the Covenant either, though the Covenanters' 'system of utter extermination was not at all disapproved of' locally.

The tales draw on the fiction of Scott and of Galt, and on the plays of Shakespeare: Hogg's Edinburgh baillie is a Polonius, and there's a Malvolio and a Romeo and Juliet. Much of the writing adheres to Gothic convention, and has the self-mockery frequent in such fiction. Keats's parody of the convention, in a letter of March 1818, threatens his correspondent with 'I'll immense-rock you, and tremendous-sound you.' The tales have a tremendous rock, and one paragraph has 'tremendeous mountains' and as 'tremendeous' a passage as any that could be conceived. Sides of beef are necessarily and sublimely immense. The *Collected Works* edition of the tales preserves, as others in the series do, Hogg's inadequate punctuation and his errors and wayward spellings. This seems to give more trouble on this occasion than it does elsewhere in the series; more trouble, indeed, than those of his ballad texts which employ his ancient style. It isn't easy to welcome such sentences as 'the toscin of war was now sounded in the distracted vallies.' 'Toscin' is a spelling which recurs, but familiarity does not keep you from fretting about whether or not it is Hogg's. The editor sees the tales as belonging together, in line with a plan of Hogg's, and as embodying the lineaments of a peace process. 'Hogg's achievement depends largely on his ability to persuade the reader that his five narratives are at once distinct and separate tales, and at the same time the progressive links of a chain of successive historical events.' His achievement can scarcely depend on the communication of such an uncertainty; nor is the achievement in question an impressive one.

CHAPTER TWENTY-ONE

Farewell to Ettrick

———

Hogg's writings went down well in nineteenth-century America, which loved them so much, claimed the Shepherd, as to dramatise *The Three Perils of Man*; and some of his best critics and scholars have been American – among them, the poet Louis Simpson. Wilson's writings were also popular there, and in September 1834, a winsome, sharp-witted citizen of that country paid him a visit at his house in Edinburgh. N. P. Willis's head was filled with the Waverley novels, by now a thriving spun-off commerce and tourist staple. He regarded Scott as 'the greatest spirit that has walked the world since Shakespeare', and called at a deserted Abbotsford to inspect the room where he had died two years before. Willis found that Edinburgh had been penetrated by railway trains: 'How sadly is romance ridden over by the march of intellect.' He was awed by the beauty of the English aristocracy. A diary account of his grand tour of the old world, *Pencillings by the Way*, was published by McCrone in the following year.[1]

Breakfast was served during his call on 'Christopher North', but Wilson, in spate, kept him from it for a long time, and when they did sit down, poured the tea in one continuous swoop which flooded the tray. His table talk began with sorrow over 'poor Blackwood', then dying. He spoke of his friend in what Willis heard as a 'very broad Scots accent', noticing, perhaps, that this was not the speech of Christopher North. He explained that the 'Noctes' were generally deemed to be real carousals: the world marvelled that a professor of moral philosophy could sink to such depths, and 'poor Hogg comes in for his share of abuse, for they never doubt he was there, and said every thing that was put down for him.' Hogg takes all that, Wilson went on, 'very good-humouredly, with the exception of one or two occasions, when cockney scribblers have visited him in their tours, and tried to flatter him by convincing him he was treated disrespectfully. But five minutes' conversation and two words of banter restore his good-humour, and he is convinced, as he ought to be, that he owes half his reputation to the "Noctes".'

Willis then asks a question which offers to relieve Maginn of the responsibility imputed by Lockhart for a particular attack on Hogg, and which brings into focus the uncertainties of anonymity:

'What do you think of his "Life of Sir Walter", which Lockhart has so butchered in Fraser?'

'*Did* Lockhart write that?'

'I was assured so in London.'

'It was a barbarous and unjustifiable attack; and, oddly enough, I said so yesterday to Lockhart himself, who was here, and he differed from me entirely. Now you mention it, I think, from his manner, he *must* have written it.'

'Will Hogg forgive him?'

'Never! Never! I do not think he knows yet who has done it, but I hear that he is dreadfully exasperated. Lockhart is quite wrong. To attack an old man, with gray hairs, like the Shepherd, and accuse him so flatly and unnecessarily of lie upon lie – oh, it was not right!'

'Do you think Hogg misrepresented facts wilfully?'

'No, oh no! he is perfectly honest, no doubt, and quite revered Sir Walter. He has an unlucky inaccuracy of mind, however; and his own vanity, which is something quite ridiculous, has given a colouring to his conversations with Scott, which put them in a very false light; and Sir Walter, who was the best-natured of men, may have said the things ascribed to him in a variety of moods, such as no one can understand who does not know what a bore Hogg must sometimes have been at Abbotsford. Do you know Lockhart?'

Willis unleashes a diatribe. Lockhart is almost the only London literatus whom he has not met, and he has no wish to meet this 'most unfair and unprincipled critic of the day ... I never heard him well spoken of. I probably have met a hundred of his acquaintances, but I have not yet seen one who pretended to be his friend.' Wilson replies that there is a great deal of good in Lockhart – in private, 'the mildest and most unpresuming of men'. The exchange is a reminder of how far these writers could be, and could pretend to be, in the dark about their own corporate anonymities and effronteries. Joint authorship had always been a factor in such cases, and distance, geographical separation, now lent further possibilities of concealment and bewilderment to past and present enigmas.

From the high ground of his breakfast table, Wilson declares that Lockhart has 'an unhappy talent' for sarcasm, 'with which his heart has nothing to do. When he sits down to review a book, he never thinks of the author or his feelings. He cuts it up with pleasure, because he does it with skill in the way of his profession, as a surgeon dissects a dead body.' After an Ambrosian meal, as Wilson has it, Lockhart had come up with the first 'Noctes', having thought it a pity that 'some short-hand writer had not been here to take down the good things that have been said at this supper' (enter, in due course, Gurney).

At this point, Wilson at last seizes the teapot 'as if it were a sledgehammer' and breakfast breaks out. Wordsworth is discussed ('wrapped up in his own poetical life', he 'thinks of nothing else'), and Wilson's alleged imitation of his verse. He invites Willis to visit him at his place near Selkirk, Thirlestane, leased for a season, and promises him a meeting with his neighbour Hogg, which did not occur.

Willis's allusion to Lockhart's lack of principle can't have escaped him when, in a review of the New York edition, he came to blue-pencil *Pencillings* in the *Quarterly*. He is 'a young American sonneteer of the most ultra-sentimental delicacy' who is unacquainted with the best society of his native country, let alone that of London's West End. He is suspected of Cockneyism. He passes on harmless things told him by dukes in private – but what if they'd been harmful things? Lockhart asks. 'Gentlemen are shy of us,' Willis's book says of the reception given in Britain to his compatriots. They are thought 'unsafe', 'odd', 'a bad thing to be'. Their 'high-wrought language', applied to trifles, is an offence.

Lockhart quotes pretty things said by Willis, and warns that they will not 'so far propitiate Lady Blessington as to make her again admit to her table the animal who has printed what then ensues'. What ensues is table talk gleaned by Willis from Tom Moore about the Reformer Lord Althorp ('a wonderful instance of what a man may do *without* talking') and the Irish patriot O'Connell. Moore had been watched at a salon, 'sliding his little feet up to Lady Blessington', another compatriot of

Moore's: 'Half a glance tells you that he is at home on a carpet.' Moore's talk, passed on by Willis, is that of a man who had in his time taken the field against Jeffrey: 'They may say what they will of duelling; it is the great preserver of the decencies of society.' It seemed that O'Connell had failed to turn up to fight a duel, pleading an ill wife, and that a Dublin wit had delivered an epigram, which Lockhart must have loved to come across in *Pencillings*:

> Some men, with a horror of slaughter,
>   Improve on the Scripture command,
> And 'honour their wife and their daughter,
>   That their days may be long in the land'.

This effigy of a detested Lockhart is hardly valid for the early days of his connection with Hogg, who was as close to Lockhart then as he was to Wilson, their relationship a study in affinity and in antithesis. Lockhart was himself among the compounds and involutes of his time, a time when difference of class was widely held to be inherent and benign, when those with long pedigrees were the givers of good things and the praisers of peasant virtue, but when a feeling for the equality of man could be experienced even among the hierarchically-inclined, as by Lockhart in his life of Burns. He was a Scottish patriot who was also a leaver of the country and a member of the British ruling class. The young Lockhart of the cigar and the Parisian morning gown believed that Scotland was torn between Calvinism and Enlightenment scepticism, and he too was torn. He was an adherent of superstition, imagination and nationality who agreed with Carlyle, in 1843, that 'we are all wrong and all like to be damned.' And yet a wee Jeffrey, a closet rationalist and internationalist, has been surmised in him. Two creeds are spoken of, successively, in rhymes of his.

> But now my creed, from nonsense freed,
>   In three short items lies –
> That nothing's new, and nothing's true,
>   And nothing signifies.

In the second poem a fourth item appears. He hopes to join his friends in the hereafter – 'That creed I fain would keep.'[2]

When Lockhart said of Burns that 'the tormenting bitterness of a mind ill at ease within itself escaped (as may be too often traced in the history of satirists) in the shape of angry sarcasms against others,' he knew that he was speaking also of himself. Keats said something, something perfect, about satirical criticism when he spoke of the attacks on him in *Blackwood's* and the *Quarterly*: 'This is a mere matter of the moment – I think I shall be among the English Poets after my death.'[3]

Lockhart's internal conflicts give clues to Hogg's contradictions and intellectual vicissitudes. It is a drastic simplification to talk of Hogg as an enemy of the Enlightenment, to lay appreciative stress, as can now happen, on his forward-looking denial of reasoned explanation. He is as forthcoming with explanations as he is with mysteries. He was interested in science. He wanted to know what could go wrong with sheep, without thinking them like to be damned. He was an enemy – while also a connoisseur – of enthusiastic madness.

Hogg's American visitors may sometimes have seen him as nature's American – as a child of nature out there in a wilderness, a suitable subject for egalitarian sentiment. One American caller published two anonymous pieces in the *American Monthly Magazine* for April and May 1834, in which Hogg was seen as 'a man whose unaffected simplicity of manner, whose boundless but unoffending egotism, whose goodness of heart, and sincerity of feeling, made him loved by all men': an impression which resembles that left on admirers by the egotistical farmer poet Robert Frost. The caller was told by his simple soul: 'Gie me ae verse o' an old sang, and the tune, and I'll cheat them a' – I've done it: Wattie Scott could na find me out.' This is a scandalous claim which sounds like Hogg, and which may well have been true.[4]

William Blackwood died shortly after Willis's visit to Wilson, and Hogg's nephew Robert died of consumption in the same year, 1834. In that year too the eternal separation between Hogg and *Blackwood's* came to an end. During the darkness of his 'Noctes' eclipse, with Lockhart attempting a reconciliation at one point, Hogg had vowed to Grieve that Blackwood 'must succumb to me not I to him, nor to the King, nor to the Duke of Wellington neither'. This was in the style of Scott's impersonation, in his journal, of 'the black hussar of literature', and in the belief that he, Hogg, had been the hero of the 'Noctes' all along.

Then, on 8 November 1834, with Blackwood dead and Scott's biographer estranged and outraged by his anecdotes of Scott, Hogg wrote to Cochrane to say, without charm, of Lockhart: 'if I liked I could tell things of him and his that would crush him like a moth.' He also told Cochrane: 'My kind and liberal friend John Wilson forced me again into Blackwood without asking my leave. He could not pull any longer without me.'[5]

An arrangement was discussed whereby he would receive so much for an article whether or not it appeared in print, and there was talk of his being paid for his ghosted 'Noctes' appearances. On the 17th of this eventful November, in correspondence with Blackwood's son Alexander, he said there was no doubt that his 'Noctes' eidolon was 'a much nobler animal than the Shepherd himself', but then there was irony in that, and he also said that the proposals for a reunion were 'rather too humiliating'. Nevertheless, an armistice was reached. He had already returned to the page in the May 'Noctes', set in a tent in the Fairy's Cleugh. Who should turn up but 'The SHEPHERD! The SHEPHERD! The SHEPHERD! hurra! hurra! hurra! hurra! hurra! hurra! hurra! hurra! hurra!' This is the English-speaking voice of 'Omnes'. The Shepherd responds in Scots – 'Hurraw! hurraw! hurraw!' – and proceeds to make a speech:

> Where's the strange auld tyke? Whare's the queer auld fallow? Where's the canty auld chiel? Whare's the dear auld deevil? Oh! North – North – North – North – ma freen – ma brither – ma father – let's tak anither intil ane anither's arms – let's kiss ane anither's cheek – as the guid cheevalry knichts used to do – when, haen fa'en oot about some leddy-luve, or some disputed laun', or some king's changefu' favor, or aiblins aboot naething ava but the stupit lees o' some evil tongues, they happened to forgather when riding opposite ways through a wood, and flingin' themsells, wi' ae feelin' and ae thocht, aff their twa horses, cam' clashin' thegither wi' their mailed breists, and began sobbin' in the silence o' the auncient aiks that were touched to their verra cores to see sic forgiveness and sic affection atween thae twa stalwart champions . . .

This sylvan reconciliation is like an aftermath of the scene evoked by Hoffmann in *The Devil's Elixirs*, where a knight fights in the darkness of a forest with his double. Here are two knights who are at variance and who are at one. They are knights who have now made it up.

The Shepherd stays with his sobbing cavaliers for a lot longer, before sweeping North up into his arms and bearing him into the tent. Meanwhile Hogg also went on writing copiously for *Fraser's*, his Southern abuser.[6]

That same November, the publisher McCrone was caught with Mrs Cochrane in his plaid. Hogg sought to know from Allan Cunningham in London: 'How were they discovered?' During a visit paid by McCrone to Altrive, the summer before, 'there was a constant correspondence carried on' between him and a Miss Salem, whose letters 'I am almost certain,' said Hogg, were in Mrs Cochrane's hand. Cunningham wrote to say that he had set down 'the attentions of Mac' in this quarter 'to a sort of forwardness for which he was something conspicious'. Mrs Cochrane had come back from Margate, where Mac had gone to see the miss 'to whom you allude', and fourteen letters had been found in Mrs Cochrane's petticoats. Cunningham had read one and a half of these. The letters referred to a 'frequent intercourse' and to McCrone as Mrs Cochrane's husband. Mac, who had been about to marry the daughter of a respectable Professor Bordwine, is no longer to darken Cunningham's door. This was to be seen as a different matter from the actions which had forced Hogg before the Closeburn kirk session, years before in Nithsdale. The scandal was miserable and calamitous. Mrs Hogg, said her man, 'is so shocked at it that she is like to faint whenever it is spoken about. Poor woman, she kens very little about London morality.' Peebles had chastity and the marital bond. Pall Mall had adultery.[7]

Hogg, who liked to be seen by Cunningham to be doing well, added: 'I have made this cottage a very fine place now. A house of ten rooms, kitchen, dairy, and five cellars!!' Prior to the 1834 Election, Hogg was enfranchised when a fresh lease was granted for Altrive which created a post-Reform Parliamentary vote, a vote which was unlikely to be withheld from the Duke of Buccleuch's candidate.

On 26 August 1834 came one of those banquets which set the face of triumph on his struggle, Scotland's reply to the Holborn thanksgiving. A dinner was held at the Tontine in Peebles – as Blackwood lay dying in Edinburgh and Lockhart nursed his wrath in London, with Willis about

to breakfast with Wilson – in order to do honour to the *Blackwood's*
maverick and Selkirkshire poacher, at which Wilson took the chair and a
sheriff served as vice-president, and Hogg reviewed his career: 'Mr
Wilson can tell ye that I hae fought very hard for my literary fame, but I
hae got it at last. Nae body can say, after this night, that I hae na got it.'
England had already saluted his fame. 'I gaed to Lunnon, an' was
received there as never ither man was received in this warld. I was made
a member o' seven learned societies. I got free tickets sent me for a' the
theatres, exhibitions, and every ither thing ... I dinna ken how mony
clubs I'm a member o'.' The Brownie of Bodsbeck had fetched the
houdy for his birth. He'd expected to die at the age when Burns did, but
had been granted something yet, like Burns's auld farmer and auld mare:
'Here stauns still the auld Shepherd.' In 1833, he had checked the parish
register and been upset to find that he had not been born on the same
day of the year as Burns, and that he was sixty-three, not sixty-one.[8]

He went on to say at Peebles that he'd been 'blamed for the
eccentricity o' my conduct, but you canna bind wi' the ordinary rules the
actions o' a genius.' A chaplet of heather and of red berries was placed
on his brow. The occasion was unruffled by political rancour. This was
one of those occasions when vanity proves itself right and is taken at its
own valuation, even by some of those who have come to mock.[9]

The kingdom itself was quiet. Reform had not destroyed it.
Revolution had not come. Cockburn and Jeffrey had benchified, settling
down as Lords of Session. But the heart of Midlothian was not quite as it
should have been. Chartism was stirring, even among the better sort.
For the 1834 Election, 'Douglas Cheape Esq. Advocate', a 'Noctes'
contributor, brought out a Chaldee Manuscript entitled 'The Book of the
Chronicles of the City',[10] a worthy successor to the original of 1817.
Cheape was one of the gifted people of the *Blackwood's* divan who are
now largely lost to fame; another was the St Andrew's professor Thomas
Gillespie, admired by Hogg. A masterful Whig chief is shown here
vacillating over the choice of the party's candidate. The Radical
candidate is James Aytoun, who had, said Cheape, the support of the
Irish – that infestation, displeasing to Cockburn, from the island of
Miletus – and of the insolvent (Tory bankrupts having slipped Cheape's
mind):

21. Now James was a strong man, skilful in speech from his youth up, a despiser of Princes, and of their servants;

22. Whose voice was as the voice of the bulls of Bashan.

23. And he gathered unto him as many as were in debt, as many as had fled to the place of refuge, which is the Sanctuary; as many as were of evil report; as many as were given to sudden change;

24. Also many from Miletus, which is the green island of the sea, whose hats and hosen were as the hats and hosen of the likenesses of the living things whereat the ravens are affrighted and flee away.

25. With sticks and staves did they come.

Hogg grew up when 'the last purely Scotch age' spoken of by Cockburn was nearing its end. Scotland did not cease to be Scottish, but was thereafter more open to England and the world. Between Trafalgar and Waterloo Edinburgh was in a bustle, an excitement caught in Hogg's *Spy* and in a contemporary account by Cockburn. The pleasures of the city included 'nocturnal parties and a sort of half-fashionable, half-literary slang about Science and reviews', wrote Cockburn in 1810. Scott 'still keeps the printer's devil chasing him for sheets, like a fool. I know no poet who has committed such suicide as Watty.'[11] Edinburgh was an intellectual and professional place, a holy place and a thinking place, and a feasting and hurrahing place, a medley of taverns, kirks and law courts, of booksellers' parlours and massage parlours. This bustle went to the formation of the countryman Hogg. Between Waterloo and the Reform Bill there ensued what Laurance Saunders calls a 'new pattern of elegant living'.[12] Edinburgh nights were lit, not just by gas eventually, but by the Theatre Royal, and by halls and assembly-rooms, where Mozart and Beethoven and the Gows were famous names. Beethoven, who had set Hogg to music, was 'starving in his native country', grieved Tickler in the 'Noctes' of April 1827, and a Philharmonic Society in the South had 'sent him a hundred pounds to keep him alive – he is deaf, destitute, and a paralytic. Alas! alas!' Raeburn, Wilkie, Nasmyth, William Allan and John Watson Gordon were among the artists of the place, from whom came portraits of the Ettrick Shepherd. Allan painted *The Celebration of the Birthday of James Hogg* in which Wilson sits with his friend, amid a divan of eminent Scotsmen in a Tibbie Shiel's-like parlour, stocked with

John Wilson toasts Hogg, by Sir William Allan (1819).
Hogg is at the far left; next to him, Scott

punch bowl, fiddle, and a guitar, a lounging Highlander at the edge of
the throng. One of Wilkie's genre paintings is of a 'distraining for rent' –
a timely treatment of the Scottish subject of eviction.

Edinburgh was at the centre of the industrialisation of publishing
which had taken hold in Britain by the 1830s. Publishing-houses could
be seen as 'factories'. There were publishers who owned the journals
that reviewed their books. Print runs were expanded, authors chased for
copy. Having chosen to be a man of letters who earned his living by the
pen, Hogg was caught up in these factories, and suffered for it.

Inherited wealth gained power, and shared it with men of parts and of
sense who prospered in a society experienced as one in which class
difference became more acute – with Edinburgh's Old and New Towns
emblematic of the new, divided, rich-and-poor Scotland – and in which
prosperity could come to grief. A 'trained and active benevolence', as
Saunders puts it, that of scientists and doctors, did what it could, in
time, to fight the overcrowding and disease of the country's spreading

slums, to cause them to be seen as a concern of government. Much of this attempt post-dated Hogg's Scotland, which stood in need of such activities. A squalor of town and country alike was there to be feared and fled. It was not absent from his Selkirkshire Arcadia.

Was it worse than the squalor of the noctes depicted in Irvine Welsh's twentieth-century novel of Edinburgh addiction, *Trainspotting*, whose violent man Begbie has the same name as the homicide victim discussed by the Ambrosians? Welsh and Hogg are alike in having at their command a subtle and expressive Scots-English, and in other respects besides. Welsh's novel contains sport and conviviality, and carnage, and a kind of ruined carnality. These features are consonant with what goes on in Hogg's *Queen Hynde* and in Hogg's carnival writings at large, whose phantasmagorias belong to a great Scots tradition, a Scots devotion to the hallucinated and the surreal, to such matters as covens of jolly beggars, balls of Kirriemuir, Tam o' Shanter's night ride, the drunk man's romance with the thistle. Nearly everyone takes drugs in *Trainspotting* and, as we have seen, there were drugs, as well as drinks, in Hogg's world also, where the 'Noctes' Shepherd confesses that he once took laudanum and 'cowped ower'. Cowping, so called, in the sense of toppling, is also found in Welsh's novel. Scotland, where the word can also now mean copulating, has been prone to proneness. James Boswell was jeered at by his English lawyer colleagues for 'adhering to the pavement' on circuit, like the spirits in Dante's *Purgatorio*, where proneness is described in the language of the Vulgate Psalms: *Adhaesit pavimento anima mea*. There's a description in *Trainspotting* of the proneness produced by grievous bodily harm: 'We left the guy slumped on the pavement.'[13] And the 'Noctes' are not without such slumps.

Hogg's Scotland had its desperate places, its circles of hell, its battalions of the lost, its beggars. The midnights of the resurrectionist assassins Burke and Hare could be considered more than a match for what can happen in Welsh's circle of junkies, with its dead baby and its gangster Begbie, its brutality and betrayal. All the same, while 'Scotland' may be too compendious a concept for it to make sense to compare past and present embodiments in search of an unqualified change for better or worse, it is possible to feel that the idea of progress in which people used to believe would encourage no one to throw nostalgia to the winds and prefer Welsh's Leith to Hogg's Innerleithen.

Hogg's own nostalgia for the old Scots countryside wells from the essay he did, dated 21 June 1831, for the third volume of Blackwood's *Quarterly Journal of Agriculture*, on 'the changes in the habits, amusements and conditions of the Scottish peasantry'. Here is an eloquent expression of the golden retrospect congenial to old age. Country people are better-off, he believes, but less cheerful, and less happy, and less devout. The diet of menials has improved. But social division has increased, and 'with regard to the intercourse between master and servant', there is, for the worse, 'a mighty change indeed'. In the large, amalgamated farms of the new age, menials have been put in to boss other menials, who feel that they are the servants of servants, members of a community no more. Once upon a time, 'every farmer had only one farm, and his family were his principal servants.' Now most farmers have several farms, 'which makes the distance between master and servant wider and wider'. 'Ruinous war prices' had turned some farmers into fine gentlemen. Less glee now. Coarser jokes. More poachers stalk the Borders with their blackened faces. Gamekeepers are insolent bad hats.

Song-singing is now kept up only 'by a few migratory tailors'. Tom Moore's songs are cursed for being sung instead of Scottish ones. When 'Mr Scott's work' appeared, the 'arcanum' of Scottish song was 'laid open, and a deadening blow was inflicted on our rural literature and principal enjoyment by the very means adopted for their preservation.' He firmly identifies the welfare of the countryside with the survival of its arts and amusements. The sexes don't get together in play as they used to. Manly exercises, but for his own efforts, would be extinct: 'For the last forty years I have struggled to preserve them in a local habitation and a name.' Such names as the St Ronan's Games and the Six Feet High Club.

He offers a threefold summary of the position. One: disuse of song. The ancient minstrelsy 'lost all its interest and romance as soon as it ceased to be chanted to its native and animated lilts'. Two: the game laws need reform, in the forlorn hope of stopping poachers. Three: the new subjugation in the labour market. 'The ancient state of vasselage was a delightful bond compared to this. It is a state of absolute slavery' – tempered by the freedom to sell yourself, each term, to the highest bidder. In the good old days, the reader might feel, a farmer's family had been his slaves. 'To the gradual advancement of the *aristocracy* of farming', district after district is being given over to big farms. The enterprising and the respectable are leaving.

An ironised nostalgia can be found in 'A Screed on Politics', five letters to the editor of *Blackwood's* which were published, with something of a belated air, in April 1835. 'You know well enough that I'm a Tory,' he begins: but not, it seems, a doctrinaire one. What follows is more screed than creed; the lay-sermoniser deploys an irony that gets out of hand. The Reform Bill encourages drinking and conversation. But there is talk now of politics, where once there had been talk of morality and religion, and an attention to song. 'Our ballad lore had been all ruined by being published.' The bill helps the fair sex by keeping them from novels and gossip. It brings a sparkle to their eye. But it also brings violence, personalities.

The fifth letter admonishes people 'not to be angry with any man for his opinions'. Let there be a decent 'medium' or mean. The old 'legitimate' road to Edinburgh was by Peebles. But other roads went by Innerleithen and Selkirk. All three roads led to Edinburgh, and it's the same with politics, and with getting to heaven. He says that he is drawing out this letter unduly, 'but I cannot help it.' And he can't help drawing this dualistic statement to an end by blaming the 'almighty crowd which shortens all disputes – whose essence is power, and whose power neither faith nor reason can stay from overleaping the pales of eternal truth'. Some poet, he says, has called them 'the scum'.

Hogg was a man of parts who rose in the world, in a cowping sort of way, and who was also in some degree enslaved. Chained to the oar of publishing, he could write carelessly and modishly. In doing so, he could sometimes be one of those many writers who have withheld the honest truth in order to please, and to make money, or a living, or a name: a refusal which may involve an inability and which is no doubt primordial. The refusal is made comic in V. S. Naipaul's novel *Half a Life*, where an Indian youth is taught the English Romantic poets and decides: 'This is just a pack of lies. No one feels like that.'[14] Some of

Hogg's writings are like that. But this is the same Hogg who wrote one of the most moving and interesting of all novels, and who wrote the tales of Marion's Jock and John Gray, and the ballad of the Witch of Fife, and other works in which a truth is told. It can be said of him what he said of himself – that he got it at last. He came true. He was like the man in the Bible who came late to the vineyard but was paid the same as the grafters. He was a man of parts with a role to play in a parable thought to expound the arbitrariness of God's grace.

From the later 1820s, he published a succession of stories and poems in the *Edinburgh Literary Journal* and in *Fraser's*. There were queer stories, adventure stories, homiletic, lay-sermon yarns like 'The Minister's Annie', which feels less for a deserted mother than for her seducer – who repents – or for her saintly minister father, who declines at first to take her in. 'The Strange Letter of a Lunatic' is a comedy of manners about a man who treats with a double, 'my whimsical namesake and second self'. The lunatic proves to be an alcoholic. Alcoholics have indeed seen and been double, in the sense known to literature: but the story is mechanical rather than electric, and stands in invidious relation to the *Confessions*. One of his less welcome duplications.[15]

Who did *Fraser's* think they were getting when they hired Hogg, about whom Maginn knew a thing or two worth sneering at? He has never been 'very backward in coming forward', said the pseudonymous Pierce Pungent (Lockhart and Maginn) in February 1832, in their series 'Literary Characters'. He is 'our old rough and round, hearty, wholesome friend', whose 'worrikow' or scarecrow appearance at Manners and Miller's Edinburgh bookshop has remained over the years in Pierce's mind. He has no sense of humour. 'Sacredness' is his poetical character. But 'The Witch of Fife' is preferred to mawkish 'Kilmeny'. There are said to be admirers of *The Queen's Wake* who have never read it.

An earlier profile of Hogg, No 1 in the series, a piece which has been attributed to Thomas Powell, contains, in contrast, a real effort at literary criticism. Powell, personally unacquainted with his subject, talks of the 'electric power' of genius, and of Hogg's fancy and facility. Hogg has imagination. Burns has understanding. Powell, too, likes 'The Witch of Fife' and not 'Kilmeny'. The faults of Mr Hogg's verse are 'the very faults which, in their greater aggravation, render valueless the greater portion of the current poetry of our day'. Hogg has 'a degree of worldly-mindedness' which is 'not often found with high poetical character'.

Maginn and Lockhart, the two London editors, continued to be close friends. Billy Maginn of the child's sweet face and stammering repartee was the archetypal scholar journalist and drunken wit. He had earlier become, as Hogg was to become, *persona non grata* at *Blackwood's*. He was a casualty of the more decorous and odorous journal that had evolved from the early outrages, with the publisher's decision that it would no longer do 'to run amuck in this kind of way'.[16] Maginn had gone south, where he was to start a London *Blackwood's*, and to make a success of it. These periodicals, together with the *London Magazine*, have been placed among the most influential of the century, beyond the province of the intellectual reviews. But the Irishman's fortunes were to founder in illness and improvidence. Debt was his vocation. He worked at it. And his life was a delirium. Cruel and kind, a helper of the immigrant Irish, a frequenter of thieves' dens, a lampooner of his friends, the often well-liked enemy of everybody. A Protestant loyalist, he was a Tory who didn't like his party and a patriot who didn't like his country. A scholar, with his Latin and his Greek and his Hebrew and his Sanskrit and his Shakespeare studies, and an oceanic journalist. A hater of Liberalism, a supporter of the Reform Bill who went on to deplore its consequences.

Carlyle – described as 'dreadfully in earnest' by Jeffrey – deemed Maginn, his editor at *Fraser's*, to be 'without earnestness': and he deemed the journal he wrote for to be one whose 'Saturnalian Toryism' was such as to out-Blackwood Blackwood. Lockhart applied to his friend a line from Maginn's own poem about the Irish giant Timothy Thady Mulligan: 'The whisky, frisky, rummy, gummy, brandy, no dandy Irishman'. Lockhart's memory served him with:

> A randy, bandy, brandy, no Dandy,
> Rollicking jig of an Irishman!

He also wrote a privately-published, single-rhyme poem of his own on the subject of 'the Doctor', as Maginn was known, which delighted the poor fellow portrayed there and was revised to furnish an elegy when he died in 1842:[17]

For the Tories his fine Irish brains he would spin,
Who received prose and rhyme with a promising grin,
'Go ahead, you queer fish, and more power to your fin,'
But to save from starvation stirred never a pin.

Lockhart's spin-doctor Maginn had few faults:

Barring drink and the girls, I ne'er heard of a sin –
Many worse, better few, than bright, broken Maginn.

Lockhart had lost his taste for the Tories, as the poem implies. In 1837 he wrote arrestingly, like some ailing knight-at-arms, to William Laidlaw: 'I have satisfied myself that the age of Toryism is by for ever; and the business of a party which can in reason propose to itself nothing but a defensive attitude, without hope either of plunder or honour, seems to me to have few claims on those who, when it was in power, never were permitted to have any of the advantages' lavished on fools and knaves.[18]

Among Hogg's other contributions to the journal was 'The Flower o' Glendale' (1831), a poem in which a wooer, a 'queer body', a 'wild little body', wins a duel for the hand of the Flower, with whom he leaves the world for a season. This dwarf is a supernatural agent who might count as a diminutive of Maginn's Irish giant. In October of the same year, a drinking song on the coronation of William IV was accompanied by a 'yepistle' to the editor which gives news of the state of Scotland ('we are a' goin' here to the pigs and whistles since Lord Jauphrey – Lord sauf us – was made Lord Advocate'), and by a parody which manages to be both democratic, in Burns's manner, and élitist:

A king may make a man a lord,
A belted knight and a' that;
But he can't make Jeff. a gentleman,
For a' that, an' for a' that.

It seems probable that these lines, and the epistle, were written in the office. An imitation of Hogg was well within the scope of the journal's replication of *Blackwood's*, and Lockhart had tried in the past to bind Hogg by such means to the Tories.

The following year, 1832, a poem of Hogg's, rather than 'Hogg's', predicts a Whig doom, an engulfing egotism: this is his 'An Auld Wife's Dream'. There are pieces in *Fraser's* about the cutting of throats, snow-smotherings, ghosts, a King James in disguise, elders in love. 'Georgie Scott, a Hamely Pastoral' (February 1831) is about a Cameronian who is turned down by the girl he falls for, unlike those

> Shepherd lads o' Tweed an' Yarrow,
> Sair exposed to Cupid's arrow.

This lively poem was followed in the next issue by a lively tale, 'The Barber of Duncow', where Rodger McFunn marries and murders a Cameronian lass. Gentlemen with secrets employed the barber. 'Whether he put any o' thae luckless lasses to a waur place than genteel service, an' the poor babies to a caulder hame than a nurice's lap, I canna say,' says the female narrator. When the wife discovers that her husband has other wives, she warns him: 'I shall be unto thee Grizel McGrief.' She returns from the dead, with the white plates on the dresser showing through her, to visit an aunt, pious but as like a witch as anyone the narrator ever saw, and to direct attention to her own corpse, which Rodger incriminates himself by touching. A sceptical listener is warned that Grizel's ghost will appear to any sceptic. 'What's that at the door?' brings to an end this 'auld world story'.

In 'The Mountain-Dew Men' (September 1832) a wife tells a hoyden on their hill farm: 'Wild and wicked as ye are, the truth whiles fa's frae your lips.' The hoyden Jane ('ill Jean') goes to the aid of her master in the snow. Drunk mountain-dew men mess about – keepers of an illicit still. The farmer and his faithful collie perish in the storm. The women survive.

Also in *Fraser's* (February 1833) was 'A Remarkable Egyptian Story', told in a modified Chaldean, divested of irony and humour. The God of Israel subdues Abdallah the Ethiopian. A similar story, 'Eastern Apologues', had figured in a Christmas annual, the *Forget me not* of 1829. The pursuit of wealth and sensual pleasure is rebuked by a prince's mutilated monitor: but a surprise is sprung when the claims of power and practicality are shown to be respected – weighed in the balance, in dualistic suspension, against an Ettrick-seeming innocence and virtue. Both Easterns are obliged to *Rasselas*.

A poem by Hogg appeared in *Fraser's* during the last weeks of his life, 'The Chickens in the Corn', the brutality of its concerns a notable feature, together with the strength and virtuosity of its Scots.[19] Jenny is a farmer's wife who is 'wae' about her wrinkles and silver hairs, and jealous of the bonny lasses, the ill Jeans, mounted by her man. She spies one gliding in at the stable door and goes after her, shedding garments as she does so.

> 'For I see by the limmer's flisky stride
>   There's a tryst in the stable sta'.'

> She kickit her stockings an' syne her shoon,
>   Gart a' her body-claes flee;
> But her petticoat she hastit on,
>   Though it hardly reach'd her knee.

The lass in the hayloft is so scared that she is only able to cry – like Hogg, on one occasion – ' 'Tis me!' She has been looking for eggs, she claims. Jenny climbs up to verify, falls and breaks a leg. The remaining six stanzas harp on her injuries. The moral is not one Hogg would have wanted for his last words in life:

> May every auld wife of jealous heart
>   Of the comely an' the young
> Get sickan a cast as bauld Jenny Gill,
>   An' gang hirpling o'er ane rung.

He appeared posthumously in the journal, like Grizel's ghost, with two tales. A letter dated 17 September 1835, which offers them to the publisher, James Fraser, damns 'the insolent, scoundrelly Whigs, Papists, and Radicals'. He'd felt 'safe' when Sir Robert Peel was at the helm. These are the words and tone of the portrait of Maginn and his politics which Lockhart did for the journal in 1831: 'Whigs, Papists, Radicals, whatever comes under the disgusting category of *Liberalism*, should be exposed, insulted, stabbed, crucified, impaled, drawn, and quartered.' The published covering letter reads as if copied from a handout. Here, too, the probability is that it was written in the office, as a last fling in the Toryfying of Hogg by these friends of his, who could see him as a true man and a steady, lightly rewarded for all he has done for the party.

Oliver Yorke – the Christopher North of *Fraser's* – introduces 'Helen Crocket' as the 'last tale' of that elderly 'child of nature'. Drunken Nol Yorke remarks in his periodical that Hogg 'erred in devoting so much of his time to such worthless labours' as periodical writing. Hogg's covering letter remarks of one of the tales that 'if it does not suit, I am sure to get it back again' from *Fraser's*. 'I cannot get one thing back' from *Blackwood's*.

'The Turners' came out first, in May 1836. It has a duped, drunken laird, a grasping attorney, Jacob Evans, and a termagant landlady. A laird-apparent runs mad. The 'auld Jew' Jacob pursues bonny Margaret, and tries to get her dominie boyfriend sacked. The wish is for 'the body that is kicking every body out, an' cheatin' every body, to be turned out himsel''. A half-blackamoor shows up, is denied a lodging, but proves to be a son and heir back from bettering himself in India.

'Helen Crocket', published in October, puts Papists down. Eppy Welch is a witch whose spells root people to the spot, such is 'the electricity of Eppy's eye'. Her friend Nans Blake says that Catholics are 'laden with iniquities' – a weary way of putting it. Eppy describes her gift in a manner that might seem intended to evoke Hogg's: 'I am no witch; but I have a certain power of my own above human nature, from whom or from whence I do not know. I never prayed for it, never bargained for it, never asked it, and yet I have it.' Tailors sin with women, and one of these sinners is frozen in the act of defecation, shot in the bum with wine-soaked wadding, and tended by Jock the blacksmith, who suggests that murder is bad, but that 'there's nae other sins atween men and women.' Jock proposes a horse plaster for the tailor's afflicted part; of all operations the patient 'hates flaybottomie the maist'. Helen Crocket loves Eppy and is her child. Having been away 'in the east kintry at the hairst work', she returns home pregnant by a vile man whom, with Eppy's help, she shoots dead. She inherits Eppy's powers. Hogg's Fraseriana indicates a failing vigilance in the matter of indelicacy, and a reversion to his early world of firesides, long winter nights, queer sights and rude jokes.

These were among the preoccupations of the last months of Hogg's writing life. Supernatural themes were invested with what has been seen as a bucolic realism. He was still a countryman, and had always written as one, for all the treaties he had signed with a sophisticated urban culture. A benign account of his later life was given by Henry Scott Riddell, poet and clergyman.[20] 'His seemed one of those hearts that do not become older in proportion as the head grows grey. Cheerful as the splendour of heaven, he carried the feelings, and, it may be said, the simplicity and pursuits, of youth into his maturer years.' Riddell spoke of Hogg's 'bien and happy home'.

Very little has been said about his relationship with Hogg, but he belongs to the electric circuit of pairs and likenesses which Hogg inhabited. This double was a Selkirkshire shepherd and poet, 'a bard from the mountains', as he called himself. He was less exposed to want than Hogg, less starving: but his education was impeded. He nonetheless went to Edinburgh University, where he was, as was the Rev. James Russell, one of Wilson's favoured pupils. He became minister of Caerlanrig, Teviothead, where he went mad and was sent to an asylum (1841–4). He then returned to Teviothead.

The memorial essay prefixed to his *Poetical Works* reveals a simplicity of heart akin to an aspect of the Hogg contemplated by his contemporaries. While still on the hill, Riddell used to carry his writings in his hat, and 'unlike most other young authors, I got a publisher unsought for. This was the wind' – which blew the contents of his hat over hill and dale, shifting them to a' the airts. Among them was a hostile piece about a farmer with whom he was disputing over a sheep and a boundary. The enemy read the piece, and trouble came of it. This is quite like Hogg. It may be that the strain of being both poet and peasant, of getting off the hill and into the manse, undid Riddell, for a while. A not dissimilar experience of translation and division had surely shaken Hogg.

The two had much in common. The Duke of Buccleuch built Riddell a cottage, fondly mentioned in his verse. He was 'a good old Tory'. He wrote about foot rot in sheep, and about the Cheviot breed. Riddell wrote about his friend, in 1847, in the *Instructor*, edited by another

James Hogg. He believed that his friend's features were beyond the power of art to portray, and was said by Burns's widow to be of all men the one who bore the strongest resemblance to her husband, whom Hogg desired to resemble. A plethora of similitudes here.

The most intriguing common ground between the two Border poets emerges in the sympathetic account of himself which Riddell received from his psychiatrist, Dr W. A. F. Browne, at the Crichton Royal Institution in Dumfries, where the patients ran a literary magazine. Riddell felt that his 'country bearing and local reputation' scarcely entitled him to mix with such a cultivated set of inmates at the hospital. His doctor held that 'a duality of consciousness had been established by the processes of disease. He spoke much of two parallel currents of thought which seemed to run constantly through his mind, one of these consisting of suggestions of despondency and despair, the other of bright imaginings,' which took shape in verse. This is the language of the advanced psychiatry of the day (A. L. Wigan's, for instance), applied to a case-history in which Hogg and his thoughts can be glimpsed.

The Shepherd sings a dactylic song by his friend in the 'Noctes' of March 1825: 'When the glen all is still, save the stream from the fountain'. It's 'ane o' the bonniest sangs you ever heard in a' your born days. I dinna ken that I ever wrote a better ane mysel'. It is by a friend o' mine – as yet an obscure man – Henry Riddell – t'ither day a shepherd like mysel' – but now a student.'

Perception of likeness is a perception of difference, and can bring an understanding of the idiosyncrasy of each of the parties to the resemblance. The affinity between these two men yields a sense of the complexity and particularity, the quiddity, of Hogg the simple-seemer, and of the depth of his achievement. He respected the boundaries he transcended, the bonds he broke. He was a friend of hierarchy who was opposed to slavery. He thought that religion held his society together, but wished to exercise a freedom of the imagination, and a right of criticism, with regard to its teachings and sectarian angers. He remained with the peasantry from which in his stardom he escaped. He was never the gentle shepherd. His art found ways of accommodating these contradictions, some of which threatened his peace of mind and were shared with Riddell. It was a part of his doubleness that he both was and was not divided. But it's hard to doubt that it could give pain.

Ten years after Riddell's stay at the Crichton Royal Institution another Border poet paid a visit to a patient there. The visitor was Thomas Aird, who knew Hogg and attended his Peebles feast and Scottish Olympics.[21] He also knew Carlyle, and was helped by Wilson to the editorial chair of the *Dumfriesshire and Galloway Herald*. His poetry, once well known, is exotic and domestic and outdoors, period-pathetic and gargoyle-Gothic, Miltonically sublime. He was a Bewick of the small birds he fed and described, this mother's son, a minute observer of the countryside, and of Selkirkshire lads, with their dreams of swimming and their winter slides. A believer in 'patriarch order'. He was said to be – rather like Hogg – aristocratic in theory and democratic in practice. In one of his best poems he impersonates a benevolent English squire of Royalist descent, Frank Sylvan. Elsewhere he reveres the dark:

> From sleepless work, and a ne'er setting sun,
> Imagination shrinking with affright,
> Turns with fresh thankfulness to thee, O Night,
> Come up the shaded East, silent, composing One.

An Afghan maid tends the wounds of a blond British soldier, and leaves the Khyber as his bride. North and the Shepherd agreed (November 1830) that Aird was 'a man of true genius'; few men so impressive in conversation, thinks the Shepherd, though hard to follow, with his 'awfu' loups frae premise to conclusion'.

Aird and Riddell – two of the prolific Border minstrelsy, both simple and sophisticated, of Hogg's heyday. Another Border poet, of the generation before, is Susanna Blamire, a Cumbrian who went to the Highlands for a spell and wrote some of her poems in Scots, and who was a source for Hogg's *Jacobite Relics*, where the highly nostalgic 'The Exile's Return' is credited by him to 'the late ingenious Miss Blamire of Carlisle'. Her poems have a lyrical shrewdness and a talented kindness.[22] One passage has Miss Sukey, famed for her pills, dispensing laxatives to the neighbouring poor. It is very sad to find her falling ill in mid-life:

No emblem for myself I find,
  Save what some dying plant bestows –
Save where its drooping head I bind,
  And mark how strong the likeness grows.

This is hardly a poor-woman plea for sympathy.

By the autumn of 1835 Hogg, too, was drooping. The year before, to Blackwood's son Alexander, he had written a letter which conveys that his 'something' had begun to fail him: 'I have been trying my hand on a "Noctes" for these two or three days but Wilson has not seen it as yet I fear it will be all to re-write. I *cannot* imitate him and what is far more extraordinary I cannot imitate myself.' On 25 January of that year, his adoptive birthday, he had told his 'sterling assistant' Robert Gilfillan: 'As this is the 64th anniversary of my birth, you need not expect much more from the old Shepherd. Yet I feel my head as clear as ever, although the enthusiasm of love and poetry is sorely abated.' The Ettrick Shepherd, moreover, was no longer readily recognised, as he'd once been, on the streets of Edinburgh. He had now suffered for some time from what his doctor diagnosed as 'water on the chest'. But he went on with his arts and his sports. Scotch airs, he felt, would die out when he'd gone, and he played them on his fiddle to the last. In August 1835 he was out shooting on the moors. At one point he climbed a hill with his son for a last overview of Ettrick; before that, he had ridden for the first time in years – over to Blackhouse, where, under the Laidlaws' roof, his poetry had begun. His vanity had not lost its voice. It was his old friend. On 18 September he wrote to Robert Chambers: 'You know or should know that my literary pride is very easily hurt, but that is no reason why we should not be friends as usual. I believe you have not a greater admirer in Scotland than myself, but I will not succumb to you that any man is superior to me as a poet.'[23] That autumn, another friend, John Galt, published his mysterious novella *Tribulations*, in which an Argyll minister takes up with two strangers and travels, in search of a legatee, to the Old Town of Edinburgh, a different world, where he treats with bad women, one of whom cowps over in a hotel. *Tribulations* has its place in the literature of indeterminacy, and its resemblances to Hogg's *Confessions*.[24]

In October Hogg fished the Tweed. He walked from the fishing to Cameron's Hotel in Innerleithen, to play bagatelle with a friend by the name of Boyd. He was seized there with a trembling which a glass of brandy could not calm. The Yarrow carrier was passing through with his parcels on the way to Edinburgh, and Hogg asked him to draw an order for twenty pounds on the Commercial Bank, founded by Cockburn. But he could not sign his name. The carrier lent him a five-pound note. He had a presentiment that he and Boyd would not meet again. Paralysis had started to take hold. He was borne back to Altrive in a carriage. Boyd took his condition to be 'what the country folks call black jaundice'; his biographer Thomson speaks of liver failure. For some days he lay unconscious. Watched over by his family, by Tibbie Shiel, and by Alexander Laidlaw of Bowerhope farm on the shore of St Mary's Loch, who had taken part with him all those years before in debates and poetry competitions up there in the hills, Hogg died on 21 November. He departed 'this life', said William Laidlaw, 'as calmly', and, apparently, 'with as little pain, as if he had fallen asleep, in his gray plaid, on the side of the moorland rill'.[25]

Wordsworth read in the *Newcastle Journal* that Hogg was gone.

> And death upon the braes of Yarrow,
> Has closed the Shepherd-poet's eyes,

ran his 'Extempore Effusion', which ends:

> No more of old romantic sorrows,
> For slaughtered Youth or love-lorn Maid!
> With sharper grief is Yarrow smitten,
> And Ettrick mourns with her their Poet dead.

The poet to whom he had once been rumoured to deny that title.

Local people did indeed turn out when Hogg was laid to rest in Ettrick kirkyard. There were not many of the Edinburgh great, and no Buccleuchs. It was a dismal winter's day, with patches of snow on the ground. The noble figure of Wilson was noted by the minister, James Russell. Wilson lingered in the graveyard, in tears, head and mane scolded by the wind. He was expected to write his friend's life, but never got round to it. He went on to live for a long time more, as did Mrs Hogg, who set up the stone in the graveyard, next to the burial-place of Hogg's parents, and of his legendary grandfather, Will o' Phaup. Many years later, in 1858, a statue was raised of the seated shepherd, with plaid and stick, a watchful collie at his feet, overlooking Tibbie Shiel's and the loch.

'All that remains of what was once Mr Hogg's,' wrote Margaret, 'belongs to his creditors, and it is my desire that they should understand that I so consider it ... My children and myself must depend upon Him who is the Husband of the widow and the Father of the fatherless, and who, I feel confident, will provide for us as He has hitherto done, and that confidence is not abated by my not seeing any visible source from whence His bounty is likely to flow upon us.'[26] She would endure by seeing Him who is invisible. Visible sources of support did, however, present themselves. The Duke of Buccleuch gave her an annuity; the prime minister, the Whig Melbourne, £150. A subscription was arranged. A state pension of £50 a year was awarded, and a later award was made to her daughter Jessie; John Wilson's pension came to £300. At the time of the Disruption, in 1843, she moved with her children to Stockbridge in the New Town, and after that to Linlithgow. She went with the Free Kirk in their break with the Church of Scotland. Her minister said that she was 'an advanced Christian', 'never flighty', and that her husband's works were pure and elevating – 'in the main'.[27]

In Stockbridge, she encountered the St Andrews philosopher James Ferrier, Wilson's nephew and son-in-law, who brought out a selection from the 'Noctes' in four volumes (1855–6), with a preface which insisted that Hogg was only a faint adumbration of the 'Noctes' Shepherd. Ferrier had a high regard for Wilson, an altogether less technical philosopher than himself, and for the Ambrosian golden age. His formidable wife remarked of her husband that his philosophy 'made you feel as if you were sitting up on a cloud with nothing on, a lucifer match in your hand, but nothing to strike it on'. A confessional game was played in St Andrew's in which he gave out that the person he most disliked was Calvin, that his favourite activity was 'driving with a handsome woman', and that the vices to which he was inclined to be most lenient were 'the world, the flesh and the devil'.[28] Another St Andrew's professor, Robert Crawford, has recently written a poem,

'Knowledge', which mentions Ferrier, to whom it credits the invention of the word 'epistemology'.

> A sore has developed, a gland gone syphilitic.
> He reads up the chemistry of mercuric oxide.
>
> Hears his Aunt Susan, the famous author
> Of *Marriage*, has died in her sleep.

A study of Ferrier by Arthur Thomson, published in 1985, saw him as an important moral philosopher – interested in the Sophists, and in Berkeley and Hegel – whose health was destroyed by a visit to the Cremorne Gardens in Chelsea.[29] The book records that Hogg once invited Ferrier to dinner at Altrive, but that he lost himself in his fishing and forgot to come.

Hogg's daughter Mary told how, on the Sabbath, his widow would frequently see Professor Ferrier and his wife in the streets of Stockbridge.[30] They would pass 'my gentle mother without so much as a recognition, although they had made Altrive a home-house a few years before. I did not then understand my mother's shrinking dislike, and the blush which mantled on her cheek', as she and her 'fatherless children' made their way, under the snub of literature, to the house of God.

Afterword

James Hogg and his works, and his friends, and his readers, have all taken part in the history and contemplation of human error. He will survive his own mistakes, and the mistakes made by those of us who have written about him. Edith Batho prefaced her critical biography of 1927 with the assurance that 'he hardly deserves to have his life fully written or his works fully edited.' Since then, his deserts have been re-imagined, and his masterpiece exalted. My own bias can be briefly stated. The involute of the *Confessions* – text and counter-text – has been seen here as a response to the Christianities of his time, and as an outcome of his experience of the double life of poet and peasant, and of the multiple personality of the *Blackwood's* collective. He is seen to have gone hungry, and to have been shaped by the hostility generated among his contemporaries in relation to the various species of social class – a hostility that can seem unquestioning, elemental, when compared with what was later to be known as snobbery. The excellence of his writings could be said (with acknowledgements to William Tennant) to be that of their intentness on a real, visible, palpable, smellable Scotland, as opposed to an absence or escape from it – which is not to deny that his flights can be wonderful.

I learnt about James Hogg from my grandmother, and grew up in a space between Ettrick and Edinburgh. His writings are mine, in the sense that they have been part of my experience of Scotland, and England, and at one or two points I have turned from the literary and documentary record to the oral tradition that runs in families and in the regional community that surrounds them. The organisation of the book – which is arranged both chronologically and thematically – was thought to be appropriate to what is, in this sense, a personal account, a personal account of the unlikely man who has helped to give to the word 'personality' the meaning it now bears.

It also seemed appropriate, at first, that annotation should not loom large in a book of this kind. But there is a good deal of it after all, and I am very grateful for the help I have received on this front, as I am for the work of previous writers and researchers on Hogg. I am indebted to the following people for advice and encouragement: to my wife Jane Miller; to Neal Ascherson, Rosemary Ashton, Betty Barrie, Robert Crawford, David Drew, Duncan Forbes, Ian Gilmour, Harriet Harvey-Wood, John Holmstrom, Douglas Johnson, Matthew Kaufman, Paul Keegan, Fiona MacCarthy, Virginia Murray, Andrew O'Hagan, Meiko O'Halloran, Christopher Ricks, Betty Rosen, Judy Steel, John Sutherland and Peter Swaab; to Iain Gordon Brown, Principal Curator of Manuscripts at the National Library of Scotland (NLS), and his staff, and to the staff of the British Library, the Senate House Library of the University of London, and the Library of University College London. I must thank James Campbell of the *Times Literary Supplement*, where some passages in the book first appeared, for his editorial guidance; and the keepers of the John Murray archive for access to their letters from Hogg to Byron.

There is a strong dependence on the probing archival work of Alan Strout: on his book, *The Life and Letters of James Hogg*, Vol. I, 1770–1825 (Lubbock, Texas, 1946, hereafter 'Strout'), and on the material for its unpublished second volume which is held at the National Library of Scotland, NLS MS 10495, which consists of transcripts of correspondence and a connecting narrative. The bibliographical information supplied in Edith Batho's *The Ettrick Shepherd* has also been gratefully consulted.

Quotations from Hogg's autobiographical writings are taken, unless otherwise identified, from one of Douglas Mack's several contributions to the understanding of Hogg's work – his joint edition of the *Memoir of the Author's Life* and *Familiar Anecdotes of Sir Walter Scott* (1972). The *Memoir* is a short book which is referred to throughout; page references are reserved for passages of particular importance. Such quotations also come from the relevant volumes of the Stirling/South Carolina Research Edition of the *Collected Works of James Hogg* (hereafter CW), general editors Douglas Mack and Gillian Hughes. The volumes of the Collected Edition which have so far appeared are as far as possible the source for quotations from Hogg's fiction and verse. These volumes are *The*

Shepherd's Calendar, ed. Douglas Mack, 1995; *The Three Perils of Woman*, ed. David Groves, Anthony Hasler and Douglas Mack, 1995; *A Queer Book*, ed. Peter Garside, 1995; *Tales of the Wars of Montrose*, ed. Gillian Hughes, 1996; *Lay Sermons*, ed. Gillian Hughes, 1997; *Queen Hynde*, ed. Suzanne Gilbert and Douglas Mack, 1998; *Anecdotes of Scott*, ed. Jill Rubenstein, 1999; *The Spy*, ed. Gillian Hughes, 2000; *The Private Memoirs and Confessions of a Justified Sinner*, ed. Peter Garside, with an Afterword by Ian Campbell, 2001; *The Jacobite Relics of Scotland*, First Series, ed. Murray Pittock, 2002; and *Winter Evening Tales*, ed. Ian Duncan, 2002. *The Works of the Ettrick Shepherd*, ed. Thomas Thomson, 2 vols, 1865, is also used for quotations from Hogg's verse: where such quotations are unattributed, this is generally the source. The first volume has his Tales and Sketches. The second (abbreviated here to Thomson) has his Poems, and a life by the editor. The spelling and punctuation followed in passages of quotation are, with minor adjustments, those of their sources.

The text cited in the book of the 'Noctes Ambrosianae' conversations serialised in *Blackwood's Magazine* is that of the American edition done with memoirs by R. Shelton Mackenzie (5 vols, revised edn, 1863), which leads off with the 'Chaldee Manuscript' by Hogg et al. A 'Noctes' selection by James Ferrier appeared in four volumes in 1855-6, and another, entitled *The Tavern Sages*, was produced by J. H. Alexander in 1992. John Gibson Lockhart's *Life of Sir Walter Scott* (2nd edn, 10 vols, 1839) has been consulted throughout (in abbreviation, *Life of Scott*), as have the *Letters of Sir Walter Scott*, ed. Herbert Grierson, 12 vols, 1932-7 (*Letters of Scott*).

Other sources are given in the select bibliography and notes which follow. Publication details are British, except when otherwise stated.

A Note on the Paperback Edition, 2005

━━━━

This edition has corrections, some of which need a word of explanation, and the book itself has omissions which I should try to put right.

Where did Gabriel's Road get its name from? More might have been said about this. Gabriel's crime, as it was known to Lockhart, was, in fact, committed, in 1717, by Robert Irvine, thought to have been called Gabriel at times; and there was also a local innkeeper of that name.

I am sorry about the absence from the book of an appreciation of Robert Morehead, a writer and an Episcopalian clergyman, a supporter and friend of Hogg, and a friend and relative of Francis Jeffrey. Morehead's rebuke of his friend John Wilson for the 'unhandsome personalities' carried in *Blackwood's* ('you are throwing around you poisoned arrows against those whom you surmise to be infidels') is a shining example of how to blame someone in an honourable fashion (see Mrs Gordon's life of her father, pp.193–5). The barriers between Whig and Tory, and between the religious denominations, in the Edinburgh of the time, were forbidding but far from insurmountable: Morehead's mediations suggest as much, and so does a letter from Hogg to Blackwood of the same time (19 Oct. 1817, see Strout, PMLA, Sept. 1950). The letter belongs to the month in which *Blackwood's Edinburgh Magazine* was launched: 1817 was the year of the new journal, and of the 'Chaldee Manuscript', and it was a year in which Hogg admired Jeffrey. The admiration conveyed in the letter was enclosed in one of the most sensible, most condignly anti-imaginative, of his critical comments. In the years to come, with barriers and personalities an established feature of the journalistic world he had entered, he was to denounce Jeffrey, and to be represented as doing so, and to be cut up by Jeffrey. His letter concedes Wilson's powers, while saying of 'the fellow', his new friend:

> The worst fault about him is that he lets his imagination run away with
> him. If he leans to one side at all he leans too much, he either praises or

blames in the extreme. Brougham is the same way. I don't like him. I would take Jeffrey for a model of all that I ever read. He gives a cut now and then with much severity and at the same time with such perfect good nature.

Of the attacks made in the magazine on Professors Playfair and Leslie (see p.175) only one was deplored in the pamphlet 'Hypocrisy Unveiled': that on Leslie came later, in 1820. An attack of Hogg's, a piece of work entitled 'The Boar' (Strout, PMLA, Sept. 1950), deserved a mention in the book. This adds an Armageddon to the Chaldee narrative, in taking account of the furore it caused. Constable goes down to defeat: 'The host of the man that was crafty was annihilated.' The leopard of the piece – Wilson presumably – is rated 'deceitful', with a sting in his tail for those who trust him.

It was wrong of me to suggest, in 2003, on page 197, that Scott gave up poetry on turning to fiction. There were further frisks, as he called them, in later life – among them, poems of his which have been especially esteemed.

Hogg may not have written the account in the *Scots Magazine* of a tour of Stirling, Perth and Kinross in 1805, according to Hans de Groot, who is engaged in editing for the *Collected Works* the various descriptions by him of his Highland journeys. The account, initialled 'H', has been credited to him, and it has, I think, its likenesses to Hogg – in the veneration bestowed on the traveller by the rudimentary double he encounters, and in its talk of a laird's gliding on his bottom down a Highland precipice. Hans de Groot also argues, in the journal of Hogg studies (8:1997), that he can't have met John Galt in Greenock in 1804, as Hogg's memoir recalls, but may have done so the year before. The journal (13:2002) has published notebook passages – found, in transcription, by Gillian Hughes – which relate to the journey of 1803: amid a discussion of sheep, cattle and kelp, he tells how 'we sailed, fished, ate skate, drank grog, leaned forward upon the table & fartd as loud as we were able,' and how he fell from the boat, and was threatened with a pressganging, off Mull, by a Naval cutter.

The 1997 issue of the journal has a text of the prayers and hymns Hogg wrote for his children in 1832, during his stay in London, where they were published in that year by James Cochrane. The prayers sent by the husband and father show an exacerbated puritan sternness. 'I am unworthy of thy notice,' his children are to pipe. They are to present themselves as poor things, sinful and polluted, 'offending and helpless'. This hardly suits the 'religion of the heart' spoken of in his *Perils of Woman*, where an inanimate female body springs up 'with a power resembling that produced by electricity', only to fall into one of the unmeaning, stricken states Hogg was drawn to describing, but is later restored to family life by a kind God.

I want to thank the *Collected Works* editor currently preparing an edition of Hogg's letters, Gillian Hughes, for the valuable guidance received from her with regard to some of these post-publication topics. The first of her projected three volumes appeared in 2004. It revealed misreadings, now adjusted, in the quotations from his correspondence which are given in published biographical sources consulted for the present book – principally, Mrs Oliphant's 'sister' for 'leister' in Hogg's account of his rural happiness on page 185 (where 'sweetheart' now seems likely to refer to his future bride, rather than to any mere 'composite'). In the boat-banning passage on page 66, parenthetical words of Hogg's, which now seem more likely to refer to the appointment of a new minister for Ettrick, have been withdrawn. Gillian Hughes has located in New Zealand the draft of a long, very angry, and yet hardly unequivocal letter of remonstrance (3 August 1818), directed at his *Blackwood's* friends, with their Greek and Latin sentences and their jealous mockeries at his expense. This 'will never do', he writes, in the language of Francis Jeffrey. His letter, which has its own Latin sentences, contains further firm praise of Jeffrey. Hogg tells his friends that his clothes may be out of fashion – what matters is his writings. And what a calumny it is to suppose him capable in his youth of sitting soaked in the shelter of a crag, drinking whisky. The volume indicates that his friendship with Eliza Izett may have carried a degree of romantic attachment, and of the uncertainty that attended Burns's friendships with married ladies of a literary disposition. Douglas Mack's edition of *The Queen's Wake* (CW, 2004) points out that Hogg's disapproving visitor John Morrison may once have been an admirer of the future Mrs Hogg: Morrison is insulted, his harp unstrung, in successive editions of the poem (which also has its tale of a 'brave Morison of Locherben'). It seems that Morrison may have hit back, with a so-called *Hoggiad*. Hogg talked of the 'hound', as I have it, that his magazine friends were making of him: Gillian Hughes reads 'hand'.

I am grateful, too, for the help given me by another Hogg scholar, Richard Jackson, from whom I was pleased to hear that a Border farmer, Harry Scott, an expert in the field of farming equipment who died in 2002, was known locally as the Electric Shepherd.

A subsequent discovery has moved me, awed me indeed, with its window on the workings of heredity, on an ancestral duplication and coincidence. At the Edinburgh Festival of 2003 I talked about Hogg, and about this book, and ended with an allusion to the present-day Canadian writer Alice Munro. The point at issue, at that stage of the talk, was literature's frequent distaste for rural life, and the intention was to place Munro in possible relation to what I called the Hogg paradox of the country writer admired and suspected. The extent to which she shares in the paradox may be doubtful, but it would seem that there are readers who have managed to mind her country matters. The following passage was quoted: 'The fullness of the country. Nowhere to breathe for the reek of thrusting crops and barnyards and jostling munching animals.' And I went on: 'Among the best living writers of fiction in the English language is Alice Munro, whose words these are, phobic words for the state of mind of one of her characters, words which belong to her concern with the inner lives of the farm people of Ontario. Her stories also attend, in their wisdom, to the puritan heritage evoked for Scotland by Hogg, to the doctrines of election and predestination, to his Cameronians, and to his Selkirkshire, with its "Royal Forest, and all the fighting with the English", its battle of Philiphaugh, and its minstrelsy of the Scottish Border.' A few weeks later I learnt that she is a relative of James Hogg, who once wrote, with his customary foresight, of 'the broad Ontario's shore'. Alice Munro is a Laidlaw, and is 'very proud' of the connection.

She is descended from Will o' Phaup, the last man in Ettrick to converse with the fairies, and related to Hogg's cousin James Laidlaw, who emigrated to America and found the Methodists there unsound in the matter of justification. As suggested in the present book, this was the same Laidlaw who held that Hogg's poems and stories were a pack of lies. He was sad to think that Hogg and Walter Scott had made more money from their artful lying than old Boston the minister ever did from his sermons.

Hogg's art has been known for its puzzles, for the uncertain authorship of a book about uncertainty, for its predictions, for coming true, and for its element of luck, good luck and bad. Hereditary genius – a Victorian expression that would perhaps have appealed to Hogg – may be apparent in his preceding of Alice Laidlaw, and so may a fresh stroke of luck, a further electricity.

K.M.

Select Bibliography

Further Writings by Hogg

Scottish Pastorals, 1801, 1988 (ed. Elaine Petrie)
The Mountain Bard, 1807
The Shepherd's Guide, 1807
The Forest Minstrel, 1810
The Queen's Wake, 1813
The Poetic Mirror, 1816
Dramatic Tales, 2 vols, 1817
The Brownie of Bodsbeck, 1818, 1976 (ed. Douglas Mack)
The Jacobite Relics of Scotland, 2 vols, 1819, 1821
The Poetical Works of James Hogg, 4 vols, 1822
The Three Perils of Man, 1822, 1972 (ed. Douglas Gifford)
Songs, 1831
Altrive Tales, 1832
The Tales of James Hogg, 2 vols, 1886
James Hogg: Selected Poems, ed. Douglas Mack, 1970
James Hogg: Selected Stories and Sketches, ed. Douglas Mack, 1982
Tales of Love and Mystery, ed. David Groves, 1985
A Shepherd's Delight, ed. Judy Steel, 1985
James Hogg: Selected Poems and Songs, ed. David Groves, 1986

Books on Hogg

Memorials of James Hogg the Ettrick Shepherd, by Mary Garden, 1885
James Hogg, by Sir George Douglas, 1899
James Hogg: A Critical Study, by Louis Simpson, 1962
The Romantic Novel in England, by Robert Kiely, 1972
James Hogg, by Douglas Gifford, 1976
James Hogg at Home, by Norah Parr, 1980
James Hogg: The Growth of a Writer, by David Groves, 1988
Studies in Hogg and his World, ed. Gillian Hughes, published annually

Notes

CHAPTER ONE: Hogg's Hole

1 Hogg's *Memoir*, pp.71–3. His account of his meeting with the Cunninghams first appeared in 1829, in the *Edinburgh Literary Journal*. See also a letter from Allan Cunningham to Hogg of 16 Feb. 1826: NLS MS 10495 f.1.

2 Hogg's dumpling hills are spoken of in an essay in *Prize Essays and Transactions of the Highland Society of Scotland*, Vol. IX, pp.281–306. See Galt's *The Entail*, 1984 edn, p.355.

3 *Scots Magazine*, Oct. 1802.

4 *Memoir*, pp.5–6.

5 The last line of his long poem *The Queens Wake*. See *A Shepherds Delight*, ed. Judy Steel, p. 6: a James Anderson farmed locally, and the name was given, in Hogg's *Confessions*, to a witness of the sinner's last days.

6 Hogg's 'Journey through the Highlands of Scotland', *Scots Magazine*, Oct. 1802–July 1803. See also his *Highland Tours*, ed. William Laughland, 1981.

7 *The Shepherd's Guide*, pp.13–4.

8 Ibid., pp.279–300, 201.

9 *Blackwood's*, Feb. 1823: from a piece by Hogg on 'the Hon. Captain Napier and Ettrick Forest', challenged in the journal by the other Ettrick shepherd. In that year Captain Napier, a writer on sheep, became Lord Napier, the eighth Baronet.

10 Saunders, p.79. Ballantine is quoted in John Heiton's *The Castes of Edinburgh*, 3rd edn, 1861, pp.6–8.

11 Ibid., p.7.

12 *Memoir of William and Robert Chambers*, by William Chambers, 13th edn, 1884, p.254.

13 *Memorials of James Hogg the Ettrick Shepherd*, by Mary Garden, 3rd edn, 1903, p.215.

14 *Statistical Account of Scotland*, 21 vols, 1791–9: Vol. II, pp.434–8; Vol. VII, pp.501–12.

15 Ibid., Vol. III, 294–7.

16 *Blackwood's*, Jan. 1825.

17 *Three Perils of Man*, 1972 edn, pp.217–32.

18 Ibid., pp.268, 276.

19 Thomson: from the life of Hogg which prefaces Vol. II of his *Works of the Ettrick Shepherd*, p.xiii.

20 *Transactions of the Hawick Archaeological Society*, 1905: 'Recollections of Sir Walter Scott (1802–4)'. See also Robert Carruthers's 'Abbotsford Notanda', in *The Life of Sir Walter Scott* by Robert Chambers, 1871, p.131.
21 *Scotch Novel Reading*, 3 vols, Vol. II, p.101; Vol. III, p.244; Vol. I, p.10.
22 Lockhart's *Life of Scott*, Vol. VI, p.349; Vol. VIII, p.17. *Life of Lord Jeffrey*, by Henry Cockburn, 2 vols, 1852, Vol. I, p.131.

CHAPTER TWO: First Poems

1 'Noctes Ambrosianae', Jan. 1831. *Memoir*, p.62.
2 From a photostat in the possession of the present writer. *A Publisher and his Friends: Memoir and Correspondence of the late John Murray*, by Samuel Smiles, 2 vols, 1891, Vol. I, pp.473–4.
3 Strout, pp.8–9.
4 *The Shepherd's Calendar*, CW, pp.103–11.
5 Lucky Hogg is discussed in the notes to Hogg's poems 'The Fray of Elibank' and *The Queen's Wake*: Thomson, pp.71, 24–5.
6 *Scots Magazine*, Feb. 1803, pp.24–5, 71, 92–3.
7 For William's words see Strout, pp.10–11. For an 'aefauld' Hogg see Mrs Garden's *Memorials*, p.151. *Memoir*, pp.8–9.
8 Strout, p.22.
9 Robert Chambers's life of Scott, p.130. On the lasses 'Jamie always turned an expressive *espiègle* glance.'
10 *Scottish Pastorals*, 1988 edn, p.ix.
11 Ibid., p.59. The wider Napier kinship contained generals, admirals and radicals – including Sir Charles, 'Conqueror of Sind' and banner of suttee.
12 Nov. 1805. Three pieces giving 'Particulars of the Life of James Hogg' appeared in the magazine in the course of that year and were probably co-written by Hogg.
13 *Memoir*, p.11.
14 *James Hogg*, 1899, p.32.
15 *Works of Robert Burns*, 1834–5, 5 vols, Vol. I, p.203.
16 Ibid., Vol. V, p.246, Vol. I, pp.222–3. *Reminiscences of Yarrow*, 1886, p.212.
17 *Anecdotes of Scott*, CW, p.3. *Lady Louisa Stuart: Selections from her Manuscripts*, ed. James Home, 1899, p.244.
18 Edith Batho's *The Ettrick Shepherd* (hereafter 'Edith Batho'), pp.166, 7–8, 120, 168.

CHAPTER THREE: Ballad Work

1 Lockhart's *Life of Scott*, Vol. VI, p.362.
2 Cunningham's dealings with the publisher of the collection are discussed in David Hogg's *Life of Allan Cunningham*, 1875, p.50: 'The idea of a volume of imitations passed upon Cromek as genuine remains passed across the poet's mind in a moment.'

3 *The Letters of Sir Walter Scott*, Vol. I, p.391.

4 Strout, p.22.

5 See William Laidlaw's 'Recollections of Sir Walter Scott', as above, and Hogg's *Memoir*, pp.61–4, 136–8.

6 *The Life of Walter Scott* by John Sutherland, pp.77–83. Edgar Johnson's life of Scott, *The Great Unknown* (2 vols), was published in 1970.

7 Lockhart's *Life of Scott*, Vol. II, pp.102, 107. Edith Batho, pp.174–5. Hogg's praise occurs in his *Queen's Wake*.

8 Edith Batho, pp.24–7. Elaine Petrie (*Scottish Literary Journal*, May 1973) argues that Margaret Hogg's knowledge of the subject, and her powers as a performer, may have been exaggerated, and that Hogg's father was a more stimulating presence in the household than some accounts suppose. His brother William spoke to the same effect about his father. Other informants discussed by Petrie are Hogg's uncle William Laidlaw and Andrew Muir or Moore.

9 *Minstrelsy of the Scottish Border*, 1931, ed. Thomas Henderson, pp.102–13.

10 'Familiar Anecdotes of Sir Walter Scott': see Hogg's *Memoir*, pp.136–7.

11 Edith Batho, p.179.

12 Thomson, pp.371–2.

13 'Abbotsford Notanda', Chambers's *Life of Sir Walter Scott*, p.132.

14 Lockhart's *Life of Scott*, Vol. II, p.131.

15 David Hogg's *Life of Allan Cunningham*, p.31.

16 *The Horner Papers*, ed. Kenneth Bourne and William Banks Taylor, 1994, p.253.

17 Vol. II, pp.61–2.

18 *Anecdotes of Scott*, CW, pp.xxxii–iii. Strout, p.36. Scott's use of 'daubings' appears in Chambers's life, p.147. See *Blackwood's*, Oct. 1823.

19 Lockhart's *Life of Scott*, Vol. II, pp.168–71.

20 *Memoir*, p.109.

CHAPTER FOUR: Sandy Tod

1 *Memoir*, p.84.

2 Edith Batho, p.57.

3 *Annals of a Publishing House: William Blackwood and his Sons* (hereafter 'Mrs Oliphant'), by Margaret Oliphant, 2 vols, 1897: Vol. I, p.285.

4 *Reminiscences of Yarrow*, p.112.

5 They were reprinted from the *Scottish Review* of July 1888, and published under the title *A Tour in the Highlands in 1803*. See also Edith Batho, pp.46–8.

6 *Anecdotes of Scott*, pp.59–60. For the resentment of the proviso see Thomson, p.59.

7 *Letters of Sir Walter Scott*, Vol. 1, pp.299–300, 352. Strout, p.37.

8 *Life of Scott*, Vol. III, p.92.

9 *Letters of Sir Walter Scott*, Vol. III, 14 August 1811.

10 *Memorials of his Time*, 1974 edn, University of Chicago Press, p.213.
11 *Memoir*, pp.17-8.
12 *Letters of Sir Walter Scott*, Vol. III, from letters to Scott's brother Thomas and to the Earl of Dalkeith.

CHAPTER FIVE: A Scene in Romance

1   This account of Morrison's activities is based on a series of articles by him in *Tait's Edinburgh Magazine*, Vol. X, 1843: 'Reminiscences of Sir Walter Scott, the Ettrick Shepherd and Sir Henry Raeburn'. William Tait was a Whig.
2   Lockhart's *Life of Scott*, Vol. VI, pp.162-3.
3   *James Hogg: The Growth of a Writer*, pp.16-7. For Gillian Hughes's essay see *Studies in Hogg and his World*, 11:2000. Hogg's review took the form of a letter to the editor, Henry Glassford Bell (30 October 1830). Sandy Elshinder's is a 'queer book', by a great goose and 'petted deevil'. Hogg has read it, though, 'with the most thrilling and painful interest'. He feels sorry for Sandy's father, who didn't want him 'popping into' the house to 'give him a call', and who had him sent to jail. The 'constitutional failings' of this 'spurious race' generally derive from the mother's state of mind at the time of nursing and before: 'disappointed affections, terrors of a discovery, and visions of infamy and want', produce a 'trembling irritability of soul'. The greatest cowards he has ever known 'were all bastards – the very thoughts of some of whom never fail to set me a-laughing. There was one – a gentleman who had, indeed, a little of the Blackamoor blood in him, but not much – the whole tenor of whose life was one uniform track of fear and astonishment.' Hogg said that he had written as he did in order to help Sandy by 'conciliating' his father. See also Hogg's 'Elegy' in the *Spy*, No. 39.
4   See Thomson, pp.270, 274, and *A Shepherd's Delight*, pp.54-5. 'Love is like a dizziness' is said by Hogg, in his *Songs* of 1831, to be a 'ridiculous' piece which caught on enduringly among the lads and lasses of the countryside; it supplied an epigraph for a chapter in D. M. Moir's Galt-like novel *Mansie Wauch*, a tailor's Annals of Dalkeith, published in *Blackwood's* in 1824. 'The Mermaid', first published in the *Edinburgh Magazine*, appeared in revised form in the *Poetical Works* of 1822; the *Selected Poems*, ed. Douglas Mack, has this text, pp.88-91.
5   *A Shepherd's Delight*, pp.11-12.
6   *Tales of Love and Mystery*, pp.163-75. The story appeared in a London annual, *Forget me not* (1830).
7   See *Cockburn's Millennium*, by the present writer, 1975, pp.175-6, 192, 195. The writer of the Magdalenism book is a different William Tait from the editor of *Tait's Magazine*.
8   *Fraser's*, Oct. 1834.
9   *Tales of Love and Mystery* has a later version, pp.48-145.
10 1888: facsimile edn, 1975, pp.339-40.
11 *Anecdotes of Scott*, p.73.

12 Strout, pp.144, 87.
13 See William Blackwood's *Quarterly Journal of Agriculture*, Vol. I, May 1828–August 1829.
14 'The Poacher': *A Shepherd's Delight*, p.28.
15 *Quarterly Journal of Agriculture*: see above.
16 *Reminiscences of Yarrow*, pp.229, 192, 135. The testimonial was written in 1833.
17 Strout, p.143.
18 Carlyle's *Reminiscences*, 1997 edn, p.238.
19 See *Doubles*, by the present writer, 1985, pp.114–5. For 'Scottish Haymakers' see *Tales of Love and Mystery*, pp.194–201.
20 Strout, p.86 (from a letter to Byron dated 11 Oct. 1814).
21 *Reminiscences of Yarrow*, pp.363.
22 *Scots Magazine* (retitled the *Edinburgh Magazine and Literary Miscellany*), from Jan. 1818.
23 *The Autobiography of William Jerdan*, 1852-3, 4 vols, Vol. IV, p.200; *Men I Have Known* by Jerdan, 1866, pp.248–55.
24 Mary Garden's *Memorials*, p.186.

CHAPTER SIX: Mr Spy

1 Thomson, p.278.
2 *Selected Poems and Songs*, ed. David Groves, pp.108–9.
3 In Cockburn's words: *Cockburn's Millennium*, p.250.
4 'The "Life" of the Ettrick Shepherd Anatomised', by 'an Old Dissector', 1832.
5 *Memoir*, pp.20–1, 85–6.
6 *The Spy*, CW, p.43.
7 See also *Tales of James Hogg*, 1886, Vol. II, pp.25–66.
8 *Anecdotes of Scott*, p.58.
9 'The First Sermon', *Selected Poems and Songs*, p.171.
10 Juvenal's *Satires*, Book Three.
11 *The Spy*, p.22. Cf. *Winter Evening Tales*, CW, p.4.
12 *The Spy*, p.200; the *Rambler*, Nos 29 and 8.
13 See, by the present writer, *Dark Horses*, 1998, pp.265–8, and *Cockburn's Millennium*, p.73.
14 *The Modern Scottish Minstrel*, by Charles Rogers, 6 vols, Vol. II, 1856, p.36.
15 *The Spy*, pp.401, 440–3.

CHAPTER SEVEN: Come down, Kilmeny

1 Thomson, p.45.
2 *New Monthly Magazine*, Vol. 46: 'Some Particulars relative to the Ettrick Shepherd', by G, evidently a relative of James Gray. The three instalments

appeared in Feb., March and April 1836. The third contains William Hogg's two letters, dated 20 Nov. and 12 Dec. 1813.

3 *Memoir*, pp.79–81.
4 *Fraser's*, August 1834: in a review of Hogg's *Domestic Manners and Private Life of Sir Walter Scott*.
5 Lockhart's *Life of Scott*, Vol. III, pp.363–4. The other letters to the Duchess are dated 20 March and 10 May 1812 and 22 March 1813; the letter to Byron is dated 6 Nov. 1813.
6 *Memoirs of a Literary Veteran* by R. P. Gillies, 1851, 3 vols, Vol. II, p.121.
7 Ibid., II, p.231–3.
8 *Memoir*, p.29.
9 *James Hogg at Home*, by Norah Parr, 1980, p.55: to his wife, 24 August 1828.
10 'Noctes Ambrosianae', Dec. 1822.
11 *Memoir*, pp.23–4. See Thomson, p.xxvii, and Lockhart's *Peter's Letters to his Kinsfolk*, 3rd edn, 3 vols, 1819, Vol. II, pp.65–72.
12 *Blackwood's*, August 1821: 'Epistle to Christopher North: From an Old Friend with a New Face'. The epistle appears to be both to and by Wilson.
13 Quoted in the commentary to Hogg's *Memoir*, p.88.
14 Ibid., pp.25–8.
15 Ibid., p.26. This was not the Dr William Dunlop, a *Blackwood's* man and a partner of Galt's in Canada, to whom Hogg dedicated his *Lay Sermons*.
16 Thomson, p.24.
17 *Memoir*, p.30. David Groves's *James Hogg: The Growth of a Writer*, pp.38–40.
18 Thomson, p.xix.
19 See David Groves's *Selected Poems and Songs*. The poem has a source in the story of Jane Brown, the Maid of Plora, near Traquair, perhaps an abused child, who went missing in 1720 (Thomson, p. 32).
20 *Miscellanies*, by Maginn, ed. R. W. Montagu, 2 vols, 1885, Vol. II, p.303.
21 Thomson, p.60.

CHAPTER EIGHT: Lies

1 *Letters of Scott*, Vol. IV, p.345.
2 *Anecdotes of Scott*, p.11.
3 The poem (1830) is 'almost certainly one of Hogg's': see *James Hogg and the St Ronan's Border Club*, by David Groves, 1987, p.19–21.
4 *Fraser's*, August 1834.
5 Strout, pp.86–8.
6 *Selected Poems and Songs*, pp.59–60, 45–6.
7 *Fraser's*, Oct. 1832.
8 Thomson, p.xxxvii. *Studies in Hogg and his World*: 12, 2001, ed. Gillian Hughes, who writes here about Hogg's response to the death of his patron.
9 To Blackwood, 8 Dec. 1816: Strout, p.116.

10 *Memoir*, pp.69–71. Strout, p.80. See *Christopher North*, by Mrs Mary Gordon,
   2 vols, 1862, Vol. II, p.142, Cunningham to Wilson, 12 Dec. 1828. Wilson became
   a professor in 1820.
11 Lockhart to his wife: Strout, p.83.
12 Ibid., p.74. *Life of Scott*, Vol. IV, p.387. '*So Late into the Night*' (*Byron's Letters
   and Journals*, ed. Leslie Marchant, Vol. V), 1976, p.38.
13 Strout, p.80. Gillies's *Memoirs of a Literary Veteran*, pp.152, 155, and Groves's
   James Hogg: The Growth of a Writer, p.51.
14 *Memoir*, pp.68–9. *Wordsworth: A Life*, by Juliet Barker, 2001, p.245.
15 Strout, pp.81–5. Hogg's *Songs* of 1831, p.117.
16 From the collection of Hogg's letters to Byron (1814–18) which is held at the firm
   of John Murray. See also Strout, pp.72–4.
17 Ibid., p.76.
18 Murray collection. The letter to Murray is dated 13 March 1819.
19 Ibid., 26 Feb. 1816.
20 *Selected Poems and Songs*, pp.31–95.
21 *James Hogg: The Growth of a Writer*, pp.58–62.
22 Thomson, p.xxxvi.
23 Groves, p.65.
24 *Memoir*, pp.33–7.
25 Ibid., pp.47–8, 90–1.
26 *Selected Poems and Songs*, pp.173–4: 'The Cutting o' my Hair'.
27 *James Hogg and the St Ronan's Border Club*, p.8. *Life of Scott*, Vol. V, pp.116–
   21. *Letters of Scott*, Vol. IV, p.141–2.
28 *Scots Magazine*, Dec. 1815.
29 *Memoir*, pp.96–7.
30 *Life of Scott*, Vol. V, pp.120–1.
31 *Letters of Scott*, Vol. IV, p.162.

CHAPTER NINE: Parodies

1 *Memoir*, p.39. Strout, pp.113–4. *Blackwood's*, August 1821: from Wilson's 'Epistle
   to Christopher North – From an Old Friend with a New Face'.
2 The *Mirror* parodies are given in Thomson. 'The Flying Tailor', an extract from
   'James Rigg', and the inferior Coleridge take-off, 'Isabelle', appear in Dwight
   Macdonald's *Parodies*, 1961.
3 *Poems* by Wordsworth, 2 vols, 1981, ed. John Haydon, Yale University Press,
   Vol. I, pp.743–6, 1027.
4 David Groves quotes in his study of Hogg from the *British Lady's Magazine*,
   p.75. For the eye see *Blackwood's*, August 1821, as above.
5 From Sept. 1829.
6 *Selected Poems and Songs*, pp.163–7.

CHAPTER TEN: Two Fine Friends

1 For the boar see *Tales of Love and Mystery*, p.39. Some of these beasts come from the menagerie assembled in the 'Chaldee Manuscript', co-authored by Hogg.
2 *Christopher North*, by Mary Gordon, Vol. I, p.331. *The Life and Letters of John Gibson Lockhart*, by Andrew Lang, 2 vols, 1897, Vol. II, p.47.
3 *Christopher North*, by Elsie Swann, 1934, pp.185–95.
4 Mary Gordon, Vol. I, pp.26, 128, 146–7.
5 Ibid., p.128. *Peter's Letters*, Vol. I, p.130.
6 Mary Gordon, Vol. I, pp.262–3.
7 Elsie Swann, pp.36–7, 202, 44. *Sir Walter*, by Donald Carswell, 1930, p.221. *New Statesman*, 12 March 1960.
8 For Scott's testimonial description, see Lang, Vol. I, pp.349–50.
9 Mary Gordon, Vol. I, p.161.
10 1845 edn, pp.15, 226.
11 Lang, Vol. I, pp.13–4.
12 Mary Gordon, Vol. I, pp.261, 266.
13 Elsie Swann, p.24.
14 Scott to Lockhart, 30 March 1820, *Life of Scott*, Vol. VI, pp.217–8. Scott's *Letters*, Vol. VI, p.222, 8 July 1820, to the Lord Provost of Edinburgh, and p.164.
15 Mary Gordon, Vol. I, p.331, Vol. II, pp.31, 351; revised American edn, 1863, ed. R. Shelton Mackenzie, p.442. Elsie Swann, pp.221, 195. Carlyle's *Reminiscences*, pp.420–4.
16 Elsie Swann, pp.210, 222, 215.
17 *Fifty Years' Recollections*, by Cyrus Redding, 3 vols, 1858, Vol. III, p.50.
18 American edn, p.429.
19 *James Hogg and the St Ronan's Border Club*, p.3.
20 John Carey makes use of these statements in the Introduction to his influential edition of the *Confessions*, 1969, p.xx.
21 Strout, pp.155–7.
22 *Memoir*, pp.75–6.
23 31 Oct. 1827: NLS MS 10496.
24 *Life of Scott*, Vol. VI, p.13. See Strout, p.170, for a letter which alludes to Scott's baronetcy. See *Blackwood's*, March 1818.
25 *Adam Blair*, 1822, pp.337, 326.
26 Lang, Vol. I, p.242. *Politics and Reviewers*, by Joanne Shattock, 1989, pp.47, 63.
27 *Peter's Letters*, Vol. I, pp.141–5.
28 *Life of Scott*, Vol. V, p.271.
29 Strout, p.13.
30 Ibid., p.137.
31 Hogg to Blackwood about the 'Chaldee' continuation: NLS MS 4807 f.34. *Memoir*, p.44. Lang, Vol. I, pp.156–7. Strout, pp.135, 143.
32 A text of the 'Chaldee Manuscript' introduces Shelton Mackenzie's edition of the 'Noctes'.

33 For the reception given to the 'Chaldee Manuscript' see Strout, pp.136–8.

34 Scott's *Letters*, Vol. V, pp.6–7, 208.

35 *Letters*, Vol. III, p.38.

36 *The Brownie of Bodsbeck*, 1976 edn, pp.159–66.

37 Ibid., p.4–5.

38 Edith Batho, pp.114–6. *Shepherd's Calendar*, CW, p.98.

39 By Douglas Mack: *Brownie of Bodsbeck*, p.194.

40 *Anecdotes of Scott*, CW, pp.50–1.

41 Hogg's *Familiar Anecdotes of Scott*: see *Memoir*, pp.103–4, 107. Strout, p.39.

42 *Brownie of Bodsbeck*, pp.172–8. For the Duke's warning about profanity see NLS MS 2245 (Dec. 1816).

43 *Letters*, Vol. V, p.154. *Life of Scott*, Vol. IX, p.178.

44 *Fraser's*, Feb. 1832, from their 'Gallery of Literary Characters'.

45 For this story see also *The Tales of James Hogg*, 2 vols: Vol. II, pp.1–25. These volumes also have 'The Wool-Gatherer'.

46 *Memoir*, pp.45–6.

47 Strout, p.196. This was said in a *Blackwood's* piece (Oct. 1820) where Lockhart is thought to be present. See p.155.

48 Quotations from the *Relics* come from the first editions and from the CW edition of the First Series: see Murray Pittock's Introduction, pp.xv–xvii and xxiv. Pittock's edition, with its command of the archives, puts Hogg's to a severe test, but is likely to gain respect for it, 'disingenuous' and 'impishly unreliable' though it is said to be. Scott's amusement at Hogg's at first mistaking Major-General Cannon, present at the battle of Killiecrankie, for some great cleric should not be mistaken for the talismanic story of the *Relics*. Hogg is thought to have looked beyond Jacobitism to the social protest of his own day in his song 'Donald Macgillavry', and to have neglected the sacred songs of the Episcopalian element in the Jacobite tradition. See also *Memoir*, p.49.

49 *Edinburgh Review*, August 1820. Hogg's Jacobites belong in part to his construction of a half-fabulous Highland past. In the story 'Ewen McGabhar' (*Fraser's*, December 1832), an infant son is hidden in a cave and suckled by a goat. This missing heir is raised by humble folk, and, after a spell of clan warfare, restored to his mother, a homicidal queen, once his legitimacy has been checked. A chief with the exotic name of Lord Downan has been meddling in the conflict (the Marquis of Downshire rumoured by some to have been the parent of Lady Scott may account for the Sassenach name). Peace comes to the region when the heir marries Downan's daughter. The theme from folklore of royalty in disguise is one which the hunting of Bonny Prince Charlie after Culloden did much to prolong, and in which clan warfare is apt to preclude class warfare. The narrator freely admits: 'Over this country the two classes are a distinct species.'

50 Strout. pp.196–7.

CHAPTER ELEVEN: Personalities

1 *Scots Magazine*, Jan. 1806, 'Letters on Poetry'.
2 'Noctes', June 1823, April 1830.
3 *Collected Works of Coleridge, The Friend* 1, 1969, p.210. In the 'Noctes' of March 1827 the Shepherd speaks to North about epoch-making Maga: 'Afore you and her cam out, this wisna the same warld it has been sin syne.'
4 *Memorials of his Time*, pp.300–5.
5 Joanne Shattock's *Politics and Reviewers*, p.23.
6 *Memoirs of a Literary Veteran*, Vol. III, p.53. Carruthers's 'Abbotsford Notanda': see Robert Chambers's life of Scott, pp.150, 129. Carlyle has a chapter on Jeffrey in his *Reminiscences*.
7 'Noctes', Vol. I, p.82. For the Macnish description see his *The Modern Pythagorean*, 2 vols: Vol. I, p.330 (from a letter of 2 Oct. 1834 to D. M. Moir).
8 For the reference to Maginn see Mrs Oliphant, Vol. I, p.207. There now exists a small literature concerning the authorship of 'The Canadian Boat Song'. Hogg's claim can be discounted. Lockhart's is enhanced by a letter of his to his wife from Inverness in 1821 which complains: 'The room is cold, my hand shakes, the pen is Highland': *John Gibson Lockhart*, by Marion Lochhead, 1954, p.86.
9 From James Ferrier's preface to his edition of the 'Noctes', 4 vols, 1855–6: Vol. I, pp.xii, xviii. Mary Garden's *Memorials*, p.141. *Essays in English Literature, 1780–1860*, First Series, 1895, by George Saintsbury, pp.45, 281. For Mackenzie's reference to 'Messieurs de l'Imagination' see Vol. I of his edition of the 'Noctes', p.385.
10 'The Authority of Some Unidentified or Disputed Articles in *Blackwood's Magazine*', by Brian Murray, *Studies in Scottish Literature*, Jan.–April 1967. Hogg's page seems to have consisted of a song sung by the Shepherd.
11 Mrs Oliphant, Vol. I, p.354, 221. Strout, p.263. Mrs Garden's *Memorials* quotes Blackwood to Hogg about the forthcoming 'Noctes', p.196.
12 Mrs Oliphant, Vol. I, p.517.
13 Ibid., p.257.
14 Ibid., Vol. II, pp.75, 103–9.
15 To the volume Jan. to June.
16 Lang's life of Lockhart, Vol. I, pp.128–31.
17 See the 'Noctes' of Nov. and Jan. 1828 and May 1829. In the writings of the American philosopher Richard Rorty are the very words of the 'Noctes Ambrosianae' . In an essay on 'The Inspirational Value of Great Works of Literature' (*Raritan*, Summer 1996), he notes approvingly that the philosopher Whitehead 'stood for charisma, genius, romance, and Wordsworth'. Rorty is a defender of inspiration, nonsense, excitement, hope and 'the idea of greatness'.
18 NLS MS 10495.
19 Mrs Oliphant, Vol. I, p.357.
20 'Hogg in the "Noctes Ambrosianae"', *Studies in Hogg and his World*, 4: 1993. See also Alexander's Introduction to his 'Noctes' anthology, *The Tavern Sages*.

21 Vol. I, pp.118-9, 35, 201-4, 213, 318.

22 Strout, pp.142-3.

23 Ibid., pp.174, 198. Mrs Oliphant, Vol. I, p.337.

24 Vol. VI, pp.241-2, 252.

25 7 Feb. 1828: *Journal*, ed. W. E. K. Anderson, 1972, p.424.

26 *Peter's Letters*, Vol. I, p.143. Maginn's *Miscellanies*, Vol. I, p.21.

27 'Noctes', April 1829.

28 MSS SLV. 14, Sterling Library, University of London.

29 Strout, pp.230-2.

30 To Scott, 16 Nov. 1821, NLS MS 393 ff. 159-60: see *Scott and his Influence*, ed.
    J. H. Alexander and David Hewitt, 1983, pp.335-6.

31 Strout, p.249.

32 *Letters of Scott*, Vol. V, p.204. Strout, pp.160, 165. The putting-up of Hogg, by
    Wilson, occurs in his 'Some Observations on the Poetry of the Agricultural and
    that of the Pastoral Districts of Scotland' (Feb. 1819). Burns and Hogg are seen
    as equal but different poets, and shepherds as possessed of 'a more intimate
    acquaintance' than ploughmen with 'the great and simple forms of nature'. But
    Hogg is also praised as an agent of the supernatural: 'poet laureate of the Court
    of Faery'.

33 David Groves's *James Hogg*, pp.86-8. *The Ettrick Shepherd*, by H. T.
    Stephenson, 1922, Indiana University Studies, No 54, p.40.

34 Strout, pp.152, 162. Scott's *Letters*, Vol. V, pp.150-1, 154-5.

35 Cockburn's *Memorials*, pp.353-4. *Cockburn's Millennium*, pp.32-3. Scott's
    Letters, Vol. VI, p.293. Mrs Oliphant, Vol. I, pp.321-2. Strout, p.106. Lach-
    Szyrma's account of his travels is remarkable both for its European view of
    Scotch bards and Scotch feasts and for its concurrence with local estimates of
    Hogg's significance. Of this feast he writes: 'The more important toasts are drunk
    standing, the lesser ones sitting with three loud shouts of Hip! Hip! Hurrah! The
    guests twirl their upraised glasses in front of them ... The toasts to the honoured
    dead are drunk sitting and in silence.' National songs are sung, on such
    occasions, in the land of hurrahs that Scotland can sometimes seem at this time.
    Hogg, 'an ordinary shepherd in the Ettrick Hills before he became a poet', has
    'not received a good education and everything in his writings is due to
    inspiration. His all too vivid imagination, which makes him often swerve from the
    path of reality, has such freshness and novelty that it appeals even to those reared
    on classics. This simple country bard is sought out by the choicest society and
    liked because of his gaiety and originality.' The writer was at this point tutor to a
    princely family on tour. His memoir (ed. Mona MacLeod Lewis) is forthcoming.

36 John Sutherland's *Life of Scott*, pp.245-7.

37 *Regency Editor*, by Patrick O'Leary, 1983, p.76.

38 Strout, p.194. *Regency Editor*, pp.141-54.

39 For Scott's view of John Scott see the *Letters*, Vol. VI, pp.342-67. Lockhart's
    Life of Scott is silent about the affair.

40 Mrs Oliphant, Vol. I, p.150. He was addressing Walter Scott on this particular occasion, with a view to evading responsibility for the 'Chaldee' scandal.
41 *Regency Editor*, p.153.
42 *Cockburn's Millennium*, p.71.
43 *Regency Editor*, pp.157–60. Scott's *Letters*, Vol. VI, p.368.
44 *Regency Editor*, pp.163, 168.
45 Mrs Oliphant, Vol. I, pp.338–9.
46 *Life of Scott*, Vol. VI, p.329. *The Ruin of Sir Walter Scott*, by Eric Quayle, 1968, p.153.
47 *Life of Scott*, Vol. V, pp.347–8.
48 *The Ruin of Sir Walter Scott*, p.274.

CHAPTER TWELVE: Marriage

1 Strout, pp.176, 50, 181. Mrs Oliphant, Vol. I, p.325.
2 Strout, pp.178, 220. *Anecdotes of Scott*, p.15. Norah Parr, p.7. *Margaret Phillips*, by Mary Garden, 1898, p.39.
3 'Some Particulars Relative to the Ettrick Shepherd': *New Monthly Magazine*, Feb. 1836.
4 Mary Garden's *Memorials*, pp.122–3. Norah Parr, p.47.
5 Ibid., pp.9–10.
6 *Anecdotes of Scott*, p.124.
7 Norah Parr, pp.14, 16.
8 Ibid., pp.54–5: 24 August 1828.
9 Ibid., p.15. *Life of Scott*, Vol. IX, p.115.
10 Strout, p.263. *Memoir*, p.54.
11 *Life of Scott*, Vol. VI, p.359. Strout, pp.213–5.
12 Ibid., pp.251–3.
13 Ibid., pp.189–93.
14 Ibid. See pp.198–215 for these letters of 1820–1.
15 Ibid., p.216: from the *Dublin University Magazine*, Jan. 1844.
16 Ibid., pp.216–7.
17 Ibid., p.224.
18 Ibid., pp.226–33.
19 See *John Galt: The Life of a Writer*, by Ian Gordon, 1972, pp.96, 100, 155. For the letter of 1821: NLS MS 4007, f.24.
20 *Ivanhoe*, pp.52, 58, 211. 'Captain Lochy' appeared in the *Altrive Tales* of 1832, Vol. I.
21 *Selected Poems and Songs*, ed. David Groves, pp.215–7. The quotations from Hogg's verse which are given at this point are taken from this edition and from Thomson.
22 The poem was published in *Blackwood's*. See Douglas Mack's Introduction to the *Selected Poems* of 1970; and Thomson, p.57.

CHAPTER THIRTEEN: Castle Cannibal

1 *Life of Scott*, Vol. VII, pp.49–65. Scott's *Letters*, Vol. VII, p.231. Strout, p.245.
    A History of Scotland, by Rosalind Mitchison, 1970, p.377.
2 *Rebellious Fraser's*, by Miriam Thrall, Columbia University Press, 1934, p.240.
3 *Doubles*, by the present writer, 1985, p.4.
4 Strout, pp.236–7.
5 *Edinburgh Literary Journal*, 3 Jan. 1829.
6 *Life of Scott*, Vol. VII, p.155. Scott's *Letters*, Vol. VII, p.269.
7 See p.136. Strout, pp.238–42, 155–6. 'James Hogg's Forgotten Satire, "John
    Paterson's Mare" ', by Alan Strout, PMLA, June 1937.
8 *Memoir*, p.55. Strout, pp.243–4.
9 Ibid., pp. 101, 213. *Memoir*, pp.101–2.
10 *The Three Perils of Man*, 1972 edn. Gillian Hughes has consulted a draft version
    of the novel in the Fales Library, New York, and a lecture by her on the subject,
    delivered in 2002, has been reported. She suggested that the work was started
    after *The Brownie of Bodsbeck*, and somewhat earlier than has been supposed,
    and that, in the autumn of 1819, Hogg was keen to see *Ivanhoe*, concerned,
    perhaps, about its relation to what he himself was up to. His friar, 'yon fat lazy
    Bacon', was shown in the draft as loquacious and concupiscent, hungering for
    the maid Delany. His part was cut back in revision, while Michael Scott became
    more dignified, his Satanism viewed as intellectual, heuristic.
11 Strout, p.248.
12 *Three Perils of Man*, pp.182, 184. *Confessions of a Justified Sinner*, CW, p.70.
13 *Three Perils of Man*, p.325.
14 Ibid., p.232.
15 Ibid., pp.242, 253–4.
16 Ibid., pp.240–2.
17 For a valorisation of the carnival Hogg see the editorial commentaries on *The
    Three Perils of Woman*, CW, p.xxxv and elsewhere.
18 Douglas Mack writes about this letter (NLS MS 5317, f.61) in *Studies in Hogg
    and his World*, 12:2001, p.18: 'Scott's irritation finds expression in the inevitable
    pig pun, as he responds to the "singular vulgarity & bad taste" of the indelibly
    "*hoggish*" Hogg. The *hoggish* quotation from Spenser comes from the final stanza
    of Book II Canto XII of *The Faerie Queene*, and refers to Grille, the companion
    of Ulysses who was transformed by Circe into a hog. This condition suited Grille
    so well that he refused to be changed back to human shape.'
19 Strout, pp.254. Norah Parr, p.46.
20 Strout, pp.249–54.
21 *Rebellious Fraser's*, p.101. Wandering by his 'glassy brooks', Byron's Juan thinks
    'unutterable things' (Canto I:90), while the eyes of Hogg's Jane speak them in the
    poem 'Halbert of Lyne' (*Winter Evening Tales*, p.127), a poem shared with
    Gillies.

CHAPTER FOURTEEN: Likenesses

1 Page references relate to the Collected Works edn. See Strout, p.262.
2 *Essays in English Literature, 1780–1860*, pp.34, 62.
3 Strout, p.33. *Anecdotes of Scott*, pp.xxxiii–iv: the proposal to Lockhart belongs to a letter of 4 Oct. 1832.
4 Strout, p.88.
5 Ibid., pp.260–1.
6 *Maule's Curse* by Yvor Winters: see his *In Defence of Reason*, 1960, p.158. The *Pilgrim's Progress* is subtitled 'Under the Similitude of a Dream'.
7 From a letter of 1805: *The Horner* Papers, p.391.
8 Professor Garside's CW edn. of the novel contains an informative discussion of eighteenth-century Scottish Antinomianism. The views on this subject which are reported in Lockhart's life of Burns (p.65) are those of the Rev. Hamilton Paul.
9 *Confessions*, pp.80–6.
10 Ibid., Introduction, p.lxxi.
11 Ibid., pp.85, 136–40.
12 'Nature's Magic Lantern' is suitably placed immediately before the *Confessions* in Thomas Thomson's *Tales and Sketches* of 1865, 1873 edn, pp.459–62. Marina Warner's *Fantastic Metamorphoses, Other Worlds*, 2002, has a passage (pp.180–3) in which Hogg's approach is contrasted with Coleridge's invocation of 'the explicable, meteorological status of the shadow double' with reference to natural phenomena such as the halo of glory and the Brocken spectre. Hogg's summit scene, 'with its phantasmagoric epiphanies, its violent, near-fatal encounter, and its hallucinatory multiplication of the doppelgänger figure, fuses modern dilemmas about the stability of the self with visual metaphors of meteorological wonders and optical illusion'.
13 *Confessions*, pp.86, 94, 47.
14 *Doubles*, by the present writer, pp.2–4.
15 *Confessions*, p.lii.
16 Strout, p.262.
17 Professor Johnson has described the situation in a letter to the present writer. During his adolescence he had taken to Hogg's novel, happening on it in the Lancaster Public Library. At Oxford in 1947 there occurred this somewhat silent seminar. The honorary degree had been conferred with an air of reluctance; the pious Mauriac had been chosen first for the honour. Afterwards Johnson regretted having spoken at the seminar. 'I had been showing off. It wasn't as if I could have talked sensibly about the book. But I will confess that a subsequent event helped me to forget about the seminar.' A man from the Oxford Registrary came to ask him if 'Mr Gide' had left his Oxford gown behind at the Maison Française, where Johnson was lodging. 'I had to show him the room where we had had the seminar. I told him that he had not been to any other rooms and that he didn't have a gown with him. He asked particularly if "Mr Gide" had been to my room. I looked him straight in the eye and said "No".' Those were

the days of Austerity, when gowns cost coupons, and when the man who helped to make Hogg respectable was hardly quite respectable himself.

The significance of Gide, for the British universities of the time, resembles that of Hogg in affording an example of the way in which considerations of propriety and status have affected academic recognition. It seems fitting that Gide's literary reputation, then on the rise among British readers at large, should have assisted Hogg's.

Hogg's French connection was enhanced, and duality's link to the prophetic re-affirmed, when, in June 1996, a young Frenchman, Emmanuel Caillet, who had taken part in sportive feudal re-enactments, was found shot through the head on top of a Scottish mountain, Ben Alder. He was thought to have committed suicide. During his last days, however, he had been seen in the company of a dark stranger, and doubts were expressed about what had transpired on the summit. Stranger than most fictions and very like Hogg's, the mystery remains. See the *Guardian* of 5 Jan. 2002.

18 *Anecdotes of Scott*, p.xiii; and see p.311.

19 *Peter's Letters*, Vol. II, p.198. *The History of Matthew Wald*, published anonymously, 1824, p.218.

20 *Memorials of James Hogg*, p.157.

21 'Abbotsford Notanda': Robert Chambers's life of Scott, p.178.

22 *Confessions*, pp.xlvii, lxxxviii. Hogg concurs in 'An Auld Wife's Dream' (*Fraser's*, Jan. 1833). Both as a shepherd and as a political shaman, he set store by dreams.

23 *Confessions*, p.lxviii.

24 To Wilson: Mrs Gordon (American edn), p.263.

CHAPTER FIFTEEN: Flesh

1 *Three Perils of Man*, pp.266–8, 275.

2 *Essays in English Literature*, p.284.

3 Strout, p.53. Norah Parr, p.91.

4 Scott's *Letters*, Vol. VIII, pp.108–9. Lockhart's *Life of Scott*, Vol. VII, p.380.

5 *Reminiscences of a Literary Veteran*, Vol. 1, pp.182–3. Lang's *Lockhart*, Vol. II, pp.53–4. The 'bothering repast' belongs to Wilson's review of *The Three Perils of Woman* (*Blackwood's*, Oct. 1823).

6 April 1830. For Maginn's Mulligan see the 'Noctes' of March 1822.

7 *Studies in Hogg and his World*, 9:1998.

8 Ibid., 4:1993, 5:1994.

9 Strout, pp.269–70. Gillies was writing in the *Fraser's* of Oct. 1839.

10 See Hogg's notes for his *Songs* of 1831, published by Blackwood.

11 Cockburn's *Memorials*, p.354. For Cockburn's opinion of Henry Brougham see below, p.251, and see *Cockburn's Millennium*, p.27.

12 The anonymous observer of Orange marches (Oct. 1831) appears to have been

Samuel O'Sullivan, a Protestant divine, chaplain of the Royal Hibernian Military School in Dublin.

13 *A Memoir of Charles Mayne Young*, by Julian Charles Young, 2nd edn, 1871, pp.96-8.
14 Strout, p.269.
15 Ibid., p.271.
16 *Life of Scott*, Vol. VII, p.96.
17 The text is that of the CW.
18 By Sharon Alker and Holly Faith Nelson, in *Studies in Hogg and his World*, 12:2001.
19 Ibid. Cardinale's essay is followed by a text of both books of the poem. This is the first time that the second book has been published since the first appearance of the poem in the *Poetical Works* of 1822.

CHAPTER SIXTEEN: Sporting Life

1 'Noctes', Nov. 1826. Norah Parr, pp.58-60.
2 'Noctes', July 1827, April–Nov. 1826.
3 *Memoir*, p.5. *James Hogg and the St Ronan's Border Club*, pp.6-7.
4 Russell's *Reminiscences*, pp.126-7.
5 *James Hogg and the St Ronan's Border Club*, pp.20-1, 39.
6 Ibid., pp.2, 4 and *passim*. John Harper was one of a sporting family. His achievements recall those of the strong-minded star athlete of that surname who lived near Abbotsford at the village of Darnick and was wanted by Walter Scott for his volunteer force (see pp.56-7).
7 Norah Parr, pp.87-8.
8 *Queer Book*, pp.xiv, 138-9, 217, 60, 159.
9 *Christopher North*, by Mary Gordon, American edn, pp.146-7.

CHAPTER SEVENTEEN: Personality Hogg

1 Norah Parr, pp.54, 80. Strout, p.262.
2 *Memoir of William and Robert Chambers*, by William Chambers, pp.255-64.
3 See *Sir Walter Scott: The Great Unknown*, by Edgar Johnson, Vol. I, p.70.
4 *Henry Glassford Bell*, by Anna Stoddart, 1892, p.21.
5 Norah Parr, p.76. A version of the song appears as 'Auld John Nichol' in Thomson, p.438. Another poem, 'Auld Ettrick John' (Thomson, pp.274-5), tells, with verve, a different story of the elderly spouse. 'John cam daddin' down the hill,' with a manful wagging of the arms, on his way to court his sonsie Nell. But their marriage proves bitter bad, a warning to young and old alike:
> She frets, an' greets, an' visits aft,
> In hopes some lad will see her hame.
6 *Selected Poems and Songs*, pp.163-7.

7 *Shepherd's Calendar*, CW, pp.xiv–xvii.

8 See p.151.

9 'The Prodigal' was published in the Blackwood *Shepherd's Calendar* of 1829, from which quotations are taken, but was omitted from Thomson's *Tales and Sketches* and from the CW edn. of the *Calendar*. Stories were left out of this last edition which had appeared in that of 1829 but had not formed part of the 'Shepherd's Calendar' series in *Blackwood's* on which the book was based. Two of them, 'The Prodigal Son' and 'Nancy Chisholm', are of a decidedly pious cast. The first seems to have been written at the time of Hogg's marriage.

10 *Tales of James Hogg*, 1886, Vol. I. Volume II of this collection has two notable stories. 'The Long Pack' is a thriller about a Trojan Horse pedlar's pack, a tale which did well when pedlars sold it in chapbook form and which was redone for *Winter Evening Tales*. 'Katie Cheyne', a class and courtship tale, contains a paean to the plaid: 'the canopy of kindly hearts', of love and kisses.

CHAPTER EIGHTEEN: Balloonist

1 The first poem was published in the *Edinburgh Literary Journal* (19 Dec. 1829). The second was collected in *A Queer Book*.

2 *Queer Book*, p.261, 268. Blackwood seems to have rejected his tale of 'The Two Vallies', a later version of which was published in the annual *Remembrance* for 1830. There are these two places: Luran (Church of England) and Dual (*sic* – Catholic). A fairy queen hands out white wands to the Luran girls, with which to beat off 'bad papist boys' and turn them into asses. See *Studies in Hogg and his World*, 11:2000.

3 Thomson, p.lii. *Memoir*, p.58.

4 Mrs Garden's *Memorials of James Hogg*, p.302.

5 Scott's *Journal*, p.405. Lang's *Lockhart*, Vol. II, p.15.

6 Norah Parr, pp.64–5, 82, 98, 101.

7 Cockburn's *Memorials*, p.427.

8 NLS MS 10495 f.29.

9 See *Doubles*, by the present writer, pp.160–4.

10 'Further Anecdotes of the Shepherd's Dog': *Blackwood's*, March 1818.

CHAPTER NINETEEN: Buffoon

1 *Quarterly*, Vol. XLIV, p.81.

2 Mrs Oliphant, Vol. 1, p.249. Scott's *Letters*, Vol. X, pp.208, 405. NLS MS 10495 f.4. References to Hogg's dealings with the Literary Fund are based in part on the manuscript collection relating to the Fund (Case No 594) which is held in the British Library. His acknowledgement of the 1827 award was 'unpleasant to my feelings', wrote William Jerdan, who felt that it ought not to be

communicated or preserved. Hogg's sulkiness may be surmised. The application for the 1832 award was made without his knowledge.

3 *Homes and Haunts of the Most Eminent British Poets*, by William Howitt, 2 vols, 1847, Vol. II, pp.27–67. NLS MS 10495.
4 *Journal*, p.640.
5 'Noctes', Vol. IV, p.xviii. Norah Parr, p.43: August 1827.
6 Ibid., p.80. *Memoir*, p.12.
7 Norah Parr, p.40.
8 NS MS 10495 f.49.
9 *Works, Letters and Manuscripts of James Hogg*, ed. R. B. Adam, Buffalo, New York, 1930. The letter to Mrs Izett, as it appears to be, is dated 1819, that to Byron 3 June 1814. When proposing to Constable, in 1813, a collection of prose tales based on 'rural and traditionary' material, he spoke of adopting the pen-name of J. H. Craig of Douglas, a lairdly step-up from his old-world, bardic Shepherd sobriquet, which he now thought 'hackneyed' and unsuitable for such a project. Ian Duncan examines this fugitive re-naming with reference to Schiller's distinction between naïve and sentimental poetry: *Winter Evening Tales*, pp.xxii–iv.
10 *Blackwood's*, Sept. 1831. *Edinburgh Review*, Nov. 1814.
11 As given in *Selected Poems and Songs*.
12 NLS MS 10495 f.54.
13 Norah Parr, pp.40, 89–91.
14 NLS MS 2956 f.162.
15 NLS MS 10495. For 'The Magic Mirror' see *Blackwood's*, Oct. 1831.
16 NLS MS 10495.
17 NLS MS 2956 f.162. The 'indomitable' letter is to Wilson. The two letters to Cunningham belong to 1828 and 1829: see the R. B. Adam materials (as above).
18 NLS MS 10495. Mrs Oliphant, Vol. II, pp.119–20.
19 *The Works of Robert Burns*, Vol. V, pp.23, 49, 61, 64, 134, 179–81, 192–245.
20 Lockhart's *Life of Burns*, p.15.
21 Lockhart's *Life of Scott*, Vol. VIII, p.277.
22 NLS MS 10495, and see Jill Rubenstein's Introduction (p.xiii) to *Anecdotes of Scott*.
23 *Thomas and Jane Carlyle*, by Rosemary Ashton, 2001, p.129. Carlyle's *Reminiscences*, pp.237–8. Norah Parr, p.92.

CHAPTER TWENTY: Ben Nevis on Blackheath

1 *Retrospect of a Long Life*, by S. C. Hall, 2 vols, 1883, Vol. II, pp.287–8. *The Ettrick Shepherd*, by H. T. Stephenson, 1922, p.43.
2 Norah Parr, pp.84, 96.
3 For the Shepherd's retrospective 'roar o' life' see the 'Noctes' of July 1834. For Hogg's response to Mrs Hall, NLS MS 10495 f.27: May 1830.

4 *The Autobiography of William Jerdan*, Vol. IV, pp.295–9.

5 Hall's *Retrospect*, Vol. II, pp.165, 287–9.

6 *Anecdotes of Scott*, Notes, p.122. In Chapter 64 of *Pendennis* there appears to be an allusion to Laetitia (whose landlady's name was Sheldon) which is followed by talk of epistolary indiscretion.

7 *Autobiography*, Vol. IV, p.295.

8 Norah Parr, pp.103–4.

9 *Fifty Years' Recollections*, by Cyrus Redding, 3 vols, 1858, Vol. III, pp.17–9.

10 NLS MS 10495 f.75. And see R. B. Adam (as above) for a letter of 14 January 1833 to Alexander Elder.

11 *Anecdotes of Scott*, pp.xxxv–vi.

12 Vol. X, p.169.

13 Norah Parr, pp.103–9. See R. B. Adam, as above.

14 Edinburgh, 1832: see p.73

15 A famous greeting, variously worded – here as in John Sutherland's life of Scott, p.354.

16 *Anecdotes of Scott*, pp.73–5, Notes, p.100.

17 *The Modern Scottish Minstrel*, by Charles Rogers, 6 vols, Vol. II, p.5.

18 *Anecdotes of Scott*, p.xxxvii. NLS MS 10495 f.79.

19 *Anecdotes of Scott*, pp.xxxix–xlii.

20 Ibid., pp.xlv–xlvii.

21 Ibid., p.li. *Life of Scott*, Vol. X, p.251.

22 *Anecdotes of Scott*, pp.6, 14, 12.

23 *Fraser's*, August 1834.

24 See his edition of Burns, Vol. I, p.57.

25 *Anecdotes of Scott*, p.lii. A letter to Hogg's widow of 10 May 1836 tells her that the Cunninghams 'are all Shepherdites': NLS MS 10495.

26 *Lay Sermons*, p.xxvii.

CHAPTER TWENTY-ONE: Farewell to Ettrick

1 *Pencillings by the Way*, pp.392–5. The Shepherd says of his American popularity in the 'Noctes' of May 1823: 'They've mair sense owerby there than here at hame, in some particulars. They turn a' my novels into plays.'

2 In *Past and Present* (1st edn, 1843, p.158) Carlyle tells the egotistical Methodist who worries about being saved: 'Thou art like to be damned. Consider that as the fact.' For Lockhart's response, and for his two creeds, see Lang's *Lockhart*, Vol. II, pp.238–9, 91.

3 *John Gibson Lockhart*, by Marion Lochhead, p.154. Keats's letter was written in Oct. 1818.

4 *Anecdotes of Scott*, p.xxvi: the two pieces are thought by the editor to be by the same writer, for whom see also p.26. NLS MS 10495.

5 Ibid. See also R. B. Adam, as above.

6 See NLS MS 10495 for the letter of 17 November. For the knight and his double, see Gillies's translation of Hoffmann's novel, 2 vols, 1824, Vol. I, p.138.

7 See R. B. Adam, as above, and see NLS MS 10495.

8 Norah Parr, p.118.

9 The speech was reported in the *Paisley Advertiser*: NLS MS 10495.

10 *Cockburn's Millennium*, p.128.

11 Ibid., p.19. *Dark Horses*, by the present writer, p.264.

12 *Scottish Democracy*, pp.86–91.

13 *Trainspotting*, paperback edn, 1994, p.309. The comparison is pursued in an essay on Irvine Welsh by the present writer in the journal *Scotland*, 5:1, 1998.

14 *Half a Life*, 2001, p.8.

15 *Selected Stories and Sketches*. 'The Strange Letter of a Lunatic' was turned down by Blackwood and then appeared, rewritten, in the *Fraser's* of Dec. 1830, the year the journal began.

16 *Rebellious Fraser's*, p.185.

17 Ibid., pp.187–90. See also Carlyle's *Reminiscences*, p.369, and J. A. Froude's *Thomas Carlyle*, 2 vols, 1882, Vol. II, p.89.

18 *Life of Sir Walter Scott*, by Robert Chambers, pp.190–1.

19 See *Selected Poems and Songs*.

20 See Riddell's *Poetical Works*, ed. James Brydon, 2 vols, 1871: Vol. I, p.x, and elsewhere in the accompanying memoir.

21 *The Poetical Works of Thomas Aird*, 5th edn, 1870, with a memoir by the Rev. Jardine Wallace, pp.xvii, 2, 27, 88, 136.

22 See *Eighteenth-Century Women Poets*, ed. Roger Lonsdale, 1989.

23 *Memoir of William and Robert Chambers*, p.393. For the letter to Alexander Blackwood see NLS MS 4039 f.31v. For the letter to Gilfillan, a poet from Leith, met around 1831, see *Lay Sermons*, Notes, p.124. A poem of Hogg's, 'Gilfillan of Leith', has been traced by Gillian Hughes, an outlandishly-rhymed exotic tale of the 'frightful' kind: a money man encounters his old wife's ominous dream, a perilous castle, a wicked lawyer, a well-meaning ghost.

24 *Selected Short Stories*, ed. Ian Gordon, 1978.

25 See David Groves's *James Hogg: The Growth of a Writer*, pp.151–2. This friend is spoken of as P. Boyd; Robert Boyd, who served as secretary of the St Ronan's Border Club, was a close fishing friend of Hogg's. See also *The Modern Scottish Minstrel*, by Charles Rogers, Vol. II, p. 40.

26 Thomson, p.lxix.

27 Ibid., pp.lxx–lxxi. *Margaret Phillips*, by Mary Garden, p.32.

28 *James Frederick Ferrier*, by E. S. Haldane, 1899, pp.142, 151.

29 *Ferrier of St Andrews: An Academic Tragedy*, pp.77, 117, 124. Ferrier was an academic potentate who wrestled with Edinburgh Town Council and the Free Kirk, and he is shown here as a metaphysician and a moralist, who spoke to his

students of the need to place virtue before happiness. The Hegelian hedonist suggested by the Haldane biography is replaced by a great man who was also a Scottish transgressor: 'Ferrier had violated the rules of his faith, and could not complain of the injustice of the terrible retribution that had followed upon it.' A preface by George Davie expounds Ferrier's philosophical distinction.

30 *Margaret Phillips*, p.18.

Glossary

ae one
aiblins perhaps
aik oak
aince once
airt quarter or direction of the wind
an if
anent concerning, about
aught anything

bairn child
barmy yeasty, mad
baw-waw child, contemptuous side-
  glance
ben inside or through the house
besom broom, mischievous woman
bide stay
bieldy shady, sheltered
birl revolve, toss a coin
birr strength, zest
birzed bruised, crushed
blaw blow (for example, pipes)
bodle copper coin
bouk body, bulk
bouzy fat, bushy
breeks trousers
buggen built
bught sheepfold
bumming humming

callant, or *callan* lad
carle fellow, man, peasant
cast a turn or twist, fate
casting swarming
cauldrife lukewarm, insipid

chiel child, chap
chirk harsh noise
creeshy greasy
crib coop, kerb
cuddy donkey, horse
cummer, or *kimmer* girl, godmother,
  midwife
cutty stool where misdoers sat in
  church

dad thump, strike
darg, or *dark* work
deil devil
deoch-an doruis stirrup cup
docken dock leaf
donneration stupidity
douk dip
doup bum
dour hard
dowie sad, dreary
dree suffer
dub puddle
dyke stone or turf wall
dwawm dream

edder adder
een eyes
ell yardstick
ern eagle
ettle try, strive, intend
even down honest, sheer, thorough

fashed vexed
fautour delinquent
feint a ane not a one

fire-flauchtis fireflies
flakes fence or sheep pen
flisky frisky
flit move house
fushionless savourless

gair strip of grass, meadow
gang go
gar make, cause
gate way, fashion
gelloch yell
gey, or *gay* very, fairly
gillflirt silly girl
gilliegaupy silly fellow
glaiket silly, vacant
gleg eager, quick
glisk glimpse, trace, gleam
gin if
gomeril fool
goose smoothing iron
grew greyhound, to be sick or to
   grimace
grumph snort
grumphy pig

hairst harvest
hale whole
hantle a good deal
harkit hearkened
heeze heave
herry rob, plunder
heftit swollen, unmilked
   (of sheep or cattle)
hirple limp, hobble
hirsel flock of sheep or their place of
   pasturage
hizzy hussy
hodge-podge vegetable stew
hog young, unfleeced sheep
   (cf *gimmer*, a ewe yet to give birth)
horse-couper horse-dealer
houdy midwife
howe a hollow
howf inn, shelter

howk dig
Hue and Cry bulletin of offenders
hurdies buttocks

ilk, ilka each
ingans onions
ingle fire, hearth

jalouse suspect, surmise
jaumph a joke, to mock
joost just
jow peal, toll
jurmummle crush, bamboozle

kenspeckle well-known, colourful
kern soldier, beggar, peasant
keude wild, mad
kist chest
kithe show, reveal
knowe knoll

lave the rest
laverock lark
law hill
leal loyal
lear learning, sense
lees lies
leme gleam
leuch laughed
lift sky
limmer loose woman, scoundrel
lister fish-spear
loups leaps
lum chimney

mae more
marrow partner, equal, like, mate, match
maud plaid
maun must
maut malt
mawkin hare
meinging mixing
messan mongrel
mony many

394

mould, or *mool* soil, grave
mow to make love (of males), a pile of grain
mowdie mole
muckle much
muckle-mou'd big-mouthed

neb beak

ower over

poolly-woolly curlew's cry
prigging haggling, pleading
pyat magpie

ream cream
reave steal
row row, wind, twist
rug tug
rumple rump
rung stick

saddit trampled, beaten hard
sair sore
sark shirt
scart scratch
shirra sheriff
shoon shoes
shouthers shoulders
sic such
smoored smothered
smeddum vigour, spirit
snuve, or *snoove* glide
sonsie jolly, plump
sook suck
soom swim
soop sweep
sorner sponger, cheat
stern star

sticket minister minister without a kirk
store-farming sheep-farming
stoure dust
stott bullock
strae straw
stravaig wander
sumph fool
swirl whirl, be dizzy or knotted

tangleness indecision
tapsalteerie topsy-turvy, turned upside down
thole suffer, bear
thrapple throat
till't to it
tint lost
tod fox
trance passage between the two main rooms of a cottage; corridor, aisle

unco strange, queer, very

wae sad
wake watch (over a flock at night)
wame stomach, womb
wan won
wauf solitary, vagabond, shabby, a waif
wedder male sheep, sometimes a gelded one
whaup curlew
wist knew
wud mad
wuss wish
wyse lead, guide

yestreen yesterday, last night
yett gate, door
yowe ewe

Index